The Crash of Delta Flight 723

ALSO BY PAUL D. HOULE

*The Crash of Piedmont Airlines Flight 22:
Completing the Record of the 1967 Midair Collision
Near Hendersonville, North Carolina* (McFarland, 2016)

The Crash of Delta Flight 723

The Worst Air Disaster in New England History

PAUL D. HOULE

McFarland & Company, Inc., Publishers
Jefferson, North Carolina

ISBN (print) 978-1-4766-8642-4
ISBN (ebook) 978-1-4766-4435-6

Library of Congress and British Library
cataloguing data are available

Library of Congress Control Number 2021052754

© 2021 Paul D. Houle. All rights reserved

No part of this book may be reproduced or transmitted in any form or by any means, electronic or mechanical, including photocopying or recording, or by any information storage and retrieval system, without permission in writing from the publisher.

Front cover: DC-9 aircraft (photograph by Cory W. Watts); Delta Flight 723 descent profile (National Transportation Safety Board)

Printed in the United States of America

*McFarland & Company, Inc., Publishers
Box 611, Jefferson, North Carolina 28640
www.mcfarlandpub.com*

To my wife, SHARI, and son, ALEX.
I hope I did not miss too much this time around.

To the victims and families of DELTA FLIGHT 723.
The truth is the most beautiful memorial of them all.

Acknowledgments

The author would like to thank the following individuals and organizations for their help on this project: Ray and Leona Chouinard, Brenda and Jack McSweeney, Dr. Joshua Tofield, Dr. Thomas Dodson, Tim Maclay, John Clayton, David Rogers, Neil McBride, Barbara Delac, Ashley L. Rudolph, Esq. and Michael Latti. I also want to thank Nathaniel Wiltzen and Daniel Fleming at the National Archives at Boston, Marta Crilly at the Boston City Archives, Melissa Gottwald at Embry-Riddle Aeronautical University, and Paul Oelkrug at the University of Texas, Dallas. I would also like to thank the staff at the Manchester (New Hampshire) City Library, the Fletcher Free Library in Burlington, Vermont, the Providence (Rhode Island) Library, and the Boston Public Library.

I want to thank my mother Paloma for buying me a green, portable Smith Corona typewriter for Christmas in 1975. Obviously, she saw something in me that I did not see at the time. It only took me forty years to prove her right.

And to my brother John whose advice, sometimes unexpectedly, helps get me through the difficult times.

Table of Contents

Acknowledgments vi
Preface 1
Introduction 5
Abbreviations 7

1. Fog Warning 9
2. Passengers and Crew 15
3. Merger 24
4. "Let Me Get Off the Plane" 33
5. "Partial Obscuration" 40
6. "He Didn't Say to Go On Down" 48
7. "I Don't Trust That Thing" 53
8. "A Large, Long Flame" 61
9. "Aircraft Down on 4R" 69
10. "My Name Is Leo Chouinard" 78
11. The NTSB 87
12. "Avoid Public Criticism of the FAA" 95
13. "We Are Going to Do Everything We Can to Save You" 104
14. "Thousands and Thousands of Pieces of the Plane All Over" 114
15. "Criminally Negligent" 123
16. "You Want to Get Warned About Hitting the Ground" 130
17. "Trying to Use This Accident in a Cheap Political Way" 136
18. "We're Dealing with a Burn That Is Normally a Fatal Burn" 141

19. "The Administration Has Made Repeated Attempts to Both Harass and Intimidate the Board"   149
20. "There Is a Record of Malfunctions"   159
21. "If He Was Going to Die, We Did Not Want Him Dying on Our Watch"   167
22. "Leo, You're an Uncle"   174
23. "The Result of Nonstandard Air Traffic Control Services"   180
24. "An Unusually Foggy Day"   189
25. "Mr. Taylor Simply Forgot About Delta 723"   204
26. "The Interrelationship Existing Between Pilot and Ground Personnel Can Best Be Characterized as One Requiring Extensive Cooperation"   212
27. "Short Circuits Caused by Particles Produced Mechanical Misalignment"   220
28. "You Are Not Going to Get Rid of Me, Mike"   227

Chapter Notes   235
Bibliography   253
Index   261

Preface

I heard the news bulletin over the radio that a plane had crashed at Logan Airport on July 31, 1973, as my brother John and I rode with our father on a short drive from Ashburnham, Massachusetts, to visit our grandparents in East Templeton, Massachusetts. I kept hushing the two of them so I could hear the broadcasters share details of the horrific tragedy that unfolded that day in Boston. That was the day my infatuation with plane crashes began.

Like many other families, we mourned the death of the eighty-eight passengers and crew in the crash and prayed fervently that the lone survivor, Leopold (Leo) Chouinard, would make it through. Even though we invoked God the Father, Jesus the Son, His Holy Mother, and all the saints, Leo succumbed to his wounds just over one hundred days after the crash. With his death, Leo disappeared from the headlines as quickly as he had arrived.

In 1979, our family moved from Massachusetts to Florida, and within a few years I joined the Army as a military policeman. After I left the Army, I earned my bachelor of arts degree at the University of North Florida. After marriage, my wife, my son, and I moved to South Carolina so that I could begin my career in transportation. I earned a master's degree in aeronautical science from Embry-Riddle Aeronautical University. Throughout all those life changes, whenever I read or heard about a plane crash, I always thought back to those lost on Delta Flight 723 and Leo Chouinard's fight for survival.

McFarland released my first book, *The Crash of Piedmont Airlines Flight 22*, in December 2015. After completing that book, I knew the next one I would write would be about Delta Flight 723.

My approach in writing about the two crashes is as different as the accidents themselves. In the first book, I focused on the crash and the National Transportation Safety Board (NTSB), as well as the congressional investigations. After the release of the NTSB report on Flight 22 in 1968, the story of Flight 22 ended. I relied mainly on primary sources, as well as official transcripts, to tell the story and bring it to completion.

In this book, I felt I needed to rely on more than just primary sources, especially as I told the story of Leo Chouinard and his fight for life. I interviewed Leo's family and his doctors, fiancée, and friends. The portrait emerged of a fine and brave young Air Force sergeant fighting a battle that, frankly, no one had ever fought before for that length of time. All shared their amazement at his strength and courage. I also felt his strength and courage through their stories. I hope you, the reader, feel it also. Leo deserves nothing less.

It took an NTSB investigation and three court cases to get to the cause of this crash. The last half of the book is steeped in court transcripts, and I used them freely because I felt that the arguments used by attorneys, the rulings of the judges, and the statements of the witnesses came closer than any description I could write of their thoughts, arguments, and conclusions. The final settlement in this saga came almost nine years after the crash.

For some, the details of the story will be difficult to read. Many factors contributed to this crash; hence the long legal process. No single cause can define this tragedy. An accumulation of errors, both man-made and technological, as well as bad weather, all combined to bring down a modern, sophisticated commercial jet aircraft and crash it into a seawall. How that happened is what this book is about. The story is long overdue.

"I have never seen wreckage so scattered, even that of a plane which hit a mountainside in Alaska."
—Isabel Burgess, National Transportation
Safety Board, August 1, 1973

Q. "Mr. Butterfield, are you aware of the installation of any listening devices in the Oval Office of the president?"
—Fred Thompson, Minority Counsel,
Senate Watergate Committee

A. "I was aware of listening devices, yes sir."
—Alexander Butterfield, Federal Aviation
Administration Administrator, July 16, 1973

Introduction

It is a testimony to the American ideal that the United States survived the summer of 1973. Public congressional testimony revealed that a president of the United States secretly recorded all his conversations in the White House, as well as bugged his telephone, and attempted to cover up a burglary. Historians call this event *Watergate*. Watergate, though, was a lot more than a break-in. Watergate was an effort by the Nixon administration to effectively take over the entire executive branch of government by installing individuals in executive agencies based on their loyalty to the president more than their qualifications for the job. It almost succeeded.

Delta Air Lines Flight 723 from Burlington, Vermont, to Boston, Massachusetts, with an unscheduled stopover in Manchester, New Hampshire, crashed at Logan Airport just a few days after the nation found out President Nixon recorded his conversations. Plane crashes happen quickly and just as quickly disappear from the news cycle as other stories take precedence. With a daily progression of Watergate headlines from July 1973 until Nixon's resignation in August 1974, the crash of Delta Flight 723 faded from public attention.

Not only were the developments in the crash investigation outshone by Watergate headlines, but Nixon's attempt to install his cronies at the National Transportation Safety Board (NTSB) also did not receive the coverage and attention it deserved. Nixon and his associates threatened and cajoled NTSB members with punishment if they expressed any desire to break away from the executive branch and become an independent department. They also faced pressure and threats from Nixon and his allies if they criticized the Federal Aviation Administration (FAA) in their handling of air traffic control and other responsibilities. That became a problem for investigators in the Delta Flight 723 crash because air traffic controllers at Logan on the day of the crash made several critical mistakes in handling Flight 723. As with Watergate itself, the courts would assign the blame.

Aviation experienced an explosion of technological growth in the early

1970s. Advancements in flying moved from relying on air traffic controllers for assistance in takeoffs and landings to installing navigational devices in the cockpit of the aircraft that put more control in the pilot's hands. Conversely, legal decisions in aviation cases moved toward a more cooperative arrangement between pilots and controllers. Rendering a verdict on the blame in an aviation disaster became more complicated under this arrangement. Older equipment, such as precision approach radar (PAR), a radar device installed at airports that allowed controllers to monitor aircraft on approach and landing and warn pilots if they were not lined up correctly, was pulled from airports before the new cockpit equipment, such as ground proximity warning systems (GPWSs) or the instrument landing system (ILS), became standard. The decision to prematurely pull this equipment sat squarely with the FAA.

Improvements in airline safety resulted from the crash of Delta Flight 723. The GPWS received renewed interest from the FAA and eventually became standard equipment on all commercial airlines. Flight directors became more user-friendly in that manufacturers installed annunciator panels on the screen to let pilots know if their flight pattern matched up with the mode on their flight director. The FAA finally installed Category II landing systems that gave pilots more accurate data when landing their planes.

It is the hope of all aviation safety professionals that lessons are learned from prior crashes so that future ones will not occur.

Abbreviations

ACAP—Aviation Consumer Action Program
ALPA—Air Line Pilots Association
ALS—Approach lights system
ATA—Aviation Transport Association
ATC—Air traffic control
BAC—British Aircraft Company
BAI—Bureau of Accident Investigation
BAS—Bureau of Air Safety
BCH—Boston City Hospital
BOS—Boston (Logan) Airport
CAA—Civil Aeronautics Authority
CAB—Civil Aeronautics Board
CAT I—Category I landing system
CAT II—Category II landing system
CVR—Cockpit voice recorder
DC—Douglas (Aircraft) Company
DOT—Department of Transportation
FAA—Federal Aviation Administration (formerly Federal Aviation Agency)
FD—Flight director
FSF—Flight Safety Foundation
GPWS—Ground proximity warning system
IBM—International Business Machine
ICC—Interstate Commerce Commission
ILS—Instrument landing system
LAX—Los Angeles International Airport
MAC—Massachusetts Aeronautics Commission
Massport—Massachusetts Port Authority
MGH—Massachusetts General Hospital
MIA—Miami International Airport
MIT—Massachusetts Institute of Technology
MTOW—Maximum takeoff weight
NTSB—National Transportation Safety Board
OAI—Office of Accident Investigation
PAR—Precision approach radar
PATCO—Professional Air Traffic Controllers Organization
RVR—Runway visual range
SAMB—State Airport Management Board
STOL—Short takeoff and landing
TRACON—Terminal radar approach control room
TWA—Trans World Airlines

1

Fog Warning

Fog has always been a part of the New England weather mystique. It was the enemy of the hardy fishermen who settled New England and bet their livelihood on the North Atlantic fish trade. Their dangerous dalliances with Atlantic fog could not have been portrayed better than in the painting *The Fog Warning* by Winslow Homer. This 1885 painting shows the deadly peril of a fisherman in his dory attempting to return to his main ship with a fabulous catch of halibut at his feet. However, in the distance, a fog bank is approaching, threatening to blind him and cut off his approach to the safety of his mates on the fishing boat. A description of the fisherman's curse, encapsulated in *The Fog Warning*, can be found in an old book describing the terror:

> His frail boat rides like a shell upon the surface of the sea ... a moment of carelessness or inattention, or a slight miscalculation may cost him his life.
>
> And a greater foe than carelessness lies in wait for its prey. The stealthy fog enwraps him in its folds, blinds his vision, cuts off all marks to guide his course, and leaves him afloat in a measureless void.[1]

While the fishing fleets diminished over the decades, the danger still lurked over the sea, and fog would commonly make landfall. Fog, like other dangerous weather conditions, created havoc for all aspects of New England life, but it always hit transportation the hardest. Throughout New England's history, trains have derailed, vehicles have collided, causing accidents and freeway smashups, airports have shut down, and planes have crashed—all due to fog. The enemy on the sea created the same chaos on land and in the air.

By early Tuesday morning, July 31, 1973, the fog had enveloped southern New England like a licentious barbarian campaigning on the land of innocents. The malignant dew metastasized itself onto everything it could, bending and molding itself until it cloaked the landscape with the unforgiving grip of a squeezing, starving python. Nothing could shake off the fog's pernicious hold.

The fog birthed offspring, spewing out smaller wisps of vapor that were even thicker and deadlier than the mother fog. The mist covered the land unevenly, draping some parts in a fine dew and smothering other parts in a blinding smog. The subsequent fog cover was left to the mercy of a god who chose today to excuse his benevolence and replace it with amorality. Even though the misty cover appeared amoral and amorphous, the fog was tangible—as tangible, and as guilty, as the iceberg that sank the *Titanic*.

Marvin Bomber arrived at the Manchester, New Hampshire, airport, Grenier Field, at 6:00 a.m. on that last day of July 1973.[2] His responsibilities as the Delta Air Lines gate agent for the day encompassed parking and dispatching Delta aircraft, as well as working at the ticket counter checking in passengers. The first passengers he met were those checking in for Delta Flight 751 from Boston, which was due to arrive at 7:05 a.m. However, Bomber had received a call a few minutes earlier that the plane had not yet left Boston due to the fog. Once the plane picked up the passengers in Manchester, the flight would proceed to Worcester, Massachusetts, and then fly on to New York City where, Bomber guessed, most of the passengers would depart. After Bomber checked in the passengers, he proceeded to the gate and informed those waiting for the flight that it would arrive at 8:00 a.m. and depart forty-five minutes later. When the plane had not arrived by 8:30 a.m., Delta notified Bomber that the flight had finally left Boston and was heading for Manchester. As the jet approached Manchester, the drone of its engines could be heard by some people near the airport, but the aircraft could not be seen through the fog. The weather was below the minimums for a safe landing, so the pilots of Flight 751 reluctantly turned their aircraft away from Manchester and flew off toward Worcester, leaving the stranded passengers at Grenier Field still waiting for a flight to New York.

Delta informed Bomber that after Flight 751 made its stop in Worcester, if the weather cleared, it would return to Manchester to take on the stranded passengers. The passengers were not told of these plans, but at that point it did not matter. Delta officials called Bomber back and told him that Flight 723 from Burlington, Vermont, would make a "flag stop" in Manchester and pick up the waiting passengers. The passengers, though, would be taken to Boston, not New York. It would be easier to get the passengers to New York from Boston than from Manchester.

The crew of Delta Air Lines Flight 723 did not plan on landing at Grenier Field in Manchester after their takeoff from Burlington that morning. Their intended stop was Logan Airport in Boston. But, because the fog wreaked havoc on air traffic from New York City all the way up through northern New England, Delta officials had to reroute their aircraft and pick up stranded passengers in the affected locations. Air traffic in northern New England was sporadic even on clear days, but whenever an uncontrolled variable, like fog, thrust itself into the mix, it could be brought to a halt. Before they took off from Burlington International Airport, the Delta gate agent there notified Pilot John Streil and Copilot Sidney Burrill that Delta Flight 751 had been diverted, stranding forty-five passengers in Manchester. Flight 723 would have to stop at Grenier Field and pick up those passengers and carry them to Boston.

Back in Manchester, Bomber informed the stuck passengers that they would be delayed further until the arrival of Flight 723 from Burlington. Thirteen of the forty-five passengers had already decided they would find their own way to their destinations, rather than wait for the relief plane. Waiting impatiently at Grenier Field, Sidney Samuels, owner of Bi-Rite, a retail store in Manchester, had to figure out another way to get to New York City. He, and several other employees, had been expecting to fly there to attend a retail jeweler show at the Hilton Hotel. They would be returning to Manchester on Wednesday, August 1, so if they were at all delayed, they would miss a good portion of the show. Samuels decided that, rather than wait for a later flight, he and his employees would drive directly to Logan Airport and catch a shuttle flight from there to New York. They left Grenier Field at 8:30 a.m.[3]

Several other would-be passengers also made the decision to drive to Logan, and a few others just decided to leave the airport and go home once they realized it would be fruitless for them to make the flight to Logan. They would just reschedule their flight for a later date. At 9:50 a.m., John Streil landed a DC-9 aircraft, Delta Ship 222, Flight 723, at Grenier Field.[4]

* * *

The DC-9 aircraft, built by the legendary Douglas Company of Long Beach, California, was the product of the natural progression of technology and machines—to make the technology more efficient while making the machine smaller. This is true of most machines built by man. The first commercial jet aircraft were powered by four engines and built mainly for intercontinental flight. They were designed to hold anywhere between 90 and 120 passengers. The crew navigating the aircraft consisted of three people, and the length of the aircraft was approximately 150 feet long with a maximum takeoff weight (MTOW) of approximately 250,000 pounds. The wingspan of these aircraft was almost 145 feet. The Boeing 707 and the Douglas DC-8 are representative of this type of aircraft.[5]

In the late 1950s, the search began for a smaller jet aircraft. The airlines were desperate to include jet aircraft in their domestic and regional fleets. They wanted jets that could land at smaller airports in areas that, at the time, were not served by jets. The criteria was an aircraft with fewer than four engines and a lower MTOW. A lower MTOW was vital because the Federal Aviation Agency (FAA), as it was called at the time, mandated that any aircraft with an MTOW over eighty thousand pounds must have a three-man crew. Anything lower would be a two-man crew, and that would be a money saver for any airline.

By this time, the French had already built a two-engine aircraft called the Caravelle. The Caravelle pioneered the use of rear-mounted engines in the tail, which gave the aircraft a clean configuration over the wings. It proved popular in Europe, and over 250 were built. However, its MTOW was 110,000 pounds, and that required a three-man crew. The DC-9 aircraft being designed by the Douglas Company had a 69,000-pound MTOW, which would save the airlines hundreds of thousands of dollars a year.[6]

As 1960 approached, Douglas Aircraft Company found itself in a precarious financial position. Sales of its DC-8 aircraft had taken off, but not in the numbers in which Boeing had sold its 707s. Douglas needed to keep the money coming in without spending large sums on aircraft investment. Sud-Aviation, builder of the French Caravelle, offered them an opportunity to sign a cooperation agreement.

> The terms called for Douglas to be responsible for sales and technical support of the Caravelle in areas outside Europe or any French-speaking regions worldwide. The arrangement also stipulated that should demand for the Caravelle exceed Sud's manufacturing capacity of approximately eight aircraft per month, a separate production line would be set up in Long Beach.[7]

Even though they had signed the agreement, Douglas engineers still explored designing and building a regional two-engine jet themselves to offer the market. Once word reached the French that Douglas was going to offer their own two-engine aircraft, the companies ended their cooperative agreement.

As the consolidation of Britain's aviation companies coalesced, they could focus on a twin-engine aircraft of their own. Hunting Aircraft Company had been absorbed by the British Aircraft Company (BAC), and their model 107 aircraft had won over BAC's brass. They renamed the model the BAC 1–11 (also known as the One-Eleven) and offered it for sale all over the world, with particular emphasis on the United States. The BAC 1–11 was announced to the world in March 1961, and Braniff, an American airline, ordered six right away. The production of the aircraft started in 1962, and this put tremendous pressure on Douglas as they had not even made a final decision yet to build a regional aircraft.[8]

In July 1962, Mohawk Airlines, another American airline, ordered four BAC 1–11s. American Airlines wanted to buy twenty-five regional aircraft but could not make up their mind whether they wanted the One-Eleven or whatever Douglas was going to offer. Without a firm commitment from

1. Fog Warning 13

N975NE aircraft in Northeast Airlines livery, 1971, JFK Airport. Courtesy of Art Brett.

Douglas that they would build the aircraft, the U.S. government faced a political crisis because they would be forced to subsidize the purchase of British planes for U.S. airlines. That was not something they wished to do. Finally, on April 8, 1963, Donald Douglas Sr. announced the conclusion "after a careful study of the potential market for such an aircraft that sufficient orders will be obtained to make the DC-9 program financially successful for our company."[9] The DC-9 was a "go," but Douglas was behind their British competition by two years.

The first flight of the One-Eleven came just four months after Douglas announced they would build a regional aircraft. However, tragedy struck the BAC 1–11 program when the prototype crashed in England on October 23, 1963, while on a test flight, killing all onboard. The crash was caused by a deep stall, when "the engine nacelles and fuselage blanked off the airflow over the horizontal tail surface."[10] In these designs, the turbulent wake of a stalled main wing "blankets" the horizontal stabilizer, rendering the elevators "ineffective and preventing the aircraft from recovering from the stall."[11] The One-Eleven program was put on hold just as Douglas accelerated their commitment to the DC-9.

To alleviate the deep stall, British authorities redesigned the mainplane leading edge and modified the elevator control linkage. They also installed a stick-pusher to "force the aircraft into a nose-down attitude if a critical angle of attack was approached."[12] Douglas engineers went a step further. In October 1964, they redesigned the horizontal stabilizer and elevators, expanding the surface area by just over 23 percent.[13]

On February 25, 1965, the DC-9 took its maiden flight and was first used for revenue service on November 29, 1965, by Delta Air Lines.[14] The One-Eleven entered commercial service on April 9, 1965, with British United Airways. Delta had closed the One-Eleven's two-year lead down to nine months.[15] The initial competition between the two airplane manufacturers was fierce, but the DC-9 quickly overtook its competitor.

It all came down to capacity, and the DC-9 was a larger aircraft. The DC-9 was over ten feet longer than the One-Eleven and had more cargo space. It could hold more passengers and had more powerful engines. The DC-9 also had an auxiliary power unit to service airports that could not power aircraft while on the ground. The jet also came equipped with rear stairs to allow passengers to enter and exit the aircraft without ramp services. Douglas also offered different lengths of the aircraft to cater to each airline's needs.[16] In the end, 976 DC-9 aircraft were built as compared to 244 for the One-Eleven.

N975NE, the DC-9–31 model aircraft, serial number 47075, was built and delivered to Northeast Airlines in the fall of 1967. It was the 166th DC-9 to come off the assembly line. With Northeast Airlines based out of Boston, the white-and-yellow-tailed DC-9s were a familiar sight to plane watchers and passengers in the northeastern United States. As it waited at Grenier Field, the aircraft had accumulated 14,639.7 flight hours with 843 flown since the last inspection in Atlanta.[17] After Northeast Airlines merged into Delta in 1972, Delta labeled it Ship 222 with those numerals painted on its tail just beneath the horizontal stabilizer. Because the aircraft now belonged to Delta, the airline painted Ship 222 white with a black stripe down both sides and branded it with the Delta widget.

2

Passengers and Crew

Although designed for a two-man crew, Delta Flight 723 had three men in the cockpit that July morning. Captain John Streil, forty-nine years of age, was the pilot in command. A resident of Lynnfield, Massachusetts, he had been flying since he was a teenager. His late teenage years coincided with World War II, and he signed up with the Army Air Corps. He trained in any aircraft he could but ended up mostly dropping bombs on Germany from a B-24 Liberator while stationed with the Eighth Air Force in England. In 1944, he was involved in a minor accident while training in an AT-6-C single-propeller aircraft at Easterwood Airport in College Station, Texas. He landed his training aircraft with the tail hanging a little too low. As the plane taxied after landing, the aircraft "started a ground loop to the right and efforts on the part of the pilot to correct with rudder failed."[1] According to his commanding officer, there was no violation of flying regulations. When asked to respond with a statement regarding the accident, Streil wrote sardonically, "I believe the cause of my ground-looping was overcontrolling with rudder to keep ship straight after landing, because of having flown heavy bombers for over a year."[2] It must have stung a little to have noncombat personnel, whose only flying experience was in training, passing judgment on the pilot of a B-24 Liberator who had dropped thousands of bombs on Germany. The accident did nothing to hold Streil back in his Air Force career, and he even flew over to Germany again, this time to save it from Soviet domination during the Berlin airlift of 1948.

After leaving the military, Streil began flying for Northeast Airlines in 1950. In July 1956, he became a pilot-in-command for Northeast. During his career, he held type ratings in many commercial aircraft including the Douglas Company DC-3, 6, 7, and 9, and the Boeing 727, as well as the Convair DV-240, 440, 880, and 990, and the Vickers Viscount. He was a well-rounded pilot with 14,840 hours' worth of flying time with 10 percent of that time in the DC-9.[3] A tall, lanky man with a large face and perpetual smile, he looked older than forty-nine years old, but that was, no doubt, probably brought on by his combat missions during the war. Within the

Northeast family, Streil was legendary, likely because of an incredible feat of flying he performed over Baltimore, Maryland, on September 4, 1961, when he saved twenty-three lives, including his own (detailed later).

Sidney W. Burrill, age thirty-one, lived in Winthrop, Massachusetts, with his wife, Susan, and his young son, Scott. Originally from Maine, he got his love of airplanes from his father who was an aircraft mechanic. In an interview the day after his death, Susan, pregnant with their second child, described her husband in an interview with the *Boston Globe*: "After graduating from high school in Orono, Maine, he became an aviation engineer at Bangor Airport and in 1967 he came down to Boston to train to be a pilot for Northeast Airlines."[4] When not flying, he liked to "hunt and fish, and often spent his vacations with his father lobstering off the Maine coast."[5]

According to the National Transportation Safety Board (NTSB), Burrill began his employment with Northeast Airlines on January 3, 1967. Northeast upgraded him to first officer in December 1968. He completed his initial training on the DC-9 on February 11, 1973, and was assigned as a first officer on Delta's approved routes. He had a total of 6,994 flight hours, of which 217 were in the DC-9. Over the past three years, he had satisfactorily completed all required training.[6]

Three flight attendants served the passengers of Flight 723. Patricia Humphreys, age twenty-nine, was senior to the other two flight attendants and had been employed by Delta since the fall of 1966. She had completed all competency training and checks on June 7, 1973. Ann L. Moore, age thirty-three, started employment with Northeast Airlines on November 22, 1971, and had last completed all her competency checks on November 10, 1972. Janice L. Wilson had a seniority date of February 26, 1973. She had successfully completed her initial training for Delta on March 23, 1973. According to investigators, all the cabin attendants were qualified in the DC-9–31 and 32 model aircraft.[7]

The reason for the presence of a third Delta employee in the cockpit of the DC-9 that day was a little more complicated. Joseph Burrell, fifty-two, was a captain for Northeast Airlines prior to its merger with Delta. Northeast hired him in the summer of 1957. He achieved the rank of captain in the DC-3 aircraft and of first officer on the four-engine Convair 880 aircraft. In 1963, he began suffering the physical effects of Parkinson's disease. In 1967, he was granted medical leave due to that diagnosis.[8] Never giving up on his dream to fly again, in 1967 he began treatment for Parkinson's with a new drug called L-Dopa. The treatment was so effective that by 1972, virtually all the physical difficulties he had suffered disappeared.[9] With the Parkinson's all but cured, Burrell applied to the FAA for his first and second airman medical certificates. At first, they were denied, but that decision was overturned by an administrative law judge, and the NTSB upheld the judge's decision. On April 19, 1973, Burrell received his medical certificate with no limitations and five weeks later began employment with Delta Air Lines as a first officer.[10]

Due to Delta's large fleet of DC-9s, Burrell was assigned to begin training on that aircraft. The three phases of training included ground training, simulator training, and flight training. On May 28, 1973, Burrell began ground training in the DC-9. On his first attempt at the written examination, he failed. However, a few weeks later, on June 22, 1973, he passed. On June 24, 1973, Burrell began simulator training. He did not pass that portion of the course. On July 3, 1973, the manager of the Delta Air Lines simulator program, Captain Herlong Averett, wrote a memo to his supervisor, Captain C.A. Smith, vice president of flight operations, stating that:

> [Burrell] has received the programmed number of hours of instruction as prescribed for initial DC-9 Simulator Course. At this time, First Officer Burrell has not achieved the level of proficiency required to complete the simulator portion of the proficiency check. He will require additional training to complete this portion of his training.[11]

From July 19 through July 23, 1973, First Officer Burrell went through the simulator course again. The DC-9 program manager, S.L. Leffingwell, wrote a memo after Burrell received training a second time, stating that:

> [Burrell] has not demonstrated significant progress toward and is not capable of, satisfactorily completing a DC-9 First Officer Proficiency Check.... Because of the fundamental difficulties he [Burrell] is experiencing, even at this late phase of training, I do not feel that further training, *at least along conventional lines*, is in the best interest of the company.[12]

On July 23, 1973, Captain Averett sent another memo to Captain Smith. It stated, in part, "Mr. Burrell's performance is deficient to the extent that we cannot forecast a time in the future when his proficiency level would be commensurate with the line requirements. I am returning him to his base manager for further disposition."[13]

The airline pilots' union (Air Line Pilots Association [ALPA]) representative requested a meeting with Burrell and his trainers on July 27, 1973. In that meeting, Burrell admitted that he was having problems with the simulator training. Burrell also recommended that the simulator training be interrupted so that he could "observe line operation aboard a DC-9 in actual service."[14] Captain Smith agreed to Burrell's request. In this departure from Delta's conventional training program, Captain Smith approved a plan that "contemplated Mr. Burrell flying as an observer in the cockpit of a DC-9, as requested by him, and thereafter resuming the conventional training program and utilizing the DC-9 simulator and training aircraft."[15]

Smith also instructed Burrell "not to participate in conducting actual flights but only to observe from the jump seat in the cockpit."[16] On July 31, 1973, Burrell found himself sitting in the jump seat in the cockpit of Delta Flight 723 as a first officer trainee–cockpit observer.

* * *

At any given time, on any given flight, at any given location, a cross-section of society flies on commercial aircraft. Passengers of diverse backgrounds such as politics, business, technology, royalty, management, and sales, all ride together to travel to destinations to enhance either their business or personal needs. Flight 723 was no different.

Representatives from all walks of life and from all over the United States found themselves sitting in the cabin of Flight 723. Ninety seats were taken up by ninety passengers all waiting to finally get to Boston. Most had connecting flights to take them to points beyond Beantown, but some had Boston as a final destination.

Chester Wiggin Jr., an interstate commerce commissioner, got ready to board Flight 723 as it drew to a stop on the airport tarmac. Wiggin was a World War II veteran, achieving the rank of lieutenant colonel. A former administrative aide to two New Hampshire senators, Styles Bridges and Norris Cotton, he had been confirmed by the U.S. Senate to the Interstate Commerce Commission (ICC) in October 1972 after being nominated by President Richard Nixon.[17] The ICC was the first regulatory commission formed by the United States under the Interstate Commerce Act of 1887. At first, it was organized to regulate railroads, but it eventually oversaw other surface transportation, including bus lines and telephone companies, to ensure fair rates. Another major focus of the commission was the elimination of discrimination. Wiggin had been scheduled to travel to Washington from his home in New Hampshire on Flight 751 but was rescheduled on Flight 723.

Count Laszlo Hadik, forty-one, was president of International Research Group, a Washington-based consulting firm. He was traveling on Flight 723 with his niece, ten-year-old Ilona deSchmertzing, to Washington. Among the papers he carried with him were those marked "Strategic Plans for the Nuclear Defense of NATO" and "Strategic Plans for the Nuclear Defense of the United States." These papers were part of the work he was doing with the Office of International Security Affairs. While not classified, the papers were deemed "sensitive" by the U.S. government. When he was a teenager, his family fled his native Hungary as Soviet troops and tanks approached to swallow up that brave land and crush any opposition to Soviet control. His grandfather, Count Laszlo Szechenyl, was the Hungarian minister to the United States from 1921 to 1933. Hadik's niece, Ilona, flew with her uncle to Washington to attend the Convent of the Sacred Heart school.[18]

2. Passengers and Crew

New Hampshire Assistant Attorney General Robert W. Moran and his wife, Patricia, boarded the aircraft in Manchester. Robert Moran had been appointed to the office of the attorney general in 1963 by Governor John King. The Morans had plans for lunch in New York City with some friends who were flying on to Europe that same day.[19]

Judy Smith, twenty-five, should not have been alive the day she arrived at Grenier Field to take Flight 751. In February 1973, she was involved in a horrific car crash in North Carolina that killed her boyfriend. She suffered a punctured lung, multiple cuts and bruises, and facial injuries, which required plastic surgery. After many weeks in the hospital, she returned to New Hampshire with her parents, determined to start her life over. She left her old job after Pandora Knitting Mills hired her as a trainee.[20] She was flying to New York for training with her new job. She decided to wait for Flight 723 when Flight 751 was cancelled.

John J. Ruane, fifty-two, of Hudson, New Hampshire, boarded Flight 723 in Manchester. He was an executive for Singer Business Machine Corporation en route to business in New York. According to a local newspaper, he was Man of the Year in Bethel Township, Pennsylvania, in 1966. He founded the Youth Hockey Program in Pittsburgh, Pennsylvania, and was vice president of a six-state hockey organization for youth. "He was also a member of the selections committee for the US World Champions and the US Olympic teams representing Pennsylvania."[21]

Robert A. Metz, forty-three, a partner in the architectural firm of Freeman French Freeman, sat waiting on Flight 723 with his eleven-year-old daughter, Lisa, and two other business associates of the same firm, Michael Longchamp, forty, and Laurence Hartigan, fifty-six. They were traveling to Boston to discuss details of an urban renewal project for Burlington, Vermont. On a prior urban renewal project for Burlington in 1971, five employees of Cousins Properties Inc., the developer for the project, were lost when their plane crashed into Lake Champlain a few minutes after takeoff on a snowy, ice-cold January night. Their bodies were never found.[22]

Five employees of International Business Machine (IBM) in Vermont were traveling to different business locations around the country. They were Robert Cummings, thirty; Richard Theriault, thirty-five; David K. Cameron, thirty; Robert H. Vallancourt, forty-three; and Adeline Cary, whose husband worked at the Burlington plant.[23]

Richard Mealy, thirty-three, boarded Flight 723 in Manchester for a meeting in New York. He knew with the cancellation of Flight 751 that he would be cutting it close but still figured he had enough time to make it. He had only been with his new company a short time and knew he at least had to try to get there. He waited impatiently for takeoff.[24]

Marion Smith, sixty-five, Yvette Patunoff, fifty, and Margaret Hoag, fifty-five, all of Vermont, boarded Flight 723 in Burlington. Their final destination was Louisville, Kentucky, where a national meeting of doll collectors was to be held. They had checked their dolls in at the Delta desk in Burlington and now waited in the aircraft while the Manchester passengers boarded.[25]

Waiting excitedly to attend Fenway Park that evening to watch the Boston Red Sox play their archrival, the New York Yankees, Scott Race, eleven, sat in the grounded jet with his mother, Shirley Race, forty-three, and his grandmother, Bertha Baker, seventy-two. The family was split on loyalties as Scott was a huge Red Sox fan and his mother was a Yankees fan. They planned on spending the night in Boston and then returning home to Winooski, Vermont, the next day.[26]

Air Force Sergeant Leopold Chouinard, twenty, boarded Flight 723 in Burlington lucky to be alive. He had arrived back in his hometown of Marshfield, Vermont, about a month earlier. His mother, along with his girlfriend, Brenda Newton, picked him up at the airport, and on the ride home their car collided with another car and was totaled. Chouinard, Brenda, and his mother, Laurette, were unhurt. It was an inauspicious start to his thirty-day leave from the Air Force and his base in Alaska. But his vacation from the Air Force was a time for celebration. His younger brother, Ray, married Leona Holt on July 7, 1973. Since Leo was not sure if he would be able to take leave from the Air Force to be home for the wedding, he decided that if he did make it, he should be an usher rather than the best man. His gift to the bride and groom was to be the photographer for the wedding. He spent most of the day behind the lens.

Leona had not met Leo before the wedding. Although she remembered being nervous about meeting him, the twinkle in his eye and his broad smile signaled her immediate acceptance into his family.

Leo became extremely excited when Ray and Leona announced they were expecting a baby in December. Leo was thrilled at the thought of becoming an uncle. The night prior to completing his leave, he proposed to Brenda, who by this time was a college student at Castleton College in western Vermont. They had been dating for three years and set a wedding date for some time in 1976 after she completed her college degree.

Initially, Leo had booked a flight from the airport in Berlin, Vermont. It was closer to his home and meant less driving for his mother. Unfortunately, the rain and fog caused that flight to be cancelled. In order to be sure he got back to Alaska before his leave was up, he booked Flight 723 out of Burlington to fly straight to Boston and then on to Alaska.

Brenda had joined Laurette and several of Leo's siblings in dropping Leo off at the Burlington airport. After saying goodbye to her son, Laurette and her younger children stepped away and let Leo and Brenda have some privacy in their farewell. After a passionate hug and kiss, and one more look at Leo in his blue air force uniform, Brenda and the Chouinards left Leo to wait for his plane.²⁷

Susan Boyle, Sandy Watts, and Mr. and Mrs. Joseph Fuller boarded Flight 723 in Manchester to fly to New York. They were members of the "Fresh-Air Fund." Upon their arrival in New York, they were to escort two busloads of low-income, inner-city youth to various communities around New Hampshire to provide outdoor summer experiences for a couple of weeks. Shirley Gagnon was the coordinator of

Leo Chouinard in Air Force uniform. Courtesy of Lee and Ray Chouinard.

the fund for New Hampshire and Massachusetts, but she could not make the trip. Sandy Watts took her place.²⁸

Mary Gosselin, twenty-three, and Patricia Fleury, thirty-one, were office supervisors of the Liberty Mutual Insurance Company. They boarded Flight 723 in Burlington to head to Boston for a business meeting. Fleury was the mother of twins and a nine-year-old girl. She only took this flight once a year. Mary Gosselin became the wife of Thomas Gosselin just three weeks before the flight.²⁹ They had just returned from their California honeymoon when she boarded the Delta jet.

Michael Provost, fourteen, along with his cousins, Perry Meehan, eleven, and R. Bradley Meehan, thirteen, boarded Flight 723 with their grandmother, Rose Marie Barnett, fifty-eight. The Meehan boys were returning to Florida to attend school, and Barnett was the escort. Provost went on the trip to accompany his grandmother back to Vermont after she delivered Perry and R. Bradley to Tampa, Florida.³⁰

Among others who boarded Ship 222, whether in Manchester or

Burlington, were Phyllis Gummere, twenty-five, who was returning to Illinois after visiting her fiancé in Vermont. They had plans to marry in September.[31] Mr. and Mrs. Maurice Brothman, both in their late fifties, were returning to their home in Arizona after a New England vacation.[32] Mr. and Mrs. Willis Paull, both in their early fifties, were returning to their home in Montana after a visit with their son who was a professor at the University of Vermont.[33] Clarence Hall, a thirty-three-year-old merchant seaman, was returning to his ship in New York after a visit with his wife and two children.[34] George Lafontaine, twenty-eight, was returning to his naval unit at Cecil Field in Jacksonville, Florida, after a visit to his parents in Vermont.[35]

Albert Penney, forty-one, was an electronics engineer who "held several patents on inventions of aircraft components."[36] Thomasina Muscato, eighteen, was traveling to Georgia to visit a sick sister.[37] Elizabeth Sauters, fifty-five, was on her way to St. Petersburg, Florida, to bring her elderly mother back home with her to Vermont.[38] Robert Thompson, forty-six, was a plant staff assistant for the New England Telephone Company.[39] Charles Hubbell, fifty-five, also worked with the New England Telephone Company.[40] Albert Holzscheiter, in his early thirties, was a general manager for an insurance company. He was en route to Birmingham, Alabama, for an insurance conference. Initially, he had planned to take his company's executive aircraft to Boston, but that trip was cancelled when he decided the plane was too small to land at Logan. He boarded Flight 723 instead.[41] Dennis Knapp, thirty-eight, was an employee of Delta Air Lines who had been visiting his father-in-law in Vermont.[42]

Linnell Kennett, twenty-four, and her sister Lourde Warren, twenty, also boarded the jet.[43] Mr. and Mrs. Wilbur Molin, both forty-four, were the owners of the Country Craftsman Store in Antrim, New Hampshire. They were flying to Florida on vacation.[44] Miriam Jackson, president of Jackson, Jackson, Wagner public relations firm, was also aboard the jet. "With her associates, she was the only triple holder of the 'Bell-Ringer Award' for the best public relations program in New England."[45]

Mr. and Mrs. William (Jane) Bergeron also boarded Delta Flight 723 after a month-long visit to Mr. Bergeron's sister in Manchester. They were en route back home to Georgia.[46] Jeannette Crowley, fifty-one, was flying to Ohio to attend her stepfather's funeral.[47] G. Minot D'Arcy, president of Inverness Corporation in New York, left his summer home on Newfound Lake in New Hampshire to fly back to New York. John G. Kester, salesman for Westinghouse Supply Company, boarded the plane en route to Augusta, Maine, via Boston.[48] Charles Brau, sixty-two, was also returning to New York after vacationing at his lake house in Holderness, New Hampshire. He was chairman of the board and chief executive officer of United Mutual Savings Bank of New York.[49]

Also boarding was Ora Kapopoulos of Manchester. She was the silver buyer for Lemay Jewelers.[50] Norman Richards was a sales manager of a Portsmouth fishery.[51] Winston Carpentiere, thirty-four, was traveling with Roger MacArthur, forty-one. Carpentiere was a marketing manager for the specialty products division of Nashua Corporation, and MacArthur was the general manager of the news insert specialty products for Nashua Corporation. Both men were traveling on business.[52]

Brother and sister Tracy and Jay Koteff, 15 and 18 respectively, boarded the plain after visiting friends and relatives in Vermont. Their parents had moved the family to Florida from Vermont in 1970. They were on their way home to Fort Lauderdale. Also returning to Fort Lauderdale was Mrs. Frances Bean.

When all the passengers had boarded, Marvin Bomber mounted the steps to the aircraft door and waited for the stewardess to complete her passenger count and sign the "stew slip." After she had signed it, Bomber then closed the passenger door and watched as a ramp agent moved the steps away. He then signaled to the captain to start the engines, and he walked around the plane to make sure all the cargo doors were shut and sealed tight. Bomber then saluted the captain, signaled him to leave the gate, and returned to the operations office and then the ticket counter. It was there he was informed by other Delta personnel that Flight 723 was heading for Runway 6 for takeoff. He knew immediately that someone had to reach the tower controllers and notify them that Flight 723 was too heavy to take off from that runway.[53]

3

Merger

Even on clear days, air transportation service in northern New England had limitations. Reliable service, comfortable planes, and local origins did not exist for most airline passengers in that area. Until 1972, the primary commercial carrier for New England had been Northeast Airlines.

Northeast received its operating certificate from the Civil Aeronautics Board (CAB), which was founded in 1940.[1] The CAB was an outgrowth of earlier aviation legislation passed by Congress. Prior to 1925, aviation in the United States was lightly regulated. In 1926, President Calvin Coolidge asked Congress to pass the Air Commerce Act of 1926. The act both promoted and regulated air commerce. It also established and maintained aids to air navigation as well as asserting "the sovereignty of the United States over its lands and waters and applying customs, navigation, and immigration laws to aircraft."[2] It also firmly placed these objectives under the direction of the secretary of commerce and added an assistant secretary of commerce to help enforce the act.

As aviation grew, the Air Commerce Act found itself outdated. In 1938, President Franklin D. Roosevelt approved the Civil Aeronautics Act of 1938. This created an entirely new agency called the Civil Aeronautics Authority (CAA) comprised of a nine-member board completely independent of any other agency or department. It had three separate parts: five members comprised the CAA, an additional individual became the administrator, and the other three became members of the Air Safety Board.

The responsibilities of the CAA as demanded by Congress were:

> In the exercise and performance of its powers and duties under this Act, the Authority shall consider the following, among other things, as being in the public interest, and in accordance with the public convenience and necessity—
>
> The encouragement and development of an air-transportation system properly adapted to the present and future needs of the foreign and domestic commerce of the United States, of the Postal Service and of the national defense;
>
> The regulation of air transportation in such manner as to recognize and

preserve the inherent advantages of, assure the highest degree of safety in, and foster sound economic conditions in, such transportation, and to improve the relations between, and coordinate transportation by air carriers;
- The promotion of adequate, economical, and efficient service by air carriers at reasonable charges, without unjust discriminations, undue preferences or advantages, or unfair or destructive competitive practices;
- Competition to the extent necessary to assure the sound development of an air-transportation system properly adapted to the needs of the foreign and domestic commerce of the United States, of the Postal Service, and of the national defense;
- The regulation of air commerce in such manner as to best promote its development and safety; and
- The encouragement and development of civil aeronautics.³

The three different groups had three different sets of responsibilities. The five individuals making up the CAA were assigned "quasi-legislative and quasi-judicial duties of economic and safety regulation."⁴ The chairman of the CAA was the conduit to the president of the United States. The three members of the Air Safety Board were assigned the duty and held the responsibility to investigate aviation accidents and make recommendations for improved safety. While the Air Safety Board was part of the CAA, they performed their duties independent of the CAA and could not be assigned any other work. The Air Safety Board was a fact-finding board and had the power to issue recommendations only. It did not have any regulatory or promotional functions.

President Roosevelt did not support creating an independent CAA. As early as 1935, he preferred aviation rulemaking within the ICC. Congress preferred an independent CAA. It did not like the idea of the CAA within the post office because the post office was the biggest customer of the airlines. Many members of Congress did not want the CAA within the Department of Commerce because that department was charged with the economic regulation of the country and safety is a primary part of that. If a conflict of interest arose between the two responsibilities, there was no guarantee that safety would be put first. The reason members of Congress were against placing the CAA within the ICC was that the Commerce Department had responsibility for the safety regulations of private aircraft. If the ICC had responsibility for the airlines, there would be two separate group of employees inspecting two different types of aircraft. It was a gross waste of manpower.

By 1940, President Roosevelt found the whole matter of the CAA confusing and felt there was an overlap of responsibilities. On June 30, 1940, Roosevelt reorganized the CAA. The act transferred from the CAA to the administrator the following functions:

1. Administration of the civilian pilot training program.

2. Issuance of aircraft, airman, and other certificates required in the interests of safety.

3. All other safety regulation, except for the establishment of standards, rules and regulations, and except for suspension and revocation of all types of certificates.

4. Enforcement of provisions relating to the construction along civil airways of structures which might be hazardous to air commerce.

5. Control over the appointment of officers and employees needed by the Administrator.[5]

Roosevelt wrote that this eliminated "the confusion of responsibilities" within a nine-man organization and provided a "more clear-cut and effective plan of organization."[6] This organization mirrored the responsibilities of the executive and legislative branches of government: The CAA made the safety rules (legislative) and the administrator enforced them (executive).

Roosevelt then sprung another surprise during this reorganization. He made the CAA and the administrator a part of the Department of Commerce. He eliminated the name Civil Aeronautics Authority and changed it to Civil Aeronautics Board (CAB). The CAB assumed the investigative functions of the Air Safety Board and transferred the organization to the Department of Commerce. While Roosevelt maintained that the functions of the board and the administrator would remain independent of the Commerce Department, the CAB administrator could only report to the president through the secretary of commerce. While the commerce secretary could not influence, delete, or revise reports and recommendations of the board, he would have an opportunity to read them and add any comments that he wished. Technically, the board, along with the administrator, was known as the "Civil Aeronautics Authority within the Department of Commerce."[7]

The aviation transportation sector soared along in subsequent years. Passenger traffic grew, more airlines formed, and the number of aircraft increased tremendously, as the industry tried to keep up with demand. However, on June 30, 1956, an accident over the Grand Canyon sent shockwaves across the United States and around the world. One-hundred-twenty-eight people were killed when a DC-7 aircraft collided with a Lockheed L-1049 Super Constellation. Both aircraft plunged into the canyon. There were no survivors. The accident made clear that more emphasis was needed on air traffic control.

President Dwight Eisenhower asked Congress to pass the Federal Aviation Act of 1958. This act would strip away the regulatory powers of the CAB and transfer them to a new Federal Aviation Agency (FAA). The FAA would "acquire, establish, operate, and improve air navigation facilities; ... prescribe air traffic rules for all aircraft; and ... conduct related research and development activities."[8]

The CAB would be primarily responsible for the "encouragement" of air service and promoting safety. It would ensure that all parts of the country had available to them "adequate, economic, efficient and low-price services by air carriers and foreign air carriers...."[9] They would also be concerned with promoting competitive market forces to "provide the needed air transportation system and to encourage efficient and well-managed carriers to earn adequate profits and to attract capital...."[10] They would also provide subsidies for the airlines not making a profit if they were serving areas where profitability did not arise on the routes served. Most importantly, the CAB still maintained the authority to investigate accidents.

In 1966, President Lyndon Johnson accomplished what other presidents had tried, but failed, to do. He brought together all the agencies responsible for transportation and placed them under one roof—the Department of Transportation (DOT). In describing the reasoning behind such a move, Johnson's Director of the Bureau of Budget Charles Schultze testified:

> Despite this vital role of transportation in the Nation's welfare and security, transportation responsibilities with the Federal Government have been fragmented among many agencies. Unlike other areas of national concern, the President and the Congress cannot look to a single official with Cabinet status for the development of coordinated and consistent transportation policies.[11]

The bill created four administrations: the Federal Highway Administration, the Federal Maritime Administration, the Federal Railroad Administration, and the Federal Aviation Administration (FAA, formerly called the Federal Aviation Agency). All four fell within the framework of the newly established DOT whose leader would be a cabinet-level secretary reporting directly to the president. The CAB would remain independent, but they would lose their responsibility for investigating aviation accidents. That would now fall on the newly formed National Transportation Safety Board (NTSB).

In theory, the NTSB was created to be an independent entity within the DOT. Its mandate from Congress was to "determine and report the probable cause of transportation accidents...."[12] They may also conduct special studies, ensure accident investigations are adequate, and send their own members to assist in other accident investigations when they consider it necessary. The NTSB can also make recommendations to the secretary of the DOT regarding safety.

While the NTSB would be independent of the DOT and FAA, it was not a separate agency. Congress believed that "to create the Board as an entity completely separate from the Department would be to create another agency exercising transportation functions."[13] It was located within the DOT for "housekeeping services and is empowered to require the Department to carry on investigations and to do other work for the Board."[14] The NTSB was not truly independent from the DOT. The act as written allowed the DOT to exercise influence over the board's decisions. Congress believed that creating the NTSB as a separate agency would be too costly and less effective than placing it within the DOT.

The NTSB had responsibility for all facets of transportation safety. They included motor vehicle, rail, and maritime transportation, and aviation. Of the four, aviation would be singled out for special importance. Within the board, Congress wanted a special section carved away to insulate itself further from outside influence, so they created the Office of Accident Investigation (OAI) within the NTSB, "which is made specifically independent of the new Federal Aviation Administration."[15] By incorporating this language, it would appear that the rest of the NTSB would not be immune from influence from the FAA or DOT for that matter. This office would be staffed by the current CAB investigators from the Bureau of Air Safety formerly located within the CAB.

The new OAI would become the "focal point for investigation of aviation accidents." Air accident investigations would maintain the same procedures as before.

    1. Investigation of fatal or large aircraft accidents would be carried out by a separate staff element (primarily composed of the personnel transferred from the CAB's Bureau of Safety) in the Office of Accident Investigation;
    2. as is presently the case under CAB delegation to FAA, investigations of designated categories of nonfatal accidents involving small planes would be carried out by the Department's Federal Aviation Administration field elements;
    3. determination of probable cause of accidents would be made by the National Transportation Safety Board, as the CAB does now.[16]

Congressional thinking determined that without the OAI, the FAA would, by default, investigate all accidents. This would not be allowed by the aviation industry nor the government as there would be a huge conflict of interest. Without the separate OAI, the accident investigation role would be "transferred to the National Transportation Safety Board, which then might be dominated by aviation concerns to the exclusion of other safety matters."[17]

Congress wanted the OAI to have a small staff concerned with coordinating accident investigations with the other modes of transportation. This would be done by giving advice on how to investigate accidents by their proven methods and allowing investigators from the other transportation administrations access to any laboratories and other investigative facilities.

Overseeing this vast transportation department was a cabinet-level secretary (secretary of transportation) answerable to the president, an undersecretary, four assistant secretaries, a general counsel, and an assistant secretary for administration. All these positions, except the assistant secretary for administration, were filled by presidential appointment and Senate confirmation. There was no specific statutory language that gave detailed responsibilities to each secretary. This provided the secretary of transportation the flexibility to assign each assistant to deal with emerging problems, crucial matters, or mundane tasks as they arose among the various administrations, boards, or offices within the department. It also allowed the secretary of transportation to reemphasize to his assistant secretaries not to interfere with the independent boards and offices within the department. This relationship between the various entities within the department worked as Congress had hoped through the waning days of the Johnson administration. With the election of Richard Nixon as president though, Congress's fantasy regarding the independence of the NTSB, and by extension, the OAI, came crashing down. Nixon had a plan for the complete takeover of the various executive departments and installing people within those departments who professed complete loyalty to him and who would bend the departments to the president's will.

* * *

The CAB retained its regulatory powers after President Johnson swept all the various transportation responsibilities into the new DOT. The CAB had the power to award subsidies to airlines if they felt it would promote air transportation to areas that were not profitable. Northeast Airlines became one of the first airlines in the United States to benefit from this government gift, but, for them, it was not at all profitable.

Scheduled air service began in New England in 1925 with contract air mail routes. The first route was awarded to Colonial Airlines, which flew mail between Boston, Hartford, Connecticut, and New York. The post office contracted with National Airways to run the mail in northern New England. Around this time, Mayflower Airlines began carrying passengers between Boston and Cape Cod. Most of these airlines were merged into Northeast Airlines. After the CAB formed, they made Northeast Airlines New England's regional airline and awarded them an annual subsidy of $300,000. Within five years, the CAB subsidized Northeast with almost $2 million.[18]

The subsidies were not without restriction. Airlines servicing small cities, such as Northeast did with the smaller communities in New Hampshire, Maine, and Vermont, received subsidies because, without them, it would not be profitable for an airline to serve those communities. With the CAB setting fares, sometimes the subsidy was not enough to cover the cost of service. Airlines had to maintain staff and facilities in these smaller communities, and from a business standpoint, even with the subsidy it was not possible to make a profit.

To wiggle out of receiving subsidies, airlines came up with a theory that "bigger is better." If the airline received longer, profitable routes, that would offset the cost of servicing the smaller communities, and they could run them profitably and without subsidies. According to Crocker Snow, the director of the Massachusetts Aeronautics Commission (MAC), management at Northeast Airlines told the CAB that "[e]ntry into the lucrative East Coast market south of New York through Washington to Miami would be so profitable that it could easily support improved New England service without subsidy." Snow continued:

> At any rate, Northeast was extended to Florida in 1956.... From then on it was all downhill for Northeast and for New England air service. Annual subsidy payments increased to a peak of $3.5 million in 1965 but Northeast's P & L statement continued to deteriorate to a $14 million net loss in 1971.[19]

There was no doubt that the only way an airline was going to make a profit by servicing northern New England was to shed many of the smaller communities it was forced to service with a subsidy.

Northern New England faced huge transportation problems. The problems were so large that the Senate Commerce Committee held hearings in 1971 at City Hall in Lebanon, New Hampshire. U.S. Senator Norris Cotton of New Hampshire spoke for his constituents when, at that hearing, he stated that "the CAB appears to have bestirred itself from its lethargy and at last recognized what I have long known and sought to bring to its attention, that air service to New Hampshire and its sister northern New England states is deplorable."[20]

In 1971, Chester Wiggin Jr. was the federal cochairman of the New England Regional Commission. He testified in front of the committee regarding the transportation nightmare faced by northern New Englanders. He stated that air service into Boston was "marginal" at best with service to New York a little better. He complained that direct service beyond New York was "practically nonexistent." He reminded the committee that a road traveler into Boston had to drive two to three hours before they could make a one-hour flight to Washington, D.C. Wiggin found it hard to believe that such limited service existed for an area that counted over two million people in its population.

He summed up his testimony by recognizing the needs of northern New England in regards to his regional commission:

> The commission recognizes the need for adequate transportation of all modes if we are to prosper and grow. Passenger rail service in our three Northern States is nonexistent. Our fine new Interstate highways are becoming congested. It is obvious to us that our economic well-being, present and future, depends in part on greater capacity to move people and goods by air, northern New England lags behind. It is time we caught up.[21]

For several years, Northeast Airlines faced staggering losses, but by late 1971, it was nearing bankruptcy. Northeast began merger talks with several airlines prior to 1971, but the most promising talks were with Delta Air Lines. The CAB had to decide whether to approve the merger because failure to act could cause the complete and total collapse not only of Northeast Airlines, but of all air service in northern New England.

The wooing of Northeast by Delta could become, if consummated, one of the most successful aviation mergers of all time. By 1972, Northeast was on the brink of collapse and could not live alone. When Delta came calling, it ranked as the fifth largest domestic air carrier in terms of traffic and revenues. With headquarters in Atlanta, Delta was known as a southern airline. Indeed, it had no routes in the northeastern United States and did not have a lot of interest in serving points within New England. However, the Boston to Florida runs of Northeast Airlines came as part of the merger package, and while they may have been tempted to snub points in northern New England, the Boston to Florida runs were too scintillating to ignore. Delta made a bid, and the CAB approved.

Delta Air Lines owned 141 aircraft: 78 DC-9s, 41 DC-8s, 16 Convair 880s, 3 Boeing 747s, and 3 L-100–20s. Their financial strength was staggering when compared to other carriers. Their average net income of 11.69 percent was higher than any other certificated carrier. Their total earnings were $284 million as opposed to only $189 million in long-term debt.[22] On completion of their merger with Northeast, Delta's rank of the fifth largest carrier would not change, but it would equal Eastern Air Lines in traffic and Trans World Airlines (TWA) in overall operating revenues.

By contrast, Northeast Airlines was a corpse. It owned twelve aircraft: six FH-227s, two Boeing 727s, and four DC-9s. They leased twenty-nine aircraft consisting of nineteen Boeing 727s and ten DC-9s. That brought it to a total of forty-one aircraft. They did not own or lease any wide-bodied jets as they could not afford it. According to the CAB, "Its operations as a whole have been consistently unprofitable; in fact, except for 1966 when the carrier showed a slight profit, Northeast has had an unbroken history of operating losses over the past 10 years."[23] In 1971, Northeast's net worth was a deficit of $39 million with projected net losses for the next few years. It served fewer than half of the New England points for which it had authority.

Things had gotten so bad for Northeast that, to get out of serving airports in northern New England, they purchased DC-9 aircraft because that type required longer takeoffs and landings than some of the runways of the smaller airports in northern New England could offer. This would exclude them from serving those communities.

On May 19, 1972, the CAB approved the merger between Delta and Northeast. Their decision was based, in part, on the following argument:

> For the Northern New England area, the benefits are readily apparent. It should be clear that we regard these benefits as a major decisional factor in the approval of this merger. The Board has viewed with concern the deterioration of reliable air transportation service in Northern New England in recent years. The deterioration has been due, in large part, to the persistent financial troubles of Northeast Airlines which is the only trunk carrier operating north of Boston. For the first time in many years northern New England will have a carrier financially capable of providing the public with the level and quality of service the area needs and deserves.[24]

On January 15, 1973, Delta Air Lines petitioned the CAB to delete eighteen of the twenty-six points north of New York that it had acquired from Northeast Airlines.[25] Delta had showed its hand and revealed they were not at all interested in serving northern New England. However, they instituted a novel idea to help serve some of the areas in northern New England they did not want to serve. They assisted certain commuter airlines in New England to service those points they rejected. They provided these commuter airlines access to their computerized reservation system and joint fares, published the commuter airlines' schedules on their publications, and provided various forms of technical assistance. While this was a help, the commuter airlines were subject to different safety and flight standards than certificated airlines like Delta, and their planes were not the most comfortable aircraft. However, in the end, Delta got Northeast's prestigious and profitable routes from New England to points south and relegated northern New England, as Northeast did before them, to the back of the line.

4

"Let Me Get Off the Plane"

As Ship 222 taxied to Runway 6, tower personnel notified Captain Streil that his aircraft was five thousand pounds too heavy for takeoff from that runway. The ground controller instructed him to proceed to Runway 24, which could handle the heavier weight. Once he arrived at the end of that runway, Streil waited patiently for takeoff clearance, but it was not forthcoming.

Air traffic controllers radioed Streil, "Boston can't handle you right now so there will be a little delay. Boston advises there will be right now at least a thirty-minute delay with the delay on ground at Manchester."

"You want us to hold on the runway?" Streil asked.

"Whenever Boston tower can take you will advise," the controller responded.

"OK, thank you, sir, little cluttered up this morning," Streil said summing up the situation.

"Getting missed approaches at Boston, that seems to be the problem," the controller responded.

"Ah so," replied Streil, trying to maintain his humor.[1]

Captain Streil announced the major delay over the public address system on the aircraft. The fog in Boston had delayed them further, and all that he, and the passengers, could do was wait for takeoff clearance.

Undoubtedly, the conversations inside the jet among passengers included the political, social, and cultural forces impacting the country at the time. Watergate was undoubtedly the most common word heard inside the cabin. Just two weeks prior, the head of the FAA and former assistant to the president, Alexander Butterfield, revealed publicly in front of a congressional committee that President Nixon had authorized the taping of all conversations inside the White House. This set off a huge legal battle as the special prosecutor investigating Watergate, Archibald Cox, subpoenaed the tapes because they might have recorded crimes committed or discussed in the White House. President Nixon refused to release the tapes. It was probably the consensus of many passengers that President Nixon would not survive his second term.

At the movies, the year began with the disaster film *The Poseidon Adventure*. This new genre of movies started out in 1970 with the successful movie *Airport*, about a passenger with a bomb on a commercial jet liner and the efforts of the crew and tower personnel to land the plane successfully. Two years later, *The Poseidon Adventure* was released. This movie followed the fictional story of passengers trapped in an ocean liner turned upside-down by a tidal wave. It became one of the highest grossing movies of 1973, splashed across many drive-in movie screens around the country, and ranked as one of the greatest disaster films of all time. The disaster genre focused on people experiencing a disaster and their ability to cope with it. Most of the time there were survivors, and the audience found themselves wrapped up in their story and enduring the trial with them until rescue came. It was Hollywood's way of letting people experience terror and horror without any of the physical, emotional, and traumatic consequences that come with them. Real-life disasters only happened to "other people."

One of the top songs of the summer of 1973 was "The Morning After," the theme song to *The Poseidon Adventure*. Ironically, it was a beautiful, soothing love song about what tomorrow may bring, sung in complete contrast to what the movie was about. Also on the radio airwaves, Jim Croce strummed a hit song about a fellow named Leroy Brown, Diana Ross pined about being touched in the morning, and Marvin Gaye wanted to get it on. Undoubtedly, many of the passengers heard at least one of the above songs on their way to the airport.

Surely, the annual misery of the Boston Red Sox was discussed on the plane. They had won the game the night before against their timeless nemesis, the New York Yankees, by a score of 4-3. The Sox had another game scheduled for that evening at 7:34 p.m. against the Yankees, and passenger Scott Race, along with his mother and grandmother, was thrilled to be a part of the thirty thousand fans to see the game at Fenway that night.

The passengers passed the time until takeoff by talking, reading, or just sitting back and relaxing. One man, however, kept looking at his watch and calculated that with the additional delay, he would miss his business appointment. He wanted to get off the plane.

Charles Mealy, of Bedford, New Hampshire, had been checking the time for the last couple of hours. When he boarded the aircraft a few minutes before, he figured he still had time to make his 2:00 p.m. business meeting in Long Island, New York. Once the captain announced the additional delay, he knew he would miss his connection at Logan Airport, so he grabbed the attention of the first stewardess he saw and asked her to let him off the plane.

She said, "No."

Mealy gently pleaded his case to her. He knew he would not make his connection.

The stewardess softened her look a bit and replied that he would have to go and speak with the pilot. She led him forward.

Once Mealy arrived at the cockpit door, he spoke to Captain Streil and explained the situation to him. He told the captain that he was not angry but that "I couldn't possibly make my appointment and there was no reason to go on."

Streil pondered the situation for a moment and then apologized for the delay. He consulted his two other crew members. At first, Streil hesitated but then relented. He told Mealy to take his seat and that he would return the aircraft to the terminal so that he could get off. He figured he might as well offer the prospect to all the other passengers.

Streil grabbed the cabin microphone and spoke into it. "This is the Captain speaking. We are returning to the passenger terminal to allow a passenger to deplane, due to the delay. If there is anybody else who would like to deplane, they should do so at this time rather than wait until later because we won't be making a second trip back."[2]

Streil then notified the tower and Marvin Bomber at Delta that he was returning to the terminal to drop off a passenger.

Mealy took a seat in first class while the jet proceeded back to the terminal. He chatted amicably with another passenger who had driven a semi truck all the way from Texas to New Hampshire to drop it off and was returning to Texas by air.

Marvin Bomber met Flight 723 upon its return to the gate. He moved the stairs to the plane, opened the forward passenger door, and allowed Charles Mealy off the plane. He handed the stewardess a copy of the Boston weather report received off the teletype and asked her to give it to the captain. He also told her to have the captain deduct two hundred pounds from the gross weight of the aircraft.[3] Bomber descended the stairs, and the plane pulled away. It was such a short return to the gate that Streil never unlocked the cockpit door nor shut off the plane's engines. He headed toward Runway 24, waited a few more minutes, and then received clearance for takeoff. Bomber watched the plane roll down the runway and head toward Boston.

* * *

Logan Airport, like the mythical Kraken, arose from the depths of Boston Harbor and emerged as a huge colossus astride East Boston at Jeffries Point. Benign at first, the airport started when Massachusetts leaders realized that the airfield in Framingham, Massachusetts, was too small to accommodate the aviation dreams of the Commonwealth. Officials chose the area because a weather station had already been established there, it already had port facilities, and the area could be expanded for airport runways by filling in Boston Harbor.[4]

At its inception, the plan for the East Boston Airport, as Logan was called until 1956, was to accommodate all types of aviation, military and civilian, for the Bay State, and ultimately New England. The airport developed a hunger for land before East Boston residents realized they lived on its food. In 1923 when it was opened, the airport consisted of two small runways serving propeller planes flown by pleasure pilots as well as military ones.

Ownership of the airport changed over several decades from the 1920s. In the beginning, the city of Boston ran the airport, but it grew too fast for an entity the size of a city to manage it.

In 1948, the Massachusetts legislature voted to form the State Airport Management Board (SAMB). The city signed over the airport to the state. Since the SAMB was controlled directly by the governor of Massachusetts and the legislature, the funding for the airport came from taxes. According to Dorothy Nelkin in her 1974 book, *JETPORT: The Boston Airport Controversy*,

> By the mid–1950s the airport, caught in the vicissitudes of Massachusetts politics, was a burden on the legislature. It had accumulated a debt of over $42 million, which cost Massachusetts $3 million annually in principal and interest payments.[5]

To remove the harmful political corruption from airport decisions and relieve the citizens of Massachusetts from the tax burden, the legislature passed the Massachusetts Port Authority Enabling Act. It created a "public instrumentality not subject to the supervision or regulation of the Department of public works or of any department, commission, board, bureau, or agency of the commonwealth."[6] The state of Massachusetts issued $72 million worth of bonds for the airport, and in 1959 the Massachusetts Port Authority took over the airport. The entity was simply known as Massport.

At the time Massport gained control of Logan Airport, it consisted of four runways. Runways 4L-22R and 4R-22L ran northeast to southwest, and they were parallel to each other. Runway 15R-33L ran northwest to southeast, and approaching planes would fly over East Boston and the neighborhoods on Neptune Road, and land on that strip. Runway 9–27 ran east to west.[7]

In 1967, Massport expanded Logan Airport. According to Nelkin, "Massport had extended runway 15R-33L by 2,200 feet and expanded landing areas, taxiways, parking and terminal facilities. Existing runways were modified to allow instrument landings...."[8] Plans were also in the works to build a new runway parallel to 15R-33L, extend Runways 9 and 4, and expand south of the airport around Bird Island Flats for cargo, hangars, and a short takeoff and landing (STOL) runway. By 1970, Logan was the eighth largest airport in the world; but it came at a price.[9]

Massport is a public authority. By 1973, there were at least eighteen thousand of them in the United States. They are usually set up for a single purpose and are independent of elected government control.[10] The only control that the governor of Massachusetts has over Massport is to appoint the seven members of the Massport board. Once they are appointed, though, the governor has no control over their votes or their priorities. Conversely, a public authority the size of Massport may indirectly exercise control over the governor and legislature. In the early 1970s, Massport employed over ten thousand people, used thousands of construction workers a year, and contributed hundreds of millions of dollars to the economy.[11] With this power, Massport could influence political decisions in Massachusetts, and there was nothing that the state government could do about it.

Edward J. King, a former NFL football player for the Baltimore Colts, was appointed the executive director of Massport in 1961. Before that, he ran Massport as its comptroller. The executive director of Massport held, in 1973, the state's highest paid governmental job at $54,000 a year.[12] In *JETPORT*, Nelkin writes that King was described by some as "competent, energetic and effective," and by others as "callous, insensitive and inflexible."[13] He directed so much control over Massport that it was rumored he visited and inspected the airport seven days a week.

> He believes that his plans to expand the airport are rational and necessary; if Massport does not expand, increasing air traffic will saturate the existing facilities and cause danger and inconvenience. Since the world is not a utopia, King claims, it is inevitable that the airport which benefits many people causes problems for some. He notes that Massport serves nearly 10 million passengers annually. Four thousand New England businessmen use the airport for commercial Shipping.[14]

Said King, "By far, the greatest good for the greatest number has been realized."[15]

East Boston was an especially important harbor before the airport came along. In 1925, its population was sixty-four thousand. By 1973, the population had dwindled to just over thirty-seven thousand residents. Most were Italian, Roman Catholic, and working class.[16] The many churches and Catholic schools in the area played an important part in the community keeping the residents homogenous. Many East Boston residents lived in "triple-decker," multifamily, wooden houses. Many families had lived in the same houses for many years. The growth of transportation caused the demise of East Boston. Since 1934, over one thousand housing units and seventy acres of recreational space had been taken from the residents.[17] The Neptune Road area of East Boston was hit particularly hard due to its proximity to Runway 15R-33L.[18]

The engine blasts from aircraft landing on Runway 15R-33L had knocked down television antennae and peeled the leaves off trees on Neptune Road. Landing systems interfered with television reception. A church steeple had to be removed because it obstructed aircraft landings. Oil pipelines to the airport raised homeowner insurance rates. But it was the noise from the aircraft that had the most negative impact.[19]

Many East Boston residents voiced their complaints directly to Massport. One stated, "I have two children at high school, they say noise is so unbearable teachers have to stop talking at their classes, it happens all day."[20] Another stated, "We shout to be heard until we get hoarse and then we just stop communicating."[21] And yet another complained, "It's impossible to talk on the phone, or listen to the radio, or watch television without being interrupted by the noise of the planes."[22] A Massport consultant responded,

> Noise is an increasing problem everywhere in urban life and how one reacts is highly dependent on his attitude and how much "pre-conditioning" was present. We are sure that few industries have given so much attention to reducing noise levels as has the transport industry.[23]

In April 1967, Massport destroyed Wood Island Park, leveling it to the same elevation as Runway 15–33. Wood Island Park was a recreational park and beach. It simply disappeared, taken from the residents by Massport. Later that year, Massport removed, by eminent domain, part of a block of Neptune Road to meet federal requirements for a clear zone and a localizer, a landing instrument used by planes.[24] On October 15, 1968, the Supreme Court refused to hear the case, which thus upheld a lower court ruling that Massport could indeed take the homes. The very next day, Massport evicted eight families and destroyed their homes.[25] Just a few months later, former Massachusetts Governor John Volpe became the U.S. secretary of transportation, and he stated, "Through the FAA I am now responsible for hub air safety. This necessitates the closure of Neptune Road."[26] On April 23, 1969, "35 men cut down 35 elm trees on Neptune Road and evacuated the neighborhood."[27]

Eventually, the plight of East Boston residents became too much for local and state government to ignore. Organized opposition to Massport formed. The city of Boston, under Mayor Kevin White, had no type of control, direct or indirect, over Massport. The only options available to the city of Boston were publicizing the problems with Massport in the news media or filing lawsuits. According to Nelkin, "[T]he city has lost all of its cases against Massport."[28]

The state government, under Governor Francis Sargent, had a bit more influence over Massport than did Kevin White. The governor could appoint members to Massport's board. On February 11, 1970, bowing to the public's dissatisfaction with the state's constant building of highways, Sargent "suspended all major highway construction in the greater Boston area," and he appointed Alan Altshuler, a professor of political science at the Massachusetts Institute of Technology (MIT), to become secretary of transportation and construction.[29] With $3.5 million in DOT funds in hand, Altshuler began to find other solutions to Massachusetts's transportation problem, and that included mass transit and public transportation.[30]

Governor Sargent wanted Massport to stop making decisions independent of those of the city and state and make them as part of an overall strategy involving the city and state. He said,

> What I do want is to have the Port Authority more responsive to the overall transportation problems and to the problems of the neighborhood. I think there should be some means of controlling them.... They should recognize that they must be part of the overall greater Boston Community.[31]

With Altshuler's input, Governor Sargent developed a new transportation policy. It stopped expressway construction and emphasized public transport. Excepted from the halt in expressway construction was a "two-lane special purpose road and tunnel to Logan Airport, open only to buses, limousines, trucks, emergency vehicles, and taxis."[32] He also wanted to freeze parking construction at Logan and build four parking garages in suburban areas around Boston and then have passengers take public transportation from there to the airport. Ed King opposed the proposal, but the board overruled King, and they supported the governor's policy.[33] Helping Sargent defeat King and gain some leverage over Massport was also the new DOT requirement that urban areas submit, with their grant proposals, a unified transportation plan.[34]

5

"Partial Obscuration"

Logan Airport employed over ten thousand people. Employment at the airport consisted of air traffic controllers, baggage handlers, line jobs, skycaps, airport police and firemen, construction workers, and many others. It took thousands of people every day to make the airport run smoothly. With the general fog condition currently enveloping Logan, the airport still had to get planes on and off the ground. The fog was not much more than an inconvenience. Planes were late, but the times were being made up. Construction crews could not work as fast, but the work still got done. Air traffic controllers still directed planes around the sky, but they were not overworked. Fog was a way of life at an airport that operated alongside a major East Coast harbor.

Charles Taylor of Concord, Massachusetts, checked into work that morning around 7:00 a.m. as an air traffic controller. His job that day was to guide planes into Logan as the approach controller in Logan's TRACON (terminal radar approach control) room.[1] This was a dark, windowless room at the bottom of the control tower. Taylor's main focus on the aircraft within his responsibility came through a radar scope and a radio as well as an intercom system connected to the people at the top of the tower who could see the outside world. The supervisor on duty assigned Taylor to the approach controller position. That meant that he had responsibility to guide incoming aircraft to the approach gate of each runway and guide them to the outer marker. The outer marker on Runway 4R was five miles from the end of the runway and the approach gate approximately one mile beyond that, about six miles out. Once an aircraft was inside the outer marker, the approach controller would transfer it to the local controller upstairs in the cab of the tower who would then take control of the aircraft.[2]

Charles Taylor had been employed by the FAA for seventeen years and had completed a four-year enlistment in the Air Force as an air traffic controller. He had worked at Logan as an air traffic controller for all of his seventeen years with the FAA. He held a control tower operator's certificate as well as a weather certificate.[3]

Jeffrey McDonald arrived to work about fifteen minutes prior to Taylor at 6:45 a.m. For his first four hours on duty, his supervisor assigned him to the TRACON room. After a few hours there, McDonald moved up into the tower cab and took over the local controller duties. McDonald had been an air traffic control specialist for several years and held a current visibility observation certificate and an air traffic control certificate.[4]

McDonald described his duties as a local controller as being

> responsible for aircraft movement from an area delegated from the outer marker in, which is five miles around the airport and all active runways and aircraft that are moving on the active runways and, through coordination with the ground controller, for crossing of any of the active runways.[5]

Once the plane lands, the responsibility for the aircraft falls on the ground controller who will then guide the plane to its gate or spot by the gate where the passengers will deplane.

Upon arriving in the cab, McDonald plugged his headset into his console and observed the radar blips on his screen to familiarize himself with the aircraft traffic situation. He had a panoramic view of the entire airport, 360 degrees all the way around. But with the foggy conditions, there was not much to see. At the southern end of the airport, he could see Runway 4L in its entirety, but Runway 4R was almost entirely obscured by the fog. What caught his attention, though, was a grey mass of fog, entirely distinguishable from the overall foggy conditions, moving from the harbor toward the airport. Specifically, McDonald described it moving from the south, southeast to the north, northwest and getting ready to completely conceal the approach end of Runway 4R in its thick, blinding veil.

Harry Terban, weather service specialist for the National Weather Service, had been employed at Logan Airport for approximately twenty years. His office, or observatory, was at the southern end of the airport in the general aviation building on the second floor of the two-story building. Around 10:45 a.m., he walked out onto the roof of his observatory to take a special observation.

There were two parts to taking a weather observation at Logan Airport. The first was looking around in a 360-degree turn and, as Terban would later explain,

> making a determination of the clouds, the amount of clouds, the types and also as to how we can see in every direction. With that information, we add that onto the read-out of the various instruments that we have in the observatory that we take a reading of all these various instruments, plus the visual end of it, and we combine them to make what we call an observation.[6]

Terban looked to the northwest and could just barely make out the Mystic River Bridge, which was approximately one and a half miles from his position. To the west, he could make out the Custom House building about a mile and a half away, and then, a half mile beyond the Custom House, he could make out the Prudential building. He looked toward the southeastern part of the airport toward Runway 4R.[7] However, as always, even on clear days, he could not see the approach end of Runway 4R because it was obstructed by airport buildings. He recorded his visual observation data onto the federal meteorological form, MF1–10A, and along with the instrument readings, walked back downstairs to his office and transmitted his report to the tower at 10:53 a.m. It read:

> Partial obscuration, estimated 500, broken, 25,000 overcast. The surface visibility was one and one-half miles. The tower visibility, one and one-half mile. The obstruction to vision was fog. The sea level pressure was 1,020.0. The air temperature, 68 degrees. The dew point temperature was 64 degrees. The wind was estimated at 100 degrees at 2 knots. The altimeter setting was 30.12 inches.[8]

Terban also wrote that the sun was visible.

Chief Charles Arena sat in his office catching up on some paperwork. Massport appointed him as chief of the fire department at Logan Airport in 1968. He had been with Massport as a fireman since 1955. According to friends and associates, Arena was well "respected from his men for his job knowledge and the way he handled himself literally, under fire."[9] He was known as a warm man who would drop everything to help those in need, according to his daughter. Having been at Massport for almost twenty years, a foggy day was not of much concern in terms of airport safety. The only real fear he had was construction or maintenance vehicles colliding with each other while traversing the taxiways. He glanced at the time, saw it was only 10:50 a.m., and went back to his paperwork.

Geoffrey Keating, a young junior engineer with the firm Fay, Spofford, and Thorndike of Boston, was working construction at Logan Airport on Bird Island Flats. Bird Island Flats was near the approach end of Runway 4L. When construction vehicles were halted around 9:00 a.m. that morning due to the fog, Keating and his fellow workers, Harris Cusick, Mark Falber, and George Conway, took a break. When the fog conditions lifted before 11:00 a.m., just enough for work to continue, Keating got into his vehicle and proceeded to the South Gate of Logan and waved the trucks in. The general prevailing foggy conditions persisted around the airport. After the last truck was waved in, Keating drove back to his construction site near Runway 4L on Bird Island Flats.[10]

Harris Cusick was a field inspector for Fay, Spofford, and Thorndike. He, like Keating, was part of a crew assigned to a land development job at Logan Airport involving the dumping of gravel fill. The job was a far stretch from the one he held in the Air Force as a weather observer.

5. "Partial Obscuration"

Cusick grew up in Winthrop, Massachusetts, and entered the Air Force in 1959. When asked what training he received at the Air Force Weather Observation School, he replied, "[S]trictly technical training that involved many things, mathematics, different weather codes, charting maps, teletype, learning the different types of cloud formations, atmosphere conditions, fog, anything pertinent to meteorology or weather."[11] He became a certified weather observer in the U.S. Air Force and served in the United States and Germany until 1963.

Because of the heavy, thick fog in the area, his training kicked back in, and he automatically started making weather observations in his head. He remembered the weather observation steps from his Air Force training: "A weather observation is made up of various data and in report form it would be reported as such: sky conditions, visibility, current weather which would be rain, sleet, fog, temperature, dew point, wind direction, wind speed, barometric pressure and any pertinent remarks added to that observation."[12] He began taking a visibility report and applied it to memory. "The visibility is recorded by utilizing different land marks say a half mile away, a mile away—and this was during the daytime, different structures, different solid items that are visible and you know the definite distance between your point and that point. At night they have red lights that are atop these structures. And that's what you look for at night, the red lights."[13]

Then he remembered the transmissometer. Transmissometers usually recorded the runway visual range (RVR). This was the distance one could see down the runway. According to Cusick, this was a device

> usually placed somewhere in the proximity of a runway of an airport, and it is a device which is precalculated utilizing a beam of light over a certain area. It has a recording device in the observatory so that when any smoke or fog or anything to obstruct that particular light from hitting the recording device would show you, like I say the precalculated—well, the mathematical result will show up on the chart if there should be any obstruction there.[14]

Cusick knew his weather. In the Air Force he performed exactly the same functions as Harry Terban did at Logan Airport. Harris Cusick, on this particular day, at this particular time, and at this particular airport, was probably one of the three most qualified weather observers, with the other two being Terban and McDonald. What made Cusick more reliable than the other two was his physical proximity to the fog. Terban and McDonald were located almost a mile away from it. Harris Cusick was right in the middle of it. So close, in fact, he was breathing it right into his lungs.

As his training taught him, Cusick divided the sky into quadrants. He quickly noticed that the worst quadrant from his vantage point was the east–southeast quadrant. This was the quadrant that covered the approach end of Runway 4R. Just before 10:00 a.m. it appeared that the fog was lifting, almost clearing, but by 11:00 a.m., it had deteriorated considerably. He remembered seeing "the fog in the channel and sort of lapping over the closure dike."[15] It was a rolling fog coming from the harbor down the channel and "coming up on the land like a lapping motion, like a wave."[16] Then it stopped and hovered over the approach end of Runway 4R, covering the approach to the runway like a white veil covers a bride's face or a black shroud covers the face of a corpse.

* * *

At 10:50:17 a.m., Ship 222, Delta Flight 723, began its takeoff roll. First Officer Sidney Burrill flew the plane, and Captain John Streil oversaw radio communications and explaining procedures to Joseph Burrell, who was only supposed to watch in his capacity as a cockpit observer.

"Bring her up," Captain Streil said to his first officer.

"Gear up," Burrill replied as the plane lifted off the ground.

"What I can do is this, Joe, is pull the gear up," Streil explained to Burrell, showing him the device used to lift the gears up.

As the plane settled into its climb, the crew concentrated on efforts to reach its cruise altitude. "Is that a right or a left turn he wanted?" Burrill asked Captain Streil.

"Left turn," Streil replied.

"Left turn," Burrell, the observer, reiterated. He had just approached the line from being an observer to performing a crew member duty, something he was forbidden to do by Delta.

Streil reached for the air-to-ground radio microphone and said goodbye to the Manchester tower. "An' we'll see you later, sir."

"Roger, good day," the departure controller replied.[17]

Streil then changed frequencies and got the approach controller at Logan Airport tower on his radio. "An' Boston Approach, ah, Delta seven two three, just off Manchester climbing out of two thousand to Lawrence," he informed them.

"Seven two three roger, cleared to Lawrence, no delay, plan vectors ILS four right, the Boston altimeter is three zero one one. Weather is partial obscuration, estimated four hundred overcast, mile an' a half and fog," Taylor replied, acknowledging Streil's transmission.[18] He had informed the crew of Flight 723 that they would be landing on Runway 4R, that the cloud ceiling was four hundred feet, and that visibility was a mile and a half.

Nothing in the weather report bothered Streil. Decision height for Runway 4R, the height where a pilot decides to land or execute a missed approach, was 216 feet. That still gave him plenty of height to have the runway in sight and then decide whether or not to land. Plus, Streil knew that the weather had to be improving. After all, they would not have released him for takeoff if the fog was getting worse. As a former Northeast pilot with seventeen years' experience flying around New England, he had landed at Logan Airport hundreds, if not thousands, of times.

All commercial pilots are familiar with weather reporting. It is part of their training. They are issued a *Pilots' Weather Handbook* that explains the different weather phenomena a pilot may encounter. Fog was a common phenomenon. The *Pilots' Weather Handbook* warns pilots that

> fog and stratus clouds, as customarily thought of, occur at or near the surface of the earth and can seriously restrict the visibility at low levels. Therefore, they are a very important consideration in aircraft operations, particularly in connection with landing and taking off.[19]

Fog is made up of many minute water droplets, which get suspended in the air. They have the capability to scatter light rays, which, in turn, decrease visibility. The average diameter of fog particles is about five ten-thousandths of an inch. It takes a huge amount of them to create fog. There are different types of fog. Radiation fog is a shallow fog, also called ground fog. A pilot may be able to see sections of the ground while flying and then other parts may be concealed by fog. Upslope fog forms as moist air moves up sloping terrain. It is most common in the western part of the United States. The most common form of fog along coastal areas is advection fog, also known as sea fog. It forms when "moist air moves over colder ground or water."[20] It can move in rapidly and tends to be more extensive and persistent than other types of fog.

"Very good, sir, we'll, uh, check with ya four thousand," Streil replied.

First Officer Burrill asked Captain Streil about the after-takeoff and climb checklist. "Did you get the checklist done?"

"We'll let Joe do it himself (okay). If you do the things and then—then we'll complete that checklist," Streil replied.[21]

With that remark, Streil anointed Burrell as a crew member in complete violation of the edict put forth by Delta's Vice President of Flight Operations Captain C.A. Smith. Smith only approved a plan that "contemplated Mr. Burrell flying as an observer in the cockpit of a DC-9, as requested by him, and thereafter resuming the conventional training program and utilizing the DC-9 simulator and training aircraft." The edict further instructed Burrell "not to participate in conducting actual flights but only to observe from the jump seat in the cockpit."[22]

Burrell agreed to these restrictions.

Streil cautioned Burrell not to perform the checklist by himself. "You gotta ask," he warned.

"Gear Uplatch check?" Burrell asked. This ensured that "hydraulic pressure is bypassed in all gear and door hydraulic components" and that the gear is resting on the doors in the UP position.

"Uplatch checked," Streil responded.

As Streil and Burrell traded questions and responses on the checklist, Boston approach called. "Delta 723, squawk ident please."

"Go ahead, ident," Streil told his first officer. Burrill pressed a button that sent their flight identification information to Boston approach so it would appear on their radar screen.

"Seven two three," Streil replied to approach control, acknowledging the request.

"Okay, thank you very much," Taylor replied as he saw the information appear on his screen. Because of the unscheduled stop at Manchester, the flight was not automatically generated and placed on the controller's screen. It had to be performed manually by the crew. The sound of a stabilizer in-motion horn went off in the cockpit, and the captain's microphone picked up a noise from one of the crew that could be construed as imitating the sound of a bugle in response.[23]

Streil got back to the checklist. "Okay, the gear was up, we got the gear up, right?"

"Yeah," Burrill replied.

Streil now spoke to both Burrill and Burrell. "Five hundred feet, we go to five-degree flaps. I'm afraid you got a little hot with the engines, just pull back a hair and crack them a little bit down here." He explained the procedure more to Burrell than Burrill, who had performed the takeoff.

"It would be better to leave climb power on till fifteen hundred feet. If they're bordering on the high, [cut?] back to maybe one point nine," Streil explained, finishing his quick lesson.

Burrill was concentrating far more on flying the plane than a critique of his engine thrust procedures. "What's our limit, Danvers, or ah, Lawrence."

"Lawrence, VOR direct," Burrell replied.

"Cross bearing or something on it, he didn't give us, huh?" Streil asked.

"Lawrence, VOR direct," Burrell repeated.

"We go the Boston VOR direct," Streil emphasized.

"From Lawrence," Burrill emphasized. He needed to be sure.

"Lawrence, we're only cleared to Lawrence," Burrell chimed in.

"Only to Lawrence," Streil stressed. "I'll get you something for coming up on Lawrence."

"Go ahead," Burrill said.

"I'll give you Boston," Streil replied.

"Okay, give me Boston. Let me have our clearance," Burrill added, wanting Streil to call out the altitude to him.

"Ah, one thousand feet to go," Streil said.

"Right," Burrill confirmed.[24]

As the pilot not flying the plane, Streil oversaw radio transmissions with the tower and had the responsibility of calling out altitude readings and any other vital communications the first officer may need. His responsibilities increased with Burrell in the cockpit as he took time out from his duties to explain things to the observer. With increased responsibilities came the likelihood of distraction. A pilot could only manage a finite number of tasks until he or she became overwhelmed. Even though First Officer Burrill was flying the plane, it was Streil who had absolute control in the cockpit. Every decision, and all responsibility, rested with him.

6

"He Didn't Say to Go On Down"

Captain Streil picked up his radio microphone. "Ah, Delta Seven-two-three approaching Lawrence," he said.[1] The crew needed to know which direction they would be heading after they got to Lawrence. Aircraft could not fly around a geographical fix and wait for instructions. In flying, you always had to stay ahead of the aircraft.

"Seven-two-three, roger, fly heading now one eight zero, radar vectors, ILS four right," Taylor instructed them.[2] He had notified the crew that they would be flying one hundred and eighty degrees off the Lawrence fix. Taylor would then send them more vectors to get them on an instrument landing system (ILS) onto Runway 4R.

"One eight zero," Streil replied, confirming the vector.[3] The flight plan would take them west of Boston and then southwest and over Castle Island to Runway 4R.

"You level at four thousand now?" Taylor asked.[4]

"Yep," Burrill told Streil, having leveled off the jetliner.[5]

Streil sent the answer onto Taylor. "That's affirmative. Four thousand."[6]

Burrill still needed to know his next step. "Did you identify Milton?"

"Identified Boston. Oh yeah, yeah," Streil replied, a little confused.

He set his receiver to Milton, which was the outer marker about five miles from the end of Runway 4R. This was the last major fix that a flight crew needed before landing their aircraft. All of the information they needed from the tower to make a safe and successful landing would be given to them before they reached the outer marker.

The receiver responded with the outer marker code. "Dah dit, dit dit--dah dah dah."[7] These were the letters B and O, which identify the Milton marker. This is a coded signal received in the cockpit via instrumentation. It occurs numerous times. After the code is sent and the aircraft flies over the outer marker, a set of lights appears on the crew's instruments notifying them they are over the outer marker.

Satisfied with the reception of the coded letters, Streil told Burrill it was identified.

6. "He Didn't Say to Go On Down"

Forty-five seconds after identification, Taylor ordered the Delta crew to descend to three thousand feet.

"Okay Air, leaving four for three, seven two three," Streil replied, acknowledging the command.[8]

"Delta seven two three, fly heading two two zero," Taylor instructed, giving them another vector toward Runway 4R.

"Two two zero," came Streil's reply.[9]

The interphone from the cabin to the cockpit rang. A flight attendant needed to talk to one of the crew. Burrell lifted the phone from its cradle but did not know how to use it. "Just press the thing in and talk to her," Streil advised.[10]

"Yes?" Burrell asked.

After all the delays that the passengers had incurred this morning, some of them had asked the flight attendants if they were going to be delayed further. Those passengers near the windows of the aircraft could see that the fog was still present. Most of those passengers with connections out of Boston realized that they would be extremely pressed for time or miss their next flight altogether. If there was any further delay in the air, it was virtually certain anyone with a connection would miss it.

"Uh, are we going to be able to go right in or are we going to be doing some circling around and all?" the flight attendant asked.[11]

"We've got a radar vector to the final approach course now," Burrell responded.[12]

Relieved that there would be no further delays, the flight attendant said goodbye.

At 10:59 a.m., Burrell reminded Streil to set the altimeter for a decision height for Runway 4R.

"This category two?" Burrell asked, wondering what kind of approach to expect.[13]

"No," Streil replied. "When you're on this speed, you know you're not pressed for much, even though it's a short ride, Manchester to Boston, we're only doing two-twenty so no hurry."[14]

A female pilot's voice came over the radio. "Ohh," one of the crew responded.

"There's an awful lot of women flying today—pilots," Burrill noted.[15] He did not elaborate on whether that was a good thing or not.

Streil reached for the fresh air control knob above his head and turned it on. "We're looking in for a high temperature up here. The DC-9's temp control is wild," he said.

"Yeah," Burrill replied, agreeing with his captain.

"I love the airplane," Burrell said.

"Relax," Burrill replied. "Love the DC-9," he added, agreeing with Burrell.

Streil explained how to turn the air vent on. "It makes a lot of noise when you open it. We've both got the same thing," he said to Burrell. "Ah, you've got one over your head too, eh?"

"Right," Burrell replied.

"It's okay. It doesn't cost anything," Streil joked. "They make a lot of noise but if you want extra air, sometimes.... Right behind ya," Streil added, pointing to the control knob. He then started talking about the weather forecast. "It's supposed to go down again tonight here," he said, talking about the cool New England summer. "It's supposed to get good today and then go down again tonight again."[16]

"Seven-two-three, fly heading two zero zero," Taylor radioed from Logan Airport.

"Two zero zero, seven-two-three," Streil replied, acknowledging the vector.

"It might be tomorrow morning when we come up from Washington for a while, it may be fog," Streil said, continuing on about the weather reports.

"Radar approach was blocked out," Burrill added.[17]

"Lost, ah, the whole day before I got back to work—by tomorrow," Streil complained. While he had complained about the fog forecast for the next day, he did not seem at all concerned about the presence of fog at Logan during the current flight. Obviously, it did not seem too bad in his view from the cockpit. The stabilizer in motion horn went off again, and as before, the captain's microphone picked up what could be confused as a bugle call.[18]

At 11:02:58 a.m., Taylor began transmitting his final vectors to Streil. "Delta seven two three, fly a heading of one five zero," he commanded.

"One five zero, seven-two-three," Streil confirmed.

Approximately fifteen seconds later, Taylor gave him a vector of one three zero and Streil confirmed it. About forty seconds later, Taylor changed headings to zero nine zero. Streil confirmed and Taylor confirmed it back.[19]

At 11:04:30 a.m., Taylor set Delta Flight 723 up for its final vectors. "And Delta seven-two-three, fly a heading of zero eight zero now. Intercept the localizer course and fly it inbound, over."

Five seconds later, Streil responded. "Okay, zero eight zero for intercept."[20]

"Fuel pumps," Burrell said, continuing the checklist.

"Localizer's alive," Streil told Burrill, advising him that the outer marker was showing up on their instruments and they were right above it.[21]

Something bothered Sid Burrill as he was setting the aircraft up for a final approach. Taylor had given him the intercept angle but did not authorize him to descend beneath three thousand feet. Maybe he missed it in the transmissions, he must have thought.

6. "He Didn't Say to Go On Down"   51

"Go down to two thousand now, can't we?" he asked Streil.[22]

The question confused Streil. "He didn't say—he didn't say to go on down."[23] Streil knew this was odd and not standard air traffic control service. The crew had been given the vectors to intercept the localizer, but they had not been given a clearance nor were they told to descend to a lower altitude. The controllers' lack of clearance and failure to give them authorization to descend meant the pilots of Flight 723 would intercept the localizer from above, not below, as prescribed in flight manuals. Above the outer marker, Streil had to ask for information that he should have already received from Taylor by this time in the flight. "Is seven-twenty-three cleared for ILS?" he asked approach control.[24]

* * *

For Charles Taylor, even with the fog, it was just a normal day. Not extremely busy but just enough where the time would not drag. His radar scope had blips floating across it like some scene out of a science fiction movie where Earth was under attack from some cartoonish dots that descended to Earth every time a sweep circumvented the screen. The cartoonish dots had identifiers attached to them though, and Taylor had them under surveillance. A mixed fleet of DC-9s, Boeing 727s, and Fairchild 227s from airlines as diverse as Delta, Trans World Airlines (TWA), Executive Air, Allegheny, and American were all flying around Logan Airport on a strict time frame like a flock of seabirds impatiently waiting to descend on a sandy beach. Taylor's job was to keep them separated and then corral them into single file and land them on Logan's runways. The goal the morning of July 31, 1973, was to keep the aircraft separated from each other at a three-mile distance horizontally and one thousand feet vertically. It was an easy goal to keep if every pilot followed the commands given them from air traffic control.

The one pilot that day who was not following the commands of air traffic control was the pilot of Allegheny Airlines Flight 666. He was flying his jet aircraft in a holding pattern approximately twenty miles southwest of the airport at the Millis intersection. At 11:02:25 a.m., as Taylor vectored Delta 723 toward the outer marker for landing, Allegheny 666's pilot contacted Taylor: "Approach Control Allegheny 666, eight-thousand."[25]

"Allegheny 666 Boston approach control. Roger," Taylor replied.

Since Eastern Air Lines Flight 1020 was in the holding pattern at eight thousand feet, Taylor thought he might have misunderstood him. "What is the altitude again, please?" Taylor queried the Allegheny pilot.[26]

"8,000," he responded.[27]

Both aircraft were in the Millis holding pattern at eight thousand feet making right turns and the potential for a midair collision existed. Taylor had not experienced anything like this during his career. Fortunately, the aircraft were going in the same direction so they would more than likely maintain their distance from each other, but it was imperative he get them out of the same height.

"Allegheny 666, squawk ident and maintain your present heading please and Eastern 1020 fly heading of 070, 070," he said, repeating the heading for Eastern 1020.[28] Taylor then instructed Flight 1020 to make a left turn out of the holding pattern to which the pilot complied. The midair collision issue was rectified in less than fifteen seconds.

Allegheny 666 was now flying southwesterly, away from the airport, and Eastern, at the behest of Taylor, cut the line and began vectoring for approach. Once Taylor verified that Eastern 1020 had made the left turn, at 11:03:28 a.m., he advised Allegheny 666 to reverse course and return to Millis and reestablish its holding pattern.

Even though Taylor's timing had been thrown off by the situation with Eastern 1020 and Allegheny 666, at this point, things went back to normal. Noticing that his landing time had been changed, the pilot of Eastern 1020 asked Taylor if he had an estimated approach clearance for him.

"Let's make it 1515" (Greenwich Mean Time), Taylor said.[29] That translated to 11:15 a.m. local time.

"Thank you," replied the captain.

Again, Taylor returned to the other aircraft in the area. He cleared several to land, including Eastern Air Lines Flight 572. He gave them their approaches and told them what kind of landing to expect. He also ordered them to switch their radios to the control tower for local control, Jeffrey McDonald's position.

Looking at his screen, Taylor saw that Allegheny 666 was, again, not following instructions. It had overrun the Millis intersection. At 11:05:22 a.m., just fifteen seconds before Captain Streil had to ask Taylor if they were cleared for the ILS, Taylor called Allegheny 666 on the radio to verify his altitude even though the altitude for that flight was clearly visible to Taylor on his radar screen. Looking at his radar screen, Taylor immediately saw that there were no other aircraft in the vicinity of Allegheny 666, but he kept calling anyway.

7

"I Don't Trust That Thing"

With one eye on the fog bank moving in over Runway 4R, Jeffrey McDonald continued to handle the aircraft that Charles Taylor transferred to him. "Eastern 572's cleared to land on Runway 4R," he said.[1] Eastern 572's pilot acknowledged the clearance and proceeded floating down toward Runway 4R.

Due to the presence of the monster fog bank moving across the entrance to Runway 4R, McDonald felt the need to warn the Eastern pilot. "Five seventy-two the fog's movin' back in from the south across the airport, now it's just approaching runway four right, your RVR for four right is showing more than six thousand," he warned.[2] That meant that when the aircraft punctured the fog bank and landed, he would be able to see six thousand feet down the runway, over a whole mile. Eastern 572 acknowledged.

Down beneath McDonald in the TRACON room, Taylor could not get Allegheny 666 to respond to his repeated attempts to gain contact. "Allegheny 666," he kept asking without luck.[3]

At 11:05:39 a.m., after Taylor's fourth unsuccessful request to 666, Captain Streil's voice came over the radio. "Is seven twenty-three cleared for ILS?" he asked.[4]

"Yes," replied Taylor. "Seven two-three is cleared for the ILS, yes."[5]

"All righty," Streil replied.[6] They were the next aircraft in line to land after Eastern 572, but 723's crew never heard the fog warning from McDonald to the Eastern jet. Taylor had not instructed them to change their radio frequency to the tower channel. It was mandatory procedure that the controller issue that command as the plane reached the outer marker.

Taylor then went back to trying to raise 666. Finally, the pilot of 666 responded. "You are level at 8,000?" Taylor asked.[7]

"Yes," Allegheny's pilot replied.[8]

And with that, Taylor acknowledged the communication but never told Allegheny to reverse course back to the Millis intersection. He obviously did not have an issue with the overshoot.

53

Landing preparations began in earnest in the cockpit of Delta Flight 723. "Gear down?" Streil asked.

"Yeah," Burrill replied.[9]

With just over a minute to land, Joe Burrell continued with the landing checklist. "Three green, pressure and quantity," he said, making sure the hydraulic system was working properly.[10]

Captain Streil looked at Burrill and noticed a little concern on his face. Something just was not right. Streil checked the flight director and saw the plane's position was above the glide slope. They were not correctly aligned for landing. "Get on it, Joe, ah, Sid," he said to his copilot.[11]

"Getting' down (ah) thousand feet a minute," Burrill replied tensely.[12]

Streil shook his head. "Leave it below one," he told Burrill.[13]

In the tower at Logan Airport, the controllers warily eyed the fog bank that had virtually concealed the mouth of Runway 4R. Daniel Tucker, in charge of tower personnel as the team supervisor that day, arrived at work that morning just before 8:00 a.m. At approximately 10:45 a.m., he signed on as the local control coordinator, assisting Jeffrey McDonald. He stood between McDonald and Paul Boriello, the ground controller. At 11:07:03 a.m., he decided he needed to alert the controllers in the TRACON room below that the fog would create some problems for them and more than likely initiate some missed approaches.[14] He reached for the intercom and asked for the arrival data page to pick up his phone.

"Yeah," Jim Merageas replied.[15] He was the page who sat between the two approach control coordinators.

"That fog's coming right back across again, so you can get ready for some. It's real thick again," he told Merageas.[16]

In the cockpit of Flight 723, Sid Burrill swore in frustration because he could not get the jet back on course for the approach. The flight director on the aircraft had started to malfunction. "This goddamn command bar shows ***!"[17]

"Yeah, that doesn't show much," Streil replied coolly, looking at the director.[18]

Jeffrey McDonald knew Delta 723 was next in line for landing, but he could not raise him on his frequency. "Ah, 723, you on the frequency?"[19]

No response came from Streil because he had not been told to turn his radio to the tower frequency yet. McDonald looked at Tucker. "Tell them to clear 723 to land," he told his boss, referring to Taylor.[20] This far inside the approach gate, the aircraft should already have been cleared to land and have already been switched over to the tower frequency.

Tucker relayed the message downstairs. Taylor contacted Streil. "Seven two-three is cleared to land. Tower one nineteen one," Taylor said, clearing the flight late and only after being told to do so by Tucker.[21]

"Seven two-three," Streil replied, now juggling both the radio and the faulty flight director.[22]

Suddenly, Streil had his eyes and ears scanning everyone and everything in the cockpit. "Going like a ####," he said, warning Burrill he was going too fast.[23] They were traveling at 165 miles per hour when their target speed should have been 143 miles per hour.

"Oh my god," Burrell chimed in from the observer seat.[24]

Streil's responsibilities now compounded exponentially. He had to keep focused on helping Burrill get the plane back on course, scanning the instruments, monitoring the radio, helping Burrell with his training, and dealing with this interminable fog bank that they had just entered. He had no point of reference to the runway, and he knew he had to get to 216 feet before a decision had to be made whether to abort the landing or not, but he had also been told that the cloud ceiling was at four hundred feet so that should still give him plenty of time to see the runway, approach decision height, and decide whether to land or go around. What John Streil and Sidney Burrill forgot to do was monitor their altitude. The weather had changed dramatically since their takeoff from Manchester, but they had not been notified by air traffic control about the deteriorating conditions even though the approach controllers had been told by Tucker about the moving fog bank hiding Runway 4R. Eastern Flight 572, the plane in front of them, had also been told about the bad weather from Jeffrey McDonald, but the crew of Delta Flight 723 had not.

* * *

John Streil did not get perturbed easily. He had an easy, calm, professional manner and had ice blood in his veins during emergencies. One such emergency took place over Baltimore, Maryland, on September 4, 1961.[25]

Northeast Airlines had been flying the Vickers Viscount airplane since 1958. The British government wanted to build a short-haul aircraft that would hold around twenty-plus passengers with four turbine gas engines. The cabin would also be pressurized, allowing for operations at higher altitudes to fly over storms and other bad weather. For British airlines, it could be used for short-haul runs to the European continent. In America, it could be used for short-haul runs and was ideally suited for the Washington, D.C.–New York–Boston triangle, exactly the routes flown by Northeast Airlines.

Northeast Airlines Flight 177 had taken off from Boston, Massachusetts, heading to National Airport in Washington, D.C., with nineteen passengers and four crew. As Captain Streil prepared to land the plane at National around 2:20 that afternoon, he noticed that the wheels failed to stretch out of the belly of the aircraft. After trying everything that the flight manual recommended to ease them out, Streil realized the wheels were not budging from the plane's belly. He notified the tower personnel who then diverted him to Friendship Airport in Baltimore, Maryland. Friendship had longer runways and less traffic than National. In the event of a crash, it would have less impact on that airport.[26]

Two of the crew, flight attendants Nancy Tierney and Mary Allen Walsh, walked back and forth in the single-aisle aircraft offering assurances to the passengers that all would be well. Tierney and Walsh, both twenty-one years of age, encouraged everyone to keep calm and instructed the women passengers to remove their high heels; they also intoned that prayers would not hurt their situation. As they sat down in their seats and strapped themselves in for the landing, they could hear the whispered holy names of Jesus, Mary, and Joseph being summoned by the passengers to offer protection to the crippled aircraft.[27]

As John Streil aligned the hog-tied aircraft for landing, he saw the rescue equipment lined up ready to render any assistance that would be needed for rescue and recovery if it came to that. He also noticed that white creamy foam covered the runway to cushion the landing. He aimed the aircraft directly for it.

As the plane touched down, passengers felt a small bump and then a skidding sensation. After that, the aircraft came to a stop and became the target of more foam as the rescue equipment covered the aircraft in the substance to cool it down.

Passengers gave the crew high grades for avoiding panic. Mattie Pinette said, "It was wonderful they kept everyone from becoming excited." Harold Tallant, a twenty-two-year-old passenger from Cherryville, North Carolina, said, "We felt nothing more than the normal jolt." The crew handled the emergency so smoothly that Margaret Charles, nineteen, of Columbia, South Carolina, said, "It was interesting at first ... but then I got bored."[28]

The damaged aircraft, with its scratched underbelly and bent propellers, was cleared off the runway only after the passengers and crew disembarked and took buses to the terminal complex. Before they too were escorted to the terminal building, Captain Streil and copilot John Caldwell posed next to a damaged propeller on the bent wing. Streil placed a fatherly hand proudly on the propeller as if he was congratulating the aircraft for not breaking up.[29] Caldwell had a huge smile on his face, no doubt feeling lucky to be alive. Captain John Streil had proven his mettle.

* * *

John Streil, with his proven ability to act calmly in a crisis, realized that things could quickly get out of hand in a jet's cockpit if a pilot did not maintain his focus. He knew that, even though Burrill was flying the plane, he retained the ultimate authority as captain of Flight 723. He had to remain steady, calm, and professional to gain control of the flight. At this point in the flight, thirty seconds from touchdown, he saw the jet was going too fast and was not aligned on the localizer beam. On top of that, with the weather report he had received, they should be breaking out of this fog and visually locating the runway. At 11:07:28 a.m., Streil told Burrill that "your localizer startin' to come back in now."[30]

"All right," Burrill replied. "Set my power up for me if I want it," he added.

"Okay. Just fly the airplane," Streil replied quickly.

Two seconds later, Streil realized why they were not stabilized on the approach beam. "You better go to raw data, I don't trust that thing."[31] That thing that Streil did not trust was the flight director, an instrument that was the absolute nerve center of information for a pilot.

During aircraft navigation using instruments within the aircraft, there are transmitters that send out radio signals in a 360-degree arc. The signals are called the localizer course, or localizer. There is a dial within the aircraft called a pictorial deviation indicator (PDI), which contains two needles. One needle is horizontal, and the other is vertical. The vertical needle indicates to a pilot if he is to the left or right of the localizer beam. If the needle is to his right, then the pilot will need to initiate a right turn to get back on the center of the line. Deviations are indicated by dots. The PDI will only read a two-dot deviation, not more than that. The PDI also has a horizontal needle. This needle indicates whether the aircraft is established on the glide slope. If an aircraft is not established on the glide slope, the needle rests either above it or below it. If a pilot keeps his or her aircraft on the glide slope, they will follow it down to the runway and make a safe landing. The horizontal needle, like the vertical, will only indicate a maximum two-dot deviation. The PDI is also referred to as raw data.

The instrument sometimes referred to as the "black box" or computer is known as the flight director. This sophisticated instrument also establishes whether an aircraft is lined up on the localizer and glide slope. A flight director would not just show you how far off you were from the beams, it would even calculate for you the rate of turn to regain it. Rather than relying on several instruments for navigation that showed only if there was a deviation, the flight director combined information onto one screen and let you see how your aircraft was lining up on the beams.

Diverting attention away from the flight director, Streil contacted Logan tower. "And Boston Tower Delta seven two three final," he said, informing them that they were on final approach.[32]

At 11:07:45 a.m., twenty-three seconds before touchdown, McDonald alerted Streil of a weather change that might affect his landing. It was the first transmission to Delta 723 regarding the weather since they left Manchester. Even though tower personnel knew that a dense fog bank was moving across the approach to Runway 4R for over two and a half minutes, this was the first they told Streil about it. He had been relying on the previous forecast and had been expecting to break out of the clouds at four to five hundred feet, giving him plenty of room to maneuver for a landing. "Cleared to land four right, traffic's clearing at the end, the RVR shows more than six thousand, a fog bank is moving in, it's pretty heavy across the approach end," McDonald cautioned.[33] The fog bank had obstructed the runway so badly that the RVR was dropping hundreds of feet per second, but McDonald did not check for a current reading and relied on an older one.

Seven seconds later, Streil acknowledged the warning. "Seven two three."[34] Now he could get back to assisting Burrill in getting the aircraft on course. With the heavy workload caused by the aircraft's excessive speed, failure to get on a stabilized approach, handling the radio calls to and from the aircraft, training Burrell, and now dealing with a fog bank and a faulty flight director, John Streil had forgotten one extremely important, critical, and mandatory procedure. With his attention scattered in several directions, handling several problems of increasing importance, he had forgotten to call out the altitude of the aircraft at this late stage of the flight. Streil had been into Logan Airport so many times that he, and other veteran pilots, could mentally calculate height from their position above the outer marker. He may not have told Burrill, a violation of a mandatory procedure, but as pilot in command, he knew how high they were as he calculated in the RVR distance he had been given as well as the cloud ceiling height. He mentally calculated the aircraft's height and deduced they were still safe.

Located just under a mile across Boston Harbor from the approach end of Runway 4R was Castle Island. The island was home to Fort Independence, which looked not unlike a giant starfish that had washed up on land. Militarily, it controlled the entrance to Boston Harbor and had a beautiful view of Boston and the waterways. Next to the fort was a shipping facility where boats would dock and drop off their containers and then get loaded with new cargo. On the morning of July 31, 1973, most of the shipping activity in the harbor had stopped due to the heavy fog bank stretching across the water. Veterans of harbor weather recalled they had never seen a fog bank that thick before. Just after 11:00 a.m., Warren Hutchins, an engineer on the tugboat *MARS*, tied up at berth 16 due to the fog, heard the tug cook ring the dinner bell, and stepped out of his room and onto the deck. Once out on deck, he heard an aircraft overhead. He looked up and, for just a second or two through the fog, saw the fuselage of an aircraft fly overhead. He could not make out any markings before it disappeared across the harbor back into the thick fog. He knew the plane was very low. As a matter of fact, he recalled saying it was so low he could "count the rivets on it."[35]

Richard Giroux, of Giroux Brothers Transportation, was loading a trailer and took a quick coffee break. Standing at the corner of the warehouse, he looked around him and saw fog in all directions. Behind him, he heard an aircraft approach, and he turned to look up. For just a few seconds, the word Delta flew by him low in the sky, but he could not recall if it was on the fuselage or on the tail. He estimated the height of the aircraft around three hundred feet, even though it was a rough estimate. He remembered following the aircraft about halfway across the channel and then saw it slip back into the fog. "It sort of hazed out, and then all of a sudden it just went out of sight."[36] After that, he continued drinking his coffee and remembered seeing two other planes passing overhead after the Delta jet. "All I know," he told investigators later, "is that the Delta plane was an awfully lot lower than the other two that I observed."[37]

Thomas Karakoudas was waiting to deliver a load of leather to the receiving warehouse. As he stood on the pier waiting, he heard an aircraft approaching behind him and looked up. For five seconds, he saw the entire aircraft descending from the sky. He clearly made out the Delta name on the tail and noticed the landing gear was down. He estimated the height of the aircraft at 250 to 300 feet. He watched it for perhaps a thousand feet across the harbor, and then it disappeared into the fog. Before it slipped into the fog again, Karakoudas remembered telling Skippy, the man who rented forklifts out at the receiving building, that he thought "it was going to hit something because it was so low."[38] Quite frankly, he had never seen an aircraft that low before over the harbor.

At the Sea-Land berth, number 16, William Rae was waiting to pick up a Sea-Land container to deliver. He had worked for the Boston Shipping Association on Castle Island for ten years prior to becoming a truck driver. He was an avid fisherman and spent many years navigating Boston Harbor in his boat. He had never seen fog come in that quick across the harbor. "It seemed to just roll right in and blanket everything right out," he commented.[39] In the outer harbor, he had seen fog as heavy as this, but not in the inner harbor. He heard an aircraft flying overhead, and when he looked up, he saw, like a shark's dorsal fin scything through murky water, the tail of an aircraft through the fog. He saw the name "Delta" on the engines of the aircraft.[40] He watched the tail slice through the fog and then disappear back into it. At no time was anyone on Castle Island able to look across Boston Harbor and see Logan Airport. The fog had blanked it out.

Suddenly, in the cockpit of Delta Flight 723, the sum of the problems facing the crew of the aircraft caught up with them, and it became too much to handle. The high workload brought on by nonstandard air traffic control procedures, the presence of an observer in the cockpit, the blinding fog bank sweeping across Boston Harbor and the approach end of Runway 4R, and, most importantly, the malfunction of the flight director, all led to the disappearance of Captain Streil's cockpit discipline.

At 11:07:54 a.m., Streil barked at Burrill, "Let's get back on course if you can."[41]

Burrill, most likely looking at the PDI needle, tensely replied, "I just gotta get this back."[42] The strain in his voice was apparent, like a driver wildly turning the steering wheel, trying to keep his car from sliding off an icy road.

It was too late for the passengers and crew of Delta Flight 723. For the next thirteen seconds, the aircraft was out of control. Without explanation, the jet abruptly descended at a rate of 1,200 feet per minute. At 11:08:05 a.m., too late to save them from harm, Joe Burrell shouted a warning. Half a second later, flying approximately 150 miles per hour, Delta Flight 723 struck a nine-foot high concrete seawall head-on. The DC-9 was 165 feet to the right of the runway centerline and three thousand feet short of the runway threshold.[43] The impact blistered the plane, its parts, and its pilots and passengers into thousands of pieces and dumped debris, death, and destruction as it slid across the end of the foggy, forbidding runway. Then, like a wooden matchstick scraped across a scraggy striker, what was left of the cabin burst into a tall sheet of flame, incinerating everything, and everyone, caught in it.

8

"A Large, Long Flame"

Most decades are not confined by a ten-year calendar, but by events that are an accumulation of shared actions that build up into commonality. Once those gelled together into one large commune, an era was born. However, there was always a catalyst, something symbolic, to set it off.

The "1920s" were a period of unparalleled growth in America. Having emerged largely unscathed from World War I, America entered a frenzied period of throwing off the chains of restraint and replacing them with loose morals, market speculation, and spending sprees. In 1924, the stock market began to rise, and President Calvin Coolidge lowered the top income tax rate to 43.5 percent. The airline industry began, and Henry Ford's employees produced cars on an assembly line, reducing the price of the automobile dramatically. However, it was only after these actions combined that what we know as the "Roaring Twenties" began, which was, ironically, four years after the beginning of the decade. The symbolic catalyst that set it off was the death of President Warren Harding in August 1923. Once that happened, pro-business vice president Calvin Coolidge ascended to the presidency. The economy grew 42 percent, mostly under Coolidge's stingy eye.

The "1930s" really began in 1929. The stock market crash in October of that year, the ultimate sum of the speculation of the "Twenties," began an era of massive unemployment, hunger, and the rise of dictators. In Europe, the "Thirties" ended with the start of World War II in September 1939. In America, the "Thirties" ended on December 7, 1941.

The "1940s" were an era of war. Dictators marched toward conquest, but the democracies combined and, led by Franklin Roosevelt and Winston Churchill, counterattacked, not stopping until most of the dictators had died in failure. With the world in tatters, it took the democracies years to clean up from the Plinian eruption of the war. It took approximately eight years of cleanup, economically, spiritually, culturally, and politically, but, by 1953, the world seemed to be lurching away from armed conflict. In its place, combatants maneuvered without guns, built up missile systems, and called each other names, but they maintained a peace, even as hostility lurked beneath the surface.

The "1950s," an era of huge economic expansion masking a simmering hatred between the democracies and communists, began symbolically with the death of Joseph Stalin and the inauguration of Dwight D. Eisenhower as president of the United States in 1953. The interstate highway system was built in America, television became the new entertainment medium of choice, and family incomes doubled, then tripled. Optimism ruled.

The optimism of the "Fifties" died with the death of President John F. Kennedy in 1963. The crack of an assassin's bullet in Dallas, Texas, left the world stunned, and a new era of volatility called the "Sixties" began. The tempo of violence ratcheted up with the increase of U.S. troops into South Vietnam. It exploded into war by 1965 and eventually claimed the lives of over fifty-three thousand American troops and countless Vietnamese on both sides of the border. Because of this, the counterculture movement began. This was a group of individuals shredding off the accepted norms and practices of society. They began to question authority, rules, God, and law. Their answers were free love, drugs, rock music, and communes. Their growing support was a direct result of the increasing dissatisfaction with the Vietnam War. They became, to some extent, the leaders of the opposition, maintaining a sense of optimism in a darkening tunnel.

The Sixties ended in different parts of the world at different times. According to English blogger Mark Dunton,

> Despite some bleak indicators in the early Seventies—I would single out the Dawon's Field hijackings of September 1970, the escalation of "the troubles," power blackouts in late 1970 and early 1972 and increasing worry about inflation and unemployment—the optimism continued in British pop culture—though the underlying attitude would be best described as a willful determination to have a good time, despite the darkening backdrop.[1]

Then, in October 1973, Syria and Egypt attacked Israel and started the Yom Kippur War. In response to United States' support of Israel, the Organization of Petroleum Exporting Countries (OPEC), mostly Arab, announced a 66 percent increase in the price of crude oil and imposed an oil embargo on the United States. The West plunged into a recession. This, according to Dunton, was the end of the "Sixties."

The same could be said of the United States. While a cease-fire had been implemented in Vietnam in January 1973, America had suddenly found itself in the midst of one the worst constitutional crises in its history. President Richard Nixon had ordered the Central Intelligence Agency (CIA) to intervene in covering up a crime that the president's men committed. While the CIA demurred, Nixon found himself facing calls for impeachment from many members of Congress. Then, in October 1973, he ordered the firing of the special prosecutor of the Watergate case, and within ten months, he had resigned the presidency. Symbolically, the "Sixties" were over in America.

Massachusetts had always prided itself on being the birthplace of freedom. The American Revolution began there. While Boston was a center of the slave trade, in the 1790 Census, no slaves were listed in Massachusetts. Case law ended the ownership of other human beings long before the Thirteenth Amendment to the U.S. Constitution. Many famous abolitionists were from, or moved to, Massachusetts, among them Frederick Douglass and William Lloyd Garrison. However, for reasons never fully explained, Boston public schools were segregated by race.

In 1954, the Supreme Court of the United States ruled in *Brown v. Board of Education* that laws establishing segregated schools were unconstitutional. While they watched the brutal responses of state law enforcement officials in the southern United States to black protests, the northern states had a reputation for integration. However, segregation existed in latent forms, and it did not generate a lot of television coverage.

Robert Kennedy, a born and bred son of Massachusetts, brother of a president, and himself the former U.S. attorney general, stated,

> In the North, I think you have had de facto segregation which in some areas is as bad or even more extreme than in the South. Everybody in those communities, including my own state of Massachusetts, concentrated on what was happening in Birmingham, Alabama, or Jackson, Mississippi, and didn't look at what needed to be done in our own home, our own town, our own city.[2]

In April 1965, just a few months after Martin Luther King was stymied, then successful, in crossing the Edmund Pettus Bridge in Alabama, a committee of Massachusetts citizens released a report on segregation in the state's public schools. In his classic book *Common Ground*, J. Anthony Lukas wrote, "Defining imbalanced schools as those with more than 50 percent black enrollment, the committee found fifty-five such school in the state, forty-five of them in Boston."[3] Thirteen of the public schools in Boston were over 90 percent black. According to Lukas, the average cost allocated to pupils in all-white elementary schools was $350 per year. In predominantly black schools, it ranged as low as $228.98 per year. Concluding that "racial imbalance is educationally harmful to all children," one remedy to alleviate the problem was busing.[4]

Even though the Massachusetts State Legislature passed a bill to outlaw de facto segregation in public schools in August 1965, by 1971, 62 percent of the city's black students attended schools that were at least 70 percent black, and 84 percent of white students attended schools that were at least 80 percent white.[5]

On March 14, 1972, the Boston chapter of the National Association for the Advancement of Colored People (NAACP) filed a class action lawsuit against the Boston School Committee claiming that Boston was experiencing de facto segregation in schools in violation of the Thirteenth and Fourteenth amendments to the U.S. Constitution and the 1964 Civil Rights Act. It was the beginning of the end of the "Sixties" for Boston. The city's residents held their breath in anticipation of Judge W. Arthur Garrity's ruling in the lawsuit. If the judge ruled that segregation existed, many knew that busing could be an answer to solving that issue, and if that was the case, opponents of that remedy would resort to anything to stop it.

On June 21, 1974, Judge Garrity ruled that the Boston School Committee had maintained de facto segregation.[6] To desegregate the schools, Garrity did indeed decide busing would be a remedy. For the next several years, many Boston residents opposed busing and resorted to violence to stop it. Fights broke out in schools between black and white students, neighborhoods drew battle lines and attacked those not belonging on their block, and schools shuttered. The violence and hatred tearing Boston apart over this ruling spread across television screens all over the country and helped define the Boston of the "Seventies."

Symbolically though, the crash of Delta Air Lines Flight 723 was the ignition of the "Seventies" for Boston. Up until the crash, the divisions in Boston had been subtle, simmering beneath the surface, waiting for a symbolic ignition point. Once the Delta DC-9 exploded onto the cement seawall at Logan, the symbolic match had been struck, Judge Garrity threw on the gasoline, and Boston ignited. However, it was nothing compared to the horror and destruction that awaited the first responders at the approach of Runway 4R.

* * *

Geoffrey Keating arrived back at his work site on Bird Island Flats after allowing the construction vehicles back in. As he got out of his pickup truck, he walked toward his crew with Boston Harbor on his right. It was too foggy to see anything out in the harbor, but as he turned and faced the approach end of Runway 4R, he saw a "large, long flame…."[7] It started from the direction of the edge of the harbor and made its way up Runway 4R toward the airport. He described it as rising "as if it were a curtain, as opposed to a ball of flame."[8] When it was done, it just disappeared into the fog. The flames were as high as the light poles that were near the runway. Then he heard a low, distant rumbling that shuddered right through him. Geoffrey Keating knew that something was not right on Runway 4R. He described the length of the flame as about three hundred feet. He never saw an aircraft.

Keating then ran up to two of his coworkers and breathlessly told them what he had seen. He asked them if they wanted to go investigate with him. All three climbed into the pickup truck and set out on the dike road on the perimeter of the airport that ran alongside the harbor toward Runway 4R. The closer they got to the runway, the thicker the fog became. As they reached the approach end of the runway, Keating could make out a shape lying on the ground. It was an airplane's tail. He could make out the letters "T" and "A" and the numbers "222." The tail was on its back, lying on its horizontal stabilizer. The front of the tail was pointed skyward, the fuselage missing and blown into thousands of pieces. Where the fuselage had been connected to the tail, there was nothing but torn metal, peeled back toward the ground like an empty bullet shell. Off to his left, Keating saw some smoke, but anything beyond that was shrouded in fog. He did not hear any screaming or any cries for help, and for a moment he stood there stunned alongside his two companions. What brought him back to reality was a sound worse than any cries for help could be; it was the sound of a jetliner above them attempting to land on top of the carnage.[9] He had a strange feeling that, with the fog as thick as it was, no one—not the air traffic controllers, not the firemen at the fire station, and, even worse, not the pilots trying to come in and land—were aware of the crash. He needed to sound the alarm fast before another crash occurred. He left his two companions at the scene and ran to his truck.

When the DC-9 struck the seawall on Runway 4R's border, it destroyed the number 25 and number 26 approach light bars. The approach light system (ALS) monitor panel in the control tower at the airport could easily be seen by the controllers in the tower cab. When Flight 723 destroyed the lights, the panel's alarm sounded, and both sets of red lights illuminated. However, McDonald considered this a false alarm due to the frequent maintenance problems with the lights that controllers seemed to encounter on every shift. Due to the proximity of the power line to the harbor water often seeped into the line, setting the alarms off. Many times, controllers were told by maintenance personnel to ignore the alarms. When he heard it, McDonald silenced the signal and ignored the red light.[10] When the ALS goes out, though, that increases the minimums that arriving flights must adhere to, and the controllers must notify the crews of the issue. This did not happen. Unknown to McDonald, the alarm was not false, and Flight 723 lay smoldering in thousands of pieces on the runway.

McDonald queried Flight 723 twice for its location on the runway so he could clear other planes to land. When he did not receive an answer, he turned to the ground controller, Paul Boriello, and asked him if he had heard from Flight 723.

"623 is just about at the gate," Boriello replied.[11]

What remained of the tail on Delta Ship 222. Courtesy of Fire Commissioner Records, Boston City Archives.

With that response and without warning the incoming pilots that the ALS was not working properly, McDonald cleared Eastern Air Lines Flight 1020 and American Airlines Flight 400 to land on Runway 4R. The problem was that Boriello thought McDonald had inquired about Delta Flight 623, which had just landed a bit earlier and was headed for its gate, and McDonald thought Boriello had replied that Delta Flight 723 was headed for its gate. Without being able to visually check for the aircraft itself, they relied on each other's perceived misstatements, and Flight 723 still lay shattered at the end of Runway 4R without anyone but Geoffrey Keating, and some of his coworkers, knowing about it.

Keating reached for the communications radio in his truck but remembered it would do him no good. The radio was on the same frequency as the Massport maintenance department and the fire station, but, due to lack of maintenance, he could only receive from it. He could not transmit to anyone that a major crash had just happened at the airport. He knew he had to make straight for the fire department and hope someone was there. It was 11:11 a.m., three minutes after the accident.

In the control tower, they still did not know that eighty-nine bodies and a broken aircraft were strewn across the approach end of Runway 4R.

8. "A Large, Long Flame"

McDonald was lining up aircraft to land, and Boriello was the traffic cop verbally maneuvering aircraft around the airport. The traffic kept him busy.

The pilot of Allegheny Airlines Flight 415 queried Boriello. "Allegheny ah four fifteen cleared to cross?"[12]

"Four fifteen negative stay with me ah short of four left till we get you clearance," Boriello replied.

"Okay, we'll hold short of four left."

"In fact," Boriello added, "hold it right there short of the outer, I have traffic coming out from ah the other side of the field."

"All righty," replied the captain of 415.[13]

Boriello directed all of his aircraft toward runways, gates, and taxiways so that they could either take off and deliver their passengers to their destinations or pull up to the gates and deposit their passengers here. It was a complicated, coordinated game of "Red Light–Green Light," each aircraft inching closer to a runway or gate then stopping or going at Boriello's command.

"This is Eastern five a seventy-two we just crossed fifteen right. Do you want inner or via the outer?" the pilot asked, looking for instructions.[14]

"Eastern five seventy-two via the inner to the apron," Boriello commanded, inching the aircraft closer to the gate.

"To the apron, all right," the pilot answered.

"And ten forty just to reconfirm you do have your clearance?" Boriello asked another flight.

The Eastern Air Lines pilot responded. "Yes sir, we do."

"Boston Ground Delta five eighty is ready to taxi and we don't have a clearance yet," another pilot chimed in.

Boriello gave him instructions to move. "Delta five eighty taxi runway nine via the inner and sierra, you'll be holding ah short of the outer behind Allegheny."[15]

Just before 11:14 a.m., Boriello gave Eastern Air Lines 1043 instructions to cross Runway 4L, and that was the moment that Geoffrey Keating skidded to a halt in front of Logan Airport's fire department, pushed open his door, and ran toward the station.

Chief Charles Arena was on the telephone when he noticed a man in construction clothes outside his office pounding on his window. "Plane down on Four Right," the man yelled.[16] "Plane down on Four Right."

Arena abruptly hung up the phone and quizzically looked at the man. Even though he had no report of a plane down from the tower or from Massport, Arena knew this could not be a joke. No prankster would come up to a firehouse on the grounds of a major international airport, bang on the chief's window, and yell there was a plane down if there was not.

Arena immediately picked up the direct line to the second floor where the alarm and patrol desks are located. He notified the man at the alarm desk that there was a report of a crash on 4R and instructed them to mobilize the men. He jumped in his chief's car and revved out to the approach end of 4R. He figured that was where the accident must be because the man reporting the accident had construction clothes on and that was the only area of the airport that had construction going on at this time. He looked in his rearview mirror and saw with relief that, behind him, his fire trucks with their lights flashing and sirens blaring were following him like a large posse that had just sniffed out its prey.

9

"Aircraft Down on 4R"

The teletype machine in Harry Terban's office started chirping around 11:12 a.m. It spit out a communication from the control tower that visibility had decreased, according to the controllers, down to one half mile, and they requested that Terban take another special observation. Since the request involved a change in visibility, he was required to make it. The other criteria for making a special observation would be a change in the ceiling of the clouds.[1] Terban walked out of his office and up to the roof of the building. He took note of his observation points and acknowledged that he could still see the Mystic River Bridge and the Custom House. Both of these structures were a mile and a half away, so he estimated visibility to be one mile. However, unlike his observation from a half hour before, he could not see the top of the Custom House. Since the top of it is 505 feet, he estimated the ceiling at 400 feet.[2] Terban knew that this was an estimate. He knew that the ceiling could be much lower than four hundred feet because his vantage point was over a mile away from the end of the runway and he could not see it. There was no doubt that the fog condition at the airport had gotten worse than it had been a half hour before.

Terban checked the readings on the ceilometer readout. A ceilometer is a machine that possesses a rotating beam, and it measures the height of clouds. This instrument is located at the end of Runway 4R. During this special observation at 11:15 a.m., while Flight 723 lay burning on the runway, the dark tracing on the recorder revealed a zero-degree reading.[3] The fog was so bad at the approach end of the runway that it penetrated all the way down to the ground. Terban also examined a ten-minute readout from the transmissometer. He determined that the RVR for Runway 4R was variable between two thousand feet and six thousand feet.[4] If the RVR falls below 2,400 feet, aircraft are not cleared to land.

The RVR reading that Terban analyzed was not the same as the reading accessed by the air traffic controllers. Terban's recorder in his office showed instant readings. He could also analyze the readings and get an estimate of the RVR over a certain time frame. In the tower, however, the controllers' device cycles every fifty-one seconds, and they do not have access to prior readings to make an estimate. Within a fifty-one-second period, the RVR could easily go from a mile to zero visibility.

According to the NTSB, an RVR value transmitted to a pilot

> is intended to represent runway visibility when his aircraft touches down near the ILS touchdown point. This value would represent the actual distance he could see down the runway, only if the atmosphere above the runway and above the transmissometer site were homogenous. Often, however, the atmosphere is not homogenous, particularly in fog conditions.[5]

The transmissometer reading might also be "misrepresentative" due to its location in relation to the runway. "For runway 4R at Logan International Airport, the location is approximately abreast of the ILS touchdown point, on a 250-foot baseline, and about 500 feet to the left of the runway."[6] Without its location directly on or adjacent to the runway, the reading at the transmissometer site can be completely different from that on the runway.

In fact, at Logan Airport that morning, the fog situation had deteriorated rapidly. Because of the buildings obstructing his view, Terban could not see the approach end of Runway 4R. He could not see the fog bank that obscured the runway. As he visually observed each quadrant from his vantage point, he could tell that the northern quadrants had better visibility than the southern ones and that the southeastern quadrant, the one in which Runway 4R was located, had the worst visibility of any of them.[7]

Terban's special observation before the accident revealed that the fog was obstructing three-tenths of the visibility of the Earth. Then, during the 11:15 a.m. special observation, while the plane lay in ruins on the runway, the fog obstructed four-tenths of the visibility, and about twenty minutes after the accident, it was five-tenths. Terban admitted to himself that the fog situation at Logan was getting worse.

* * *

Once he saw the fire trucks racing toward the crash site, Geoffrey Keating hopped back in his pickup truck to return to the scene. As he raced toward his construction site, he noticed Harris Cusick standing by the road. He stopped his truck and told Cusick to hop in, and they continued toward the approach end of Runway 4R.

Chief Arena had a strange feeling that neither the tower nor anyone other than Keating or the firemen following him knew about the crash. Almost seven minutes after the crash, someone finally alerted the air traffic controllers in the tower at Logan Airport.

"Ground Control Easy one," Arena said forcefully into the microphone of his vehicle.[8]

9. "Aircraft Down on 4R"

"Easy one ground go ahead," Boriello replied, thinking it was a radio test or some routine matter from the chief.

"Ah we're going to go down Charlie, may I cross the runways?" Arena asked.[9]

An uneasy feeling enveloped Boriello, and he wondered why the chief would ask to cross active runways. "What's your destination?" he asked the chief.

"Four right, aircraft down on four right," Arena responded.

Aircraft down? No one had said anything to anyone in the tower about a downed aircraft. "Aircraft down on four right?" Boriello asked the chief for clarification.

"That's what I was told," Arena replied, confirming his suspicion that the tower had no idea a crash had occurred.

"Standby, we have no knowledge, you can cross four left hold short of four right," Boriello told Arena.[10] He then looked at his supervisor, Dan Tucker, and repeated what Arena had told him, that there was an aircraft down on four right.

Tucker picked up the phone that directly connected him downstairs to approach control. "Hello?"

"Yeah," Jimmy Morrissey answered.

"Somebody says we got something wrong on four right, we don't know anything about it," he informed Morrissey down in approach control.

"Oh yeah?" Morrissey answered incredulously.

"So, ah, we're sending everybody around," Tucker warned.[11] Everybody meant everybody, and no one was leaving or landing at Logan Airport until Tucker figured out what was going on at the approach end of Runway 4R.

Following protocol, Tucker picked up the phone and called the assistant chief on duty. "Yeah, ah Easy One just came out of the barn, says there's an aircraft down on four right, we don't know anything about it," he explained to his boss.

"What?" he exclaimed. "Okay, wait a minute let's suspend operations then."[12]

Tucker told him he had already done it. "Yeah, everybody's goin' around."

"Okay," the assistant chief replied and then hung up.

Morrissey called back up to Dan Tucker. "Danny, hold the departures till we get squared away?" he asked. He sought clarification on which operations to suspend.

"Everything's holding right. Gimme some freqs [frequencies] for the Air Canada, Jim." Daniel Tucker finally realized how bad the situation had become. He still had planes trying to land. The two behind Delta 723 had executed missed approaches based on their own observations. If the pilot of

Air Canada 675 did not execute his missed approach and the aircraft landed on top of the debris on Runway 4R, another crash was imminent.

"Air Canada six seventy-five just made a miss, he's going straight ahead on four right to three, he wants to go to Montreal at twenty thou, you want to vector him up there?"

The departure controller got on the line. "Yeah, gimme, I'll take his."

"Okay," Danny Tucker replied, relieved nothing more could land on 4R until they knew what was going on.

Now that all aircraft operations on the runways had been halted, Boriello continued talking with Arena. "Easy one cleared on four right all equipment cleared on four right all other, er aircraft on the ramp come to a full stop. Easy one Boston ground cleared out to four right, proceed to four right."[13] All aircraft on the ramps, taxiways, and runways had now come to a sudden and complete halt.

As managers of the airport, as soon as Massport officials had heard of the situation, they ran to their vehicles and headed toward Runway 4R. "Easy one is cleared on the airport, your discretion," Tucker told the Massport officials, letting them know they could proceed anywhere they wanted.

Approach control called Danny Tucker seeking clarification on what was going on at the airport. "What's the status on four right?" Jimmy Morrissey asked. He had all the controllers asking him for information, but he did not have any details. All he had heard was that there was something wrong on Runway 4R.

Tucker told him what he knew. "Four right, we got vehicles on it checking, they said there's a downed aircraft we don't know anything about it," he said truthfully.[14]

"Okay," Morrissey responded.

Boriello sent a message to all aircraft on the ground to go to his frequency so they could keep informed as to what was going on. By this time, word had gotten out, even to the pilots, that there was something wrong on Runway 4R. "What happened out on four right?" one of them asked over the air.

"I really don't know," the ground controller replied.[15]

As soon as Chief Arena pulled up to the crash site, he knew it was bad. His first thoughts were to look for survivors as quickly as possible and extinguish the flames that were burning. It did not dawn on him to let the air traffic controllers know that there was indeed an aircraft down on Runway 4R.

The Massport officials pulled up to the scene right behind the fire department. One of them grabbed the radio in the car. "Ground control, ground control, this is easy ah port one o two, we have an aircraft down on four right, burning," he said breathlessly.[16]

9. "Aircraft Down on 4R" 73

The crash scene from the edge of Runway 4R. Note the utter destruction caused by the impact with the seawall. Courtesy of Fire Commissioner Records, Boston City Archives.

Morrissey could not believe it. Burning, he repeated to himself. The fog prevented any controller from seeing anything.

"Understand, you have an aircraft give me his number as soon as you can." No one in the tower knew of any missing aircraft. As far as they knew, every plane they had under their control had been accounted for, including Delta 723. McDonald had questioned Boriello about it, and he had been told it was proceeding to the gate after it landed.

The Massport men at the scene of the accident had one request for ground control. As soon as they saw the wreckage, they knew they had a major aircraft accident on their hands, one of a magnitude that the airport had not seen in years, if ever. They contacted ground control with a request. "Ground Control, this is ah Port one o two, would you press the six twelve please, press the six twelve."[17]

The ground controller did as he was told and pressed the 612 alarm. The alarm announced to the surrounding communities and neighborhoods of Boston that a disaster of the first magnitude had struck the city and that emergency help was desperately needed. A more urgent plea had not been heard near Boston since Paul Revere announced two hundred years prior that the British were coming.

* * *

Once he had clearance to proceed down Runway 4R, Chief Arena had to quickly decide whether this was a rescue or recovery effort. He saw no signs of life and lots of lifeless bodies covering the runway. The fog in its density led to the chief responding slower than he liked.

Arena parked his car and walked briskly to the approach end of the runway. He noticed a fiery glow off to his right along with some smoke. Off to his left, he noticed more bodies. He warned arriving rescue and fire trucks "to watch for survivors and debris" as they approached.[18]

Engine One pulled up by fire that had been the red glow that Arena had noticed first on his arrival. A roaring fire had enveloped a large, jagged piece of what remained of the skeleton of the passenger cabin. The plexiglas windows had been incinerated into oblivion, leaving two vacant holes like owl eyes trying to comprehend the madness of what they were looking at. The firemen jumped from their trucks and started dousing the fire with water and foam. Others aimed the truck's water turret at the fire, and it was soon extinguished.

Fog had limited the visibility of the crash site, but Arena could make out the aircraft's landing gear just forward of the smoldering piece of fuselage. There were pieces of wreckage all around the site with numerous bodies scattered and lying on the runway. He could not see the runway's approach lights, nor could he see the tail of the aircraft that Keating had seen earlier. He had his men concentrate on what they could see and then had them fan out for rescue efforts, but he had a feeling that was a wasted effort.

At 11:20 a.m., Arena heard ground control calling him over the radio. "Easy one Boston Ground how do you hear now?"

"Easy One," he responded.

"Yes sir, do you have anything you can give us as information?" Boriello asked. They still had not figured out what aircraft had crashed.

"Man and equipment Tower on four right here," Arena replied.

"I'm sorry," Boriello replied. "You broke up badly. Did you find the aircraft?"

"That's affirmative, we have a major crash here."[19]

Arena had confirmed what most had figured out by then, that a major crash had occurred. "Major crash," Boriello established for himself and others. "Ah, can you give me the type aircraft?"[20]

There was no response from Arena. There was no use attempting to identify the aircraft from the thousands of pieces that lay around Arena. It

9. "Aircraft Down on 4R"

A section of the landing gear, one of the few large pieces found at the crash site. Courtesy of Fire Commissioner Records, Boston City Archives.

could not be done. If he was wrong in identification, there could be severe repercussions. However, if the visibility had been better, he would have been able to identify the aircraft from the tail lying at the end of the runway. It clearly had most of the Delta widget visible, the "T and the A" of DELTA, and the 222 would have identified the ship number. This would have cleared up the mystery of the missing aircraft among the air traffic controllers.

"Easy one, thank you and ah more equipment is on the way," Boriello reported. "Easy one, at your discretion give us the aircraft type and company, we'd appreciate it."[21]

Engine Four now asked for permission to proceed down Runway 4R. "Easy one," Boriello replied, using the wrong call sign. "The whole airport is yours, no aircraft will be moving, Easy one."[22]

Aircraft were still moving, however, and Boriello had to stop them.

"Ground Delta seven ninety taxi out," a Delta pilot informed Boriello.

Boriello shook his head. "Delta ah seven n-ninety roger, hold at the gate, there will be delay."

"Okay, we are we blocking the taxiway if we hold right here off the end of gate thirty four," the Delta pilot asked.

Boriello looked down onto the tarmac and had gate thirty-four in sight. "Ah, I don't believe so, you look okay from here. I'll have Ex Air check you when he moves in."

"All right, thank you," the Delta pilot responded.

The pilot of Executive Air 1350 chimed in. "Ah, Ex Air with you on Foxtrot."

Boriello needed his help. "Ex Air thirteen fifty at Fox if you'd make a one eighty proceed back to the gate areas of twenty-four there will be delays. We have an emergency on the airport and when you go by the Delta in the corner if you could advise me how much space there is behind him."[23]

"Okay, sir," the pilot of Flight 1350 replied.

"And ground control Eastern five seven two." This was the pilot of the aircraft that landed just in front of Delta 723.

"Five seventy-two, Boston ground."

"Okay we're at the gate. Was that the Delta behind us that dropped on the runway now?" the pilot asked, verbalizing for the first time that it might indeed have been the Delta DC-9 from Manchester.[24]

"We really don't know[,] sir, we have no information other than there is an aircraft involved," Boriello stated.[25] Delta 723? He had not heard from that aircraft. He knew Delta 623 was probably at the gate now, but he had not heard from 723. Surprisingly, he did not ask for its location. Even if Boriello knew what aircraft had "dropped on the runway," there was no way he would announce it. Like Arena out at the scene, if he identified the wrong aircraft, severe consequences would await. No rumors needed to spread.

An unknown voice came over the radio. "What's that Delta you're questioning now the nine here?" the voice asked. Boriello's silence did not do its work. The rumors had started. He ignored the question.

Dan Tucker had spent the last three minutes trying to figure out what aircraft had crashed under the command of his controllers. He had it narrowed down to three. His intraphone rang. It was Jimmy Morrissey from downstairs. Approach control, cocooned in the windowless room downstairs, still did not know what was going on. "What, anything, these guys are all chirping down here about what's wrong," Morrissey asked.

"It's a major crash on four right, we don't know ah…."[26] Tucker was going to say flight number but thought better of it until confirmation.

"It's a major accident on four right." A few seconds later Tucker added, "The airport is closed."

Charles Taylor got on the line. "We are closed, how long?"

"Da indefinitely—"

"Okay thanks—"

Tucker reiterated. "A major crash on four right, all vehicles are responding, every—" he trailed off, figuring his controllers had the picture. "It's indefinite," he finally added.²⁷

Daniel Tucker had the three aircraft suspects in his mind. He took the next couple of minutes to make quite sure the crashed aircraft was one of these three jets. All of them were from Delta Air Lines. He picked up the phone for the Delta office at the airport. After a perfunctory greeting, he read the flight numbers of the suspected culprit to the Delta representative. "Can you account for those three?"²⁸

"Yeah, let's see six twenty-three, twelve fifty-one," and then he paused. He could not account for seven twenty-three.

"And seven twenty-three?" Tucker asked.

"And seven twenty-three," the Delta representative repeated, still looking, letting the statement hang in the air without resolution.²⁹

Daniel Tucker had the answer he needed. He picked up the phone to the approach controller desk downstairs in the tower.

"Jimmy Morrissey," said the voice on the other end.

"Arrival data," Tucker ordered, wanting to speak with one of them.

"Yeah," Taylor came on the line.

"Yeah, can you ah, Delta seven twenty three you got the inbound strip there?"

"Yeah, I got it in my hand someplace," Morrissey replied on the call with Taylor and Tucker.

"All right, give me a copy of it."

"Help me find it," Morrissey said to Taylor.

"Delta seven two three you say," Taylor replied.

"Yes," said Tucker.

Then, Jimmy Morrissey said two words that summed up everyone's thoughts. "Holy shit."³⁰

After finding the strips, Morrissey told Tucker they had them in front of them. "All right, we got 'em all in front of us, Dan."

"All right, it's a hand-written strip," Taylor said, remembering it was generated by Boston Control because the flight made an unscheduled stop in Manchester. "A DC nine ah time one four one zero and we had radar at fifty-two," he said, giving Tucker the details on the aircraft.

"Okay, he came from Manchester, was it," Tucker asked.

"Four thousand, yep."

"Okay, Jimmy, thanks," Dan Tucker said, having the information he needed.³¹ He had identified the missing aircraft.

10

"My Name Is Leo Chouinard"

Keating and Cusick got out of their pickup truck in approximately the same area as Keating did when he first arrived and discovered the accident. It was near the southern end of the runway, closer to the harbor than the firefighters were who had arrived from the fire station to the accident site. When the men got out of the truck, they stood on the edge of horror.

They stood in the grey, wet drizzle breathing in the salt-heavy air. Cusick looked off to his right but could not see any approach lights and had difficulty making out the harbor. If there were any vessels in the harbor, he could not see them. He estimated visibility at around two-tenths of a mile and the ceiling at about one hundred feet. The control tower was not visible to him. He took a hesitating step into the mist when two other men approached him. They were the two dropped off at the site on Keating's initial visit to the crash site. "Don't go near there, there's no sense," one of them told Cusick.[1]

Cusick did not listen to them and ignored their warnings. He stepped onto the runway, leaving his companions behind to go check on the dead. His sense of sight dimmed as if the fog intentionally shrouded the area lest it be found guilty of the murderous deed it had done. He could feel the wetness of the fog on his face and hands and the crunch of the crumbs of the burnt aircraft beneath his boots as he walked on the runway. He could see the twisted jumble of metal and smoke and bodies all scrambled together like an obscene omelet. He took care not to touch anything lest the jagged ends of aircraft slice off pieces of his exposed skin. All he could smell was the salt from the harbor, jet fuel, smoke, and death. All combined in a sticky stew that filled the air and clogged the nostrils.

The one sense Cusick relied on was his hearing. He could hear the roar of incoming rescue equipment and the verbal commands of first responders in the critical first moments of a disaster operation. As he pierced walls of fog and cloud and glimpsed scenes of pure terror, he relied more and more on his sense of hearing to remind him he was still part of the living world. Firefighter commands of "Over here" and "Watch out" cut through the fog, and he allowed them to echo in his ears to keep his sense of reality and life aligned together.

"Keep looking!"

"Watch out for survivors!"

"You see anyone alive?"

Cusick heard the commands coming from his left as Chief Arena directed his men to scatter throughout the wreckage and check for survivors.

"Put that out!"

"Careful what you touch!"

"Park your truck there!"

Cusick walked further and further away from the firemen toward the rear of what remained of the aircraft. He thought he could make out a jet's engine and its tail. The tail had been rudely snapped off from the rest of the aircraft and was resting on its hind quarters, with no support underneath, tilted and gaping toward the foggy, dull sky.

"*Help me.*"

At first Cusick may have thought he was talking to himself, urging himself the strength to go on with his search. He still heard the muffled orders coming from the firemen. While they were further away than before, he could still hear the authority and the staccato of urgency in their voices.

"*Help me,*" Cusick heard again.

It was a soft, pleading voice coming from the soot-covered runway. Harris Cusick stopped to listen for the words again, the ones he never expected to hear here. He would not have been more surprised than if a corpse suddenly sat up in its coffin and announced to the mourners that it was not dead. Here, in the valley of death, in a netherworld of cataclysmic destruction, caught in a purgatorial realm of despair and impossible hope, here, Harris Cusick heard the faint whisper of life.

"*Help me.*"

Cusick looked down and, on the runway beneath him, saw a young man who, from the neck up, looked like "he was in perfect health."[2] He was a Caucasian male with black hair. He had an unblemished face except for some minor smudges of soot caused by the crash. His right arm was also untouched by any of the horrors of the crash. "Help me," the man said again. To Cusick, the figure looked to be in his early twenties. His clothes had been ripped off him by the force of the crash. He was lying on his back. When Harris Cusick looked at the man from the neck down, he suppressed a dreadful gasp. What he saw was not unblemished skin, but the red and black burnt membrane of a roasted body. Cusick knew there was nothing medically he could do for the young man; however, he bent down and knelt beside him. He leaned in closer as the young man struggled to talk. "My name is Leo Chouinard," the young man whispered.[3]

The melted fuselage caused by the high heat of the flash fire. Courtesy of Fire Commissioner Records, Boston City Archives.

Chouinard was born in Barre, Vermont, two days before Christmas in 1952. He graduated from Twinfield Union High School in Plainfield, Vermont, in 1970. He had been a Boy Scout and an altar boy for the church. He also played athletics during his school years, loved riding his motorcycle—in fact, he and a friend rode their bikes all across Canada, visiting relatives on their way to Alaska—and joined the Air Force in October 1970.[4] He became a chaplain's assistant at Elmondorf Air Force Base and was well liked by all who knew him.[5]

"Leo Chouinard," he repeated to Cusick. He struggled to lift his head but could not. He told Cusick he was in the Air Force and he lived in Vermont. He asked the young man to contact his parents to let them know he was all right. Chouinard was far from all right. Unknown to him, and Cusick, he had suffered third- and fourth-degree burns over 80 percent of his body, and his legs were crushed.

Cusick soothingly spoke to Chouinard and then told him he was going to find help. He would be right back. Cusick found Chief Arena and ran up to him. The chief stood among the wreckage directing his men and giving orders. Due to each man's single-minded focus, Arena on smothering the

10. "My Name Is Leo Chouinard"

fires and searching for survivors and Cusick on Leopold Chouinard, neither pondered the incongruity of their quick conversation.

"Chief, I need to borrow a pen," Cusick said.[6] He explained he had found a survivor and needed an ambulance.

Chief Arena reached into his shirt pocket and removed his gold Massport pen. He gave it to Cusick. Cusick ran back to Chouinard.

With Cusick gone, Chouinard tried to remember how he ended up here, burnt and laying naked on Runway 4R at Logan Airport. The flight seemed routine, he remembered. Suddenly, as they were coming in for the landing, everything shattered, and his mind went blank. When Leo regained consciousness seconds later, he was still strapped in his seat. He remembered the passenger next to him reached over and unbuckled his seatbelt. The passenger pushed him toward the aircraft's missing window and Chouinard started climbing out.[7] He got his right arm and head out of the window when a flash fire roared through the fuselage incinerating everything left inside, including Chouinard's clothes and lower body. The next thing he realized he was lying naked on the runway and everything around him was death.

Cusick returned with the pen. He saw a torn, blood-spattered magazine next to Chouinard. He picked it up and started to write down Chouinard's information.

Leo struggled to give him the information but overcame the challenge. He spelled out his name. "L-E-O-C-H-O-U-I-N-A-R-D." He gave Cusick his parents' phone number in Vermont and asked him to call them. A few minutes later, an ambulance came for Chouinard and took him to Massachusetts General Hospital (MGH) to try and save him.

Chief Arena was satisfied with the amount of help that arrived on the scene from the Boston Fire Department within minutes of his call. Engine companies 5, 11, and 40 had responded from Boston as well as three ladder companies (2, 18, and 21), and rescue 1 and 2 had shown, along with a fireboat (Engine 47) and the department wrecker. The longest time spent pumping out foam and water was by Company 11 for a period of thirty minutes. Companies 5 and 40 only pumped for about fifteen minutes each. They stayed on scene for two to two and a half hours.[8]

The response also included about one hundred police officers, nurses, paramedics, priests, and other religious personnel. Ambulance drivers arrived, reporters climbed on top of rescue equipment to take photographs, medical examiners prepared the dead for transport, and Delta and Massport officials came to try and figure out what had happened.

The foam used to extinguish the aircraft fire covered the ground as if it was snow left from a stubborn nor'easter. It clung to the boots and pants of rescue personnel like fresh algae. Everywhere they looked, there was

Media on top of Engine 5 to the left. Courtesy of Fire Commissioner Records, Boston City Archives.

nothing but blackened charred remains of aircraft and humans. Some passengers were still strapped into their seats, leaning forward or to the side like one does at the end of a roller coaster ride. Many were barefoot, or had no feet at all, as their socks and shoes were torn off by the impact of the crash. Of those strewn across the runway, many were spread-eagle as if they were tossed there by a fierce gale. There was no conceptual design as to how the wreck looked; it was only chaos.

Some of the firefighters stumbled across what they thought were well-dressed babies, and the thought sickened them. They quickly realized, however, that the figures were not babies, but the dolls checked onboard by Marion Smith, Yvette Patunoff, and Margaret Hoag just a few hours earlier.

Nurses and doctors fanned out among the wreckage, as well as newspaper reporters, chaplains, and ambulance drivers. Nurse Maureen Kennedy worked at the Logan Airport Medical Center. This was a facility used for sick passengers either waiting to board their planes or having just arrived. Generally, they dealt with nervousness, chest pains, or flu symptoms. Around 11:30 a.m., Kennedy stated, "Lt. Carney of the State Police here called down and told us there had been a Phase 5."[9] A Phase 5 was code for a plane crash. Carney arrived outside the Medical Center, picked up the nurses and their emergency kits, and raced them out to the crash scene on Runway 4R.

"The first thing I saw was people. People scattered all over the ground. The fire was mostly out. There were the fire crews and a priest, I think, but the bodies were all over the ground. There was no sound. They were all dead," she explained in an interview with a reporter from the *Boston Globe*.[10]

"I really don't know what I expected when I first got out there," she continued. "I have an excellent medical background, but there was nothing humanly possible to be done for those people. We just started covering them up with sheets. I never felt so helpless in all my life, I never felt so inadequate."[11] As she covered the dead passengers in sheets, someone made the decision to start transporting them to the fire station where airport officials created a makeshift morgue.

The day before the crash, Monday, July 30, 1973, Dr. S. Arthur Boruchoff, medical director of the New England Eye Bank, received some good news. A patient at Burlington General Hospital in Vermont had died, and his eyes were a match for two patients waiting for corneas. The corneas were loaded into a small crate surrounded by dry ice and placed on Flight 723 in Burlington for the Tuesday morning flight to Boston. The container was destroyed in the crash, both corneas lost, destroying the hopes of two patients who had been waiting for their sight-saving package. A disappointed Boruchoff stated that one of the patients needed an "emergency cornea transplant before his own cornea perforates, causing irreparable damage. The other patient had been reportedly waiting for months on a compatible cornea."[12]

As word spread around the city about the crash, reporters descended onto the airport determined to be the first one on the scene. Their appetite for reporting the story knew no bounds as they interviewed first responders, airport officials, and even passengers waiting in the terminals. Cameramen were even seen on top of rescue equipment pointing their cameras onto the runway to take graphic photographs. Others wandered around the wreckage, taking pictures of the shattered aircraft, recovery workers, and dead passengers, some still strapped in their seats.

Boston Globe reporter Frank Mahoney was one of the reporters with access to the entire crash site. He knew more about disasters, fires, and safety than most firemen. It was not unlike Mahoney to show up at a disaster site, whether a building or home fire or other major accident, wearing rubber boots and a coat and a white fireman's hat with the words "Chief" and "Boston Globe" written on it.[13] He was known by virtually all the fire chiefs in New England and was even the public relations director for the New England Association of Fire Chiefs. In 1953, he was the only reporter to gain access to the U.S.S. *Leyte*, an aircraft carrier undergoing conversion to a submarine hunter, right after it exploded in the Boston Naval Yard, killing thirty-seven people.[14]

Mahoney's instincts as a reporter were razor sharp. To cover a story like this, he needed to smell, feel, and see the crash. He had to gather all relevant material to form a cohesive outline of the story he would write on the crash. Other reporters scouring the site may see something they deemed unimportant, but Mahoney's skills in attention to detail, as well as his perseverance, were what made him such a respected reporter. He saw what others did not, or did not want to, see. Experience and diligence paid off for Mahoney, for as he searched the site, seeking information and clues for his story, he found a bundle of papers in the wreckage. He picked the bundle up and, reading the blood and dirt-soaked cover letter, realized, incredulously, that he was holding in his hands the plans for the nuclear defense of the United States and the North Atlantic Treaty Organization (NATO).[15]

Count Laszio Hadik, president of International Research Group, had the papers in his possession onboard Flight 723. His death minutes before in the crash had broken the chain of custody, and they lay unclaimed on the runway. Hadik had studied the papers over his holiday in Vermont and had planned to hand them over to his research group on his return to Washington, D.C. The papers, prepared by researchers at the Los Alamos Scientific Laboratory in New Mexico, were officially titled, *Strategic Plans for the Nuclear Defense of NATO* and *Strategic Plans for the Nuclear Defense of the United States*. According to O.G. Willoughby, a public information officer with the Department of Defense, "Hadik and his firm were doing consulting work for the Office of International Security Affairs, which deals with NATO matters. He had possession of the papers in a thoroughly above-board way."[16] Willoughby continued, "Our understanding, which is second-hand, is that the papers were sensitive but unclassified."[17]

Count Hadik proudly claimed membership to Hungarian royalty. In 1948, three years after the Soviet Union stationed thousands of troops in Hungary, Count Hadik and his family fled the country and its increasing dependence on the Soviets. The Soviets focused particular attention on the Hadik family as Laszio's grandfather, Laszio Szechenyi, was the Hungarian minister to the United States from 1921 to 1933. Szechenyi had also married a Vanderbilt. Laszio Hadik graduated from the Brooks School in Andover and Georgetown University in Washington.[18]

Immediately sensing the importance of the papers, Mahoney looked for a top-secret, or secret, government classification and did not find any. He quickly perused the papers. "They were each about 12 pages of small type single spaced," Mahoney explained in a later interview. "They were treatises on nuclear defense. It was very technical and appeared to be very much national security stuff."[19] They were dated July 17. To remove himself from any type of legal ramifications for possessing the papers, Mahoney turned them over to FAA officials.

10. "My Name Is Leo Chouinard"

Something had to be done with the bodies. When Walter Bonita, supervisor for the ambulance department for Boston City Hospital, received the emergency call regarding the crash, he rushed to Logan Airport to check the status of the passengers on the crashed plane. He later told the *Boston Herald American*,

> When I arrived to determine how many were injured and who must be moved out first to what hospitals, I found an incredible scene of about 40 bodies all over the apron of the runway. The plane … what plane … there was no plane. It was totally wrecked. What was left was burned and buried in the dirt area where some construction was going on. I saw the wheels.… Yes, the wheels were there and I knew they were the wheels of a plane. But nothing else could be distinguished as the remains of an aircrash.[20]

When asked about the bodies, Bonita replied, "A few of them were unrecognizable. They were burned very badly and from what I saw of the rest of the bodies they were pretty mangled. I think it will be a long process to identify them."[21]

The fire department and ambulance services began moving the bodies to a makeshift morgue at the airport fire station. When Chief Arena decided it would not be big enough, arrangements were made for them to be taken to the Boston City Morgue across the street from the Boston City Hospital at the intersection of Massachusetts Avenue and Albany Street. This was the same mortuary where over four hundred bodies from the Cocoanut Grove fire were brought. Within ninety minutes of the crash notification, the bodies started to arrive.

After the first few arrivals came, an official pattern began to emerge. The ambulances came in from the expressway and parked in front of the morgue. Attendants removed the sheet covered bodies and paused at the entrance to the morgue where several priests had gathered to give the last rites to the victims. Once the rites were given, the victims were brought into the lower room where the refrigerated drawers were located and then stored, but there were not enough drawers.

Dr. Michael Luongo, the long-time and legendary medical examiner for the North District of Suffolk County, rushed to the morgue as the bodies were brought in. He was an investigator in the high-profile cases of seaman Willem Van Rie and the Boston Strangler. He had seen a lot of death over his years as a medical examiner but never so many so quickly.

He had to get his office's response to this disaster organized and functioning quickly as many family members would need help in the coming days. One of the first calls he made was to the director of Boston City Hospital. They arranged some necessary services such as a central office in the administration building.

To receive families and provide help in shepherding them about. Included were psychiatric and social service workers. Sandwiches, coffee and other refreshments were provided at the mortuary for the many family members, friends and workers there.[22]

Luongo then called Delta Air Lines. High officials of Delta agreed to "pay whatever extra costs might be incurred to expedite the process of identification."[23] They agreed to pay for "medical examinations of all the victims, protect and itemize personal property, etc."[24] Knowing that the limited space to store bodies would be overextended, Luongo asked Delta to rent a forty-foot refrigerated van "to house a large number of the victims since ordinary facilities could accommodate only about 25% of the victims during the hot summer weather."[25]

Delta also agreed to provide accommodations for the families of the victims, provide a group of men to help staff the mortuary, and fly all medical information to Boston to help with identification. Luongo also coordinated with the FBI to have them fingerprint all the victims as "nearly all [bodies] were badly crushed or burned, making identification a very serious problem."[26] Many bodies were identified from personal artifacts, jewelry, etc., found on the bodies.

Security and traffic control around the mortuary was provided by the City of Boston Police Department and hospital security guards. Dental examinations of the victims were conducted by Dr. Stanley Schwartz. Luongo and three other examiners conducted medical examinations on all the victims with no type of remuneration considered.[27]

11

The NTSB

Soon after taking office in 1963, President Johnson started toying with the idea of combining all the governmental departments charged with safety and placing them under one roof. He knew the benefits of having all transportation-related agencies placed under one large department. Hence, the Department of Transportation (DOT) Act of 1966 was born. Johnson shoved the FAA under the DOT shell but as an autonomous department. Highway safety, pipeline safety, etc., were all carved away from their predecessor agencies and placed under the DOT umbrella. Johnson stripped the CAB of its investigative functions, moved the entire CAB air safety board to the DOT, and renamed it the National Transportation Safety Board (NTSB). While it operated under the DOT name, it was, in theory, an autonomous department with a large degree of independence.[1] The board's success, reputation, and credibility rested on its ability to investigate accidents without interference from outside influences. Congress baptized the board with independence at its birth because they believed it could not successfully operate any other way.

With the CAB's air safety board now fully entrenched as the NTSB, the board lacked leaders. President Johnson wanted the board set up like the CAB with five members appointed by him for staggered terms. To assure fairness, the members had to be from both political parties. On April 17, 1967, the U.S. Senate held a hearing on the nominations Johnson sent down from the White House. He assigned Joseph J. O'Connell, Francis H. McAdams, Rear Admiral Louis N. Thayer, Governor John H. Reed, and Oscar M. Laurel to the board to await Senate confirmation.

A lifelong Democrat, Joseph O'Connell came to the board with a lawyer's background in aviation. He formerly headed the CAB, having been appointed to that position by President Harry Truman. He served many clients over the years, including Japan Airlines and Beech-Nut Life Savers, and he was also chairman of the board for Lake Central Airlines.[2]

Attorney Francis H. McAdams, assistant to CAB member Whitney Gillilland for the last seven years, came before the Senate; Gillilland described him as a man who does not make mistakes. At McAdams's Senate confirmation, Gillilland stated, "I have never known him to fail or make a mistake, which is a pretty strong statement, but it happens to be accurate in his instance."[3] Gillilland further gushed that "[t]here has been no case that the board decided in this field during that length of time that did not meet his very careful scrutiny and study.... I think perhaps that he has had more to do with the final form that the safety decisions have taken than anyone else at that level."[4] McAdams became one of Johnson's Democratic appointees to the board.

Coast Guard Admiral Louis Thayer was at the end of a distinguished career with the Coast Guard and Merchant Marine. He had safely escorted over five thousand refugees from Cuba and directed many rescue operations, including saving many passengers from a fire that broke out on the *Yarmouth Castle* luxury liner. His expertise included radar plotting and antisubmarine warfare.[5] He came to the NTSB as an independent.

John Reed became the only Republican appointed to the board. An extremely successful potato farmer, Maine voters elected Reed to the Maine House of Representatives and then the Senate. His colleagues voted him president of the Senate, a position that placed him next in the line of succession to be governor. When Governor Clinton Clausen died in office, Reed suddenly found himself governor. After winning a term as governor in his own right in 1960, he was reelected again in 1962. In 1966, however, Maine voters turned Reed out and elected Kenneth Curtis as governor. Even though he was a Republican, Reed was a staunch supporter of Democratic President Lyndon Johnson and the Vietnam War.[6]

Johnson found his fifth member from his home state of Texas. Oscar Laurel was a former investigator for the district attorney's office in Laredo, Texas. Voters in the Eightieth District in Texas elected him as their Democratic state representative for two terms. In 1964, he became a state coordinator of the Viva Johnson clubs of Texas, helping run the Texas presidential campaign for Johnson.[7] The president rewarded him with a spot on the NTSB.

O'Connell became the chairman of the board, and at the confirmation hearing he spoke for the board as a whole. In discussing the responsibilities of the new board, O'Connell supported the policy of the board's independence. "We will exercise the responsibility completely independent of the secretary of the Department of Transportation," he told the confirmation panel.[8]

In an interview two years later, he still maintained his faith in the independence of the NTSB. "We are the least subject to pressure and influence of any agency I know," he said proudly. "We don't even have to resist pressure—there is no way to exert it." He continued,

The circumstances are not conducive to anything else. We conduct our investigations and, in the case of aviation, seek information from the Federal Aviation Administration, the airlines, and the manufacturers. Then we are left alone to make our findings and say what we want.[9]

O'Connell and the Senate panel engaged in fantasy if they believed that the board would remain independent from outside influences. Each member of the board owed his position to the president and would be reappointed, or not, depending on his pleasure. The transportation secretary also controlled the purse strings of the board. Their upcoming budget for 1968 was made up by analysts within the DOT.

The administrative duties of the board were also handled by DOT personnel.[10] The board members and their employees at the NTSB were held accountable to those who had the power of appointment and the power of the purse. Conflict of interest issues also arise when a government agency such as the NTSB investigates another government agency such as the FAA, especially when both are under the umbrella of a larger department, in this case the DOT. In turn, the executive branch of the government controlled the DOT, and the president controlled the executive branch.

Even worse, as Joseph O'Connell hinted at in his interview, investigators of a major aviation accident were, and still are, dependent on other organizations, those with a financial interest in the crash, to help them determine the probable cause of an accident. This practice is called the party system, and it is still used by the NTSB today. Because of the small size of the NTSB, the board is not adequately staffed to investigate all aspects of an aviation accident without outside help. For example, if a Douglas aircraft crashes, Douglas Company employees help the NTSB investigate the accident. Pratt and Whitney employees are called in if that company's engines are involved. The Air Line Pilots Association (ALPA) is generally always a party to the investigation if the involved aircraft was conducting a commercial flight. Representatives of the involved airline are also asked to take a seat at the investigative table. All of these groups have a financial interest in the outcome of the case and generally become defendants if a case goes to trial. The party system allows future defendants to investigate the crash. Under the party system, the conflicts of interest are so obvious that it is doubtful that a thoroughly complete and unbiased investigation could ever be conducted by the NTSB. This situation was magnified when the NTSB investigated the midair collision of a Piedmont Airlines Boeing 727 and a Cessna 310 on July 19, 1967.

Titled the "Brother Act," the article about the Saunders brothers appeared in over five hundred papers on Tuesday, August 1, 1967. Jack Anderson called the government's investigation of the Piedmont crash a "family affair."[11] He explained that the government appointed a team of investigators headed by the brother of the vice president of Piedmont Airlines. Anderson wrote, "The government investigators will attempt to determine who was to blame for the collision—the Piedmont plane or a small private plane whose three passengers were killed."[12] Anderson then added why the matter was so important, why any hint of partiality toward one side or the other could have such a profound impact on the investigation. "At stake are possibly millions in insurance. There might be a temptation to pin the responsibility upon the small plane, whose owners are beyond any further harm."[13]

Bobbie Allen, head of the Bureau of Air Safety for the NTSB, had an answer for Anderson's questions. He completely dismissed them. He did not even admit that such a situation would arise or happen. He could not admit that there might be someone somewhere who would want to question the NTSB, or him, about such a thing. In reply to Anderson's charge, Allen stated that "the investigation cannot be subverted."[14] He went on to say, "It's a fishbowl operation ... so many officials are involved that no one person, not even the chief investigator could get away with altering the facts."[15] He admitted that he knew the two men were brothers when the team was selected. "We saw nothing wrong, and we see nothing wrong," he said defiantly. "No other investigative team was available," he added, as if daring Anderson to question his authority further.[16]

Allen's responses belied reality. A lot of things could be done with facts other than altering them. Washington, D.C., was ground zero for spinning facts. Someone could present one fact in Congress, and by the end of the day you had so many spins on the fact that everyone involved forgot what fact was being discussed. More importantly, facts could be ignored. If a fact or, in the instance of the NTSB, a piece of evidence was ignored, the fact would disappear. If a fact was never presented at a public hearing, no one would know the difference, which was the same as altering the facts.

* * *

However, it was politics that ultimately decided how the NTSB would function. On November 5, 1968, the American people elected Richard M. Nixon as president of the United States. Nixon, a Republican, would now be able to switch the balance of the NTSB's members from a Democratic majority to a Republican majority.

Just over six months into the Nixon administration, the chairman of the NTSB decided to retire. Even though his term did not expire until the end of 1969, O'Connell decided he would end his term early. In an interview just before he quit, O'Connell shared a conversation he had with his wife when he first took the job. "Don't you think you're a little old for this—isn't it about time to start thinking about retirement?" she asked.[17]

"I started thinking about it November 5, 1968, the day after the elections," O'Connell told the newspaper reporter.[18] The lifelong Democrat decided he could not work for Richard M. Nixon. With O'Connell's departure, Nixon promoted John Reed to the chairmanship of the board. Now, Nixon would need to appoint someone to fill Reed's vacant spot. He looked to Arizona and plucked Isabel Burgess, a Republican state senator from the Grand Canyon state. This, of course, was on the recommendation of his political buddy Senator Barry Goldwater.

Burgess had impeccable transportation credentials. She was the mother of three children and spent ten years in the Arizona State House of Representatives. After election to the Arizona State Senate, she became chairman of the Joint Senate and House Interim Transportation Committee and was a member of the National Legislative Transportation Committee. Before elective office, she was a Republican political operative. In 1950 she organized precincts for the Republican party in Arizona and served as first vice chairman of the Republican State Central Committee. She served on the executive committee of the Arizona Federation of Republican Women and served as chairman of the Suffrage and Elections committee.[19]

Senator Burgess also had the knack of saying the wrong thing at the wrong time. While reviewing her credentials for the board, she stated in an interview, "That's why I was considered for the post. I'm the only state legislator in the nation who is chairman of a joint transportation committee and is also a woman," implying that part of the reason she got the job was because she was a woman.[20]

However, the next transgression was a little more serious. President Johnson had proposed the NTSB to be an independent agency within the DOT. Congress had approved this arrangement but knew how easily exposed the board would be to political interference from the DOT. Congress jealously guarded the independence of the NTSB as much as they guarded their own legislative branch from interference by the judicial or executive branches. During her brief 1969 confirmation hearing, Senator Burgess was asked about the relationship between the board and the secretary of the Department of Transportation.

"What is the relationship of the National Transportation Safety Board to the Secretary of Transportation?" asked Senator Howard Cotton of Nevada.[21]

"Well actually," Senator Burgess replied, "the National Transportation Safety Board is part of the Department of Transportation but as you know, we are independent of the Secretary though we work for him."[22]

"Does the Board have—perhaps I should ask Mr. Reed this—does the Board have a very close liaison with the Secretary?" Cotton asked.[23]

Instead of letting John Reed answer the question, especially since he was on the board and she was not, Isabel Burgess chose to answer. "From what I understand, they do. I think it would be highly constructive."[24] There would be one or two members of the safety board who would disagree vehemently with Burgess on this. Their thoughts, and the thoughts of many in Congress, were that you cannot be an independent agency if you are part of another agency, especially when that agency is an executive branch agency under the direct control of the president of the United States and his cabinet. That created an environment of control and coercion, which was not to be expected of an independent agency trying to undertake its mission.

In a department with as many groups attached to it as the Department of Transportation, it was important that senior staff meetings of all the different organizations attached to it be held during the year. Some among the board members of the NTSB did not think they should attend due to their independent status. Joseph O'Connell, as chairman, attended the meetings. He did not feel that the NTSB's independence was threatened by attending these meetings. Francis McAdams, though, had a different opinion. For a time during O'Connell's tenure, McAdams was acting director. In deference to O'Connell, he attended a senior staff meeting of the DOT. It became quickly apparent to McAdams that no board business was to be discussed— "it was mostly DOT business, and politics, that type of a discussion."[25] When O'Connell returned, McAdams advised him that anytime he was acting chairman, he would not be attending those meetings. He felt it undermined the independence of the board.

On September 9, 1969, in the midafternoon with beautiful, clear weather, Allegheny Airlines Flight 853 collided in midair with a small Piper PA-28 airplane over Fairland, Indiana. Allegheny Flight 853 was a DC-9 aircraft carrying seventy-eight passengers and four crew members. The Piper was occupied by a student pilot on a cross-country trip. The impact tore off the tail of the DC-9, and it plunged into the ground, raining debris and body parts onto a trailer park. The Piper aircraft also plunged to the Earth, killing the pilot. The NTSB determined

> the probable cause of this accident to be the deficiencies in the collision avoidance capability of the Air Traffic Control system of the Federal Aviation Administration in a terminal area wherein there was mixed instrument flight rules (IFR) and visual flight rules (VFR) traffic. The deficiencies included the inadequacy of the see-and-avoid concept under the circumstances of this case; the technical limitations of radar in detecting all aircraft; and the absence of Federal Aviation Regulations which would provide a system of adequate separation of mixed VFR and IFR traffic in terminal areas.[26]

In releasing this probable cause, board investigators did what they had never done before: they directly blamed the lack of oversight by the FAA on aviation matters for a crash.

11. The NTSB

John Shaffer, FAA administrator appointed in 1969 by President Nixon, did not agree with the NTSB's determination of probable cause. In a letter he wrote to NTSB Chairman John Reed, Shaffer complained that the NTSB should have, at least, attributed to the pilots of both aircraft the blame of not seeing and avoiding one another as the board's final report indicated that both pilots had fourteen seconds to see each other. He also added, "With regard to radar, there is no current method available for perfecting radar to curtail the limitations outlined in the report."[27]

Shaffer also wrote a second letter to Reed accusing the NTSB of "prejudging the cause of the accident before convening a public hearing." He wrote,

> We suggest that in cases of accidents where the board has made its determination regarding the probable cause of the accident prior to the hearing, the board does the public and the participating parties a disservice in holding the hearing. Since a hearing is not mandatory in the accident investigative procedure, it appears desirable in future cases of this type that a hearing not be held and that the board simply publish its report. This course of action would not only save the time and effort of the participating parties but should expedite the publication of the report.[28]

Shaffer was so upset by the probable cause statement of the NTSB's report that he requested a meeting with the board to go over his complaints face to face. At that meeting, Shaffer and Deputy FAA Administrator Kenneth Smith asked the board members if it was possible for the "FAA to receive advanced copies of board reports and recommendations before they were released publicly."[29] Shaffer also brought up the issue of public hearings. He felt that the NTSB treated the "FAA like any other party to a proceeding and he seemed to have the impression that that was not proper."[30]

At a congressional hearing, Senator Howard Cannon (D–Nevada) asked McAdams about Shaffer's response. "He was advised at that meeting," McAdams responded, "that the Board would not give the FAA advance copies for purposes of comment, and that insofar as the FAA status at a hearing was concerned, they were to be treated as any other party."[31] McAdams continued, "Either Mr. Shaffer or Mr. Smith seemed a little taken aback by this, and they seemed to think that we were part of DOT and that in some way, the FAA should have, perhaps favored treatment from the Board. But he was disabused of that idea."[32]

When pressed by Senator Cannon regarding any suggestions as to how Congress could ensure the board's independence, McAdams replied, "Yes. I think that by legislation, I think the Board should be removed from the DOT."[33]

President Richard Nixon and his senior staff had other ideas. Their solution to effective government was to install personnel into the many different bureaus, boards, and departments across the executive branch who had an almost fanatical loyalty to the president. This would ensure that the federal bureaucracy would be completely under the control, and under the orders, of the Nixon administration. Independence was a bad word in Richard Nixon's world.

12

"Avoid Public Criticism of the FAA"

Watergate. Left by itself, the word conjures up images of wiretaps, testimonies, transcripts, and tapes. Whenever the word is mentioned, giant caricatures of Richard Nixon, H.R. Haldeman, John Ehrlichman, and John Dean usually hover in our mind, each accusing the other of high crimes and misdemeanors. The whole political saga, as known to the average citizen, can be broken down into this chronology: break-in, cover-up, trial, congressional testimony, resignations, special counsel appointed, revelation of tapes, special counsel fired, second special counsel hired, transcripts of tapes released, Committee of House of Representatives authorizes articles of impeachment, Nixon resigns. Some part of that chronology may have been left out, or erased, but that sums up Watergate as we know it.

Watergate, however, was more than that. Watergate was nothing short of an attempt by Richard Nixon to replace career, merit-based bureaucrats with individuals whose only credentials were a fierce, personal loyalty to him. This was a comprehensive effort encompassing all of the executive branch as well as independent agencies.

After the assassination of President James Garfield in 1881 at the hands of a disgruntled office seeker, Congress passed the Pendleton Act, which replaced the concept of political patronage with a merit-based system. Individuals would be tested and appointed based on merit for positions in the federal bureaucracy rather than for whom they knew.

Richard Nixon felt that this merit-based system filled the bureaucracy with individuals who were unresponsive to the needs of his executive branch, and he wanted to ensure that his policies would be carried out rather than left to die by uncooperative bureaucrats. According to his book *The Plot That Failed: Nixon and the Administrative Presidency*, Richard P. Nathan writes, "The President's men—trusted lieutenants, tied closely to Richard Nixon and without national reputations of their own—were to be placed in direct charge of the major program bureaucracies of domestic government...."[1] Nathan called this the "administrative presidency."

Not only was Nixon infiltrating the federal bureaucracy, but he was also creating his own. Nixon was so distrustful of the federal bureaucracy that he doubled the size of the White House and executive staff as compared with that of Lyndon Johnson, Nixon's immediate predecessor. His own bureaucracy was led by John Ehrlichman. Ehrlichman had worked for Nixon on his unsuccessful 1960 presidential campaign as well as his unsuccessful California gubernatorial campaign in 1962. After his election to the presidency in 1968, Nixon appointed Ehrlichman to be presidential counsel, and then in 1970, Nixon appointed him to be the assistant to the president on domestic affairs. Without any congressional oversight or any form of checks and balances, Ehrlichman expanded Nixon's private bureaucracy to bend to the political will of the president.

From this group, Ehrlichman created "the Plumbers." He appointed his assistant, Egil "Bud" Krogh, another loyal appointee of Nixon, to lead it. The Plumbers were formed to stop leaks from making their way into the press. This was an especially important assignment from Nixon because of the release of the Pentagon Papers in 1971, something the president vehemently opposed. The Pentagon Papers made up a study of American involvement in the Vietnam War going back to the Truman presidency and through Lyndon Johnson's administration. Much of it consisted of confidential information that Nixon felt must not be placed into the hands of the press. When the study made its way into the *Washington Post* and *New York Times*, Nixon was furious and demanded the leakers be found and prosecuted. In the case of the Pentagon Papers, the leaker was a former military analyst and employee of the RAND Corporation named Daniel Ellsberg. To discredit Ellsberg, Krogh ordered his Plumbers unit to break into Ellsberg's psychiatrist's office and find files on him. Ehrlichman approved the plan. E. Howard Hunt, a team leader of the Watergate burglars, led a group of three men into Dr. Lewis Fielding's office and broke into a filing cabinet purportedly containing information on Ellsberg. According to Krogh, though, they found nothing on Ellsberg. With this act, the Nixon presidency went from an "administrative presidency" to a criminal presidency.

In 1969, Harry Flemming led a group of White House staff assistants in reviewing and recommending political appointees. His father, Arthur Flemming, was a liberal Republican cabinet officer under President Dwight Eisenhower. Harry Flemming's responsibilities included filling commissions and special posts. He was transferred out of this position in 1970 and replaced by Frederick V. Malek, a former undersecretary of health, education, and welfare (HEW). He reported directly to Haldeman. "Malek's forte at HEW had been the removal and Siberian placement of HEW officials

12. "Avoid Public Criticism of the FAA" 97

felt to be a problem for the new Administration, as well as the selection of management-oriented new appointees.... Hereafter, the White House role in the selection and approval of key agency officials would be much stronger."[2]

After Nixon's huge reelection victory in 1972, he felt he had earned a mandate from the American people to do what he felt he needed to do to make government more responsive to him. He replaced many cabinet officers after the election and moved many of his loyal aides into different federal agencies. Three Ehrlichman aides were moved into different undersecretary and assistant secretary positions. Many other White House aides were moved into different federal departments.

One of the main dumping grounds for the president's men was the Department of Transportation. In 1969, Nixon appointed John Volpe, former governor of Massachusetts, as secretary of transportation. After Nixon's reelection, Volpe was out and replaced by Claude Brinegar, a former oil company executive. In March 1973, President Nixon nominated Alexander Butterfield as FAA administrator, guardian of the nation's skyways. He got the job because he had been the guardian of the president's door. As a deputy assistant to the president, Butterfield coordinated all paperwork and visitors to and from the president. He was Bob Haldeman's assistant and ran the White House staff when Haldeman was away. He also oversaw the installation of Nixon's White House taping system and was one of the few men in the world who even knew it existed.

One of the great debates in Washington prior to 1975 was the nature of the independence of the NTSB. Was it an umbrella organization of the DOT, was it part of the FAA, or was it completely independent? At its inception, Congress did not know quite what to make of the NTSB. There was a degree of independence, but, despite the protestations of some in it, the board could still be subject to undue influence. Some of the board members wanted Congress to legislate an NTSB completely separate from the DOT and FAA. Others felt the organization was better served remaining a part of the DOT as it allowed them cabinet-level access to the president.

There was no doubt where Richard Nixon stood on this issue. He wanted the board to remain within the DOT so he could keep an eye on them. To achieve that, he appointed Egil "Bud" Krogh, the leader of the White House Plumbers, as undersecretary of transportation. Nixon also appointed William S. Heffelfinger as assistant secretary for administration (the one part of the DOT that the NTSB relies on for assistance). Heffelfinger, in turn, assisted in the removal of the executive director from the NTSB and replaced him with Richard Spears, a man politically aligned with Nixon.[3] Spears in turn attempted to remove the director of aviation safety from the NTSB, Charles O. Miller, and replace him with someone more attuned to Nixon's thinking. Then Nixon himself acted to make the NTSB members more malleable to him: he sought to replace board member and Democrat Francis McAdams with close friend Timothy J. Murphy, a man who called himself a Democrat but supported Republicans.[4] This would, de facto, leave the NTSB without a Democratic member, and that was a violation of the legislation used to create the NTSB. There is no doubt that this formula was used throughout the federal bureaucracy to bend it toward Nixon's will and create fear, pressure, and intimidation all over the executive branch of government.

Nixon himself summed up how he wanted the bureaucracy to operate during his presidency. He stated, "We have no discipline in this bureaucracy. We never fire anybody. We never reprimand anybody. We never demote anybody. We always promote the son-of-bitches that kick us in the ass."[5] He was talking about disciplining the director of the Office of the Small Business Administration in San Francisco. Nixon wanted him disciplined publicly "as a warning to a few other people around in this government, that we are going to quit being a bunch of God damn soft-headed managers."[6]

* * *

The NTSB had many functions other than determining the probable cause of accidents. One very important duty was that "the Board shall report to the Congress annually on the conduct of its functions under the Act and the effectiveness of accident investigation in the Department, together with such recommendations for legislation as it may deem appropriate."[7]

Annual reports are written a year after the period they summarize. The 1969 annual report was released in 1970, the 1970 annual report in 1971, the 1971 annual report in 1972, etc. By the time the 1971 report was released in 1972, it became clear to the NTSB, representatives in Congress, as well as the general public that the perception of the board as truly independent of the DOT was not realistic anymore.[8]

The NTSB's staff resided in the same building as the FAA. Responsibility for accounting and payroll support, printing, guard services, personal support services, and other administrative functions of the NTSB fell to the DOT. The NTSB paid over half a million dollars in 1971 for these services. Board member Thayer summed up conversations he frequently had with aviation officials and reporters. They would say to him, "I saw your boss yesterday, Mr. Volpe. Please tell him I said hello."[9] Volpe was the secretary of transportation, and if the NTSB was truly independent of the DOT, he would not be confused as Admiral Thayer's boss.

In a letter to the director of aviation safety at the NTSB in 1971, General

12. "Avoid Public Criticism of the FAA" 99

Manager Spears wrote, "In response to your memo of Nov. 17, I am attaching the revision of the first paragraph of Mr. Child's presentation. He incorrectly stated that the Safety Board is 'an independent federal agency' which as we know, is simply not the case...."[10]

Spears also gave a speech to NTSB personnel in which he stated, "It is a matter of public record that several of our board members believe we should be made independent of the Department of Transportation. This may also be my personal desire. However, the day has not yet arrived when any of us of the staff can say the NTSB is an Independent Federal Agency."[11]

In early 1972, a draft of the 1971 annual report to Congress was distributed to the five board members. In it, there was no mention of independence. Francis McAdams wrote a memo suggesting the time had come for them to include a statement on independence from the DOT. The five board members held a meeting and voted on whether to include the statement of independence or not. Chairman Reed and member Isabel Burgess voted against including the statement. Members Francis McAdams, William Haley, and Louis Thayer voted to include the statement. The statement read, in part,

> Unfortunately, since the inception of the Board, its status within the Department has been misunderstood by the media, the public, and other government agencies. Too often it has been assumed that the Board is not independent, but a subordinate part of the Department, despite the legislative history of the Act, which makes it clear that the Board is fully independent of the Department....
> The appearance of a lack of independence which is broadly accepted by the Public is nearly as detrimental as would be actual infringement because it serves To create doubts as to the objectivity, the integrity and credibility of the board....
> In Light of the above, it is the view of the Safety Board that this problem should be given careful consideration and analysis, looking towards an organizational solution which would remove any doubts as to its independence.[12]

After the report's release, Secretary of Transportation John Volpe contacted Board Chairman John Reed. Volpe expressed that he was hurt by the inclusion of the independence statement in the NTSB report because he felt he had done everything to make sure the board was not interfered with in any way. He also stated he had been contacted by people within the Nixon White House asking if there was a problem with the NTSB. Reed calmly informed Volpe that this was not about him but about the appearance of the lack of independence.[13] Volpe's feelings, though, were not given much thought by the board. He had resigned after Nixon's reelection, and John Brinegar took over the DOT.

John Reed knew that the 1972 annual report needed to be submitted to Congress soon, and he had a feeling that the Nixon administration was not going to look kindly on another independence statement. In March

1973, he made a call to the newly appointed undersecretary of transportation and the former head of the Plumbers inside the Nixon White House, Egil Krogh. Reed asked him if the administration had an issue if the board included a statement of independence. Krogh had Heffelfinger communicate to the board that "[t]he administration was not interested at this time in sending forward a reorganization plan which would further separate the Department of Transportation and the Board."[14] Not only that, according to Reed, Heffelfinger told him that they were to refrain from publicly criticizing the FAA and that if the Republican members did not follow these orders, they would be disciplined.[15]

Reed contacted the Republican board members immediately. On March 23, Reed called a recuperating Louis Thayer at home and relayed to him the stern White House communiqué. Even though Thayer was an independent member of the board, Reed felt it necessary to warn him of the White House position due to, according to Thayer, "our long friendship, and because he thought I should know it in view of that fact that I would be coming up for consideration for reappointment before long."[16]

Republican member Isabel Burgess received a phone call while she was on NTSB business in Anaheim, California. Reed told her by phone about the administration's edict that "the Secretary was furious that Members of the Board would consider including in our 1972 Annual Report a statement on our independence as it appeared in our 1971 report."[17]

On either March 15 or 16, Chairman Reed invited Republican member William Haley to his office to relay the White House directive. He relayed to Haley that if any Republican member supported the inclusion of a statement of independence, "those Republican members will be disciplined."[18] Haley was also advised that a "DOT official had told him that the NTSB should avoid public statements that would be in disagreement with the policies and programs of the various agencies administered by the DOT and that the NTSB should avoid public criticism of the FAA and its programs."[19]

Democratic member Francis McAdams did not hear directly from Reed regarding the White House decree, but he heard it from Burgess and Haley. They told him that "there should be no public criticism of either the Department of Transportation or its components by the National Transportation Safety Board."[20] They also relayed the information that the statement of independence was not to be placed in the 1972 annual report to Congress, and they added that "if they voted to include the section they would be disciplined."[21]

Nixon's attempted overthrow of the executive branch had reached the NTSB. This intrusion of executive overreach and the intimidation of members of an independent bureau of the U.S. government signaled that Richard Nixon, through the cabinet offices of his loyal soldiers, wished to extend

12. "Avoid Public Criticism of the FAA"   101

his complete control and authority over the entire federal government with no dissent allowed.

As Nixon's grip tightened on the federal bureaucracy, James McCord, recently convicted in the Watergate break-in, wrote a letter to Judge John Sirica who had presided over the trial. In his letter, McCord wrote that:

1. There was political pressure applied to the defendants to plead guilty and remain silent.

2. Perjury occurred during the trial in matters highly material to the very structure, orientation, and impact of the government's case, and to the motivation and intent of the defendants.

3. Others involved in the Watergate operation were not identified during the trial, when they could have been by those testifying.[22]

The letter tore the dirty, bloody bandage off the Watergate cover-up and laid bare to the world that Richard Nixon and his men were criminals. The president's men fell quickly. John Dean, the president's attorney, began cooperating with federal authorities on April 6, 1973. The media reported that the Committee for the Re-Election of the President (CREEP) made cash payoffs to the Watergate burglars for their silence, and on April 27, 1973, the acting director of the FBI, L. Patrick Grey, resigned after admitting he destroyed evidence relating to Watergate. On April 30, Robert Haldeman and John Ehrlichman resigned, and John Dean was fired. On May 9, 1973, Undersecretary of Transportation Egil "Bud" Krogh resigned from the DOT as the media uncovered his role with the Plumbers. Congress responded with a ferocity never seen in Washington and convened the Ervin Committee, named after its chairman, North Carolina Senator Sam Ervin, to investigate Watergate. The Commerce Committee also commenced hearings on Monday, May 21, 1973, to investigate the subterfuge perpetrated on the NTSB by the Nixon White House.

The committee listened with rising anger as it heard about the pressure brought to bear on the NTSB by Nixon's men. They heard about the removal of Eric Weiss as executive director of the NTSB and how Spears came to the agency on the recommendation of the White House. Nixon administration officials wanted Spears to replace Weiss. Weiss had been with the NTSB as executive director since its inception in 1967. As far as Chairman John Reed was concerned, Weiss did a fine job and there was no reason to replace him. Then the White House Office of Personnel called and asked him to find a job for Spears, preferably as the replacement for Weiss. Reed acquiesced and forced Weiss to retire and replaced him with Spears.[23]

Spears possessed no prior management experience in aviation. He had worked for Aero Jet General Tech in California for several years. Their main responsibility was building rockets, and Spears worked in the public relations department. Once he left there, he worked as an aide for Nixon ally Senator George Murphy of California, and once Murphy was defeated in 1970, Reed was told by the White House Personnel Office to hire him as a consultant to the NTSB and then make him general manager. For Spears to replace Weiss, Reed had to change the name of the position from executive director to general manager. This allowed Spears to qualify for the position because of his lack of aviation training and protected Reed from any criticism from the Civil Service Commission. It was well known that Weiss was a registered Democrat and Nixon wanted him replaced with a Republican. Reed followed his orders even though he had a perfectly satisfactory working relationship with Weiss and could find nothing wrong with his performance. The White House, though, had heard "complaints" about him but did not share the nature of those complaints with Reed.[24]

1972 was also the year Democrat Francis McAdams's term as a board member expired. By law, no more than three members can belong to the same political party. The chairman of the board, Democrat Joseph O'Connell, was replaced by Republican John Reed. Reed's vacancy was filled by Republican Isabel Burgess. Democrat Oscar Laurel left in 1972 and was replaced by Republican William Haley. Louis Thayer was an independent, and Democrat Francis McAdams's term was up in December 1972.

Nixon could not replace McAdams with a Republican but Nixon wanted to flout that restriction. Nixon nominated his friend and former naval shipmate Democrat Timothy J. Murphy of Massachusetts to replace McAdams. Murphy had an impressive résumé. He was the former national commander of the Veterans of Foreign Wars (VFW), a former Democratic member of the Massachusetts House of Representatives, and an assistant attorney general. The problem was that Murphy had no safety experience and was a Democrat in name only. He had seconded the renomination of Richard Nixon as vice president in 1956 and, as a Democrat, had said he would "campaign for the Eisenhower–Nixon ticket if they request me."[25] If his nomination was approved by the Senate, the NTSB would, in reality, have no Democratic members. It was in this environment that Nixon's subterfuge of the board reached Senator Cannon's ears, and by this time, Congress had had enough of Nixon's shenanigans. Senator Cannon refused to hold hearings on Murphy's nomination. This would be extremely embarrassing to Nixon because Murphy, without any safety experience at all, was already working at the NTSB and was being called McAdams's replacement.

In the summer of 1972, Chairman Reed received a phone call from Secretary of Transportation John Volpe relaying instructions from President Nixon. These instructions demanded that the DOT find a job for Nixon's friend Timothy Murphy. Secretary Volpe did not want to hire Murphy, so he instructed Reed to "put Mr. Murphy on the payroll of the National Transportation Safety Board."[26] The White House also notified Dick Spears of their interest in Murphy. A short memo written on July 12, 1972, read:

> Per your telephone conversation with Helen Browder, I have attached biographical information on Timothy J. Murphy. We are very interested in seeing that he receives a consultancy with NTSB and would consider Mr. Murphy to be a Must.[27]

Reed hired him as a consultant with the stipulation that he would be McAdams's replacement. As introductions were being shared at NTSB headquarters, Murphy was introduced to Director of Aviation Safety C.O. Miller as the next probable board member, and Miller testified that "we should provide him with detailed briefings of the Bureaus operations, which we did."[28]

That was as far as Timothy Murphy would climb in the NTSB's hierarchy. Murphy had no safety experience. Congress sent word to the White House that Murphy "will never be confirmed."[29] Senator Cannon was opposed to Murphy "because he does not consider him a legitimate Democrat and that he won't be re-nominated for this post."[30] The letter sent to the White House described Murphy as a "low quality nominee."[31] Two other candidates the president wanted to nominate for that position were also dismissed. The Senate committee was putting pressure on the White House to renominate McAdams. Even though they did not consider him a team player because of his insistence on making the NTSB a separate unit from the DOT, McAdams's credentials carried the day. He was "highly qualified in the field of air safety, the only Board member with these credentials, and is a thorough professional, well-respected by the airline industry."[32] The White House surrendered and, seeing itself surrounded by hostiles, sent McAdams's name up to the Senate committee for renomination so that "we can pick up a chip with the Committee."[33] Congress had started fighting back against Richard M. Nixon's takeover of the NTSB.

13

"We Are Going to Do Everything We Can to Save You"

When the stretcher carrying Leopold Chouinard crashed through the MGH emergency room doors, the range of reactions from medical staff veered from shocked silence to audible gasps at the charred figure lying on the white sheets. While their reactions to the sight of Chouinard may have been different, their thoughts were all the same: there was no way this young man was going to make it through the day alive. One other survivor had made it alive to MGH but had died within thirty minutes of his arrival. If there were to be any survivors of this crash, those hopes rested on Leo Chouinard and the doctors waiting for him.

Chouinard begged for water.[1] He pleaded for it to anyone who could hear him. His pleas were ignored as he was whisked at high speed into the main emergency treatment room where Dr. Joshua Tofield stood waiting for him.

Tofield graduated from the University of California, Los Angeles medical school in 1967. He started his internship in general surgery at MGH soon after graduation and completed it in 1968. Tofield then began his residency at MGH, becoming the first resident at MGH to have an integrated program—his general surgery residency would be combined with a plastic surgery residency. One of the responsibilities of his residency in plastic surgery was to oversee the burn unit at MGH under the supervision of the plastic surgery staff.[2]

MGH had gained worldwide recognition as a premier burn center unit after the catastrophic Cocoanut Grove fire in 1942. A popular nightclub in Boston, the Cocoanut Grove caught fire and 492 persons were killed. One hundred and thirteen survivors were brought to MGH. Boston City Hospital (BCH) received over three hundred. At BCH, the Grove's burn victims were treated with tannic acid. Tannic acid formed a leathery scab over the wound and helped prevent infection. It was a lengthy process and extremely painful to the patient as the wound had to be scrubbed before

13. "We Are Going to Do Everything We Can to Save You" 105

the application of the acid. A month after the fire, 40 of the 132 initial survivors died at BCH from their wounds. MGH used a different technique. They covered a soft gauze with boric acid ointment over the burn. MGH also strictly adhered to sterilization processes in their burn unit: none of the initial thirty-nine survivors died from their burns. Tannic acid was thus phased out in the use of burn treatment.[3]

Of greater importance, Drs. Charles Lund and Newton Browder led the burn team at BCH. Their treatment of burn victims led them to create one of the most important documents in the history of burn treatment: "Estimation of the Area of Burns," also known as the Lund and Browder chart. This chart, informally known as the "Rule of Nines," divided sections of the body into different areas. The chest was 9 percent, the back was 9 percent. The front of the head was 4.5 percent and the back of the head 4.5 percent for a total of 9 percent. The front of each leg was 9 percent, and the back of each leg was 9 percent. Upper arms were 4.5 percent each, lower arms also 4.5 percent for a total of 9 percent. The groin area was 1 percent.[4] By dividing the body into these parts and assigning a percentage of body total, a doctor can quickly add up the burnt areas and provide a percentage of total burns over the body.

This tragedy also led to the term "Cocoanut Grove" being assigned by MGH to any mass casualty event. With the crash of Flight 723, MGH had issued a "Cocoanut Grove" code.[5] Once the code went out through the hospital, Josh Tofield rushed to the ER to await the arrival of any victims.

From Tofield's arrival six years prior, staff knew him as more laid back and less deferential to superiors than his fellow surgeons. Some said he arrived in Massachusetts with a surfboard on his back. At one point during Tofield's internship, a professor of pediatric surgery had performed a tricky suture maneuver during an operation and wanted to know what Tofield thought of it. "What do you think of that, California?" the surgeon asked Tofield.[6] "Not much, Kansas City," Tofield dryly replied.[7] His casual relationship with his superiors did nothing to hide his tremendous surgical skills, and as he took his first look at Leo Chouinard lying on the table in front of him, he knew he would need all of his skills, and those of his team, to give the young man even a whiff of a chance at survival.

Tofield immediately took command of Chouinard's life. Every order, every technique, every move, and every decision he made had a direct impact on whether Leopold Chouinard would live or die. Doctor Tofield instantly analyzed his patient, and an extremely critical picture formed. One of the first instructions for a medical student working with burn patients was to teach them to ignore the burns and focus on the patient. The sight, and smell, of the burns had overwhelmed many a med student to where they could not give the proper care to their patient. Tofield pushed

Leo's injuries out of his mind and focused on treatment. The crash had burned Leo so badly that Tofield applied the Lund and Browder chart in reverse. Rather than add the different areas that were burned together, it was quicker to just subtract the parts that were not burned and use the difference rather than the sum. Except for his head and face, right arm, and upper back, burns covered all of Chouinard's body. His legs were battered beyond repair. Parts of the tibia protruded from underneath the burnt skin, and Tofield knew those legs would never work again. They had to go. If they were not removed, what minuscule chance Leo had of surviving would be erased. Removing the legs would decrease the burn space on his body by almost 25 percent.[8] But first, he had to stabilize Leo, and that would take a few days.

Then, there were the burns that covered the rest of Chouinard's body. A first-degree burn, known as a superficial burn, affects only the outer layer of skin. The burn site is red, painful, dry, and with no blisters. A second-degree burn, known as a partial thickness burn, involves the epidermis and a part of the lower layer of skin, the dermis. The burn site looks red and blistered and may become swollen and painful. A third-degree burn, also known as a full thickness burn, destroys the epidermis and the dermis. The burn may also penetrate the innermost layer of skin, the subcutaneous tissue. The burn site will look white, blackened, or charred. Fourth-degree burns go through all the layers of the skin and underlying tissue as well as deeper tissue, possibly involving the muscle and bone. There is no feeling in the area since the nerve endings are destroyed.[9] Eighty percent of Leopold Chouinard's body was covered in third- and fourth-degree burns.[10] As a specialist in burns, and with his experience as a surgeon as a guide, Josh Tofield could not recall anyone recovering from burns this bad. He went to work anyway.

"IVs," Tofield commanded. His staff moved immediately to every command. The nurses in White 12, an informal name for the burn center at MGH, inserted large bore IVs into Leo's veins to replace the massive amounts of bodily fluids he had already lost and would continue to lose. They also inserted a large bore IV into Leo's bladder to monitor urine production. This was the primary manner to determine how much fluid a patient needed for survival. Tofield began removing any burnt skin that was in the way of immediate treatment. With the IV treatments, electrolytes flowed into Leo's body from the tubes as well as antibiotics, nutritional supplements, and massive doses of protein. "Monitor the intake and output of his fluids and chart them hourly," Tofield instructed. The nurses moved quickly and methodically to Tofield's every command. Josh Tofield knew that Leo's survival depended on the actions of these nurses. The doctor also knew he had the best nurses in New England with him here at

13. "We Are Going to Do Everything We Can to Save You"

MGH. They would become the frontline warriors in caring and treating Leo Chouinard.

As Josh Tofield began to remove foreign material from the burns and clean them, he looked at Leo, and both men immediately locked eyes. All doctors know that there is one patient they will work on in their career who they will never forget. The look in Leo's eyes made Josh Tofield realize he had just met that patient. Leo's piercing stare was not one of defeat. It was the look of defiance. Tofield could tell by Leo's look that the young man was going to defy death for as long as he could.

"Hello, Leo," Tofield said to his patient, having gotten his name from the ambulance staff who had received it from Harris Cusick. "You're at Massachusetts General Hospital and you've been in a plane crash. We are going to do everything we can to save you."[11]

Holding the doctor's gaze with his own defiant stare, Leo nodded and understood the reason he was at the hospital. He took a deep breath, and then, with his head cocked to the left and chin out, he nodded earnestly at Tofield.

"Doc, I know what's gonna happen. This is Mass General and you're gonna work like crazy on me but then I'll die of an infection in four to six weeks."[12] The statement, this prediction of the future, was uttered with such conviction that, at first, it startled the staff into silence. But because of the instant connection doctor and patient shared, the statement became a catalyst to save Chouinard. Leo's rebellious tone indicated he wanted to be proven wrong, and Tofield wanted to be the one to prove it to him.

Leo described to Tofield the events inside the airplane after it crashed. In the few seconds after the crash, he told his doctor that "someone next to him unbuckled his seatbelt and pushed him towards the window."[13] He then realized he must have fallen onto the runway, and the next thing he remembered was asking Harris Cusick for help.

There were many factors making burns a high mortality injury in the years prior to 1973. One of the most misdiagnosed factors was burn shock. With burn shock, patients become disoriented, vomit blood, and become manic. It would lead to death in a few days. In their study, "The Management of Burns with Silver Nitrate Solution," Drs. Jude Aldo and John King of Norfolk, Virginia, discovered that the shock was initiated by the depletion of sodium from the patient. They concluded that the "logical therapy for reversing the shock is replacement of sodium."[14] They determined that a diluted silver nitrate solution (0.5 percent $AgNO2$) helped replace the sodium. Their study indicated that

> [w]hen burns are treated with dilute silver nitrate solution, fever and wound infection are abolished without the use of antibiotics. Additional benefits from this therapy are reduction of heat loss from the denuded surfaces and

facilitation of spontaneous epithelial regeneration in deep second degree and superficial third degree burns.[15]

After stabilizing Chouinard as best as he could, Tofield gave the nurses the order to prepare the gauze dressing with silver nitrate and apply it to Leo's burnt skin. For the remainder of his hospital stay, the nurses in White 12 would respond to Leo's every need. They would change his gauze, turn him over when necessary, and monitor his fluid intake and outflow. They would make sure he had the correct nutrients and change his sheets. With their training, dedication, and professionalism, the nurses at MGH were fully prepared to care for Leo Chouinard.

* * *

Laurette Chouinard had dropped Brenda Newton off at home. After promises to stay in touch now that Brenda would soon be part of the family, Brenda waved goodbye to her future mother-in-law and walked inside her house. She lived on a farm in Marshfield, Vermont, with her parents. Behind her parents' house was a barn and between the barn and the house, on Hollister Hill, stood her grandparents' house. Brenda went to her room and started gathering items she would need to go back to college in a few weeks. She had plans to graduate within a few years with a degree in education. Around one o'clock, she walked into the kitchen to get a drink from the refrigerator. Before entering the kitchen, the phone rang, and her mother, Lorraine, answered it.

"Hello," was the only word she heard her mother say. Lorraine Newton's face tensed on the phone, and she quickly clamped her hand to her mouth as if reacting to a shock. She focused her eyes on her daughter and then glanced away every few seconds. Concerned, and sensing something was wrong, Brenda slowly moved toward her mother, straining to hear whatever news had so startled her. Lorraine softly waved her daughter way. Suddenly, through the large kitchen window behind the sink facing the barn, Brenda saw her father running from the cow pens to the house as if being chased by angry wasps. Brenda Newton knew something drastic had occurred to her family as she had never seen her father run in his life. Bud Newton entered the house breathlessly as his wife put down the phone.

Lorraine looked at her daughter. "Honey," her mother said. "There's been an accident."

Brenda glanced from one parent to another, not understanding. She tried to figure out who had caused this strange response in her parents. It could not have been someone too close as neither parent was crying, yet their reaction was one of extreme anxiety and worry. "What do you mean?" Brenda replied. "Who's been in an accident?"

13. "We Are Going to Do Everything We Can to Save You"   109

"Brenda," her father replied. "Leo's plane has gone down."

Leo? Brenda thought. No, you must be mistaken, she wanted to say. Not Leo.

Her parents waited for her reaction. None of the three knew what to say to the other.

Brenda took a deep breath. "Are there any survivors?" she asked. No one asked if there were any deaths because in commercial plane crashes in the 1970s, there were mostly always deaths. There was no need to ask. Survivors were a slim commodity in plane crashes, so there was always a need to ask about them.

Brenda Newton (left) and Leo Chouinard, winter of 1971–1972, Vermont. Courtesy of Brenda Newton McSweeney.

"I heard it on the radio in the barn," her father replied. "There are two survivors but from what they are saying they are not in good shape."

Brenda's mother chimed in. "Honey, Miss Betty just told me on the phone. The rumor is that Leo is one of the survivors."

Leo survived? Brenda said to herself. Of course, Leo survived, she told herself! It was Leo! He had just survived a crash from the airport last month, made it through Air Force bootcamp, and safely ridden a motorcycle from Vermont to Alaska without incident. He was an avid hunter, hiker, and Air Force sergeant. Of course, Leo survived; he could do anything.

Before Brenda had a chance to plan her next move, her father told her to pack some clothing and toiletries. "We've got to get you to the Chouinards."

Yes, she thought to herself. My new family. I will be one of them soon. She ran into her room and packed to go be with the Chouinards.

Laurette Chouinard was the proud matriarch of seven children. Her husband, Roger, worked in a granite firm supporting Vermont's number one export. With seven children residing there, the Chouinard home always attracted neighborhood children and friends like a magnet. They lived on Creamery Street in Marshfield, Vermont, in a small, light blue, white-shade, two-story house with a tin roof, next to a bridge with a barn across from the house where Leo and his brothers raised rabbits and had a fishing worm business as kids. The two Chouinard girls had their own bedroom, and the five Chouinard brothers shared two bedrooms upstairs. With school out for the summer and not scheduled to resume until after Labor Day, the Chouinards' residence became the neighborhood block playground.

Laurette worked the night shift at a local factory, so after going to the airport, she dropped her youngest child, Robbie, off at the neighbors, one house away, so she could rest before fixing lunch and getting ready for work. At the neighbor's house, Robbie and the neighbor child were playing inside in front of the television, when a news flash interrupted scheduled programming. It told of a plane crash in Boston of a flight from Burlington. It was the first time Robbie had seen a breaking news flash, and it immediately caught his attention. Even at six years old, he knew the importance of that news. He told his babysitter he thought his brother was on that flight because he remembered Leo's plane was going to Boston. They listened to the broadcast together, and then Robbie dashed out of the house to go tell his mother the news.

Plane crash? Laurette thought. I have not heard anything about a plane crash. When Robbie entered and spoke, she glanced at the television where news reports of a Delta plane crash from Burlington and Manchester broke in. The television anchor relayed the news that there were two survivors in extremely critical condition, but the rest of the people had died. Watching the broadcast, Laurette knew that Leo was involved in the crash. It was his plane.[16]

Laurette picked up the phone and called Roger at work. She was told he knew and was already on his way home. Slowly, the Chouinard children who were home came out of their rooms and gathered around their mother and the television set. They wanted to ask questions but did not quite know which ones to ask. The telephone rang incessantly. Laurette's responses were quick and curt. "We don't know if it was his plane. We haven't heard if he survived. We don't know." She kept repeating it over and over while trying to gather what little news she could from the television. Neighbors arrived for information but, most importantly, asked what they could do to help. Some did not even ask. They just went into the kitchen and started making sandwiches.

By this time, Roger had arrived home, and Brenda Newton was not far behind him. The phone rang again, and this time it was Massachusetts

13. "We Are Going to Do Everything We Can to Save You" 111

General Hospital. Laurette calmly listened as her optimism was tempered by the staff at Mass General. The caller explained that Leo was in extremely critical condition and that the family should proceed to the hospital at once. The Vermont and Massachusetts State Police had both been notified and were lining up cars to escort the Chouinard family to Boston. Within five minutes, babysitters had been found for the children, bags had been packed, and several members of the Chouinard family, including Brenda Newton, jumped in their car. They connected with the Vermont State Police waiting for them at the end of the street and, with sirens blowing and lights twirling, began a high-speed trip to Boston.

Delta Air Lines had already booked rooms for the Chouinard family at the Holiday Inn next to MGH. Delta put the word out to all staff at the hospital and hotel that all the Chouinards' needs were to be met and Delta would take care of the bill. After the journey from Vermont, which included a flat tire as the family crossed the state border into Massachusetts, the family dropped their few belongings off in the rooms and Delta personnel escorted them to the hospital. They then boarded an elevator to White 12, the burn center at MGH, and sat in a waiting room until the doctors arrived for their briefing. After several minutes, Drs. John Constable, Josh Tofield, and two others entered the waiting room. Roger, Laurette, Ray and Leona Chouinard, along with Brenda Newton, eyed them warily.[17]

"He's alive and resting at the moment," Constable stated.

Laurette clasped her hands together in prayer and then reached for her husband's grip. They both let out a long sigh of relief as if they had just breathed for the first time in hours. They, and the others, sat and listened as the doctors explained Leo's injuries. The doctors described their son as in "extremely critical condition." There was no guarantee he would make it through the night. Josh Tofield gave the family a rundown on Leo's injuries and burns.

Tofield explained to the Chouinards that Leo had third- and fourth-degree burns over 80 percent of his body. The doctor described how the depth of the burns had damaged and destroyed most of the nerve endings and that Leo was not suffering a lot of pain. However, he was on IVs and being treated with silver nitrate.

Tofield described how infection would now be the greatest enemy they would be fighting. "The skin is a blanket," he explained to the Chouinards. "Right now, Leo does not have that protective blanket and his vital organs and bloodstream are exposed to infection. There is no protective barrier keeping out germs. What we have to do," Tofield said, "is replace that barrier with skin grafts."

The doctor told them how the only areas unaffected by the burns were Leo's head, right arm, and upper chest and back. While those areas may be small compared to the rest of the body, he told them there might be enough good skin to cover the exposed, burnt areas back up. He explained that it was a painful process but one that must start as soon as possible.

Tofield ended on an optimistic note. "Your son is young," he said. "He is in extremely good physical condition and, just as importantly, he did not breathe in any fumes or smoke as his head was outside when the fire tore through the fuselage. He has no lung damage from the fire. Above all, he and I spoke in the emergency room. He has an incredible will to live and I can assure you, we will do everything we can to save him," Tofield finished.[18] He then gave the orders for the Chouinards to get prepared in hospital gowns and masks to visit their son. The nurses assisted the family into their gowns.

Roger and Laurette entered the room first. Leo recognized them immediately. Laurette just wanted to reach down and give her son a huge hug, but because of the burns, she could not do so. It was Leo who comforted them. "Mom, Dad, I'm going to be all right," he told them. He asked about his siblings and friends at home and was told everyone loved him and would see him soon. Roger and Laurette only stayed a few minutes and wanted their son to rest. "I'm going to be all right," he told them as they left the room in tears.[19]

Brenda Newton waited as Ray and Leona Chouinard took their turn. She started to get nervous. What am I going to say to him, Brenda thought? What could we talk about? She feared she may break down when she saw him; but she kept on a brave face. When Ray and Leona returned from their visit, Brenda knew it was bad. Ray looked badly shaken at what he had just seen. Brenda walked to the door to Leo's room and opened it. His handsome face was untouched by any injuries, and his thick, black hair still hung like a mop just above his eyes. She swore he smirked as she walked in. Before she could say a word, Leo looked at her and confessed, "As I was laying on that runway," he said, "the only thing I thought was that I would never see you again."[20] Tears streamed lovingly down her face. She wanted to hold him but knew she could not, so she just sat there letting him know if he needed her, she was right there.

After the Chouinards and Brenda completed their visit, Tofield gathered the group of surgeons together and went over their findings. Among the surgeons were Dr. Matthias Donelan and Dr. Constable. Donelan received his bachelor's degree in biology from Harvard and his medical degree from Tufts University. His general surgery residency brought him to the burn unit. John Constable, professor of surgery at Mass General and the most experienced staff member in the treatment of burns, received his bachelor's and medical degree from Harvard University. Having been born in England, his voice was still tinged with an English accent even though he had lived in America for well over thirty years. He had spent several years treating the injuries of hundreds of civilians in the killing fields of Vietnam.[21] During his time in Vietnam he had seen injuries of all types; and then, in Boston, he saw Leopold Chouinard's. Twenty years later, Constable remembered Chouinard clearly and reminisced to the *Boston Globe*:

> At first, his case raised ethical questions because so much of his body was so severely damaged and some parts were perfectly normal. We grappled with how much pain we should expect him to suffer for the life that may await him. But he tried so badly to live that we did our very utmost to save him....[22]

Night supervising Nurse Prudy Cullen, RN, had followed the news of the crash on the radio and television for most of the day. She had responsibility for the nurses in the burn unit for the 11:00 p.m.–7:00 a.m. shift. She had full confidence in the doctors at MGH as well as her nurses. She knew that if there was any place on Earth a plane crash survivor would wish to be taken after a crash, MGH would be it. When she got to the supervisory desk, the small AM/FM radio on the desk still shared details of the crash. She heard how eighty-eight people had died and one had survived but he was not expected to live. Suddenly, it dawned on her that many patients had radios in their rooms. There was no way she would allow Leo Chouinard to hear that he was not expected to live. She sent out orders immediately to confiscate the radios in the burn unit and bring them to other rooms.[23]

14

"Thousands and Thousands of Pieces of the Plane All Over"

The management at Delta Air Lines knew they needed to respond to all the needs the families of the victims of the crash. All requests from Dr. Luongo were met with an immediate "yes." Delta flew in friends and family members of the victims to help identify the bodies. Delta paid for all the accommodations. The airline also flew all medical information to Boston, and dispatched local airline staff, as well as staff from their headquarters in Atlanta, to assist the medical examiner. Delta paid for all X-ray examinations of the victims as well as the transportation of them from the airport runway to the morgue. Delta picked up the cost of all dental examinations involved in the identification of the bodies.[1]

Three other medical examiners assisted Luongo in the identification of the bodies. None of them ever billed Delta for their services. Theirs was strictly a volunteer effort. All victims were identified within five days of the accident.[2]

Back at the runway, response efforts had wound down as the afternoon progressed. Police officers and fire fighters still crept through the debris searching for more victims. The airport eventually reopened early that afternoon, and five hours after the crash, all that remained on scene for the fire department was Ladder Company 21. After all the bodies had been recovered and the fires extinguished, Company 21 remained to provide support to the investigators who swarmed on the wreckage when it was safe to do so. Removal of the plane's carcass began as the afternoon wore down into twilight. A cost analysis of the crash scene by the various responding departments was made a few weeks later.

The Boston Fire Department responded to the crash with seven department cars, four engine companies, four ladder companies, two rescue companies, one department wrecker, and one fireboat. Because of the massive response of equipment to Logan Airport, other companies had to cover for those units responding to Logan, and engine companies 26 and

20 covered for those units responding to the crash. The engine companies supplied water to the airport apparatus foam operations. Engine Company 5 pumped for fifteen minutes, Engine Company 11 pumped for thirty minutes, and Engine Company 40 pumped for fifteen minutes. Fifty feet of 2.5-inch hose and 750 feet of 1.5-inch hose were used by the fire department. In their analysis, the Boston Fire Department wrote, "Most of the duty at the scene consisted of searching and recovery of bodies of the passengers of the ill-fated airplane."[3] Among the personnel responding from the Boston Fire Department were the fire commissioner and his aide, chief of the department and his aide, deputy chief of fire prevention and his aide, along with deputy fire chief (acting) for Division 1, district fire chief for District 1, and district fire chief for District 2.[4]

The superintendent of maintenance, the assistant superintendent of maintenance, as well as a lieutenant (maintenance) showed up to help move some of the wreckage to get to the bodies. Two engineers, three members of the arson squad, and two department photographers also showed up to assist with the recovery as well as take photos of the accident scene. The companies were at the scene for an average of two to two and a half hours, and Ladder Company 21 remained on the scene for five and a half hours. The cost for fire department personnel was $1,130.04, and the cost of the equipment was $1,025.00, for a total of $2,155.04. In 2019 dollars, this would be $12,432.22.[5]

Luongo turned in his estimated cost of the disaster for his medical examiner's office and their pathological services. Luongo was only interested in reimbursement for his employees as it related to overtime. Luongo did not want any reimbursement for himself or the other medical examiners. He billed his overtime at $8,596.00, or $49,590.21 in 2019 dollars.[6]

The Boston Police Department broke down their receipts as: personnel costs at $4,158.09 plus $1,771.49 overtime, and the cost of the vehicles used as $680.40, for a total cost of $6,609.98, or $38,132.89 in 2019 dollars.[7]

The largest cost for the city was from the Department of Health and Hospitals. Personnel services included those giving assistance at the South Block of the hospital, porters, plant engineering, security administrative services, social services, radiology, and mortuary personnel. Those costs were $7,566. Supplies and equipment ran the gamut from electric line installation, food, sheets, blankets, air scrubber rental, trailer rental, ambulances, and radiology. Those supplies and the equipment came to $5,497, with the demand for white sheets being the highest cost of supplies at $2,470. The sheer number of white sheets gave a clue as to the condition of the broken bodies on their arrival at the hospital morgue. The total from Health and Hospitals came in at $13,003, or $75,014.13 in 2019 dollars.[8] The total cost to the city of Boston was enormous, and while Delta incurred much of this cost immediately, they were going to want reimbursement from those they felt caused the accident, and the Delta legal team was already looking at the FAA, as the employer of the controllers in the tower, for the blame of the crash. Once the lawsuits started, those found at blame could be responsible for paying out millions of dollars in compensation to the victims' families. The first step in that process was the NTSB investigation, and its investigators had arrived on the scene at Logan the afternoon of the crash.

* * *

Isabel Burgess and Arnold Holstine arrived at Logan Airport just hours after the crash. When Flight 723 went down, Burgess was the on-call board member and hence had responsibility to represent the board at the crash scene. Holstine was director of the NTSB's New York office and had responsibility for the Boston crash.[9] The two represented vastly different aspects of the safety board.

Holstine was a civil servant and had been with the safety board for decades. His primary region of responsibility was New York, Pennsylvania, and the New England area. Holstine had handled many high-profile crashes in that large geographic area. He was professional and meticulous, chose his words carefully, and relied on the facts of a case when answering questions. As the investigator in charge of this crash, he would coordinate all aspects of the investigation and attempt to solve the riddle of why it crashed. For this investigation, Holstine had close to fifty investigators assisting him. He split them into groups. Those groups included human factors, weather, witnesses, cockpit voice recorder (CVR), systems, etc. All of the groups had chairmen, and once they investigated their areas of responsibility, they would write a report on their findings. Holstine would take those group reports and transform them into one final report. He just hoped that he would have time to complete the investigation without pressure from NTSB General Manager Richard Spears. Spears had recently criticized investigators for taking too long to complete accident reports. His comments had rippled through the ranks of the investigators, and they could only reject Spears's complaints for so long. Holstine probably doubted he would get the time to completely figure out what happened as he saw from the beginning that this was going to be a very complex case; to unravel it would take a lot of time, more time than Spears was probably willing to give.

Burgess's authority came directly from the president. She was a political appointee acutely aware of the seriousness of the president's threats of retribution should they find fault with the FAA. She did not believe the NTSB should be independent but reliant on the DOT and thus exposed to outside political influences. There is no doubt that the distractions of

14. "Thousands and Thousands of Pieces of the Plane All Over" 117

Watergate, and how it affected the NTSB, weighed heavily on her. She did not know if she would have a job within a year as there was a push within Congress to have the board reorganized and run by a single administrator. By this time, she was almost four years into her term as a Republican board member. With the souring of the Senate on Nixon and his cronies, her reconfirmation could be in jeopardy. What she did not know was that she herself had already laid the groundwork for her eventual dismissal from the board by the U.S. Senate.

Burgess had the highest rate of absenteeism among board members. From 1969 to 1973, she was absent 27.5 percent of the time from regular and special board meetings, almost double that of other board members.[10] She racked up more travel time than any other member during her tenure, and traveled aboard equipment owned by companies in which the NTSB had pending investigations. She went on an "orientation" tour of the southwestern United States on Southern Pacific railways. She claimed to Congress that the trip helped her understand how railroads worked.[11] The NTSB, though, had some concern about the number of railroad accidents in the Southwest on Southern Pacific railways. When pressed for clarification, Burgess replied that it was coincidental.

The most damage Burgess caused to herself was her purchase of stock in Allegheny Airlines in June 1972. The NTSB barred members from owning stock in any transportation company because conflict of interest issues might arise. In June 1971, an Allegheny aircraft crashed in New Haven, Connecticut, killing twenty-eight people. While Burgess did not own Allegheny stock at this point, she owned it before the final report was finished and thus had a vested interest in the outcome of the report. When asked about her Allegheny stock ownership as a board member, she replied, "It was very unwise on my part."[12]

She and Holstine spent much of the afternoon of July 31 at Logan Airport traipsing through the debris of the DC-9 aircraft. Burgess had seen a lot of wreckage in the many crashes she worked on during her time on the board. What struck her hard about this crash was the utter devastation of the aircraft. The jet was splattered into, literally, thousands of pieces. The only recognizable pieces were the tail, a couple of tires, and a small part of the cabin. The wreckage was charred from the flash fire that swept through it. After conversing with Holstine and other investigators, she retired for the night and got ready for her press conference the next morning.

Burgess and Holstine met with the press the next day. NTSB policy and practice preach one thing when dealing with the press during an investigation: stick to the facts and do not speculate. Burgess began by stating that she had never seen wreckage so scattered, even that of an Alaska Airlines Boeing 727 that hit a mountainside in Alaska in 1971. She said the

Delta jet had "just disintegrated." Burgess explained how mostly everyone had been killed on impact because there "were scattered fires amongst the wreckage and thousands and thousands of pieces of the plane all over. It's just incredible."[13]

Holstine stated that the flight recorder recovered from the jet "indicates that there is some meaningful data that can be obtained." He did not reveal, though, what the data held. Holstine also revealed that his investigative team had interviewed Leopold Chouinard that morning and that Chouinard said he did not notice anything unusual with the approach to the airport. He also explained that after impact, the person next to him had unbuckled his seatbelt and pushed him partially out the cabin window before the fire engulfed what was left of the cabin.

Burgess added that the CVR had also been recovered and that both recorders were "found intact and sent to Washington."[14] She also stated that the jet had approached too low and at an angle with the runway. She clarified that even had the jet cleared the seawall, it would have crossed the runway at an angle and still have caused a major accident. She added that on first impact with the landing lights, the aircraft's speed was between 100 and 120 miles per hour. Burgess added that the jet's engines would be moved to a hangar at Logan for analysis. She said there was nothing unusual about the engines, that "they seemed to work."[15]

With the end of the conference rapidly approaching, the press seemed satisfied with the answers to their questions. Holstine and Burgess stayed on script and answered with the facts as they had them, and then, for whatever reason, Isabel Burgess decided to state her opinion. "It's like anything else. An accident is hardly ever the result of any one thing. It's usually several things that just happen to occur at once. Some people compare it to a slot machine," she said.[16] Then she picked from the slot machine one of the things she thought may have caused the crash.

"Because of noise pollution requirements here, some pilots have to come in high and then come down very quickly," she said. "It's possible that something like that could lead to this sort of tragedy. We don't know yet. We will be looking into that," she explained at the end of the press conference.[17] Within a few minutes, the newswires hummed and spread the news that the lead member of the NTSB investigation believed that the crash had been caused by noise requirements, requirements that were initially implemented by the FAA and CAB to keep people safe.

After the September 1969 midair collision between an Allegheny Airlines DC-9 and a Piper P-28 killed eighty-three people, the FAA began a study into the causes of midair collisions. At the same time, the FAA wanted to tackle the problem of aircraft noise in communities around airports. Perhaps, they thought, there was some equipment, or a procedure, that could decrease both noise and the collisions. In March 1970, a hearing was held by Senator Edward Kennedy at the John F. Kennedy building in Boston regarding the operations at Logan Airport. Stanley Lyman, vice president of the National Association of Government Employees (NAGE), an organization that represented some air traffic controllers at Logan Airport, told Kennedy and his committee that "federal money was needed immediately to modernize the ILS at Logan."[18] James E. Hayes, president of the Professional Air Traffic Controllers, told Kennedy's committee that "the FAA had failed to carry out a safe and orderly air traffic system."[19] He further related that in the late 1950s, studies showed a daily average of four reported near misses. In 1968, the FAA reported the near misses were up to six a day, but Hayes's organization had "reason to believe there were from 10 to 40 unreported close calls a day."[20] Both Lyman and Hayes called for "more qualified men to man the air traffic control posts at Boston and at other U.S. airports."[21]

Another witness, Captain George Drew of the Air Line Pilots Association (ALPA), testified that "Logan's lighting system is not up to that of airports at Syracuse, Rochester, Buffalo, Detroit or New York's LaGuardia airport."[22] Drew also protested the construction of a new taxiway at Logan, saying it was too close to an active runway. Richard Mooney, director of aviation for the Port Authority, replied that the authority had spent "about $50 million in developing landing areas."[23]

After the hearings, Kennedy, along with Mooney, visited the control room at Logan, and Kennedy told reporters the reason for his visit was to "make Logan the safest airport in the country, regardless of expense."[24] He added that "it was not a question of looking for scapegoats, but with the combined effort of the FAA, the pilots, the controllers, to determine the problems."[25]

Part of the solution was suggested to the FAA in the summer of 1970. It was suggested by the CAB, the NTSB, the president's Aviation Advisory Commission, and virtually every group involved in aviation planning. In late October 1970, FAA Administrator John Shaffer ordered new procedures to be implemented at airports around the country. One program was called "Get 'Em High, Keep 'Em High."[26]

"Get 'Em High," Shaffer explained, meant "[c]limb-out will be accomplished as rapidly as aircraft performance capabilities, noise reductions procedures, and passenger comfort permit."[27] This would get the aircraft away from populated areas as quickly as possible.

"Keep 'Em High" holds jet aircraft at ten thousand feet or higher. When they are within thirty miles of the airport, they must stay above five thousand feet. Only when they reach the "final turn into the descent area and enter the final maneuver in preparation to land," can they descend.

Shaffer noted that "[a]rriving aircraft will be descended as steeply as passenger comfort permits."[28] The FAA, CAB, and Environmental Protection Agency (EPA) hoped that would reduce the noise level in surrounding communities.

In addition to reducing noise, FAA Administrator John Shaffer stated that "the new system should also separate high-performance turbojets and slower aircraft in airport areas, reducing mid-air crash possibilities. This 'Keep 'Em High' procedure will reduce exposure between the higher-performance turbojets and the smaller, slower aircraft that usually fly at lower altitudes."[29]

Shaffer cited an FAA study on midair collisions that was initiated in 1969 after the Allegheny crash. The DC-9 had descended to 2,900 feet and collided with the Piper P-28 on approach to Indianapolis. The study also revealed that most midair collisions occurred at altitudes below eight thousand feet and within thirty miles of airports.[30] It was hoped that the new programs would not only reduce noise around those communities close to airports but also keep jet and propeller aircraft segregated and apart from one another.

Crocker Snow also concurred with these programs. Snow was the chairman of the Massachusetts Aeronautics Commission (MAC). By Massachusetts law, MAC was responsible for investigating accidents at the state level. Snow was also a leading figure in the promotion of aviation, not just in New England but nationally. President Nixon chose Snow to lead a study of the problems facing the country's aviation community and suggest remedies for it. His report, prepared in conjunction with a variety of industry leaders around the country, suggested that one remedy to alleviate noise immediately was the approaches recommended by the FAA. The report stated,

> The impact of noise would be reduced by altering airport approach and take-off patterns. Planes would approach the airport at higher altitudes than is usual at present and descend more steeply in either one or two segments; on takeoff, their climb angle would also be steeper, the object of both approach and takeoff procedures being to reduce the time the aircraft is in the vicinity of the airport at relatively low altitudes.[31]

With the almost universal support of "Get 'Em High, Keep 'Em High," many in the aviation community were aghast when Isabel Burgess suggested the program they had implemented for aviation safety and noise abatement could be the cause of this crash.

Snow hurriedly fired off a letter to Burgess. He began by stating that the Boston papers had quoted her as saying that anti-noise procedures may have caused the accident and that the plane came in at an angle.

14. "Thousands and Thousands of Pieces of the Plane All Over" 121

It would be most helpful to us in the investigation which Massachusetts law requires us to make, if you would elaborate on these observations, if in fact you made them. Specifically—

- Just what are the anti-noise procedures involved and what effect might they have had on the approach
- If the pilot came in at quite an angle, an angle from what plane of reference?

Thanks for your help.[32]

At least one Massachusetts newspaper gave Burgess the benefit of the doubt. The editorial staff of the *North Adams Transcript*, a newspaper in western Massachusetts, demanded action. At first, they rejected Burgess's words as speculation, that they "might be an injustice to the pilot." However, if Burgess was correct about the noise requirements, then "some important questions arise."[33]

The editors wrote that, "If noise regulations at Logan are such that under certain conditions—as in Tuesday's fog—the lives of passengers are risked by compliance, then clearly a long look at the regulations is advisable and even imperative."[34] While admitting that "the roar of jetliners at major airports" is a huge problem for the residents in that area, curbing that noise is appropriate. "But if human lives are to be in the balance, then obviously the regulations must be studied to determine if they can be revised in the interests of passenger safety."[35] They went further:

The anti-noise regulations surely could be studied to determine if they could be linked with comprehensive safety factors that would take into consideration the delicate navigation problems that are peculiar to landing at Logan Airport. This is a matter of widespread concern, because Logan is one of the busiest airports in the country. Many from this area are familiar with it and its particular problems and can testify that they have known nervous moments in takeoffs and landing there. If the noise regulations are found, indeed, to have been a factor, then at least air traffic at Logan should be suspended during fog and storms and other adverse conditions for longer periods than was the case Tuesday.[36]

The paper ended by stating that the noise regulations must be implemented for the benefit of both the passengers and the communities surrounding an airport. "Every effort should be made to do so."[37]

In addition to the "Get 'Em High, Keep 'Em High" program, Logan Airport had their own local noise abatement program. It included:

1. The first preferential runway system in the United States. This system influences the use of runways from which takeoffs cause the least community noise.

2. The prohibition of run-ups between the hours of midnight and

7:00 a.m. A run-up is defined as any operation of a stationary aircraft engine above idle power except to overcome inertia to begin taxiing.

3. The prohibition of flights over Boston proper at less than three thousand feet unless required to do so by air traffic control.[38]

In answer to her critics, Burgess denied she had said anything about noise procedures being a factor in the accident. "It is unfortunate but true," she replied to Crocker Snow, "as we in public life well know, that the press has the habit of quoting us out of context. During an informal morning session, anti-noise procedures were discussed, among other things. I have no recollection saying that these procedures might have contributed to the accident." She also explained that the plane did come in at an angle as this "was evident by the distribution of the wreckage which indicated that the plane came in at an approximate 15° angle to the runway."[39]

The anti-noise pollution measures at Logan were the least of the problems affecting the safe arrival of aircraft at that airport. The cost-cutting measures implemented by the FAA several years before, to help pay for the Vietnam War, shut down radar units at major airports all around the country. Most importantly, precision approach radar (PAR) had been discontinued, and had it still been in effect at Logan, the crash of Delta Flight 723 would probably not have happened.

15

"Criminally Negligent"

Like a hungry moth feeding on forgotten clothes hung in a closet, it was apparent by the late 1960s that something was eating away at aviation safety in the United States. With two midair collisions within four months of each other in 1967, Harley Staggers, the chairman of the House of Representatives Committee on Interstate and Foreign Commerce (now known as the Commerce Committee), summoned aviation safety officials to appear before his committee and testify about the deterioration of aviation safety. After the second midair collision, General William McKee, head of the FAA, and his assistant, David Thomas, found themselves in front of the House Sub-Committee on Aviation being asked some serious questions. Congressman Paul Rogers of Tampa, Florida, asked the first pointed question: "What is your budget request for radar systems in the present budget, and for towers?"[1]

"There is nothing in the budget request for radar systems or towers in the current budget," Thomas replied.[2]

"Nothing?" Rogers repeated incredulously.[3]

"That is correct," Thomas replied.

McKee chimed in and explained that radar had two purposes. The first was that it speeds up traffic, and that is why it is used mostly in congested airspace. The second was that it identifies where an aircraft is, and if it is in the wrong place, the controller can warn the pilot. "With regard to the Asheville problem [the midair collision of Piedmont Flight 22], as the chairman pointed out I am in a position now, as the administrator of the FAA, where I cannot appropriately comment on what could or might have happened or what radar would or might have done," he answered, wiggling out of commenting on the Asheville crash.[4]

"I understand that," Rogers added sympathetically. "You don't have the facts. We are not asking you. You don't make a determination of that. I am saying assuming."[5]

Instead of excusing himself and refusing to answer an assumption, an extremely common tactic used by public officials to deflect an uncomfortable question, McKee chose to answer the assumption, and the fight started. "As a general matter with money no object, as I pointed out, obviously there are many areas of responsibility we have; sure, we would like to have radar. But there is a question of priority in the budget, looking at the overall national programs."[6]

"But you have none requested in the budget this year," Rogers retorted.

"There is none before Congress," McKee admitted.

"There are no new ones," David Thomas chimed in, clarifying the confession of his boss. "We have funds for the operation this year for six new radars going in as well as ten towers. But they were all in last year's budget. As far as new radars are concerned, there are none in the budget."[7]

Congressman Fred Rooney of Pennsylvania eyed Chairman McKee suspiciously. He had been in talks with the FAA for a couple of years trying to get radar installed at the Allen–Bethlehem–Easton Airport in his district. Now he had the opportunity to push McKee on answers that he could not get over the telephone or via letter. "You speak about radar and you see the need for radar," Rooney began. "You wish you could establish radar facilities at every airport in the country. You made that statement, is that correct?"[8]

McKee fidgeted. "I said it would be highly desirable, obviously, if money was not an object," he replied.[9]

Rooney shook his head. He hated computing lives versus the value of a dollar. "Every reply I have had from your office is always in dollars and cents versus lives. Last year, in fiscal 1967, under the facilities and equipment, how much was requested by FAA?"

"In fiscal 1967?" replied McKee, stalling for time.

"Yes."

"On radar?"

"Well, new facilities and equipment," Rooney responded impatiently. "Doesn't that include radar?"

"The total for facilities and equipment that was requested of the Congress was $28 million. Our request was $73 million. That was to the Bureau of the Budget."

Rooney did not care about the Bureau of the Budget. He wanted to know how much was requested to Congress. Congress controlled the purse strings, not the Bureau of the Budget. Rooney saw through the charade quickly. "You requested $28 million in fiscal 1967 and you were granted $28 million."

"That is right," McKee admitted.

Rooney looked at McKee quizzically. "This was $11 million less than you requested in fiscal 1966. So why don't you request more money?" McKee decided to give Rooney and the committee a brief overview of administration policy. He told them that he was just a part of the whole

15. "Criminally Negligent"

picture and that he had to take into account what he thought other departments might want. In other words, it was not just the FAA that McKee concerned himself with; it was every executive department in the U.S. government. "I am only part of an administration. We have to take into account the other problems. We have a problem in Vietnam. We have problems of highway safety. We have problems of marine safety. So there are a lot of things that are highly desirable but, nevertheless, in the priority system we can't justify them."[10] With this explanation, McKee revealed the priorities of the Johnson administration with the first and foremost being the Vietnam War.

The Vietnam War was not part of General McKee's problem. It did not fall under his areas of responsibility. Yet he felt that because an unwinnable war raged in Southeast Asia, federal agencies other than the Pentagon needed to limit their spending even at the cost of innocent lives.

Rooney smirked at McKee. "You are now talking like the director of the Bureau of the Budget. You told me that you needed the money, that we needed the facilities, and yet you don't request the money to install radar installations throughout the country." Rooney knew his line of questioning exposed the FAA administrator as remiss in his FAA responsibilities. "General McKee, I would like to ask one other question about the 1966 request of $51 million for new facilities and equipment. You were granted $49 million. How much of that was spent?"

"This was in 1966?" McKee asked, shuffling through some papers.

"Yes," Rooney responded.

"We asked for $51 million and were granted $49.8 million. Do you want the status of the expenditures?"

Rooney nodded. "You were granted $49 million in 1966," he said approvingly. Now was the moment Rooney had waited for, the moment he could lay bare and expose General McKee as a failure in his job. "How much was unexpended?"

"I don't have that figure with me," McKee answered quickly.

Rooney raised his hand as if to let the general know there was no need to worry if he did not have the answer. "It is in the neighborhood of $25 million."[11] William McKee did not even spend all of the money he was given to develop and improve aviation safety.

With the election of Richard Nixon, John Shaffer was appointed as the new administrator of the FAA. Shaffer inherited the same problems that McKee had left, and the need to fix them was immediate.

* * *

Landing accidents had long been a problem in aviation. Indeed, the takeoff and landing segments of any flight are the most dangerous. The aviation industry searched for a landing aid that would assist pilots in landing their aircraft in all weather conditions. Previously, precision approach radar (PAR) assisted the air traffic controllers in monitoring flights as they came into the airport. In testimony in front of Congress, representatives of the FAA explained their attitude toward PAR. They stated that PAR

> provides precise lateral and vertical guidance information which is furnished to the pilot by a ground-based radar controller. Because of the communications lag and the ever present possibility of pilots misunderstanding ground instructions, PAR does not provide the same degree of precision as an ILS. Further establishment of PARs at ILS equipped airports is a redundancy we can ill-afford in view of the far more pressing airport problems previously discussed. Therefore, very few PARs have been installed at civil airports and their use has been limited primarily to ATC monitoring of ILS approaches. Accordingly, the FAA is considering the elimination of the remaining PAR systems as their use as a monitoring aid has been shown to be unnecessary and merely adds to the workload of the already over-burdened traffic controller.[12]

The FAA was more interested in an instrument landing system (ILS). They described that system this way: "The ILS glideslope furnishes the pilot precise and instantaneous information with respect to deviations from the approach path trajectory which permits him to make fine corrections in airspeed and rate of descent which results in a highly stabilized approach plus a very accurate trajectory to the touchdown point of the runway."[13] They also stated that funds were not available for all airports to receive an ILS, so its establishment would be based on traffic activity and "installed on the basis of where they will do the most good."[14] What FAA personnel failed to realize was that if the they removed PAR too quickly, before pilots were completely comfortable with the ILS, air traffic control could not warn the pilots if they were making a mistake.

Chairman O'Connell of the NTSB admitted that pilots were to blame for most landing accidents. "Most," he said, "have been attributed to improper operational procedures, techniques, distractions, and flight management."[15] Being that the landing was the busiest part of the flight for pilots, it seemed premature to pull PAR at this stage of the process since many pilots were not familiar with ILS approaches; he stated that the NTSB was recommending that "the air carrier industry review their policies, procedures, practices, and training to increase crew efficiency and distractions and nonessential crew functions during the approach and landing phase of flight."[16] This should have been done before the FAA discontinued the use of PAR.

Two fiery crashes, one in West Virginia and one in Chicago, as well as two spectacular crashes off the coast of California, led the FAA to believe they might have been hasty in removing PAR. On August 10, 1968, Piedmont

15. "Criminally Negligent"

Airlines Flight 230 crashed on landing in Charleston, West Virginia. No PAR had ever been installed at that airport, and the glide slope feature of the ILS had been out of service since June of that year. The FAA stated that the reason the glide slope was out was because the monitoring system for this component was unsatisfactory in the event of an out-of-tolerance glide path width.[17]

On November 22, 1968, a Japan Airlines DC-8 aircraft approached San Francisco airport on an ILS approach and splashed down in San Francisco Bay almost three miles from the airport runway. One hundred and seven souls were onboard Flight 2 when it landed in the bay, and miraculously no one onboard died. The pilot had attempted an automatic coupled ILS approach (which uses a glide slope), something he was not familiar with and had not attempted before. As he descended the aircraft, he did not realize he was below the glide slope and crashed into the bay. The PAR at the airport would easily have detected that the aircraft was too low, but it had been removed by the FAA sixteen months before.[18]

Just two days after Christmas in 1968, a North Central Airlines Convair 580 crashed at O'Hare Airport in Chicago, Illinois. PAR was not in use at the airport but was on standby, if requested. Twenty-seven people were killed as the pilots became disoriented due to the weather and the aircraft crashed into a hangar.[19] Had PAR been in effect, the controllers could have told the pilot he was in trouble.

The discontinuance of PAR had frightened residents of the neighborhoods around O'Hare. At the beginning of the year, members of the Barrington Village Council petitioned the FAA, urging them to require the use of PAR at O'Hare on a full-time basis. The resolution was dropped when Council President Jack Pahl read a letter from the FAA explaining why PAR is not used for every landing.[20]

The letter from the FAA was the same one it used to defend its discontinuance of PAR at all airports. Through a spokesman, the letter stated that PAR "is not favored by airline pilots who prefer to use an instrument system which leaves them in full command of the landing." The FAA defense also states that the PAR systems are on standby at eight major airports—two in Chicago, and one at each Seattle, Los Angeles, Kansas City, Atlanta, New York's Kennedy International, and Portland.[21] The FAA continued by stating that pilots can request the use of PAR, but most of them do not do so.[22]

Congressman Roman C. Pucinski (D–Illinois) represented those home owners in the residential areas surrounding O'Hare. He fully believed that the FAA valued the efficiency of air traffic control over the lives of those he represented. At a press conference, he lashed out at the FAA. He accused them of being "criminally negligent" for not making PAR mandatory at

O'Hare. He continued that "PAR would have instantly told the tower that the North Central aircraft had deviated from its final approach pattern because it is designed to be used by ground controllers as a backup to pilots' instruments." Leonard Kmiecek, president of the Chicago Area Pilots Association, said radar "definitely could have helped the pilot."[23]

Stanley Lyman, vice president of the National Association of Government Employees (NAGE), an organization that represented over eight thousand air traffic controllers, knew how little the FAA had spent on radar during the last few years, and he was determined to increase the pressure on that organization to increase their air safety funding. During the rash of midair collisions in 1967, he had been instrumental in pressuring the Johnson administration to increase aviation safety spending. He even publicly called on President Johnson to fire FAA Administrator William McKee due to Lyman's belief that McKee was not up to the job. Lyman had been involved in aviation safety for years and had testified before Congress on many occasions on the need for increased spending on safety. He had predicted in front of Congress back in March 1967 that aviation safety was in peril and that there would be more crashes. Within a few days, a TWA DC-9 collided with a small plane over Urbana, Ohio, and killed twenty-six people. When Lyman spoke, the FAA community nervously listened. He accused the FAA of culpable negligence by their persistence in discontinuing PAR. He also stated that had PAR been in use in San Francisco, O'Hare, and Charleston, West Virginia, those crashes could have been avoided.

On January 13, 1969, just a few days after Lyman accused the FAA of negligence, a Scandinavian (SAS) DC-8 jet crashed on approach to Los Angeles International Airport (LAX). The pilot thought he had a problem with his landing gear, and as he became preoccupied with the issue, the plane descended beneath the ILS glide slope and crashed into Santa Monica Bay, killing fifteen passengers and crew. PAR was not available at LAX while coming in from the bay as most landings occurred on the east–west runways at that airport. The runway over the bay is used infrequently and only in stormy conditions, precisely the weather in which PAR is needed.

Danny Jones, regional counsel for the Professional Air Traffic Controllers Organization (PATCO), a union representing air traffic controllers, claimed at a news conference that the aircraft landing aids on the seaward side of LAX were of pre–World War II vintage.[24] He urged that PAR be installed to cover this seaward approach before another crash happened. Acknowledging that pilots prefer an ILS over PAR, Jones added, "We are recommending it only as a monitoring system so that incoming flights can be watched and alerted if their position with respect to the glide path appears to be dangerous—an emergency situation."[25] Jones attributed the lack of landing aids to insufficient funds and personnel available to FAA.[26]

15. "Criminally Negligent"   129

The cry to keep PAR was not only heard in the United States. Eric Lubbock, member of Parliament (MP) for Orpington, England, and members of the English Air Safety Group met with the Board of Trade to protest the removal of PAR from Heathrow Airport in London. A few weeks prior to their meeting, an Ariana Airways Boeing 727 crashed at Gatwick Airport south of London and killed fifty people. They argued that had PAR not been decommissioned from Gatwick, the crash would not have happened. The captain of the aircraft had allowed the plane to fall below the glide slope due to a bad sequence in extending the flaps for landing. PAR would have alerted the Gatwick controllers he was below the glide slope. Five thousand members of the British Air Pilot Association also called for the extension of PAR at Heathrow.[27]

Finally, at the cost of hundreds of dead, the FAA rescinded its order to decommission PAR and ordered its recommission at eight major U.S. airports. ALPA said it did not object to the tower monitoring aircraft but reiterated that modern jetliners "move too fast for foolproof communication between [the] radar operator of PAR systems on the ground and pilots of inbound aircraft."[28] The move to recommission PAR became only a temporary move as ILSs continued to be installed at airports around the country. Ironically, San Francisco Airport had their PAR system dismantled and moved to Oklahoma City, Oklahoma, which is where the FAA's operational headquarters is located. Eventually, that PAR system was shipped to Vietnam to assist the American military in their war efforts against North Vietnam.[29]

16

"You Want to Get Warned About Hitting the Ground"

A few days after the crash of Flight 723, families began to bury their dead. Ministers of all faiths donned their vestments. Mothers and fathers buried their children, and children buried their mothers and fathers. Husbands mournfully buried their wives, and wives buried their husbands. Undertakers cracked the earth with their shovels and burgled the dirt in their way. They dug, and dug, until a crater four feet by eight feet appeared in the ground, and they lowered a coffin into the hole. Then, they returned the earth to its rightful place. Eighty-eight holes had been dug into the earth, and eighty-eight coffins filled them-eighty-eight times.

Churches all around New England opened their doors to let mourners grieve in their houses of worship. At night, stained windows glowed from the candles that had been lit in memory of the dead. They could be seen in most of the mourning villages in New England. Mourners came to pray for the eighty-eight souls lost and the one survivor.

The *Manchester Union Leader*, the largest newspaper in New Hampshire, started the days of mourning off with a simple message on its front page:

> The editors and entire staff of this newspaper join in expressing our very deepest sympathies to the relatives of those who lost their lives in the traffic crash at Logan Airport. Certainly all New Hampshire shares their sorrow. Under the circumstances, words are of no avail, but we here at the paper want the friends and parents and relatives of the victims to know that you are in our thoughts and prayers.[1]

Manchester Mayor Sylvio Dupuis announced that on Friday, August 3, a memorial service would be held in Victory Park for the victims of the crash. It would be led by the Clergy Association of Greater Manchester. All residents of Manchester were invited to attend.[2]

The Vermont Ecumenical Council and Bible Society asked that "this weekend churches and synagogues in Vermont offer prayers and dedicate their worship to the memory of those we have lost."[3]

16. "You Want to Get Warned About Hitting the Ground"   131

In Massachusetts, at the Lynnfield Center Congregational Church, family and friends bid goodbye to Captain John Streil. Eighty-five employees from Delta filled the pews to say farewell to their friend. At the conclusion of the service, they stood outside and formed a long line on both sides of the pathway as others departed the church. As the pallbearers escorted their dead captain's coffin outside the church, some mourners saluted, others removed their caps, but all remained silent in deference to their lost friend.[4]

A few miles away, at Logan Airport in the Catholic chapel of Our Lady of the Airways, Humberto Cardinal Medeiros led a Mass of the Resurrection. The Catholic diocese of Boston, under Archbishop Richard Cushing, built the chapel and opened it in 1951. Its primary mission was to become a church Logan Airport staff could attend when they worked long shifts and might miss a Mass because of their work schedule. The diocese renovated the chapel in 1965 to hold 250 people, and priests frequently held Masses there. On August 4, 1973, just four days after the crash, Cardinal Medeiros led a Mass for the dead of Flight 723. Worshippers attending were Massport Director Edward King, Director of Logan Airport Hubert Gainer, as well as Harris Cusick, Geoffrey Keating, and Mark Felber, the three construction workers who were first on the scene of the accident.[5]

While planes took off and landed just outside the chapel, Cardinal Medeiros humbly prayed: "We ask Him in His mercy to make safe our airways and our airports. We ask Almighty God in His Mercy to assist all travelers safely to their destinations."[6] But Logan Airport was not safe. The ground surveillance radar still did not work. It had been pulled out by the FAA in 1966 because it was not reliable. The PAR had been removed, and state officials as well as those at Massport were locked in a heated battle about which runway should get a new, modern landing system. Until these problems were addressed, Cardinal Medeiros's humble prayers could not be answered by the Lord.

To fix the problems at Logan, investigators first had to figure out why Flight 723 had crashed. To do that, thousands and thousands of feet of recorded tape had to be analyzed. Tapes from the traffic control towers in Boston, Manchester, and Burlington, as well as tapes from the aircraft had to be studied. Immediately after the crash, FAA personnel took possession of the tapes, and that was a huge problem for Delta's attorney, Frank F. Rox.

Frank Rox had represented Delta Air Lines as one of its attorneys for decades. A combative lawyer, he fought for Delta on all fronts regarding its interests. The FAA stymied Rox on his request to copy and transcribe the complete set of tower tapes between air traffic controllers and other aircraft in the hours leading up to the crash. Rox knew, as did every other airline attorney in the world, that the FAA had erased portions of tower tapes from a plane crash the prior December. That was the plane in which Mrs. E. Howard Hunt, wife of a Watergate burglar, and forty-two others were killed as it attempted to land at Midway Airport in Chicago.

Rox did not want the tapes in the possession of the FAA, he argued, because prior tapes "were erased by mistake and if they remain in the custody of the FAA they may be inadvertently erased or otherwise destroyed."[7] Rox was not being paranoid in his demand. Even the NTSB complained to the FBI about the investigation of the Chicago crash. Chairman John Reed wrote the following to the FBI:

> Our investigative team assigned to this accident discovered on the day following the accident that several FBI agents had taken a number of non-typical actions relating to this accident within the first few hours following the accident. Included were: for the first time in the memory of our staff, an FBI agent went to the control tower and listened to the tower tapes before our investigators had done so; and for the first time to our knowledge, in connection with an aircraft accident, an FBI agent interviewed witnesses to the crash, including flight attendants on the aircraft prior to the NTSB interviews.[8]

The day after the Chicago crash, Egil "Bud" Krogh, one of the White House "Plumbers," was named as the undersecretary of transportation, a role in direct control of the NTSB. Rox argued that, at safety board hearings, transcripts are provided to the involved airline, but he stated, "We want to make our own transcript. We want to make sure the written word we see is what was recorded."[9] When Rox did not get the tapes he wanted, he sued the FAA to get them. One week after the crash, arguing in front of Judge Garrity of school busing notoriety in Boston, Assistant U.S. Attorney Richard Bachman promised Rox and Garrity that the FAA would give Delta re-recordings of the tapes so that Delta could make their own transcripts.[10] Rox had won this round.

Round two concerned the controversial party system. A new party wanted to join the investigation. The group's name was the Aviation Consumer Action Program (ACAP). It was founded by Ralph Nader, and the attorney representing the group was Neil G. McBride. It was that name that raised the ire of Frank Rox.

Nader became famous for his exposé on the automobile industry, particularly the Chevrolet Corvair. In his book, *Unsafe at Any Speed*, Nader alleged that automobile manufacturers chose comfort over safety, even when faced with facts that showed an increase in injuries and death. Nader then led a group of volunteer law students to investigate the Federal Trade Commission. Their exposé led to massive reforms within that organization. Nader became a crusader against what he considered to be organizations of big business and government that did not protect the ordinary citizen. Without Nader, laws like the Clean Water Act, the Freedom of Information

16. "You Want to Get Warned About Hitting the Ground" 133

Act, and others would never have been passed. In a plane crash investigation, the companies involved would consider any group run by Ralph Nader as, at the very least, the last organization they would ever want probing around. All anyone had to do was ask Eastern Air Lines.

On December 29, 1972, Eastern Air Lines Flight 401, a brand-new Lockheed L-1011 wide-body jet, carried 176 people from John F. Kennedy International Airport (JFK) on a flight to Miami International Airport (MIA). As the jet approached MIA, the pilot lowered the aircraft's landing gear, but the gear light indicator did not come on. This was due to a burned-out lightbulb. The pilot asked air traffic control at MIA if the aircraft could enter a holding pattern. When he received permission to do so from the tower, the pilot dispatched the flight engineer to go below and look through a small porthole to see if the landing gear was indeed down. While the crew preoccupied themselves with this issue, unbeknownst to them, the plane's automatic pilot disengaged, and the aircraft began to descend. The aircraft came equipped with an adjustable altitude alert warning system, which the crew could set, and if the aircraft deviated from its assigned altitude, the system would emit one chime (C chord) over a period of seconds.[11] With the flight engineer out of his seat and the crew distracted, they never heard the warning. The L-1011 descended until it crashed into the Florida Everglades eighteen miles from MIA, killing 101 persons.

The NTSB held public hearings on the accident in March 1973. Chairman John Reed presided over the hearings. He gave Neil McBride permission to question parties involved in the crash. This was the first time at a safety hearing that the customer had been represented with an official spot in the investigation.

McBride's questioning revolved around the ground proximity warning system (GPWS) within the Eastern Air Lines L-1011 aircraft that would have notified the pilots that they were too close to the ground. After a spate of accidents in the late 1960s, in 1969, the NTSB formally recommended that the FAA mandate all commercial aircraft possess a GPWS. The FAA replied that they would study the proposal.

By the time Eastern Flight 401 crashed into the Florida Everglades in 1972, the FAA was as far away from requiring commercial aircraft to carry this device as they were in 1969. No action had been taken, but Flight 401 did have an adjustable altitude alert warning. The captain of Flight 401 set the adjustable altitude alert warning to warn them if the aircraft departed more than 250 feet from their assigned 2,000-foot altitude. When they did depart from that altitude at the beginning of the crash sequence, the warning device issued only a single chime note. The pilots never heard it.

Trans World Airlines (TWA) was another Lockheed customer for the L-1011. TWA had Lockheed install a terrain avoidance system on all their aircraft. Indeed, all TWA aircraft, whether built by Lockheed or not, were equipped with a terrain avoidance system. TWA's system "automatically goes off every time an airline passes through 500 feet altitude indicated by the radar altimeter whether or not the altitude change is intentional. A 1,000-cycle tone [roughly one octave above middle C] sounds for 2½ seconds."[12]

McBride wanted to know why GPWSs were not mandatory on every commercial aircraft. His questions on the subject were so pointed that NTSB Chairman John Reed repeatedly cut McBride off. Reed replied that the NTSB had already requested the FAA to make the systems mandatory. McBride responded by asking who at the FAA made the decision not to require the ground warning device. Reed told McBride that this hearing was not the place for that type of question.[13] Lockheed responded that they build their aircraft according to customer specifications, and Eastern Air Lines did not ask for the terrain avoidance system. TWA did ask for it.[14]

Frank Borman, former Gemini and Apollo astronaut, and at this time a vice president for Eastern, was asked if the TWA systems were installed on Eastern jets. He replied he did not know because "we fly the plane according to our procedures manual."[15] The negative publicity regarding Eastern's failure to purchase the terrain avoidance system prompted Borman to change his tone. He soon revealed that Eastern would reveal a warning system and install it on their planes. This system would emit a loud continuous horn blast if the plane descended to within one thousand feet of the ground without being on a glide path—or airfield landing approach. Borman also stated that they had been experimenting with these types of systems for three years but dropped one system because Eastern pilots complained "about being distracted so close to the ground."[16]

Only because of McBride's persistent questioning did these deficiencies in Eastern's operations come out. As the *Chicago Sun-Times* reporter William Himes wrote,

> Thanks to McBride, some vital points were brought out about the incredible botch that ended in a Florida swamp. They impinged directly on basic questions of airline safety that were pointedly unasked by other parties who were still playing the game according to the old rules.[17]

It was no wonder Delta's Frank Rox did not want McBride as a party to the investigation: Delta aircraft N975NE, also known as Delta Flight 723, was also not equipped with a terrain avoidance device.

The day after Delta Flight 723 crashed, Wednesday, August 1, 1973, Neil McBride obtained permission from Isabel Burgess to survey the crash site and observe the investigation.[18] After his tour of the site, McBride spoke to several reporters regarding the crash. Again, he mentioned that

16. "You Want to Get Warned About Hitting the Ground" 135

the aircraft did not possess a GPWS and that if it had been equipped with one, the crash may not have happened. McBride also accused the NTSB of "pussy-footing" around and insinuating that the board was not doing enough to push for that system.

Critics responded that the answer to these types of landing crashes was not more systems or instruments in the cockpit. Personnel from the American Transport Association (ATA) responded, "There's enough stuff in there already designed to alert the pilot if he'll only use it and listen to it. There are so many lights and bells and sirens now that sometimes the pilot just unconsciously tunes them out."[19]

McBride acknowledged they had a point, but he said "that if there is this danger, the logical thing is to eliminate some of the signals that warn of relatively minor dangers." He added for emphasis, "If you want to get warned about anything, you want to get warned about hitting the ground."[20]

Later that evening, after the interview, McBride attempted to attend some meetings of the NTSB investigative teams regarding the Boston crash. When he arrived, he was told that the NTSB had reconsidered Burgess's permission to allow him to observe and barred him from participating. McBride was told that representatives of Delta Air Lines had "bitterly" protested his participation and pressured the NTSB to reconsider, which they did.[21] McBride observed that "[i]f Delta did oppose our participation, they have done a great disservice to themselves and the board for they have raised the obvious implication that there is something to this investigation that they don't want the public to know about."[22] After McBride's performance in Miami back in March, Chairman John Reed may have remembered the warning given him by people in the Nixon administration that they did not want the DOT or the FAA blamed for anything. Undeterred, McBride applied as a party to the investigation at the public hearing to be held in September. So far, the NTSB and federal investigators had done what they could to limit the damage of the GPWS controversy. Also forgotten by most aviation observers was the fact that authorities at the airport had stripped and removed Logan's PAR several years prior.

17

"Trying to Use This Accident in a Cheap Political Way"

A pile of wooden crates sat unseen and unused in a warehouse in Winthrop, Massachusetts, just across from Logan Airport. The crates contained components of the most advanced landing system available. This Category II (Cat II) ILS would allow jets to descend all the way down to one hundred feet at Logan Airport before the pilot must make the decision on whether or not to land. Currently, only a Cat I system guided pilots down onto a runway, and they made the decision on whether to land around two hundred feet. The Cat II system also decreased the visual runway distance for a pilot to land from 2,000 feet to 1,300 feet.[1] The Cat II system was certainly more accurate, and the more accuracy a landing system possessed, the more aircraft could land in inclement weather. More landings meant more money for an airport.

The FAA had already installed the Cat II system at thirty airports around the country. These airports met certain criteria based on traffic and weather conditions. Logan Airport, known for its tricky winds lurking over the harbor, became a prime candidate for the Cat II system.

The decision to name Logan Airport as a recipient of the Cat II system was as far as the FAA got in installing it. Disagreements, accusations, and threats flew back and forth between appointed Massport officials and the elected state officials over the choice of the best runway to install the Cat II system. Massport favored Runway 15R, where planes must fly over the neighborhoods of East Boston to land, and state officials, mainly Governor Frank Sargent and Transportation Secretary Alan Altshuler, favored Runway 4R, where planes must fly over Boston Harbor to land.[2]

Massport, the FAA, ALPA, and the Air Transport Association (ATA) all favored putting the system on Runway 15R because 2,500 feet of the 10,000-foot Runway 4R could not be used because of the runway's proximity to Boston Harbor. Captain George Drew, a spokesman for ALPA, also said of Runway 4R,

You're playing with numbers and with cross winds and wind shear aloft.... It's just a matter of time ... the only reason that 4-R has survived so far is due to the pilot's ability to handle the planes and cope with the winds.[3]

That group also opposed Runway 4R because of the restriction imposed by the FAA regarding ships sailing through the harbor. Ships over one hundred feet in height would interfere with planes landing on 4R. However, a study by the Raytheon Corp for Massport in 1969 concluded that only one and one-third ships per day were of a height and location to interfere with aircraft landing on 4R. Crocker Snow suggested that an electronic surveillance system around the harbor be built that would warn the air traffic controllers that a ship over one hundred feet in height was in the area. Coast Guard representatives, however, stated that they "did not have the requisite authority to bar marine traffic solely to facilitate the operations of another mode of transportation."[4] They also had concerns about the stopping capability of large ships and explained that without an electronic surveillance system, or two Coast Guard cutters stationed on either end of the harbor, there was no way to stop an uncooperative ship.[5]

Runway 4R was, at first, considered the ideal runway to place the system by the FAA, ALPA, and Massport from a utilization cost and environmental view, but not from a safety performance point of view. Runway 4R came in fourth, while 15R came in third. The cost of the Cat II system on 4R came in at $45,000. However, the FAA then approved 15R and had agreed to pay over $2 million for the project with Massport supplying just over $800,000.[6]

The idea to place a Cat II system on Runway 15R began in 1969 when Massport wanted to construct a second and parallel runway to 15R. Seeing that this would greatly increase the amount of aircraft traffic over their neighborhoods, the residents of East Boston, along with elected officials, engaged in mass protests until, finally, the parallel runway project was abandoned. Unelected officials do not have to answer to voters, but the governor had to answer to them every four years. The governor also appointed the secretary of transportation, so they were both answerable to the residents of East Boston, and East Boston residents had had enough of aircraft flying over, and ruining, their neighborhoods. Massport sent Governor Sargent their permit to install the Cat II system on Runway 15R on December 2, 1972. He returned it, unsigned, on July 10, 1973, just three weeks before Flight 723 crashed into the seawall.[7]

The main reason state officials did not want to place a Cat II system on 15R was because aircraft coming in to land on that runway not only have to come in at an extremely low altitude over the East Boston neighborhoods, but they also have to clear the natural gas tank farms in Everett, which store millions of gallons of fuel at any given time. The aircraft then must clear the highest point on the Mystic River Bridge and then proceed over another set of fuel tank farms beside Chelsea Creek at just several hundred feet. If an accident like Flight 723 had happened over East Boston rather than on the edge of Boston Harbor, thousands of people could have been killed.

The failure of either Massport or the state of Massachusetts to act on the Cat II system burst onto the front pages of newspapers as open warfare a few days after the crash. That this crash might have been prevented had a Cat II system been installed on either runway made users of Logan Airport shudder. Each side quickly and venomously blamed the other for their failure to act.

When asked about the failure to install the Cat II system, Edward King responded, "The Federal Aviation Administration has an allocation for all [complete] installation. They said we could put it in as quickly as we could get clearance to set a foundation…. The Cat 2 system is particularly useful in guiding down a plane in foggy weather like that in which a Delta DC-9 crashed Tuesday, killing 88 people."[8]

In reply, Altshuler replied that Logan is a safe airport and that installation of the system had been delayed due to Massport's insistence on placing it near a residential area. "I gather Mr. King is trying to use this accident in a cheap political way. I am astonished that anyone would stoop so low," he added.[9]

King responded through the media to Altshuler. "Isn't that amazing. That statement is absurd and totally contrary to the circumstances. Politics is certainly more Mr. Altshuler's way of life than mine. It's most unfortunate that he'd make such an intemperate statement unsupported by any facts."[10] King also added that he did not believe there was a danger to the neighborhoods near 15R. "If instrument landing is a danger, I'm surprised," he said.[11]

By this time, state officials watching the bickering, as well as Altshuler and King themselves, decided their arguments were doing nothing to fix the problem. Each man reached out to the other later in the day and stopped their public fracas. "We've decided to bury the hatchet," Altshuler said. "We've decided to work together to have the instrumentation on both runways."[12]

As the NTSB's investigation into the crash entered its second day, an analysis of the CVR of Delta Ship 222 revealed a major clue in the crash, and it revealed a hidden danger of instrument landings. Edward King, director of Massport, was about to get an education and a surprise on the dangers of instrument landings.

*　*　*

Playing the CVR tape and listening through his earphones, Arnold Holstine heard the late Captain John Streil tell his copilot twenty-five

17. "Trying to Use This Accident in a Cheap Political Way"   139

seconds before they died, "You better go to raw data, I don't trust that thing." Holstine rewound the tape and played it again ... and then again. "You better go to raw data, I don't trust that thing," he heard over and over.[13] Holstine passed the earphones around to let other investigative team members listen to the tape, and they heard the same thing. "That thing," Holstine knew, must have been the flight director. A pilot would only tell his copilot to use raw data if the flight director was malfunctioning.

This was not the first piece of evidence Holstine had reviewed in the investigation, but it surely was the most important thus far. He had pored over witness statements that had been collected by his investigators. He had listened to tapes of the airport tower, gone over photos of the wreckage, and reviewed pilot and passenger files. He had held meetings with his investigative groups. Holstine briefed Charles Miller, director of aviation safety for the NTSB, but neither of them brought the matter to the attention of the board members just yet. They needed to review the maintenance records of Delta Ship 222 and find out if this malfunction was a one-time thing or if it had happened before. Holstine dispatched two investigators to Delta's headquarters in Atlanta. The records those two investigators returned with put the NTSB on a collision course with the FAA. On receipt of the maintenance reports, Charles Miller and Arnold Holstine had no choice but to brief the five-member board and advise them on how to proceed.

Two weeks after the accident, members Reed, Haley, Burgess, Thayer, and McAdams listened intently as Holstine and Miller explained that there were numerous complaints regarding the radio and flight instruments onboard Ship 222. These complaints, however, only started after Delta modified the avionics from their original Northeast Airlines configuration to the Delta configuration. There were seven write-ups alone on the accident aircraft between July 25 and July 29, 1973. Many of these were of a "chronic and recurring nature."[14] Compounding the situation, it was not only aircraft N975NE (Ship 222) having the issues. The Northeast Airlines DC-9s (N979NE and N978NE) immediately preceding and following the accident aircraft also had similar complaints to those reported on N975NE. Fourteen DC-9s from Northeast were affected by this modification plan.[15] The five board members decided to write a letter to the FAA with their analysis and recommendations.

Dated August 29, 1973, the letter to FAA Administrator Alexander Butterfield outlined the above complaints. Signed by William Haley for Chairman Reed, it read, in part,

> Although our investigation has not progressed far enough to assess the role of avionics and instrumentation in this accident, we are concerned about possible operational implications of these chronic discrepancies and the apparent difficulty that Delta Air Lines has experienced in correcting them.[16]

The safety board made three recommendations to the FAA. The first was to "investigate the adequacy of the modification program, its implementation, and the quality control aspects monitored by the appropriate FAA office."[17] The second recommendation was to "review the adequacy of the Delta Airlines' quality control procedures in detecting and correcting the reported discrepancies."[18] The third recommendation was the most drastic. With it, the NTSB knew they would put the financial and reputational aspects of Delta Air Lines at risk. The recommendation also put the FAA's paradoxical mission to the test. Unanimously, the board wanted the FAA to "consider the necessity of imposing appropriate operational restrictions on the modified DC-9 aircraft until the underlying reasons for the avionics discrepancies have been identified and corrected."[19] A spokesman for the board confirmed that the NTSB "wanted the planes to conform to altitude minimums for takeoffs and landing during bad weather."[20] The harshness of the recommendation stung both Delta and the FAA. Passengers would not want to fly on an aircraft that the NTSB did not completely trust to be airworthy. Now, the FAA would have to balance their mission of safety as well as promoting commercial aviation interest. Would the FAA come down on the side of safety or economics?

The NTSB received their response from Administrator Butterfield the same day. Butterfield replied that the FAA had already conducted a comprehensive audit of the technical aspects of Delta's modification program. FAA investigators found "nothing in the modification program that could have contributed to the introduction of spurious signals or system failures in the flight director system."[21] Butterfield also explained that their southern regional office had already initiated, before the crash, an in-depth inspection of Delta Air Lines' entire operations and maintenance systems. The final determination of the inspection had not yet been concluded, but he promised to send it to them when it was complete.

> Based on the results of our investigation, we do not believe that there is any basis for placing an operational restriction on these aircraft. In every case, there is adequate back up or other navigational intelligence to apprise the flight crew of any misinformation.[22]

Alexander Butterfield decided to let the modified DC-9s fly without knowing what was causing the problems of a chronic and recurring nature.

18

"We're Dealing with a Burn That Is Normally a Fatal Burn"

Within forty-eight hours of Leo's admission to the hospital, the doctors there all agreed that amputating his legs might give him a fighting chance to live. The medical team held a conference with the Chouinards and explained the situation to them. "In order for Leo to have any chance of survival," Tofield told the Chouinards, "his legs will need to be amputated."[1] The doctor was blunt. Without the removal of Leo's legs, there was no way the young man would survive. The lower legs suffered fourth-degree burns all the way down to the bone. The burns to his legs were so severe that, even if the rest of his body had escaped the fire untouched, amputation would still be necessary.

Laurette and Roger insisted that Leo be involved in all the decisions regarding his treatment. They told their son that without amputation, he would not survive. Leo consented to the doctors' recommendation and comforted his mother that he would be okay. The surgeons immediately scheduled the surgery to remove Leo's legs the next day.

As the sole survivor of the worst plane crash in New England's history, Leo drew continuing attention from news media, whose demand for information on his progress forced his physicians to brief them when possible. Tofield and Constable dampened any enthusiasm the press and public might have for Leo's long-term survival. "In burn cases of this magnitude," Constable explained, "the delayed onset of infection in the burned tissue usually determines the survival factor."[2] He added that "anytime the burns exceed 50 to 60 percent, survival is in question. The critical period will be the next several weeks."[3] Without amputation, Constable warned that the burned and damaged legs were "an overwhelming threat to his survival."[4] Constable finished by stating that "[w]e're dealing with a burn that is normally a fatal burn, because of its depth and extent." Tofield added that Leo's chances of recovery "are extremely poor at this point."[5]

Tofield and Constable had examined all the medical evidence available to them. As burn specialists, they knew that Chouinard's burns were lethal but still.... Chouinard's words and actions infused the doctors with a sliver of hope. Josh Tofield saw it in the young man's face. He watched in awe how Leo set his jaw and winced through the pain inflicted on him while undergoing treatment. Tofield heard the young man's determination to survive when Leo was asked how he was doing. Tofield never once, except when they first met and Leo was lying near death on the gurney, heard Leo complain about his situation or consider giving up. The doctor knew that Leo's chances of survival were extremely poor, but there was something going on with this young man not medically explainable. The consensus among the doctors was that there was no medical reason why Leo Chouinard should still be here ... but maybe, just maybe....

Considering his medical state before he entered the operating room, Leo survived the amputation without complications. He received two pints of plasma and one pint of blood. A hospital spokesman reported that "Chouinard is showing tremendous courage in his fight for life and they are encouraged by the sergeant's strong will to live."[6]

Residents of Leo's hometown, Marshfield, Vermont, were also encouraged by the fact he was still alive and fighting. Marion Ennis, health officer of Marshfield, spoke for the town's residents when she said in an interview, "It's been a miracle so far. Some of us think he is going to make it." She coordinated a fund drive to help the Chouinard family. She confessed that the whole town felt the impact of the crash deeply. "You hear about these things, but you don't pay attention to them," she added. "But this is really hitting home."[7]

For some, though, it was hard to believe that Leo would survive; the odds were just not in his favor. One of them was Bud Newton, Brenda's dad. While everyone was thinking about Leo, Bud thought of his daughter Brenda. He had not seen her since the crash. The college semester was starting soon, and he wanted her to get back to school. One day she came home for a quick visit from the hospital to see her parents. Bud sat his daughter down, and the two spoke. "Brenda, you know there is very little chance Leo will survive," he started. "You need to decide what you want to do. School will always be there for you, but you will have to live with your decision for the rest of your life."[8] Brenda despised the negativity that surrounded talk of Leo. She even overheard the doctors say on several occasions that "[t]here's no reason he's here today."[9] She knew her father meant well and was putting her interests first, but she was disappointed her father was in the pessimist camp. She needed to delay her decision until she spoke with Leo.

Brenda and Leo had not had much time to talk since his arrival at Mass General. Doctors and nurses came in and out every few minutes monitoring his vitals, filling IV bags, and changing his bandages. Laurette and Roger hardly left his side, and Brenda respectfully gave them precedence on visitation. On the few occasions she and Leo had alone, they discussed their future. Amazingly, Leo was able to sit in a wheelchair. On several quick occasions, Brenda was able to wheel Leo out on the semicircular balcony that extended from the hallway of White 12. There, they were able to be alone. Both could even see the planes take off and land at Logan. Leo shared his dream with her that he wanted to become a pilot. When talk of the future came up, he adamantly told her he wanted her back at school. There was nothing medically she could do for him, and it would be unfair to expect her to stay here with him while school was in session. The hard part of his recovery was coming up—he would have to endure skin grafts over most of his body. Once they started, there would be no more trips to the balcony off White 12, he would be in great pain, and he did not wish her to witness that.

On the one hand, with Brenda, Leo kept up a brave front. It was as if his injuries, which would have killed anyone else, could just be ignored and he would get better. He told her over and over that "we will get through this." On the other hand, Brenda wanted to hold him tight and just scream, "It's not fair, why did this happen!" But she would not give in to despair and would try and match Leo's optimism ounce by ounce.[10]

Brenda Newton decided to balance the wishes of Leo and her father. She decided to go back to school for two days a week. She could then take a day to travel and take two days to be with Leo.

Media requests for interviews and updates on Leo bombarded his parents. They were quiet, reserved, family people who shunned any type of publicity. Speaking no English, they had moved to the United States from Canada in 1952. Their oldest son Leo was born in Barre, Vermont, where they lived in a small apartment near other granite workers until their third child was born, before moving to the house in Marshfield. Roger and Laurette became proud citizens of the United States several years after their move. They learned English by talking and reading newspapers because they did not want their children speaking just French, they wanted them to be American and speak English.[11] Now, these two humble, hardworking, and proud parents found themselves at the center of the biggest news story to come out of Vermont since, almost fifty years to the day, John Coolidge swore in his son Calvin as president of the United States.

A friend suggested they hire a family spokesman to help them with media requests. They spoke with attorney Richard Davis who ran a law firm in Barre, Vermont. Three weeks after the crash, on Friday, August 17, they held a press conference at the Holiday Inn across from Mass General, which had been their home since the crash.

The conference began with Laurette thanking everyone for their thoughts and prayers throughout the ordeal. She relayed all the good thoughts to Leo, and it did much to cheer him up. She said her son was in "good spirits."[12] She clarified that Leo was not a pilot in the Air Force but that "[h]e served as an assistant to the chaplain."[13] She added that he "did have goals to be a commercial airline pilot."

Laurette went on.

> Leopold won't say anything about the accident when he talks to us. Most of the time, he asks for his brothers and sisters, and is concerned about us and how things are going at home. He doesn't seem to be worried about himself.[14]

When Laurette finished, Brenda spoke up. "I talk to him about anything. I tell him of friends who sent him cards, I say anything that pops into my head, just to relax," she explained. "His thoughts are about what we want. He just lets the doctors go ahead and do what they think they should do, he helps the nurses with the other things. He's cooperating completely."[15]

What Laurette did not explain was that not only was Leo receiving cards from friends but also from complete strangers all over the country. Thousands of people were sending him their best wishes. At first, the mail contained a few cards, and then, gradually, every week, more and more people sent more and more cards until Leo was receiving hundreds of cards a week. The cards contained words of encouragement and photos of other amputees with their spouses telling him he could live a normal life. Some even stuck money in the cards to help the Chouinard family financially. It was a great comfort to the family, and to Leo, that he had not been forgotten.

Roger Chouinard stayed silent. He could not bear to talk about the injuries of his eldest son. It was too emotional and personal for him. Richard Davis spoke next. "His outlook at the present time can be best described as one of courage," said the attorney. "He expresses great concern for his family, and fully expects to recover from his injuries." Davis explained that the family spends most of their days at the hospital with him and has only been home to Marshfield one day since the crash. "This has all been a strain on them," Davis added. "That is why we've waited until this time before deciding to grant interviews. They're still in a state of shock."[16]

Four days later, Leo's progress faltered as he had difficulty breathing. Doctors quickly diagnosed pneumonia in both lungs, and they found an infection in an area of his burns caused by blood poisoning. Over the next several weeks, Leo made several appearances in the operating room as doctors tried to clear his lungs and stop the infection. By the middle of September, they had succeeded.

The nurses continued their incredible job of providing extraordinary, total care for Leo. Silver nitrate solution, the kind the doctors used to treat Leo's burns, instantly stained any surface with which it came into contact. Nurses had to take extreme care in avoiding contact with the solution, while at the same time, soaking Leo's gauze in it. They provided total care for the young sergeant, including seeing to his psychological health. A smile and a friendly touch went far in soothing him. Like the doctors, the nurses felt Leo's determination to survive, and they continued providing him with remarkable care. In a *Boston Globe* article written on September 17, 1973, by Gloria Negri, she described the nurses in the burn unit at MGH. "They worry about 'Leo,'" she wrote. "Leopold Chouinard, the Air Force sergeant who survived the July 31 Delta crash, because, like most of the other patients there, he is about their age and they identify with him."[17]

* * *

Josh Tofield had made the decision within a few days of Leo's arrival at Mass General that he would aggressively attack and remove any crust, dead cells, dirt, and any other type of debris from Leo's burnt skin as quickly as he could. This process was known as debridement. Not only does it remove debris from the burnt skin, it allows a doctor to create a "neat wound edge to decrease scarring."[18] It also promotes healing in severe burns such as those suffered by Leo. Scissors and scalpels are used to remove the infected areas.

Again, staff wheeled Leo to the operating room. Tofield removed more debris from his patient's wounds in an aggressive tactic to start skin grafts immediately. Leo faced days of intermittent debridement as Tofield and others cut and sliced away dead skin. His attitude throughout the procedures indicated he knew that these debridement sessions were necessary to save his life. He never once complained to the doctors or the nurses about the procedure. His only goal, the only goal that mattered to him, was survival, and if he had to endure days of agony then it had to be done. Once that skin came off, new skin had to be placed over the removed skin, and Leo had precious few areas of his body that were untouched by the burns: his right arm and hand, a small section of his back, his torso, and, fortunately, his scalp. Chouinard's effort to escape the flaming fuselage had protected these vital areas, and that is where the doctors began removing his skin.[19]

The scalp was an ideal place to gather skin for a graft. Hair follicles there ran deep, meaning the excision would heal quickly and could be used repeatedly, if needed. The scars left from the grafts recede to invisibility as hair grows back and covers the marks.[20]

Like most young men, Leo had his vanity points. His hair was the first feature you noticed about him. Even while in the Air Force, he kept the length longer than he should have, and it was hibernation thick. It made him look more like he came from Liverpool, England, than Marshfield, Vermont. Had an audition been held for a fifth Beatle, he would have won on hairstyle alone; now it had to come off. Again, once the doctors explained the reasons for hair removal to him, he acceded to their wishes as it was one of the means to get better. Whatever misgivings he had, he kept to himself.

After debridement came the graft itself, and, once again, Tofield had to make a life-saving decision: What thickness of skin should he remove from Leo's unburned areas? The thicker the graft, the more time it would take for reharvest. Neither Leo nor Tofield had that kind of time to spare. Because such a large area needed to be covered on Leo, Tofield decided to go for a thin-split thickness skin graft. This way, Leo's skin would regenerate quicker and the area could be used again and that would allow Tofield to cover more of Leo's burnt body more quickly.

With a black marker, Tofield measured the amount of skin he needed for each graft. The markings were rectangular in shape. He also had to apply a formula for each graft as the removed skin would be stretched through a Mesher to increase the area of the graft. Depending on how much was needed, Tofield would mark an area 2:1, 3:1, up to 5:1. These measurements included length, width, and depth of the graft to be performed. They were measured at one-thousandths of an inch.[21]

Before removing the skin, it had to be prepared with saline to be ready for use. One of Tofield's assistants carefully aimed a syringe at the marking and slid the needle under the skin. He then pushed the plunger until the saline formed a puddle under the skin, pushing it up and away from the skull so it could be thinly sliced like a round of cheese. Once done, the edges were flattened out for removal.

Tofield used a Brown dermatome, named after its inventor, Dr. Harry M. Brown, to excise Leo's skin. The dermatome resembled a handheld plastic ice scraper and worked like a wood plane shaving thin slices of wood off a board. Once the target skin was lubricated with mineral oil, the dermatome would be placed flat on the marked skin surface to be excised. An assistant would gently push down on the area adjacent to the target to apply tension, thus making the skin taut and easier to remove. The doctor grasped the handle of the tool and gently pushed forward. One electric-powered blade in the dermatome sliced back and forth at a high rate of speed and removed the skin. The assistant gently grasped the excised skin in a pair of forceps and held it up and away from the dermatome. Once Tofield reached the end of the marking, the assistant snipped away with scissors any remaining skin, and that finished the procedure.[22]

Once removed, the skin graft was cleaned with saline and gently spread out until no air bubbles or creases were present. It was then placed onto the Mesher plate, which has small plastic ridges on it that make longitudinal incisions into the skin as it is cranked through. It is the same technique used to stretch pie dough. The incisions are made into the skin to facilitate any drainage needed so that the skin can reattach itself to the body over the burnt area and grow. The graft is then placed dermal side up over the wound and stapled into place. Once in place, the graft is wrapped in bandages soaked with silver nitrate until they can be removed approximately seven days after the graft.

Leo Chouinard endured this process and pain over and over until most of his abdomen was re-covered with his own skin. Human skin is the largest organ on the human body, so this procedure could be considered an external organ transplant, and Leo Chouinard was enduring one of the largest organ transplants ever performed on a human being. Against all odds, the grafts took hold. However, to dampen unrealistic expectations of his imminent survival, Tofield gave an infrequent press conference about Leo's condition.

When a reporter asked about Chouinard's condition, Tofield immediately spoke about Leo's will to live. "I will say that throughout, psychologically, he has been most unusual in that he has kept up a very fierce determination to keep on going, which he can really verbalize," Tofield said.[23] He then explained the difference between trauma patients and burn patients. "Ordinary trauma patients who receive good, prompt treatment have increasing survival chances with every passing day," he explained.[24] However, "[A] burn patient looks best after about a week and then he gets worse for a long time before he gets better," Tofield explained.[25] Chouinard was in that time period now.

Tofield explained that he and his staff took unusually aggressive steps to save Leo. He spoke of the amputation and the quick debridement of the burns. "Our feeling is that people seem to do a little bit better if we get right at it. Over the last couple of years, we've become progressively more aggressive."[26] He explained that most of the burned areas on the front of Leo's body had been covered in grafts. Next, they would have to work on Leo's back while he spent weeks lying on his front or sides while they applied the grafts. Tofield spoke of the secondary problems Leo faced. He spoke of Leo's loss of weight and malnutrition. "The body," he explained, "uses up enormous amounts of calories trying to heal itself." Leo also suffered from "intermittent internal bleeding, blood poisoning, pneumonia in both lungs and hallucinations as well as disorientation."[27]

Tofield added that Leo had been to the operating table eight times for the amputations of his legs, skin grafts, and procedures to clean out his lungs from infection. "A person with 75 percent of his skin removed can't do many things. For example, he can't regulate his own temperature very well, he loses massive amount of fluid. Evaporation takes calories away. He still has all this raw area that essentially oozes protein, protein that he needs to reconstitute himself and to heal skin grafts and spread them out and heal the wounds."[28]

The doctor explained about the meshing process of the skin before it is grafted onto the wound. "We sort of crank it through this machine and it puts a pattern on the skin. It's much like when one puts holes in pie dough to stretch it out. You sort of get more for your money and you're able to cover a bigger area."[29] He added that Leo was fed intravenously about six thousand calories a day and had been able to drink some liquid by mouth. "He hasn't asked for a steak yet but that may come in time," he added with a smile.[30] What Josh Tofield did not tell the reporters was that Leopold Chouinard was exceeding all expectations and then some. He wanted to tell them that Leo had experienced, and so far survived, wounds and burns rarely, if at all, recorded in the history of human medicine. Leo should have been dead weeks ago, and Tofield had no explanation for why Leo was still here. All Josh Tofield knew was that he and Leo, one with his fierce determination to live, the other with his extraordinary surgical skills, had partnered together since that first meeting on the emergency room table, to hopefully pull off what could be considered one of the greatest death-defying feats of all time.

19

"The Administration Has Made Repeated Attempts to Both Harass and Intimidate the Board"

The NTSB had reached the public phase of its investigation into the crash of Delta Flight 723. Isabel Burgess would not be the hearing officer; that role would fall to Francis McAdams. He convened the public hearing on September 18, 1973, at the Holiday Inn in Peabody, Massachusetts, at a time when the full impact of Richard Nixon's war on the government bureaucracy was in full swing. Turmoil wracked the NTSB. Senior managers engaged in a war of words and subterfuge with each other. Managers blamed investigators for not being thorough in their job performance, and board members were threatened with reprisals by the White House if they did not follow the administration's lead. Individual board members had different definitions for their various responsibilities (i.e., the definition of a probable cause, why public hearings were held, etc.). The situation at the NTSB had gotten so bad that congressmen prepared hearings on whether to even keep the board in its current form or make it completely independent with a single administrator rather than five board members. The board, as it was currently being run, was viewed by some in Congress to be obsolete and untrustworthy.

Charles Otto "Chuck" or "C.O." Miller began his career in aviation as a U.S. Navy and Marine Corps instructor pilot. After the war, he earned his bachelor of science degree at Massachusetts Institute of Technology (MIT) in aeronautical engineering. He worked for Douglas Aircraft Company as an engineer, worked for Vought Aircraft Industries as a test pilot, and worked on missile programs. He served in the Marine Corps Reserves and qualified as a commercial pilot. In 1963, he began work at the Flight Safety Foundation Inc. (FSF). He earned his master's degree in aerospace operations management from the University of Southern California and spent five years at the Institute of Aerospace Safety and Management as a lecturer and director of research. In 1968, Joseph O'Connell appointed Miller as the director of aviation safety for the NTSB when Bobbie Allen resigned.[1]

When Congress created the NTSB, they were mandated with finding the probable cause of transportation accidents. "It shall be the duty of the Board to ... [determine] the cause or probable cause of transportation accidents and [report] the facts, conditions and circumstances related to such accident."[2]

The probable cause statement mandated by Congress had always stirred controversy within the aviation community and within the NTSB itself. Board member Francis McAdams, an attorney by trade, wrote that the definition of probable cause is "the most reasonable cause, the one having more evidence for than against."[3] C.O. Miller did not agree. When he took over his duties at the NTSB, he explained in a speech that a probable cause statement is too simple. "There is one overriding principle in safety that requires a diminution of emphasis on a singular probable cause. Accidents are a combination of events with numerous chains or cause–effect relationships determinable therein."[4] He felt the reason Congress limited the NTSB to finding a probable cause to an accident was that "[w]e, the public, prefer simple answers; we like a nice, convenient, singular cause–effect relationship. It avoids adding another confusing segment to our already complex lives."[5] On Miller's arrival at NTSB headquarters, he surveyed his investigators, both verbally and in writing, and came up with some startling results. He found that NTSB investigators lacked a clear understanding of probable versus proximate cause and that there was a tendency for them to structure reports toward a singular cause. Even Chairman O'Connell found merit in Miller's thinking. In a speech to safety technicians, O'Connell said,

> We must not become so preoccupied, in sifting through the wreckage and seeking out that one alternative of omission or commission that caused the event, that we ignore other lessons which may be lying on the surface.... We place a great premium on pursuing the many alternatives, narrowing down the areas of consideration, and arriving at that one specific cause. I have been wondering whether it is so important that our choice of the cause be so exact.... Is it always vital that we identify beyond peradventure which one as the culprit? I think not. If the alternatives are all possible causes, shouldn't we seek remedies for all? I think so.[6]

Miller also had another reason for diminishing the probable cause statement. "Implicit also is a concern that if the Bureau is ever exclusively identified with a probable cause determination, then its product will tend to be vectored away from safety promotion in the minds of the public and will be identified with fault finding, pure enforcement, or legal functions."[7] Miller wanted the Bureau of Aviation Safety to promote all aspects of safety, including analysis and recommendations that would be placed into the final accident report.

General Manager Richard Spears disagreed. He wanted the probable cause statement changed, or "defined," as he put it in congressional testimony. On February 15, 1973, he made a speech to the board's professional staff indicating other items he wanted changed in accident reports. In it he said, "Relative to our accident reports themselves, you would do well to reduce extra or extraneous analysis, select those recommendations which are obvious, never mind wasting your time trying to think up a few extra recommendations."[8]

In Senate testimony a few months later, Senator Cannon called Spears out regarding his statement. "How do you justify that kind of interference with the Board's professionals who are involved in making recommendations involving the saving of people's lives?"[9]

Spears responded. "I did not regard that as interference.... The Board, individually and collectively in its meetings, has been extremely critical of both bureaus in that they seem to be, in the Board's view—this is the words of one or two of the members—trying to impress their professional peers with their great intellectual ability in these matters...."[10]

Spears went on:

> It seems to me, since the bureaus come to the Board at any time with recommendations for safety ... that to hold up a report for extra recommendations certainly didn't make us look very good. And in many cases, in an accident report, the recommendations to a modal administration or to a manufacturer or to a career are made long before the report is passed by the Board. I saw nothing wrong with including those recommendations that are obvious from an accident, making other recommendations before or after the report is issued. I was talking about the administrative side of preparing a report.[11]

Cannon responded to Spears. "When you are telling them how to do their job, and you have no expertise in that field, it seems to me that actually what you are trying to do is tell them they should do less than a total job in making recommendations regarding safety improvement."[12]

"I would disagree with that description, with all due respect, sir," Spears replied indignantly.[13] The U.S. Senate had put Richard Spears, and the NTSB in its current form, on notice that they were being watched and the senators did not like what they saw.

Senator Cannon and the Senate Committee on Commerce struck back at the NTSB with the swiftness of a disrespected boss toward an insolent employee. On September 12, 1973, just one week before the public hearing into the crash of Delta Flight 723, Cannon opened hearings on eradicating the NTSB of its five-member, politically appointed board and replacing it with a single administrator appointed for his or her expertise in the field of transportation safety.

In his opening remarks, Cannon summarized the prior hearings on NTSB activity. He said those hearings provided "solid documentation that the administration has made repeated attempts to both harass and intimidate the Board and to politicize it in so serious a fashion as to divert the Board's attention and resources from its sole mission which is transportation safety."[14] He explained that there was confusion among the public as to whether the board is indeed independent and said "the testimony in our hearing adds further evidence to the view that the Board, in important respects, is merely an arm of the executive branch and a subservient unit of the DOT." He added, "I instructed the staff to prepare legislation directed toward making the Agency totally independent and restructuring it in such a way as to minimize the opportunities for the executive branch to interfere with its important safety mission."[15]

The U.S. Congress had lost all confidence in the NTSB's ability to function independently. With these new hearings, Congress told the public that the NTSB was being run by the corrupt Nixon administration, was not putting the safety of travelers first, and was not to be trusted. It was under this umbrella of confusion, distrust, and doubt that the hearings into Delta Flight 723 opened inside the ballroom of the Holiday Inn hotel in Peabody, Massachusetts.

* * *

Public hearings are a dress rehearsal for any court cases that may arise from an airplane crash. No monetary award is issued; no one is found guilty. It merely reveals, publicly, the evidence that the NTSB has discovered during the onsite investigation of the crash. Witnesses are questioned at the discretion of the hearing officer. Tapes are played, or transcripts are read, at the discretion of the hearing officer. Charts, photos, and other exhibits are revealed at the discretion of the hearing officer. It is also at the discretion of the chairman of the NTSB whether a hearing is even held.

The function and purpose of a public hearing evolved as each year passed with its definition expanding or constricting depending on the circumstances of the crash. Its importance to the outcome of an investigation is so minimal that many times they are not even held. If they are held, the investigators have already completed the on-scene investigation, taken witness statements, and analyzed wreckage, and most group chairman reports have been completed. It should be no surprise that by the time a hearing is held the investigators have concluded what, or who, caused the crash.

Public hearings have been part of the investigative process since the 1940s. However, participation of parties to the investigation during the public hearing has not. Since the early 1940s, only members of the Air Safety Board could question witnesses. In 1956 that changed: the CAB

19. "The Administration ... Attempts to ... Intimidate the Board" 153

allowed parties to the investigation that privilege also. Again, air carriers, manufacturers, and other parties whose equipment or procedures, or personnel, may have caused the accident are allowed to participate in another facet of the investigation. Family members, though, and attorneys representing them, are not allowed to participate and question witnesses. To excuse this inequity, the CAB explained that the purpose for allowing certain parties was "not to enhance the position of these parties but to assist the board in developing a more complete factual record."[16] They also had a safeguard measure to ensure that the rules would be followed: the public hearing officer wielded as much power over the hearing as a judge did over a trial.

NTSB Chairman John Reed appointed Francis McAdams as the hearing chairman. McAdams, an aviation attorney and long-time employee of the CAB, and also the only Democratic member of the board, garnered respect throughout the aviation community. However, like the probable cause statement, the purpose of holding a public hearing was confusing. At the beginning of a hearing in 1967, McAdams began by stating, "Apparently, there is some misunderstanding as to the purpose of the hearing. This hearing is a part of the investigation. It is an integral part of the preliminary fact-finding process, and that's all it is."[17] A few minutes later, he contradicted himself. In explaining the role of the NTSB as it pertains to public hearings, he said, "As part of the Board's responsibilities, it investigates accidents. In some accidents it holds a public hearing to assemble facts. There is no need for the board to hold public hearings to assemble facts. In fact, the great majority of the Board's determinations of probable cause are based upon facts that were not adduced in a hearing of this type."[18]

* * *

Since the NTSB's letter to the FAA in late August asking for restrictions on the Delta DC-9s inherited from Northeast Airlines, everyone attending the meeting knew that a problem existed regarding the plane's flight director. Rumor had it, and was reported by the press, that one of the pilots of the doomed aircraft had left a cryptic clue recorded on the CVR seconds before the crash. Obviously, a main focus of the crash would be what instrument failed and caused a crash with such devastation that Edward E. Slattery Jr., longtime spokesman for the board, stated, "You could pick up almost any of the pieces in your hands."[19] Other areas that would be discussed would be the extremely foggy weather conditions that enveloped Runway 4R at the time of the crash, communications between the tower and the pilot, and why the shattered plane and its mostly deceased passengers lay undetected on the runway for almost twelve minutes.

As is customary, the lead investigator of the crash was called on to summarize the investigation up to this point. Arnold Holstine testified that the Delta aircraft did not suffer from any structural damage that could have caused the crash. He acknowledged that no fire existed prior to the crash and that the engines operated normally up until the jet's impact with the seawall.

From his report, Holstine shared that "one minute prior to impact, the first officer stated 'this so and so command bar shows ... [words unidentifiable].'"[20] It was customary for the NTSB not to release offensive words a pilot said so as not to embarrass the family. "So and so" was more than likely replaced with "fucking" or "God damn," and the unidentifiable word was more than likely "shit." Holstine stated that twenty-three seconds later, Streil replied, "OK, your localizer [radio navigation aid] is starting to come back now...," and five seconds after that, he told Burrill, "You better go to raw data, I don't trust that thing."[21] Ten seconds before impact, Streil said to his copilot, "Let's get back on course if you can."[22] Holstine also mentioned flight director issues in his opening statement. He stated that after Delta modified the electronic equipment from the Northeast DC-9s, "chronic" maintenance problems with that equipment continued. Delta swiftly issued a statement that the modification program was within "established standards and that in the four days before the crash, approximately 40 landings had been made without malfunctioning of the instruments."[23]

Holstine also mentioned the weather. He revealed that "a special weather observation taken at 11:14 a.m. showed partial obscuration estimated 400 feet overcast, surface visibility of one mile and tower visibility of a half mile."[24] The lead investigator had left out a vital piece of information regarding that special observation. Perhaps in deference to the threats that came from the White House regarding blaming the FAA or other executive departments, Holstine knew that the observation indicated that the RVR by that time was 1,600 feet, and that if it was under 2,400 feet, tower personnel could not let aircraft land.[25] Holstine also did not indicate that by the time that special observation had been taken, Flight 723 had been burning for five minutes on the runway.

When Holstine finished, the next people to testify were the ones who saw the plane seconds before the crash and others who saw the remains of the plane minutes after the crash. Thomas Karakoudas, who had been on Castle Island making a truck delivery, explained he saw the plane on approach to Runway 4R and yelled to others near him that the plane was extremely low and was going to crash. "The wings were level," he said. "I heard an increase in the engines' power and two seconds later I heard an explosion."[26]

Next up was Geoffrey Keating of Lynn, Massachusetts. He told the story that led him to Chief Arena's office to report the crash.

19. "The Administration ... Attempts to ... Intimidate the Board" 155

I saw fire and thought it was the Logan fire department practicing. Then I realized it wasn't a practice fire and I called to two guys nearby and we drove out to the scene. It took us five minutes to drive to the scene and the fog got thicker as we went along and then I saw the accident. I let the other two out and drove to the fire station. A plane went over me as I was driving back.[27]

When Chief Arena spoke, he indicated that he "could not recall any other instance of the Fire Department receiving word of a crash without the tower knowing it." He further stated that arrangements "have now been made for the tower to be notified when the fire department moves on any alarm whether it involves an air crash or fires in any of the airport buildings."[28]

Dr. Luongo testified next that the problems his department faced at the morgue were the transportation of the bodies from the runway and their identification thereafter. He testified that many victims were so badly burned that identification could only be confirmed by dental and X-ray records. He reiterated that the response of the emergency services to the crash scene was outstanding. He also made a recommendation to the NTSB that "a national identification team, made up of forensic dentists, radiologists and experienced pathologists be formed which could fly in to function as the FBI special team."[29]

None of these first five witnesses were active participants in the flight or crash. None were in the tower. They were passive witnesses laying the foundation for what had happened. They made recommendations for different scenarios as pertained to the consequences of future air crashes; none had been active participants in the events that led to the crash. The spectators in the ballroom—the lawyers, family members, the press—wanted to hear from the active participants in the crash. They wanted to hear the controllers and the recordings of the dead pilots talking to each other. They wanted light shed on the actions of those individuals who had been cast in this tragic aviation production, and the first actor they saw and heard from had talked to the pilots during 99 percent of the flight that led them into the seawall at Logan Airport: Charles Taylor, approach controller.

Taylor explained to the panel that when a plane reaches the "outer marker," a point approximately five miles from touchdown, he usually transfers the plane to the local controller. However, it was during this time, Taylor explained, that he had trouble with the separation of Allegheny 666 from other aircraft. He was preoccupied trying to get that pilot to maintain flight in the holding pattern. It was not until the aircraft was two and a half miles from the airport that Taylor gave Flight 723 permission to land, and that was only after Captain Streil had requested it and eight seconds after Streil's copilot had first noticed that there was a problem with the flight director. This involved Streil having to change frequencies to the local controller.[30]

Frank Rox did not let Taylor speak uninterrupted. He cross-examined Taylor on several occasions, and Francis McAdams admonished Rox against arguing with the witnesses and asking repetitive questions. But Delta paid Rox not only as their legal counsel, but also as a vice president of the company, and he had financial interests to protect. He knew the focus of the safety board would be on the pilots' actions in the cockpit. Rox needed to make sure that he shone the spotlight on the air traffic controllers because he knew that their lack of protocol in handling Flight 723 contributed to the crash.

Rox asked Taylor why he delayed the landing clearance to Flight 723.

Frustrated with Rox's aggressive tactics, Taylor fairly yelled his answer. "Delta was not a problem," he barked.[31] He said he "took first thing first" and needed to rectify the situation with Allegheny 666. "He [Streil] has the option to go, hold, or exercise a missed approach. You can't work airplanes if you don't talk to them," he explained, exasperated.[32]

With Taylor's questioning finished, local controller Jeffrey McDonald came next. While McDonald had only spoke to Captain Streil once before the crash, his conversation with him was so critical that he spent almost a full day giving testimony on it.

Frank Rox started on McDonald right away. He asked the controller why he had waited so long in warning Flight 723 about the approaching fog bank.

If Streil had "called me when he should have, I would have given the weather as I saw it," he replied.[33] He admitted that visibility at the end of Runway 4R had been deteriorating rapidly and told the pilot that "the RVR shows more than 6,000. A fog bank is movin' in. It's pretty heavy across the approach end."[34]

Rox asked why, if the visibility was dropping rapidly, McDonald did not get a current RVR reading rather than relying on one from earlier.

"I usually check the RVR reading every minute and a half," he replied. "Other duties prevented me from seeing it."[35]

Rox asked him why he did not switch runways if the fog was so bad.

McDonald replied, "There was no reason for it. Runways are chosen by wind conditions," he explained.[36] Day one of the hearing ended during McDonald's testimony. He resumed his testimony the next day.

Air traffic controllers receive the transmissometer readings at Logan in intervals of fifty-one seconds. When visibility drops by hundreds of feet per second, a fifty-one-second gap can be deadly. For Runway 4R at Logan Airport, the location of the transmissometer is approximately abreast of the ILS touchdown point, on a 250-foot baseline, and about 500 feet to the left of the runway.[37] Because of the distance from the end of the runway, a fog bank could completely envelope the end of Runway 4R and not even be picked up by the transmissometer. Seconds after the crash, the transmissometer on Runway 4R picked up an RVR reading of two thousand feet.[38] The runway should have been closed.

Rox also asked McDonald why he had cleared two planes to land on Runway 4R when a warning light came on notifying the tower that the approach lights had suddenly stopped working.

McDonald replied that he did not tell the pilots "because the alarm often went off because of a continuing maintenance problem with the wires."[39] In response to his answer, the safety board asked the FAA to provide repair records and witnesses from Logan's maintenance department.

McDonald also explained why he did not know the whereabouts of Flight 723 after the crash. "When I asked the ground controller if he [the Delta plane] was at the gate, he responded that he was going to the gate or at the gate," McDonald said. Delta Flight 623 had landed just before Flight 723. "It's possible that I misunderstood the first number. But to the best of my recollection, I got the answer that I was looking for," he said.[40]

Ground Controller Paul Boriello replied, "He [McDonald] turned to me and asked if I had Delta, and I understood he said 623. I don't believe he said 723. I replied that 623 was just about at the gate."[41]

Day two ended on a sour note as Francis McAdams admonished Frank Rox at least twice during the hearing. A lawyer for the family of one of the victims complained that Rox was trying to "shift the blame" from the malfunctioning flight instruments to others.

The next two witnesses called by the inquiry board were pilots onboard the planes directly ahead of, and behind, Delta Flight 723. Keith Chappell of Atlanta flew the Eastern Air Lines jet as the copilot in front of Flight 723, and Captain Ralph Queener flew the Eastern jet behind them.

Chappell testified that his aircraft "came out of the fog below 300 feet and that at the point of touchdown the runway was clear."[42] Chappell described coming out of the fog "as if I was in a semi-darkened room and someone opened a curtain."[43] He explained how the plane came in on automatic pilot and at a normal rate of descent. He added that the glide scope was captured inside the outer marker. "The weather was no surprise. We take things as they come," but he also added that he received a late clearance from the tower to land and that caused Flight 723 to get a late clearance.[44]

Queener testified next. He told the hearing he did not see the runway when he reached the decision height of 216 feet because of the fog. Due to his weather report from the tower, he had expected to see the runway at four hundred feet but did not. "There was no ground contact. There was no visibility at D.H. [decision height] so I initiated a missed approach," he explained. "There was fog that I couldn't see through," he said, giving the hearing spectators an inkling of what Streil and Burrill faced in the cockpit with a malfunctioning flight director and old, unreliable weather reports.[45] Queener powered up his aircraft, regained altitude, and headed to a different airport where he landed.

Delta Flight 723 tried to land in the gap between Chappell's landing and Queener's missed approach. There can be no doubt that the fog bank had already enveloped Runway 4R at the time Flight 723 approached it. Chappell's aircraft had landed before the fog's arrival and Queener's aircraft after the fog arrived. Delta Flight 723 flew through the combination of two different types of air masses that created a destabilized front. It created a weather picture so confusing that, coupled with a malfunctioning flight director, the crew had no time to recover or react to their environment, and they crashed into the seawall.

20

"There Is a Record of Malfunctions"

On the fourth day of the hearing, Harry Terban walked to the witness table and talked about the weather. He relayed to the inquiry that he did not notice any movement of the fog bank at the time of the crash. "From my vantage point it was a constant fog situation," he said, contradicting what other witnesses said about the weather.[1] Even the controllers spoke about a shifting and moving fog bank. Harry Terban sat too far away from Runway 4R to be any sort of witness as to the weather conditions there. He reviewed the instruments the weather service used in estimating visual conditions. He testified that during a ten-minute period, including the time of the crash, the visibility range was between 1,400 and 6,000 feet. Due to the location of the transmissometer away from the runway and the lag time before those numbers are posted in the tower, the actual visibility as compared to the visibility read-out on the instruments could be over one thousand feet different. It would be easy to find out the actual conditions that hovered over and around Runway 4R at the time of the crash. Harris Cusick could have told the NTSB at the hearing the actual conditions that existed on Runway 4R. He could provide the most accurate and detailed fog conditions in the area of Runway 4R; but the one man trained in weather reporting at airfields, the one man who was so close to the runway that he actually breathed in the fog that had enveloped and obscured Flight 723, the one man who rescued the only survivor of the crash, did not get to speak at the hearing. The NTSB did not think his testimony was as important as that of Harry Terban, who was located almost a mile away from the scene.

The hearings dragged on longer than anyone had expected. Frank Rox's questioning of Taylor and McDonald, expected for a day but stretching into two and a half days, delayed the other witnesses from testifying on time. Francis McAdams had no choice but to reconvene the hearing in Washington, D.C., the following week. The impact of the flight director on the crash had barely been discussed. FAA Inspector Murrell Johnson and

Captain Richard Henrickson of Delta had both testified that on July 26, 1973, just five days before the crash, the equipment on the accident aircraft had malfunctioned during a flight in adverse weather conditions from Atlanta, Georgia, to Dallas, Texas. Henrickson stated that he had "experienced difficulty with the pitch bar which shows the angle of the aircraft to ground."[2]

To refute that testimony, Frank Rox introduced five statements from five different Delta captains, which all read that the navigational equipment onboard that aircraft was in "good working order." Rox asked to introduce the statements into the record for the hearing. McAdams assented to their admission. Rox had to deflect any testimony that showed that the flight director may have malfunctioned. It became rather a futile effort with the pilots' voices on the CVR complaining about it, as well as the almost thirty write-ups on that equipment.[3] It became obvious to all that, more than likely, a main culprit in this crash was the malfunctioning flight director that nobody, up to this point, seemed to want to talk about. The hearings broke up on Friday, September 21, 1973, to reconvene the following Tuesday.

* * *

On Monday, September 24, the day before the hearings were to reconvene in Washington, MAC, led by Crocker Snow, surprised all the participants in the federal crash investigation by announcing that not only had they conducted their own crash investigation, but that they had also released their report as to the cause. MAC's investigation concluded that "pilot error, created by a natural psychological reaction was the proximate cause" of the crash.[4] They further stated that "[t]here is no evidence of any malfunction of the ground electronic equipment, but there is considerable evidence that it was operating properly in view of the flight which immediately preceded and followed the accident." In explaining the "psychological reaction of the pilots," the MAC staff wrote,

> Twelve minutes before the crash, the flight was given weather which predicted a very simple approach with both the ceiling and visibility way above the prescribed minimums. However, this was an observation taken far from the approach path, and the weather not only could have been, but obviously was, very different over the waters of Boston Harbor in the approach to the runway. Just one minute before the crash, the crew was informed that the runway visual range was more than 6,000 feet, again way above the minimum requirements of 2,400 feet. This must have confirmed the crew's feeling that the approach and landing would be a simple one.[5]

The MAC report also concluded that the first officer flying the plane distrusted the flight director, and the captain confirmed he did also. The report also verified, before the NTSB had discussed it in depth during their hearings, that issues with the Delta modification program also contributed to the crash. "There is a record of malfunctions, largely of the newly installed flight directors, both in this airplane and in the other DC-9s acquired from Northeast."[6]

The report stunned the participants in the federal investigation. Delta Air Lines, through Frank Rox, indicated that they were unaware the commission had even investigated the accident, and many could not understand how the report could be valid if, of all parties, Delta had not been asked to participate in it. A spokesman for ALPA said that "it was highly unusual that MAC would release such a report before the official findings were determined by the NTSB." The spokesman further stated that "Congress charges the NTSB with determining an accident, not MAC or other states agencies."[7] The NTSB dismissed the report and through a spokesman stated that "our investigation still has many weeks to go. We have 12 witnesses left to hear and findings will not be available until the end of the year."[8] However, like ALPA and Delta, the NTSB spokesman did admit that he was "surprised by the action of the state agency but I don't question their authority. I have no idea, however, of the extent of their investigation."[9]

* * *

When the hearing reconvened in Washington at Onassis Hall, the board still had unanswered questions about the weather and visibility, and the instruments used to read them. Alcott Larsson, chief of the FAA weather service, testified regarding the discrepancies between the RVR readings on Runway 4R that morning. The readings are reported two ways, one on paper on a rotating drum. This allows anyone to access the information at any given time. They are also reported by electronic pulses to the tower. Those are the readings that are given to the pilot from the tower, but they are only reported at forty-eight- to fifty-two-second intervals. At 11:08 a.m., when McDonald had told Streil that his RVR was six thousand feet, the drum recorded the range to be below two thousand feet. No flights may land if an RVR reading falls below 2,400 feet. A minute after the reading of six thousand feet, and while Flight 723 lie burning on Runway 4R, another controller advised pilots of a minimum below two thousand feet.[10]

Frank Rox prepared a report he wanted submitted to the NTSB that correlated the discrepancy from the actual RVR of less than two thousand feet, recorded on the drums, to the reading given to Streil from the tower of six thousand feet. McAdams refused to admit the report as an exhibit but told Rox he was free to include it in his conclusions at the end of the hearing.[11]

Now the time had arrived to start testimony on the doomed aircraft's flight director. Anticipation had been building for days regarding the flight director and the ominous words of Captain Streil recorded on the CVR saying, "Go to raw data, I don't trust that thing." Mostly everyone following the hearing speculated that "that thing" was the flight director.

A flight director (FD) is a sophisticated instrument that interfaces with other equipment onboard the aircraft. It can be defined as an instrument that tells a pilot how to get where they are going by following the command bars and flying according to the location of the command bars on the display.

Northeast Airlines used the Collins FD in their DC-9s. When Delta bought them out, they replaced the Northeast DC-9s, including Ship 222, with Sperry Rand FDs. There were immediate differences noticeable to any pilot who used the different FDs. The Collins FD was a dual system with dual indicators, whereas the Sperry Rand FD was a single system with dual indicators. Each Collins FD had its own mode selector switch, whereas the Sperry Rand FD had one mode selector switch located on the left side of the center instrument panel. The Collins FD had a single command image, whereas the Sperry Rand FD had two, a pitch command bar and a roll command bar. Other differences were minor.[12]

The guidance display on the Sperry Rand FD has two command bars. The vertical bar presents roll, steering, VOR, and localizer course tracking; the horizontal bar presents pitch guidance for glide slope capture and tracking. The single rotary mode selector switch provides pilots with the following commands: SB (standby), BL (blue left), FI (flight instruments), VOR/LOC (visual omni range/localizer glide slope), APP (approach), and G/A (go-around). Commands are selected by rotating the switch in a clockwise direction.[13] The Collins FDs provided pilots with the following commands: Off, FI (flight instruments), VOR/LOC (visual omni range/localizer glide slope), and APP (approach). The go-around mode was located on the throttle and activated with a palm switch.[14] Perhaps the most important difference between the two systems was that the mode logic presented to the FD on the Collins system was seen on an annunciator panel. The Sperry Rand system did not have an annunciator panel.[15] If a pilot inadvertently selected the wrong mode or the switch did not stay in the correct mode, there was nothing on the display to tell the pilot that something was wrong.

During simulated flights with the Sperry Rand FD at Delta headquarters in Atlanta after the accident, the instructor switched the mode selector from APP to G/A. When this was done, the pitch command bar came into view at the top of the instrument and commanded a fly-up maneuver. It was identified by the pilot because it was different than the information the pilot received from raw data. However, the anomaly was not quickly apparent from observation of the FD roll bar. Although localizer guidance was removed from the FD display, the roll command bar remained centered until an inadvertent roll of little magnitude was initiated. At that time, the roll bar deflected opposite the direction of bank and commanded a return to wings-level flight in accordance with the FD's G/A mode. Attempts to follow the roll command invariably led to large deviations from the localizer centerline, which was detectable only by reference to the raw data displayed on the PDI.[16]

Incredibly, according to the NTSB, the G/A mode could be selected inadvertently by rotating the FD mode selection knob slightly past the approach mode detent. Even if the knob was returned to the approach mode detent, the G/A mode continued to be displayed on the FD. There were, obviously, serious issues as to the design of the Sperry Rand Flight Director.[17]

The evidence that it did not work how it was supposed to was evident from the maintenance issues it caused. The FD computer on Ship 222 had been replaced six times since the completion of the aircraft's modification program in April 1973. After maintenance crews removed the computers and analyzed them further, they showed no discrepancies.

The aircraft's logbook found forty-nine discrepancies related to the interface between the radio and flight instruments that were involved in the modification program. This, according to the NTSB, was a "relatively high number" compared with other discrepancies that occurred between April 21, 1973, and July 31, 1973.[18] The records of the aircraft immediately preceding and following N975NE—N979NE and N978NE—also contained recurring discrepancies like those reported for N975NE. Two FD mode selectors were removed from N975NE between April and July 1973. The first mode selector, serial no. 6111109, was removed from the aircraft about three months before the accident because the FD pitch bar was reported to be unreliable. When analyzed by mechanics after they removed it from the aircraft, it was found to be within specifications.[19]

The second mode selector, serial no. 7061174, was removed July 27, 1973, because "both flight director bars did not give correct pitch and bank indications to fly ILS."[20] When analyzed after removal, it too was found to be within specifications. The third mode selector, serial no. 7081183, was removed from the wreckage and could not be checked electronically.[21]

During airways operations or VOR and ILS approaches, the pilot selects the VOR/LOC mode and sets the desired radial or localizer course to be flown on the first officer's PDI. In the standby mode, the vertical bar is out of sight from the pilot, but when the VOR/LOC mode is selected, the bar will present roll and steering commands to capture and track the selected course. If heading guidance is needed before capture of the selected course, the FI mode is selected. As the aircraft approaches the selected heading, the vertical bar will show a command to roll out of the turn. When the aircraft is established on the intercept heading (the ILS beam or over the VOR radial), the VOR/LOC mode is selected. Once the FD detects the ILS beam, then it automatically switches to capture operations and places the system in VOR or localizer capture mode; the vertical bar commands direct the aircraft to roll out on the radial or localizer course and follow it. According to Delta and the NTSB, it is preferable to capture the glide scope from below. If capture is made above the glide slope, the horizontal pitch bar would be out of sight, presenting no glide slope capture guidance. If this happened, the pilot would select the APP mode, and that would provide immediate glide slope capture and tracking guidance. In order to regain FD guidance for an ILS approach, the selector switch should be rotated counterclockwise from the G/A position to either the FI or the SB mode and then back to the desired position.[22]

Delta Air Lines Assistant Manager of Flight Training Herlong Averett of Atlanta, Georgia, began the FD testimony. He testified that Streil and Burrill both had two days of retraining on the FD the previous winter. "This involved a day of ground instruction and two hours in a flight simulator to familiarize them with differences between the two airlines' equipment."[23] Averett also stated that Streil had additional training in a jet but did not know if Burrill did the same.[24] Averett discussed the differences between the Collins and Sperry Rand FDs but stated he could not discuss the pilots' reactions to those differences. He also explained that the reason the Collins system was replaced was to have uniformity on all their DC-9 aircraft across the Delta system.

During Averett's testimony, the NTSB planted a seed that would throw focus from the design flaws of the FD to pilot error. Without any proof to back up their claim, members of the board pointed out that the FD switch mode was found in the G/A position rather than the APP position where it would have been during the landing. David Rogers of the *Boston Globe* wrote that investigators compared the two FD systems, Collins and Sperry Rand, and found that the "go-around" position, which would be used in a missed approach, is in the same position that "'approach' is on the equipment Streil used with Northeast."[25] The implication was clear: John Streil, the veteran World War II pilot, the twenty-year veteran of Northeast Airlines, the pilot so cool that he landed a Vickers Viscount without wheels at Baltimore's Friendship Airport saving twenty-three lives, simply turned the mode selector to the wrong setting.

In order for their theory to be taken seriously, they had to conclude that all pilots who flew, not only Ship 222, but also the planes before and after that aircraft, in the modification process were simply turning the mode selector to the wrong position. If they truly expected the public to believe that this happened, then there should have been a huge indictment of Delta Air Lines' training process.

20. "There Is a Record of Malfunctions"

Both Averett and Rox picked up on this point right away. Averett quickly switched from Delta to the controllers in charge of Flight 723. "In my review of this, the controllers did not show an awareness of this pilot's needs throughout the whole approach."[26]

C.O. Miller, determined to put blame on the dead pilots, asked Averett why the pilots had not called out their altitudes as is mandatory per FAA regulations.[27]

Averett defended the pilots by stating that "a highly qualified pilot sometimes relied on his mental clock to tell him where he was above the ground."[28]

Asked to elaborate more on this response, he replied that "a pilot's mental clock may begin at the airport's outer marker and, knowing his speed, believes he has a good estimate of where he is."[29]

When asked about the flight observer, Joseph Burrell, preparing the checklist, even though he was not qualified to fly the DC-9, Averett replied that "[a]nyone who can understand the English language could do it."[30]

* * *

Frank Rox had to quickly rebut the evidence that their Sperry Rand FDs had worked erroneously since they had been installed in the Northeast DC-9s. Fortuitously for Delta, a mechanic decided to strike the switchbox that had been removed from Ship 222 four days prior to the accident. Miraculously, the blow "duplicated malfunctions reported in the system earlier by pilots."[31] D.P. Hetterman, Delta vice president for technical operations, testified that "after each change the directional system worked satisfactorily for many flights and landings over many days."[32] Since the crash, the attention of the investigators had focused on the FD. However, he said Delta took it upon themselves to focus on the switch box.[33] Like magic, the accidental tap replicated the "squawks" that had been written up and complained about in the ship's log.

After the tap by the mechanic, Hetterman stated that mechanics took apart the switch box and found "small slivers of metal" that were "found to be causing the switch to send sporadic incorrect signals into the FD system."[34]

"To the best of Sperry's and Delta's knowledge this type of fault is a first," Hetterman admitted.[35] He added that the investigation had not yet determined where the slivers in the sealed box originated, but he claimed, "There may have been some friction in there," and it caused the bits of metal to break off.[36] The argument Delta wanted investigators to believe was that the cause of all the squawks up to the crash was the switch box, which, because it had been replaced, meant that there was nothing wrong with the FD in Ship 222 at the time of the crash.

Hearing Officer McAdams waited until the last day of the hearing to bring in an engineer to rebut any testimony regarding a malfunctioning FD. Sperry Rand engineer Richard E. Schaffer blamed the pilot for not selecting the proper switch mode on the FD, which caused the improper commands. He explained that when a plane intercepts a glide path from below the localizer beam, which is the correct way to intercept the path, the FD switch should be turned to the VOR/LOC position. Because Delta Flight 723 intercepted the glide path from above, he offered that the better choice would be the "approach" mode because it would pick up the localizer at a wider range.[37] Since the selector switch found in the wreckage was in the "go-around" position, Schaffer had insufficient evidence to jump to this conclusion.

Boston Globe reporter David Rogers wrote that "the argument is speculative and depends on a set of assumptions some observers were reluctant to accept with the information now before the board."[38] Rogers also wrote, "However, the analysis does fit the tracings drawn from the flight data recorder...."[39] For the investigators, only one reason existed for Streil making the mistake: the "approach" mode on the Collins FD was in the same location as the "go-around" mode on the Sperry Rand FD. The board mentioned in passing that Streil might not have made a mistake and, instead, selected the "go-around" position moments before the crash when he realized the aircraft was in danger or that the switch moved on impact.[40] Either way, the evidence did not exist to strongly support such a conclusion.

The safety board concluded the hearings later that afternoon after Schaffer testified. After filing his last story on the hearing, David Rogers remembered that he had been impressed with the professionalism and knowledge of the investigative team, but with that, Rogers said, he often thought the "investigators already knew the answers before the questions were asked and they were just waiting for him to catch up and see what they had already concluded."[41]

21

"If He Was Going to Die, We Did Not Want Him Dying on Our Watch"

The first trickles of normalcy started to return to those affected by the tragedy. With the burials performed, services over, and the tremendous shock that such an event had even happened, summer quickly turned into fall in New England. Slowly, terribly slowly for some, families endured the grieving process and hoped that one day things would get back to normal— as normal as it could be after losing a loved one so quickly and violently.

For those who still worked, they had to get up each day and perform their jobs. If the family provider was the one killed in the crash, the surviving spouse and/or parent had to find work to support the family. Wills had to be submitted. If no will, then filings had to be submitted to probate court. Children had to go back to school, and with the holiday season approaching, surviving parents and grandparents struggled to provide their children and grandchildren with the best season they could under the circumstances. The families also searched. They searched for answers, searched for reasons, and searched for attorneys who, they hoped, would give them answers to both. Once the attorneys found those answers in court, then settlements could be reached, and money gained to recover from the loss.

Sidney Samuels, owner of Bi-Rite Merchandiser in Manchester, New Hampshire, related his story for years after the crash. He would explain how he would have missed his connection to New York had he continued waiting at the gate in Manchester for Flight 723. He told how he rented a car, drove to Boston, and got a connection out of Logan Airport and made it on time for the Retail Jewelers Association show at the New York Hilton. Only later that afternoon, when employees at his office in Manchester called the Hilton after they found out he may not have been on the flight, did he find out about the crash. "What can I say," he added. "I missed another one." Mrs. Samuels would add, "He's a very impatient man. He's always been that way...."[1]

William Wozmak, twenty-three, and the father of a three-year-old boy, who rode from Manchester with Samuels to Boston, would also relate his story for years. "We were down at 225 Fifth Avenue buying chess sets, when someone said 'Hey, did you hear about the crash in Boston? A plane from Vermont.' We weren't sure it was ours, because it was from Vermont, but I sat down for awhile."[2]

A unique estate settlement concerned the possessions and effects of Marion Smith of Burlington, Vermont. Smith, sixty-five years old, was a doll collector and en route to Louisville, Kentucky, for a national doll convention. She lived alone in the house her parents owned and had no brothers or sisters. Her friends knew her house held a variety of stamp, button, and coin collections. Her photographs of birds had been exhibited around the world. When a court-ordered appraiser for the estate surveyed and inventoried her house, he walked around in disbelief at the items she had amassed. Not only were her collections housed there, but her deceased parents, also collectors, still had their collections stored there. Appraiser Warren Smith, no relation to the deceased, stated that, in his twenty-five years of experience, he had "never seen so many extensive collections as in the estate of Miss Marion Smith."[3] He went on and explained that the collections were a result of "two generations of avid collectors who seemed to have had a great knowledge of what they collected."[4] He found over four hundred pieces of costume jewelry, one hundred pieces of antique brass, and a collection of over one hundred buttons. However, it was the doll collection that caught his eye. There were over seven hundred dolls, some worth as much as $800. The number of dolls in the collection was so vast that they would have to be sold at an auction separate from the rest. He described the auctions to be held in the coming weeks to be "among the most notable ever held in Vermont."[5]

* * *

As families in towns and villages in Vermont and New Hampshire dealt with the deaths of their loved ones, back in Boston, Leo Chouinard still survived. That he had reached the month of October alive stunned most of the doctors at Mass General.

Dr. Thomas Dodson graduated from the University of Alabama School of Medicine and began his internship at the burn unit of MGH just a few weeks before the crash. He remembered being notified of the crash and felt heartbreak when only two survivors showed up at the hospital. Even though Leo's injuries appeared fatal, everyone, every staff member, gave Leo 100 percent. "We gave him 100% because he gave it back to us," Dodson recalled.[6] He remembered Leo as a handsome young man who, before the crash, was in incredible shape. "I could just tell," Dodson said. "If anyone was going to survive those burns, it would be him."[7]

21. "...We Did Not Want Him Dying on Our Watch"

Dodson recalled the medical details that Leo had working in his favor that gave him a slim, but nonetheless fighting, chance. "His heart and lungs were clear, and he was in great physical condition." Dodson remembered the young sergeant's attitude as one of never giving up hope. Among the interns helping take care of Leo, they all expressed one wish: "If he were to die, we did not want him dying on our watch. Our goal was to keep him alive."[8] Dodson started to believe Leo might make it.

Ever the realist, Dr. Josh Tofield reminded everyone that Leo was still in critical condition, but even he too had a few doubts erased when he saw how well the grafts were taking to Leo's skin. "I remembered making progress with the grafts and, one morning, Dr. Constable came by. The dressings had been removed and I showed John the grafts."[9]

"This is absolutely fantastic," Constable exclaimed, pride welling up inside of him that his doctors had taken the patient this far in the healing process.[10]

On a weekend visit home from school, Brenda Newton stayed with her parents rather than going to see Leo. She still expressed disappointment that her father had, a month earlier, revealed his true feelings to her about Leo's chances of survival. On this visit though, his pessimism had been replaced with optimism. That evening, as they sat on the porch of the farm, her father revealed his change of heart. "You know, Brenda, with Leo coming along like he is, once your grandparents' house becomes vacant," he said, pointing to it across the field, "you and Leo will need a place to live."[11]

Bud Newton took a deep breath and spoke like he had been thinking about this for awhile. "We can build some ramps up to doors and make the house wheelchair accessible," he said. "I'll make it to where you and Leo can live there comfortably."[12]

Brenda reached over and, with tears of joy in her eyes, hugged her father. She actually felt the pessimism of Leo's survival ebbing in those around him.

However, Tofield was correct that Leo remained in critical condition. He still struggled with breathing problems, so much so that Tofield performed a tracheotomy, decreasing Leo's speech function. The threat of severe infection remained the number one enemy to Leo's survival. The burn unit provided Leo with a wheelchair for limited and infrequent use, but the mobility it gave him increased his optimism, and he could at least get out of bed and move around.

Leo had not seen Harris Cusick since the engineer had found him naked on Runway 4R lying among the burning debris. While the family had been in touch with Cusick to keep him up to date on Leo's progress, a meeting between the two men had been put on hold until Leo was stabilized enough for a visit. Laurette Chouinard decided in October it was time her son met his rescuer again. Ironically, Laurette had never met Cusick even though they exchanged phone calls, letters, and cards over the last few months. The Chouinards met Cusick for dinner to get to know him before his visit with Leo.

After each of the Chouinards had been introduced to Cusick with either a hug or handshake, they sat at the table, and he told the story of how he had found Leo. Then he brought up a subject that the Chouinards had tried to keep at a distance—the crash and the investigation.

He told them he had not been called to testify at the public hearing. "When Jeff Keating was called to testify," Cusick said, "I thought that with my experience in the past [with his aviation and weather training] that I should also testify, so I contacted the National Transportation Safety Board and the evening before the hearings got underway, I met with them at the Holiday Inn in Peabody."[13] He explained to the family that, because of his training and finding Leo, he had been extremely concerned about the accident and, having worked in meteorology for four years, he had a great interest in it. He confessed to the Chouinards that the investigators had relied on Terban's weather observations rather than his, even though Terban was a mile away from the accident scene and Cusick had been standing on it. He then admitted that his main concern was the delay in the response of the emergency services. He looked at each one of them as he explained verbatim what he had told investigators: "I wanted to know why seeing that you have all of that electrical equipment coming out to light runways and approach lights, why there is not at least one emergency telephone placed at the end of the runways so that in case of emergency, my point being that this is a very isolated area of the airport.... For the sake of one telephone, we could have had help out there a long time before it arrived."[14] He believed the investigators were not interested in his comments. They perfunctorily thanked him and ended the interview. The NTSB never called him to testify at the public hearing.

After dinner, the family escorted Cusick to Leo's room and stood outside in the hallway to give the two men privacy. As Cusick walked toward Leo's bed, he glanced at Leo's injuries and tried to figure out how to greet him. Ever the person to make those around him feel at ease, Leo reached his right hand out, and Cusick clasped it in a light grip as both men stared at each other intently. Their eyes communicated what words could not. They were both too emotional to speak. Cusick's eyes expressed amazement that this man lying in bed, who he last saw burnt and broken on Runway 4R, was still alive and fighting for his life. Cusick could sense the determination and will to live in Leo's stare. Leo's eyes reflected thankfulness at the man who found him and gave him a second lease on life. Cusick did not want Leo to expend too much energy on this visit, and after a few more minutes, they exchanged pleasantries and promised to meet again.[15] Cusick thanked the family and thanked Laurette for this "intensely emotional moment." Cusick left just before the tears fell down his face.

A visitor early in Leo's recovery was not as welcome as Harris Cusick. In late August, just weeks after the crash, Leo's parents entered their son's room and told him about a special guest named Sergeant Smith who had arrived from Leo's Air Force base in Alaska. Delta Air Lines had flown him from Alaska to visit Leo as the airman insisted that he and Leo were extremely close friends, and he knew that his visit would help the young man recover. Delta had put the airman up at the same hotel the Chouinards used at no cost. The next morning, with Brenda at Leo's side, his airman friend walked in, greeted Leo like a long-lost buddy, pulled up a chair, and started chatting about Alaska. Leo tensed up as soon as the man entered the room. He had never before seen this man in his life.[16] Leo quickly told Brenda, and she called hospital security. The man was quickly removed from Leo's room and dismissed from the hotel and sent packing. The hospital initiated extra precautions to protect Leo from outsiders and charlatans.

A low point in Leo's recovery arrived when he saw the toll his injuries, as well as his recovery, had taken on his head and face. Leo had always prided himself on his full mop of black hair and his good looks. The hair had to be shaved off for the doctors to gain access to unburnt skin for his grafts. The impact of the crash had swollen his face, and it still had not gone down to its precrash proportions. Family and staff all knew about Leo's youthful pride, and they took extreme care to keep him from seeing his reflection. Staff hid any mirrors to which he might have access, and curtains were always pulled so he could not see his reflection in a window. The one thing they forgot, though, was the television. Many times, the television was placed on a wheeled tray that extended over his bed. The screen was not very large, and Leo liked to have the television close to his face. One day, when he shut it off, he saw himself in the screen's reflection. Brenda noticed the issue immediately and removed the television from his view; but he had seen enough. Brenda remembered that moment as the only time she saw Leo stream tears.[17]

It only took the mention of Leo becoming an uncle to pull him out of any doldrums. His brother's wife Leona had become pregnant, and she and Ray were expecting their baby in December. Leo cherished his role as the eldest of the Chouinard brood and he could not wait to add another generation to the family name. The thoughts of hunting and fishing and hiking, the things he did with his brothers and sisters as they all grew up, with a new generation filled him with pride and gave him more incentive to continue his fight against his injuries. His condition had improved to the point where he encouraged Brenda to visit her parents, rather than him, on the weekends, and he reassured his parents that he would be fine if one of them went home and watched his brothers and sisters rather than stay at the hospital and worry about him.

Leo's neighbor Tim Maclay came to visit. The two young men grew up together hunting and fishing. Leo felt better when he could talk about home and the things he did growing up because it gave him the hope that he would still be able to do these things again. The two men spent hours reminiscing and reading the letters that Leo received from strangers around the country. The letters that really gave Leo comfort were those from other amputees.[18] They wrote things like, "Try and survive, you will be able to do anything you want."[19] Tim saw how easily fatigued Leo got, so he kept his visit short. Tim promised his friend he would return before Christmas.

Even Tofield, as realistic about Leo's survival odds as anyone, began to feel the optimism that radiated from Leo. He watched in amazement, and pride, as the skin grafts took, and spread out, on Leo's chest and arm. There was no doubt that they were making incredible progress. But Tofield saw that chinks in Leo's armor remained; parts of his body still lay exposed and susceptible to infection. The doctors could only graft so quickly, and Tofield just hoped he and his team could get Leo completely covered in fresh skin before a large and potentially lethal infection set in.

* * *

Delta's testimony from the last day of the public hearing had not stuck under scrutiny. Frank Rox had argued that small particles were found in a flight director switch removed from Ship 222 a few days before it crashed. Delta's theory was that the particles could have caused it to malfunction. He acknowledged that the fragments were not discovered until after the crash, and if the part had not been put on hold by a federal investigator, it would have been returned to inventory. The switch removed from the wreckage had not been available for examination at the public hearing. No one from the NTSB was present when the mechanic reproduced the malfunctions, none had observed the phenomenon, and none were present when the part was broken down by Delta and FAA personnel.

NTSB investigators had given the switch to Sperry Rand, and in October, after the hearings had ended, investigators went to the offices of Sperry Rand Corporation in Phoenix, Arizona, and examined it. According to federal investigator Francis D. Rock of the NTSB, heat and impact damage limited the conclusiveness of the findings, but "no identifiable fragments were discovered."[20]

Reporter David Rogers wrote, "Delta's own theory about the significance of such fragments is still regarded skeptically by some Federal investigators who are not sure the metal slivers found were large enough to have caused trouble."[21] Investigators would have to find another way to explain why the flight director malfunctioned.

* * *

Perhaps one of the most consequential events in the NTSB's history of plane crash investigations during the early 1970s took place on October 20, 1973. That evening, President Nixon unwittingly loosened his grip of fear and intimidation on the NTSB, and other federal agencies, when he ordered his Solicitor General Robert Bork to fire Special Prosecutor Archibald Cox.

Since the moment FAA Director Alexander Butterfield revealed the existence of the White House tape recording system, there was a view among lawyers, politicians, as well as the special prosecutor, that the tapes might contain evidence of the crimes that Richard Nixon had been accused of by John Dean. The crime Dean accused Nixon of was the cover-up of the Watergate break-in. Since the tapes were voice activated, they may have picked up evidence of Nixon talking with his aides about the cover-up.

Archibald Cox wanted those tapes. Nixon refused to hand them over citing executive privilege. The president offered a compromise to diffuse the standoff. Nixon suggested that Senator John Stennis (D–Mississippi) listen to the tapes and transcribe what he heard. All of Congress, indeed most of Washington, knew that Senator Stennis was notoriously hard of hearing and almost deaf. On Friday, October 19, 1973, Cox refused the compromise and set in motion the plans to sue for the tapes. The next afternoon, October 20, Nixon ordered his Attorney General Elliot Richardson to fire Special Prosecutor Cox. Richardson refused to do so as he had promised the U.S. Senate that he would only fire Cox for gross improprieties or malfeasance. Richardson then resigned. Nixon then ordered Deputy Attorney General William Ruckelshaus to fire Cox. He, too, refused and resigned. Robert Bork, solicitor general of the United States, stood third in line at the Justice Department. Nixon ordered Bork to fire Cox, and Bork did so. Moments later, a car took Bork to the White House where he was sworn in as acting attorney general. The events of that evening became known as the *Saturday Night Massacre*. The negative reaction from Congress, as well as the public, resounded loudly in Washington, and over fifty thousand telegrams arrived denouncing Nixon's actions. Within ten days, twenty-one members of Congress introduced resolutions calling for Nixon's impeachment. The beginning of the end had arrived for the Nixon presidency. Nixon's firm grip on power eased, and those opposed to his interference and officials in those agencies breathed a sigh of relief that they could now act without fear of repercussions from Nixon and his henchmen; this included the NTSB. No longer did they have to fear criticizing the FAA in their reports.

22

"Leo, You're an Uncle"

Fall abated and the holiday season awaited as October melded into November. With Thanksgiving just a few weeks away, the Chouinard family had much for which to be thankful. Leo progressed along, against all odds. Grafts covered most of his chest and abdomen, but his back still had areas that needed to be covered with new skin. As the middle of November arrived, Leo began to eat solid foods for the first time since the crash. His mother and father were comfortable enough with their son's condition to both be home in Vermont for Thanksgiving with the rest of the family A hospital spokesman updated the press on Leo's condition: "He's been eating solid foods, including turkey, for about two weeks now."[1] Still, the spokesman cautioned that while Leo had shown signs of improvement, he remained in critical condition. The spokesman added that Leo was "periodically put on a respirator to give him a rest from breathing on his own."[2]

Leona and Ray Chouinard visited Leo at Thanksgiving time. Their baby was due any day, and Leo could not contain his excitement about becoming an uncle. It strengthened him to know there would be more Chouinards. As Ray and Leona left, Leo escorted them to the elevator in his wheelchair. He asked to touch Leona's stomach and feel the baby. He raised his right hand and lightly rubbed her belly. He smiled and closed his eyes contentedly as he felt his niece or nephew with his own hands. The elevator door opened, and Ray and Leona got on it as they waved Leo goodbye.[3]

On the first day of December, Dr. Tofield did not like what he saw. Leo appeared sluggish, but, more ominously, the skin grafts began to discolor like fall leaves transitioning to the winter gloom. Tofield knew this was not good. He ordered tests done on his patient and discovered new infections in Leo's heart and brain along with pneumonia. As painful as it was to admit, especially after all his hard work and the fact that Leo had become such a special patient, and person, to him, Josh Tofield knew Leo would not be able to overcome these infections. As much as it broke his heart, Tofield knew he had to rely on his professional demeanor to get him through these next few days. He had staff call the Chouinard family and advise them they needed to come back to the hospital quickly.⁴

Brenda Newton sat at her desk in the dormitory studying for her final exams when her parents called her. "Brenda, you need to get to Mass General. Leo slipped into a coma and he's not going to recover," her father informed her.⁵ She left the books on her desk and grabbed a few clothes, and a friend drove her to the hospital.

Laurette and Roger arrived late Sunday afternoon, but it was too late to talk to their son again as he had slipped into a coma. Each parent took turns by their son's bedside talking to him, stroking his face, just wanting to hear his voice or see his caring eyes one more time. They had heard whispers about the lengths the doctors took to save his life and if it was worth the pain he had to endure. But Laurette and Roger had no regrets. Since the crash, every decision had been Leo's. His determination to overcome the brutal battering and burns that his body endured could not be extinguished, and he exuded confidence in his tenacity and resolve to get back to his life in Vermont. Everyone who witnessed Leo during his improbable battle for survival knew that the young man possessed a strength beyond human endurance. He had, for months, fought against medical odds that would have killed a normal man within hours.

Just one more time, Laurette thought. Just one more time to see her son's eyes open, she prayed. Just after 8:00 p.m. on Monday night, December 3, her husband walked into the room and gave her the news for which she had waited. Roger whispered to her that Leona had given birth to their first grandchild, a girl, and she and the baby were fine. In her first act as a grandmother, Laurette bent over her son's bed and whispered, "Leo, you're an uncle." Leo's eyes flashed open, and a small, thin smile arched across his face. Leo received his wish of becoming an uncle, and Laurette received her wish of seeing her son's eyes open one last time.⁶ Ray had been told Leo had slipped into a coma and was on his way to Boston right after the birth of his daughter.

On Tuesday, December 4, hospital spokesman Martin Bander issued a special bulletin from Mass General. He advised that Leo's condition was extremely critical and was "more serious now than it has been at any given time."⁷ He explained that the pneumonia had concentrated in Leo's lungs, and "this is our main concern right now."⁸ He added that there was no evidence of brain damage.

Leo Chouinard's ominous prediction of July 31 came true on December 11, 1973, when he passed away after battling his injuries for 133 days. Roger Chouinard and Brenda Newton kept vigil at the hospital until the end. Roger and Laurette decided that she should go home before Leo passed so that she could tell their other children that their oldest brother had died before they heard it on the television or the radio. Just after 10:00 p.m. that evening, Mass General issued a bulletin: Leo Chouinard died this evening from "complications from suffering severe burns."[9]

* * *

Harris Cusick, who had visited his friend as he lay in a coma, arrived at the hospital after his friend's death that evening. He escorted Brenda Newton and Roger Chouinard to the hotel across from Mass General. Roger called Laurette and broke the news to her. "They were well prepared for Leo's death and they seemed to be relieved that he was no longer in pain," Cusick said the next day. "He had suffered for so long. His mother told me it was for the best."[10]

As she packed her bags in the hotel room to go home the next day, Brenda Newton had kept her composure, but she felt she had witnessed a robbery. Her fiancé had been robbed of his life, and she did not see how she could ever forget that. She turned the television on to the eleven o'clock news that evening and heard the newscaster announce Leo's death. She broke down in tears when she heard the words, "He was only twenty years old."

She repeated it out loud. "Twenty years old!"[11]

At the same time, Leona Chouinard sat in an old chair at home in Plainfield, Vermont, rocking her eight-day-old daughter. As the 11 o'clock local news flashed Leo's high school picture across the screen and announced his death, Leona gently kissed her daughter on her head and told her that her uncle Leo, who had never gotten to see her, had loved her dearly.

On December 15, 1973, a hearse pulled up in front of St. Monica Church in Barre, Vermont. As snow fell from the sky on that cold, cloudy day, over three hundred family and friends of Leo Chouinard, as well as media from all over New England, came to say goodbye to him. Doctors and nurses from Mass General sat and stood throughout the crowd as they waited for Leo's coffin to be escorted to the altar. The Air Force provided a full military honor guard. Three priests waited at the altar, while two others fell in line in front of the military procession escorting Leo's coffin into the church. Muffled sobs echoed throughout the congregation as the military escorts placed the coffin at the front of the church. Fr. Donald Ritchie was the principal celebrant of the Requiem High Mass. The Rev. George Murtaugh, the priest at North American Martyrs Church in Marshfield when Leo served there as an altar boy, was a cocelebrant of the Mass. The Rev. Roland St. Pierre, Catholic priest and mayor of Plattsburgh, New York, where Leo had served in the Air Force, also helped celebrate the Mass, as well as a priest from Logan Airport and Massachusetts General Hospital.[12]

22. "Leo, You're an Uncle"

At the conclusion of the Mass, a long line of cars followed the hearse containing the flag-draped coffin to Hope Cemetery in Barre, Vermont. While the military honor guard fired their rifle salutes to the brave sergeant and American flags whipped in the cold wind, an airman presented the now folded flag that had draped Leo's coffin to his mother. Flanked by her family, with Roger on her left with his arm around their youngest, Laurette received the flag gracefully and then laid her cheek on it, wanting to touch a remnant of her son one more time. The cold wind snapped around the mourners, and the snowflakes fell as the mourners repeated aloud one final prayer for Leo's soul. Soon after the crowd dispersed, Leo's coffin rested at the bottom of the grave. The undertakers gently shoveled the frosted, chilled soil on top of it as if it were a balm, eternally easing his suffering and burns.

Nearly half a century later, Dr. Tofield remembered the valiant efforts to save Leo. "The nurses in the burn ward were the frontline warriors for Leo. One to two nurses stayed on duty in his room virtually 24/7," he said. "They had to constantly monitor Leo's vital signs, feed him, manage the wounds by changing the gauze every several hours and turning him," Tofield remembered, extremely proud of their efforts. "When you treat someone with silver nitrate, you must constantly beware of getting it on yourself as it easily stains anything with which it comes into contact. It is extremely difficult to remove. No nurse once complained or faltered in their care of Leo. When he passed, it affected all of us. We had put so much work into saving him."[13]

* * *

Two days after Leo's funeral, Iberia Airlines Flight 933, a DC-10 wide-body jet flying from Madrid, Spain, crashed at Logan Airport as it attempted to land on Runway 33L. All 167 passengers and crew aboard the aircraft survived, but several suffered injuries. The circumstances were eerily similar to the crash of Delta Flight 723 as both planes were on approach to the airport. After the Iberia crash, electronic technicians at the airport expressed their view that the reintroduction of PAR could have prevented both crashes. Most importantly, the technicians expressed their expert view that PAR would also prevent future crashes.

Kenneth Lyons, president of the National Association of Government Employees (NAGE), the organization that pressured President Lyndon Johnson into hiring more air traffic controllers after a spate of midair collisions in the late 1960s, said this about PAR: "We warned after the Delta crash that it could happen again. It did happen again … and it will happen again unless something is done."[14]

Stanley Lyman, now national vice president of the Federal Aviation

Science and Technological Association, which represented radar operators and electronic technicians said, "[C]old brutal facts show that accidents in the last several years, claiming at least 94 lives … at Boston's Logan Airport might have been avoided had PAR been in use."[15]

New England's FAA Regional Director Ferris Howland admitted that the use of PAR might have prevented the Delta and Iberia crashes. He added the FAA decision "to discontinue use of the precision approach radar was the result of overwhelming pilot preference for conducting landing approaches in the cockpit with the aid of sophisticated instrument landing systems."[16]

Lyman retorted that the FAA had removed ground surveillance radar at Logan "due to economy." He emphasized that "the controller did not know there was no movement on the landing runway after the Delta crash and was not immediately alerted to the fact that there was something wrong."[17]

Lyons said that PAR was still available at Logan and required only one man to operate it. "There are plenty of extra controllers who could do the job. It is located within the tower and takes no additional manpower to operate."[18]

Howland did not agree. He argued that PAR had already been moved from Logan Airport. He said that decision had been made seven or eight years ago, and "I don't think the FAA will reverse itself."[19] He explained that the equipment was intended to serve the principal landing runway, 4R, the one Flight 723 had crashed on. "Even if we had PAR, it could never serve more than one runway at a time."[20]

Lyons had the last word. "If the Federal Aviation Administration doesn't do something about utilizing PAR, and if they allow planes to continue to land at Logan in fog, then they are going to pile up more planes at this airport."[21]

It seemed that after the Saturday Night Massacre, which had weakened President Nixon's executive authority, officials started gathering the courage to criticize the FAA again and expose weaknesses in the aviation system.

* * *

Lawsuits against Delta Air Lines started in earnest by the end of 1973. The family of Roger MacArthur filed the first suit in New Hampshire. They asked for $2 million in damages from Delta. In their response to the suit, Delta claimed that the air traffic controllers at Logan caused the crash. Delta officials explained that the crash was "caused directly, proximately and solely by the airport's controllers who are employed by the Federal Aviation Administration."[22] They named the United States as a third-party defendant in the suit. Delta added that the controllers "negligently and wrongfully observed, cleared, directed and controlled the movement of air traffic approaching and landing at Logan ... as a result of which Delta flight 723 was caused to crash, whereby 89 persons aboard the aircraft were killed."[23] The airline denied "that any negligent or wrongful act or omission of any agent, servant or employee of Delta had caused or contributed to the crash."[24]

23

"The Result of Nonstandard Air Traffic Control Services"

The NTSB final report is the culmination of the board's investigation into a crash. It is the summation of all the facts gathered, evidence collected, and witness interviews wrapped up into one report. The report does not assess blame, nor does it proclaim liability. That is left for civil court. The final report only assigns a probable cause to the accident. Most accident investigations, from the time of the accident until the final report is issued, take over a year to complete. However, due to the pressure put on the NTSB during the Nixon years to complete reports more quickly, the final report into the crash of Delta Air Lines Flight 723 was completed in just eight months. The board released the report on March 4, 1974.

The NTSB determined that the probable cause of the accident was

[t]he failure of the flight crew to monitor altitude and to recognize passage of the aircraft through the approach decision height during an unstabilized precision approach conducted in rapidly changing meteorological conditions. The unstabilized nature of the approach was due initially to the aircraft's passing the outer marker above the glide slope at an excessive airspeed and thereafter compounded by the flight crew's preoccupation with the questionable information presented by the flight director system. The poor positioning of the flight for the approach was in part the result of nonstandard air traffic control services.[1]

The board retraced the approach flown by Flight 723 in a simulator with different modes selected on the flight director. They found that when the VOR/LOC mode was selected for a localizer intercept turn, the approach would "invariably result in centerline overshoot."[2] Glide scope capture occurred on these tests above the glide scope centerline, and while the flight director was still in VOR/LOC mode, glide scope capture did not take place until the aircraft was two or more miles past the outer marker and at an altitude of seven hundred feet or less. "Descent rates of 1,300 feet per minute were consistent with a closed throttle descent and were required for these glide slope intercepts."[3] In some approaches, the necessary descent

23. "The Result of Nonstandard Air Traffic Control Services"   181

rate was not achieved and impact occurred. Glide scope reference was displayed only on the pictorial deviation indicator (PDI). This is called "raw data."[4]

According to the NTSB results, "[T]o obtain a pitch command display on the flight director indicator before glide scope capture, it was necessary to change the flight director mode selector to the approach position; after such a selection a fly-down command appeared."[5] However, due to the faster than normal approach rate, caused by intercepting the localizer from above, glide scope capture was difficult. The need to decelerate to approach speed compounded the problem.[6]

During at least five approaches, the flight director mode was switched, unbeknownst to the simulator pilot, to the go-around (G/A) mode after outer marker (OM) passage. When this happened the pitch command bar came into view at the top of the instrument and commanded a fly-up maneuver.

> Since this command was contrary to the raw data displayed, the pilot recognized the anomaly with little delay. The anomaly was not readily apparent, however, from mere observation of the flight director roll command bar. Although localizer guidance was removed from the flight director display, the roll command bar remained centered until an inadvertent roll of little magnitude was initiated. At that time, the roll bar deflected opposite the direction of bank and commanded a return to wings-level flight in accordance with the flight director's G/A mode. Subsequent attempts to follow the roll command invariably led to large deviations from the localizer centerline, which were detectable only by reference to the raw data displayed on the PDI.[7]

After the tests, the NTSB made a startling conclusion regarding the mode selector switch. "They found that during these simulations, the G/A mode could be selected inadvertently by rotating the flight director mode selection knob slightly past the approach mode detent. Even if the knob was returned to the approach mode detent, the G/A mode continued to be displayed on the flight director."[8]

The NTSB then turned its attention to the "non-standard air traffic control services." The *FAA Terminal Air Traffic Control Handbook* regulation 7110.8C, dated January 1, 1973, required that "whenever the reported weather is below basic VFR minima, an aircraft shall be vectored to intercept the localizer course at least 2 miles from the approach gate and at an altitude not above the glide slope."[9] Paragraph 1351 of the handbook stipulated that "the maximum angle for localizer interception is 30 degrees."[10] In the case of Flight 723, the intercept angle was 45 degrees. Since ATC did not give the clearance to descend to two thousand feet until they were beyond the beam, the pilot of Flight 723 was forced to intercept the beam from above.

Paragraph 1360 of the handbook requires the approach controller to provide approaching aircraft with certain arrival instructions or an approach clearance before the aircraft reaches the approach gate. These instructions are:

1. The position of the approaching aircraft relative to the final approach fix,
2. An approach clearance, and
3. Instructions to the approaching aircraft to monitor the local frequency, to report to the tower when it is over the approach fix, or, alternatively, to contact the tower on the local control frequency.[11]

The NTSB concluded that in the case of Flight 723, the approach clearance was not issued in accordance with prescribed procedures. They cited that "public hearing testimony revealed that at the time the approach controller should have issued this clearance he was occupied with a potential traffic conflict between two other flights. As a result, an approach clearance was not given to Flight 723 until the crew inquired about it."[12]

The approach profile contained in Delta Air Lines' operating manual, *Flight Training*, dated August 15, 1972, describes a "stabilized" approach as an approach where:

1. The glide slope is captured from below, before the aircraft reaches the outer marker (OM);
2. The aircraft arrives over the OM on the glide slope, with wing flaps extended 15 to 20 degrees and speed reduced to 160 knots, or as directed by approach control, with a minimum speed of 1.4 Vs; and,
3. After the aircraft has crossed the OM, the wing flaps are extended slowly to 50 degrees, while the aircraft is stabilized on the glide slope, and the speed is adjusted to maintain 1.3 Vs + 5 knots for the remainder of the approach.[13]

In the report, the NTSB analyzed the crew's actions:

As Flight 723 was proceeding inbound toward the localizer course at the assigned altitude of 3,000 feet, the BOS AR-1 controller's attention was drawn to an aircraft transferred to him by Boston Air Route Traffic Control Center which was in potential traffic conflict with another aircraft at the same altitude. At a time when BOS AR-1 [Taylor] should have been clearing Flight 723, as regulations require, he was trying to resolve the potential conflict and to avoid a possible mid-air collision. Consequently, an approach clearance was not given to Flight 723 until the flight crew first requested it. Subsequent communication difficulties with one of the aircraft involved in the potential traffic conflict further occupied BOS-AR-1 [Taylor] and delayed release of Flight 723 to Boston tower control. Nevertheless, proper monitoring of the flight's progress would have provided the crew with indications that should have caused them[14]:

1. To have been aware of their position relative to the localizer and the OM;
2. To have anticipated localizer interception outside the OM; and
3. To have reduced airspeed to that which would have been compatible with the aircraft's arrival over the OM in a stabilized condition which would have permitted the continuation of the approach and landing.[15]

The aircraft's airspeed at the OM was about 206 knots. That speed was 46 knots above the maximum speed recommended by company procedures. During most of the approach inbound from the OM, the airspeed was maintained well over the computed 1.3 Vs + 5 knots (about 123 knots).[16]

"The faster than normal airspeed during the approach, together with the delay in initiating the descent, resulted in two other problems for the crew. First it increased the difficulty they had in capturing and maintaining the glide slope."[17] Descending at more than 1,300 feet per minute would have required an interception of the glide path before reaching decision height. Second, "through experience and exposure to instrument approaches during instrument meteorological conditions, pilots generally learn to pace their activities while flying such an approach."[18] The high speed required the crew of Flight 723 to act more quickly than usual.

The flight director system is also affected by a high and fast approach.

> In normal use, the VOR/LOC mode of the flight director system would be selected. Operation in the VOR/LOC mode requires following the roll command bar to maintain the heading necessary to intercept and capture the localizer. Sensing the localizer signals, the command bar will command the lateral maneuvers necessary for localizer intercept and final approach guidance. Concurrently, the system arms to capture the glide slope; after capture, pitch command information is displayed as a function of glide-slope deviation. However, the system is designed so that an aircraft operating in the VOR/LOC mode must be on or below the glide slope [at] the time the localizer is intercepted in order to capture the glide slope. If the aircraft is too high and the glide slope is not captured, the pilot will not have flight director pitch guidance information for the initial approach. Consequently, he cannot use the instrument to make an asymptotic interception in the VOR/LOC mode. The flight director system can accommodate an interception from above the glide slope if the APP mode is used. Selection of the APP mode presents a fly-down command which will force capture of the glide slope.[19]

When Captain Streil told his copilot, "Get on it, Joe, ah Sid," the aircraft's altitude was 1,600 feet, still above the glide slope at an excessive airspeed.[20] During their analysis, the board believed that "this comment was a reference to the aircraft's position above the glide slope and that it prompted a change from VOR/LOC to APP to obtain pitch guidance information. The subsequent lateral-steering problems, however, would have been understandable only if the flight director system had been inadvertently placed in the G/A mode at that time."[21] Because the APP mode in the Collins flight director system that Northeast Airlines used is in the same position as the G/A mode in the Sperry Rand flight director system that Delta used, the board believed that a crew might, by habit, inadvertently select the G/A mode in the Sperry Rand system instead of the APP mode.[22]

The Sperry Rand flight director did not have an annunciator panel that would indicate on the display what mode had been selected. The NTSB found it possible to unintentionally select the G/A mode while rotating the mode selector switch to the approach position. A very slight overshoot of the APP position detent caused the flight director to display cues associated with the G/A mode of operation. Even if the selector switch were returned to the APP detent, the system would remain in the G/A mode because of its design. Without an annunciator panel, the crew would not have known this.

"Since the investigation disclosed a history of repetitive discrepancies of the flight guidance and navigation systems, a system malfunction was also considered as the cause for abnormal flight director guidance. However, examination of the recovered system components revealed no evidence of a system malfunction in the accident aircraft."[23] The board determined that there was insufficient evidence to establish the underlying cause of the flight director malfunction.

The board also focused on the weather at the end of the runway as Flight 723 attempted to land. The investigators revealed that the radio transmission from the tower contained two statements that contradicted each other. The statements were, "The RVR shows more than six thousand, a fog bank is moving in, it's pretty heavy across the approach end."[24] When this information was given to the crew, the actual RVR was closer to 1,600 feet. This was due to the delay in receiving the information in the tower due to the 51.1-second delay in the cycle reading.[25] Another discrepancy is the location of the transmissometer equipment in relation to the runway. On Runway 4R, the location is approximately abreast of the ILS touchdown point, on a 250-foot baseline, and about 500 feet to the left of the runway. Fog covering the runway may not be covering the equipment, and that would result in an inaccurate reading.

An RVR value transmitted to a pilot is intended to represent runway visibility when his aircraft touches down near the ILS touchdown point. "This value would represent the actual distance he could see down the runway, only if the atmosphere above the runway and above the transmissometer site were homogenous."[26] During fog conditions, it is not always homogenous.

The board also stated that before the RVR can be representative, "the aircraft must be near the touchdown point on the runway. Testimony during

23. "The Result of Nonstandard Air Traffic Control Services"   185

the public hearing revealed that not all pilots may be aware of all of the limitations of the RVR reporting system."[27]

The board's analysis demonstrated how an accumulation of discrepancies, none of them critical, can rapidly deteriorate, without positive flight management into a high-risk situation. In this regard, the most significant factors were[28]:

1. Vectors given by BOS AR-1 to intercept the localizer course were not according to standard operating procedures; nevertheless, the flight crew accepted the vectors and continued the approach at an excessive speed.

2. Approach clearance and other required instructions first had to be requested by the flight crew, before they were given to the flight, which delayed the flight's descent to the correct approach altitude.

3. The first officer, who was flying the aircraft, was preoccupied with the information presented by his flight director system, to the detriment of his attention to altitude, heading, and airspeed control.

4. The captain divided his attention among the problem with the flight director system, the communications with air traffic control, and the weather and visibility information given by the local controller.[29]

In summary, "[T]he Board believes that the crew's preoccupation with the flight director's presentation was the most detrimental factor during the critical phase of the approach. This preoccupation led directly to the crew's failure to monitor altitude and to recognize passage of the aircraft through decision height."[30] The board could not determine why the captain had not exercised positive flight management.

Ironically, the board did not give a summary regarding the failure of air traffic control to give Flight 723 timely information and instructions during their approach. The controller's attention on a potential conflict between two aircraft at the same altitude lasted only a few seconds, and that provided no excuse for not delivering mandatory and timely communication to Flight 723. This omission could partially be explained by the pressure put on the board from Nixon administration officials not to criticize the FAA. In March 1974, Richard Nixon, though weakened, was still the president of the United States.

The NTSB made several safety recommendations to the FAA regarding this crash. The first had been issued just days after the crash when the NTSB recommended that Delta's DC-9 aircraft that had been modified from Northeast Airlines be placed under an operational restriction due to the many complaints received about their flight directors. The FAA vetoed the recommendation.

In that recommendation, the NTSB had also asked the FAA to review the adequacy of Delta's quality control procedures in detecting and correcting reported discrepancies. The FAA admitted in their response that their study revealed that Delta needed to improve in the area of procedures and standards in the aircraft and the engine reliability programs. They identified "documentation, alert values and follow-up systems as the specific areas of concern."[31] Delta's

> computerized reports used by the systems maintenance coordinator and the aircraft maintenance analyst did not provide the input necessary for adequate and timely analysis and correction of repetitive items.
>
> Delta Airlines is in the final evaluation of some major management changes. A change being contemplated is to combine Maintenance Coordination, Technical Analysis and Aircraft Maintenance and Central Planning into a single department. The company has revised its computerized "exception report" to identify two repeat write-ups in four days with a second identification at five repeat write-ups in 31 days. We believe the above changes will provide an acceptable level of control of repetitive write-ups. We are performing continuous surveillance to determine if the program is completely satisfactory.[32]

A second letter sent to the FAA regarding the crash involved the approach light system (ALS) at Logan Airport. It concerned the two sets of red alarm lights that warned of a problem with the ALS, specifically if they were destroyed or damaged during an aircraft landing. The alarms often illuminated because water was frequently found in the lines. Maintenance personnel determined the status of the lines by inspecting them for water. If they found water, maintenance personnel would tell the air traffic controllers to ignore the warnings. Up until the time of the crash, "No effort had been made to install automatic pumping devices, nor to prevent the water from getting into the lines."[33] However, the NTSB did admit that airport personnel eliminated the problem by installing waterproof lines.

During the crash of Flight 723, light bars 25 and 26, along with their sequence flashers, were destroyed. "Destruction of the lights caused an alarm to sound and both sets of red warning lights to illuminate. When the alarm was detected, controller personnel silenced the signal and ignored the red lights."[34]

The board explained further that an inoperative ALS requires increased landing minimums for arriving flights. "Tower controllers are directed to advise inbound flight crews of an indicated malfunction in the ALS, pending visual verification of the system's status. This was not done."[35] Had the two flights behind Delta 723 not executed missed approaches, it is feasible that each would have landed on top of the destroyed Delta DC-9 debris field and suffered catastrophic damage also.

The board stated that controllers at Logan did not receive formal training in the use of the ALS monitoring panel and that they minimized the significance of the alarm because of the frequency they went off due to water in the lines. The board also mentioned the lack of communication

23. "The Result of Nonstandard Air Traffic Control Services"   187

between the tower ground controller and the local controller regarding the sequence of incoming flights. This was due to the ground controller telling the local controller that Flight 623 was taxiing toward the gate when the local controller really wanted to know the location of Flight 723. "Because of the confusion, airport operations continued without interruption and the location and status of Flight 723 was not known. Since the tower ground controller was not provided control information pertaining to the arrival sequence, he was not aware that two arriving flight had similar flight numbers."[36] The board recommended that:

    1. Controllers receive formal training in procedures for using the approach light system monitor panel.

    2. Revise air traffic control operational procedures to assure that the ground controller is provided, concurrently, with the same arrival sequence information that is provided the associated local controller.[37]

The FAA responded that, in the past, "controllers were briefed on the ALS system and applicable monitor procedures as part of their local control on-the-job training. While not formal per se, the training was considered adequate."[38] The FAA also explained that the line problem had been corrected by the installation of waterproof lines. They also relayed that the Boston Control Tower "has developed and implemented a controller training program on both the ALS systems installed at Logan Airport. This training is all inclusive and covers all the systems components and functions as well as alarm system operation and controller's responsibilities."[39] The FAA also emphasized that they were looking at this issue nationally to determine if it was happening at other towers.[40]

In regard to controllers being provided the same arrival sequence information, the FAA admitted that, one week after the crash, on August 7, 1973, management at the Boston Control Tower issued an internal order requiring flight progress strips be passed to the ground controller, thus making sure that that controller had the same information as others. The FAA, again, relayed that they had supplemented their *Terminal Air Traffic Procedures Handbook* to make this a national directive at all towers.[41]

The NTSB forwarded their testing results to the FAA regarding the Sperry Rand flight director. They revealed to the FAA that "if the mode selection switch is moved slightly past the Approach mode detent toward the Go-Around mode, the G/A mode indication will be displayed on the flight director."[42] Even if, they explained, the selector is returned to the approach mode, the G/A mode will continue to be displayed. "In the G/A mode, the ILS signals are eliminated from the flight director system and may be regained only by switching to the Standby or Flight Instrument modes, and then back to the VOR/LOC or Approach modes."[43]

The board recommended that the FAA

1. Require that the Sperry flight director mode selection switch be modified to prevent inadvertent selection of the G/A mode.
2. Require an annunciator panel whenever any flight director system is installed. The panel would indicate electronically the mode in which the flight director is operating, regardless of the position of the mode selector switch.[44]

It took six months for the FAA to reply, but on June 26, 1974, after the final report had been published, the FAA replied that the flight director system command display needed no modification for additional annunciation and/or mode selector switch change for the reasons below:

1. The DC-9 flight director system provided for pilot monitoring of the display which gives him positive indication of computer mode, in addition to his selector switch position and comparison with other instruments.
2. The DC-9 flight director system was given an extensive flight evaluation before being approved for Category II all weather landing operations. These systems have been carefully designed, tested, certificated, and proven effective in the thousands of operations conducted day after day using these systems. We oppose additional annunciations or changes to such systems without a comprehensive design review of the total system involved, since such changes may cause increased workload and/or distractions leading to degraded safety in a critical phase of flight.[45]

The FAA determined that a flight director, which did easily and inadvertently display the wrong approach modes, was a safe and appropriate instrument to use while transporting hundreds of thousands of passengers in the air on aircraft and required no changes.

24

"An Unusually Foggy Day"

Two years lapsed between the publication of the final report by the NTSB and the beginning of the court case that would determine fault for the crash. Delta Air Lines' legal team knew it was futile to state that their pilots had no fault in the accident. Ultimately, the pilot has the final say on whether to continue an approach or initiate a go-around, and Captain Streil did not order a go-around. What Delta attorneys wanted to argue was *why* John Streil did not initiate a go-around. Their argument pointed to the negligence of the air traffic controllers directing the fatal flight.

At the end of June 1975, Delta Air Lines offered a $200,000 settlement to the families of those killed in the crash.[1] However, Delta reserved the right to recover money from the federal government to offset their settlement as the federal government employed the air traffic controllers at Logan.[2]

Delta exercised their right to sue in a civil trial. In a civil trial, a judge or jury must determine whether there is a "preponderance of evidence" that the defendant should be held legally responsible for the damages alleged by the plaintiff. This case, *In re Aircrash Dis. at Boston, Mass., July 31, 1973* (412 F. Supp. 959, 998 [D. Mass. 1976]), was argued in front of District Court Judge Andrew Caffrey.

Judge Caffrey hailed from Lawrence, Massachusetts, and was born in 1920. He received his education from the finest schools available in the Bay State—College of the Holy Cross (A.B., 1941), Harvard Law School (LL.M., 1948), and Boston College Law School (LL.B., 1948). He interrupted his schooling to serve in the U.S. Army Signal Corps, Intelligence Branch, from 1942 to 1946. After the war, he became an associate professor at Boston College Law School and served from 1948 to 1955. In 1955, he became assistant U.S. attorney for the District of Massachusetts. He became chief of the civil division in 1955 and first assistant U.S. attorney in 1959. In 1960, President Dwight Eisenhower, through a recess appointment, made Caffrey a judge for the U.S. District Court for the District of Massachusetts. Eisenhower, just days before his presidency ended, nominated Caffrey to the same position, and the U.S. Senate confirmed him to that position on August 9, 1961. He was appointed chief judge in 1972, and he became a member of the Judicial Conference of the United States in 1973 and a member of the U.S. Judicial Panel on Multidistrict Litigation in 1975.[3]

In 1955, Caffrey represented Logan Airport air traffic controllers in *Smerdon v. United States* (135 F. Supp. 929 [D. Mass. 1955]). On the morning of November 23, 1953, Forrest V. Smith flew an airplane owned by Old Colony Aviation, Inc. from Martha's Vineyard to Logan Airport. David H. Barnes and Albert West were passengers on the plane. Smith filed an IFR flight plan before take-off.[4] At approximately 11:00 a.m., the Boston Approach Control Center established radio communication with the aircraft. Approach control was handling several other aircraft and advised Smith to hold at six thousand feet altitude. Weather conditions at Logan Airport were extremely poor and below the minimums for VFR.[5] During this time, "all planes, including Smith's, were advised that the visibility at the field itself was three-eighths of a mile as determined by the Boston Weather Bureau."[6]

The control center "asked Smith what type of approach he would be making. and he requested a Ground Controlled Approach. Control Center advised that they were unable to furnish a ground-controlled approach due to precipitation clouding the scope of its precision radar equipment."[7] The controller then furnished for all planes holding at Boston, including Smith's, "the weather conditions at Bedford Airport, which were well above the minimum for VFR approach and landing."[8]

Smith mistook this information for weather conditions at Logan Airport. He reported seeing the Squantum Naval Air Station, six miles southwest of Logan, and Deer Island and Long Island, two islands in Boston Harbor about two miles southeast of Logan. He also said he could see one runway at Logan itself.[9] Smith believed that any obscuration he observed on the harbor was thin and would be a temporary impediment to visibility. "Based upon this mistaken impression coupled with his own observation, he requested VFR clearance to enter an approach for landing at Logan Airport."[10] Approach control cleared Smith. "While on his glide path, Smith was in constant communication with the control tower and was advised of his distance from the field and his relative position to the runways as his plane approached."[11] When the plane was a "half mile from the end of the runway Smith entered an area of fog; but, believed it to be a temporary obscuration. At this point, visibility was between fifty and one hundred feet. The fog did not pass as Smith expected."[12] At 11:39 a.m., the plane "crashed into the waters at Boston Harbor. Pilot Smith and passenger West escaped the plane before it sank. Barnes drowned as a result of the crash."[13] Douglas Smerdon, the plaintiff in the case, was the administrator of Barnes's estate.

24. "An Unusually Foggy Day"

While the plane was under the control of the control center, personnel exercising control did not have visual access to the field. They were "located inside a canvas tent for the accommodation of radar viewing, and they receive and transmit weather information based upon official U.S. Weather Bureau reports. In granting a VFR approach, the Approach Control Center issued instructions to insure that there would be no danger of collision with other aircraft under its control."[14]

The plaintiff in this civil case had to prove "a preponderance of evidence that the government was negligent, that the government's employees [the controllers] were negligent in the performance of their operational duties, and that such negligence was the proximate cause of the injury complained of."[15]

Title 49 U.S.C.A. §551 authorizes the Civil Aeronautics Board and the administrator of civil aeronautics to prescribe:

> (a)(7) Air traffic rules governing the flight of, and for the navigation, protection, and identification of, aircraft, including rules as to safe altitudes of flight and rules for the prevention of collisions between aircraft, and between aircraft and land or water vehicles.[16]

Part 617 of Title 14, C.F.R., contains the specific rules governing the question of negligence before the court. This section contains the Air Traffic Control Rules affecting the operation of an air traffic control center or tower by personnel certified by the Civil Aeronautics Administration:

> The primary objective of the air traffic control service shall be to promote the safe, orderly, and expeditious movement of air traffic This shall include: (a) Preventing collisions between aircraft and between aircraft and obstructions on the movement area. (b) Expediting and maintaining an orderly flow of air traffic. (c) Assisting the person in command of an aircraft by providing such advice and information as may be useful for the safe and efficient conduct of a flight.[17]

The plaintiff argued that the "air traffic controller had a duty to assist Smith and his passengers by providing advice and information to help him land safely, and that the defendant's employee failed this duty by authorizing a VFR landing in an area where visibility was unsafe to permit such a landing."[18]

The defendant countered that the "limits of the Air Traffic Control operator's duties are to clear aircraft to enter a control area, based upon the prevention of collisions in the air, or danger of collision to an aircraft from an obstruction on the movement area."[19]

The judge concluded that the regulations are designed for use by air traffic controllers in order for them to

> maintain aircraft within their control area safe from collision with one another, and from danger arising from obstacles on the surface of the movement area,

such as other moving aircraft, construction vehicles, and facilities, or depressions in the surface of the runway, and the like. Their duties do not go as far as the plaintiff urges. These regulations do not place upon Air Traffic Controllers the responsibility of determining whether or not a given weather condition is safe for landing. The operator's duty in this case was limited to maintaining control of the airways to prevent collision between aircraft under his control.[20]

State Attorney Caffrey won that case in 1955, and now, over twenty years later, Caffrey was on the other side of an aviation case—not as a fact stater, arguing a point, but as a fact finder, determining if that precedent should still stand. Much had changed since 1955 in the field of aviation. Many other civil cases had been argued that extended the responsibilities of air traffic controllers. The Federal Aviation Administration had taken over from the Civil Aeronautics Authority the responsibility of the airways, and technology had vastly improved in those twenty years—technology that assisted both the pilot and the air traffic controller.

* * *

Many of the same witnesses who testified at the NTSB hearing testified at the eleven-day civil trial, although there were some new faces, especially for the plaintiff, Delta Air Lines. Since Delta had brought a direct action against the United States claiming a right of contribution equal to 50 percent of the total amount Delta was required to pay out in settlement to the estates of the passengers as well as recovering the value of the destroyed aircraft, the focus of the trial would be on the actions of the air traffic controllers, not the pilots, as Delta had already settled their liability.

The plaintiff's theory of negligence was premised on the claim that the air traffic controllers on duty at Logan Airport on the day of the accident were negligent in the following ways:

1. They violated the provisions of the *Terminal Air Traffic Control Manual* in effect on the day of the accident by failing to provide the crew of Delta 723 (D 723) with accurate and complete and current advice that banks of sea fog were obscuring visibility at the approach end of Runway 4-R on which D 723 was about to attempt a landing.

2. They violated the provisions of the *Manual* by failing to advise D 723 to intercept the localizer course at least two miles from the approach gate at an altitude not above the glide scope.

3. They violated the provisions of the *Manual* by failing to order D 723 to intercept the localizer at an angle of 30° or less

4. They violated the provisions of the *Manual* by failing to provide D 723 with information establishing (a) its position relative to the final approach, (b) a proper approach clearance, and (c) instructions to

24. "An Unusually Foggy Day"

contact the tower on local control frequency or to monitor local control frequency, and

5. They issued non-standard confusing and distracting radio communications during the final phase of D 723's approach.[21]

The defendants took and maintained the position that this disaster was caused solely and exclusively by the negligence of the crew of Delta Flight 723. The government argued that the negligence of the Delta crew was gross in nature in, and that the data obtained from the flight path and voice recorders established that this crew:

1. Failed to scan their instruments and/or chose to ignore the information reflected thereon.
2. Intercepted the localizer at an excessive rate of speed.
3. Failed to maintain the localizer course.
4. Failed to intercept and maintain the glide slope.
5. Failed to make the required course deviation call-outs and the required altitude call-outs.
6. Relied on information provided from a flight director which was found in the wreckage to have been set to the wrong mode.
7. Failed to heed conflicting information being supplied by the more reliable primary instruments.
8. Assigned a non-crew member the responsibility of participating in the approach checklist and descent checklist in violation of Delta's procedural manual.
9. Failed to stabilize the aircraft during the approach both altitude-wise and speed-wise.
10. Allowed the aircraft to dive below the glide slope during the last three miles of the approach.
11. Ignored warning from the decision height flashing light and the fact that that light illuminated prior to the middle marker light.
12. Failed to make the required decision regarding continuing the approach when they reached decision height.[22]

After hearing arguments in the eleven-day trial, Judge Caffrey wrote his opinion on the case about a month after its completion. Caffrey started his opinion with official observations of the weather and the warning from the Manchester airport tower controllers to Delta Flight 723 that "Boston can't handle you right now so there will be a little delay."[23] The controllers explained to the crew that missed approaches seemed to be holding up traffic at Logan Airport. Delta Flight 723 acknowledged. The Manchester weather station reported patchy fog that morning. At 10:00 a.m., they reported "partial obscuration estimated 1000' ceiling, overcast 3 miles visibility in fog." Air Met, a weather warning issued by the U.S. Weather Bureau, stated for the period of 9:00 a.m. to 12:00 p.m. that day that "coastal waters, coastal New England, New Jersey and lowlands into New England, eastern New York, ceiling and visibility well below 1000', 2 mile visibility in fog, coastal waters and coastal sections and ground fog elsewhere. Fog continuing coastal waters becoming patchy outer Cape Cod with fog patches occasionally drifting over immediate coastal sections and remainder of Massachusetts, New Hampshire and Maine, and dissipating elsewhere."[24]

Caffrey then listed the last official observation made by Harry Terban of the U.S. Weather Service at Logan Airport at 10:53 that morning, fifteen minutes before the crash. Terban relayed an observation of "partial obscuration, estimated 500, broken 25,000 overcast. The surface visibility one-and-one half miles, tower visibility one-and-one half miles, the obscuration to vision fog, air temperature 68°, dew point 64°, wind estimated at 100° at 2 knots."[25] Judge Caffrey emphasized that Terban was "a veteran weather observer who has been employed by the National Weather Service for 24 years. Mr. Terban, who I find to be a highly credible and well-qualified weatherman, was responsible for taking all weather observations that were subsequently sent out for transmission as the prevailing weather for Boston."[26]

Caffrey explained the regulations that govern a pilot on control of his aircraft as it pertains to the weather. "Each pilot in command shall before beginning a flight, familiarize himself with all available information concerning that flight. This information must include (a) for a flight under IFR ... weather reports and forecasts, fuel requirements, alternatives available if the planned flight cannot be completed."[27] He also quoted the Code of Federal Regulations (C.F.R.) 121.599–121.603, which requires

> [n]o aircraft dispatcher may release a flight unless he is thoroughly familiar with reported and forecast weather conditions on the route to be flown; The aircraft dispatcher shall provide the pilot in command all available current reports or information on airport conditions and irregularities of navigation facilities that may affect the safety of the flight; During a flight, the aircraft dispatcher shall provide the pilot in command any additional available information of meteorological conditions ... that may affect the safety of the flight; Before beginning a flight, each pilot in command shall obtain all available current reports or information on aircraft conditions ... that may affect the safety of the flight.[28]

While climbing out from Manchester en route to Boston, Boston approach relayed that "the Boston altimeter is 30.11, weather is partial obscuration, estimated 400' ceiling, overcast a mile and a half and fog."[29]

Caffrey admitted that there was no doubt July 31, 1973, was an "unusually foggy day."[30] However, "the degree of density of the fog, the altitude of the lowest portion thereof, and whether or not it was in the configuration of a definable bank were the subject of conflicting testimony."[31] He described the witnesses on Castle Island observing the aircraft overhead just before landing as credible in that Delta Flight 723 "was making an abnormally low approach to the runway to Logan."[32]

Judge Caffrey was ambiguous toward Geoffrey Keating's testimony. He did not rule on his credibility one way or the other. However, Caffrey was not ambiguous regarding Harris Cusick's testimony. Even though Cusick attended an Air Force Weather Observation School and completed three years of service on active duty as an Air Force weatherman, Judge Caffrey completely disregarded Cusick's testimony. "I do not credit this witness' testimony," Caffrey wrote, "since I find him to be strongly biased in favor of the plaintiffs, as he conceded under cross-examination. He likewise conceded, in substance, that he was 'miffed' because the National Transportation Safety Board did not call him but did call Mr. Keating as a witness at the post-accident hearing it held in Peabody, Mass."[33] Caffrey went on that Cusick resented this because he felt he was a far more qualified and reliable witness due to his training. "Mr. Cusick showed further bias by making an attack on what he believed to be the deficiencies of the transmissometer system for Runway 4-R. His attack was based primarily on his own *ipse dixit*. I totally discount Mr. Cusick's testimony."[34]

Caffrey then explained his thoughts on the weather regarding the inaction of Captain Vernon H. Young. Captain Young commanded Eastern Air Lines Flight 945 and was waiting for takeoff at the end of Runway 15R. Just before 11:00 a.m. Young noticed fog between Runway 4R and Castle Island. He considered it to be "unusually dense for that time of year."[35] At 11:05 a.m. he estimated half the airport to be obscured by fog and all but the most northern end of Runway 4R. During the trial, Captain Young was asked if he was aware of a regulation that required pilots to report to the tower any change in weather conditions that may be essential to the safety of others. He replied that he was aware of the regulation but did not report it. Since Young did not report the change to the tower, Judge Caffrey did not consider his testimony factual.[36] However, Judge Caffrey did accept Captain Young's testimony when Young conceded that the only person who could know the visibility at decision height (DH) would be the pilot himself. Caffrey continued, "This is true, he [Young] testified, no matter what anyone other than the pilot saw or reported about the visibility. He testified unequivocally that it is *completely* up to the pilot to make a decision at DH as to whether a safe landing can be executed and this decision is to be based on what he then can or cannot see of the runway or its environment."[37]

Captain Keith Chappell landed his aircraft, a DC-9, Eastern Air Lines Flight 572, immediately prior to Delta Flight 723 on Runway 4R. He testified that when his flight landed, weather conditions as reported by the tower were different from those encountered on landing, but, significantly, not so different as to cause him to report them to the tower as required by an FAA regulation. Again, since he did not report it, Judge Caffrey did not credit Chappell's testimony that "any significant weather change had occurred since he received his last weather advisory."[38]

Caffrey then turned to air traffic control opinions as to their views on weather reporting. James Morrissey worked as the approach control coordinator in the TRACON room. He testified that he heard no messages about fog that indicated any change in previously existing weather conditions. He admitted that he heard internal transmissions about fog from the tower as merely "messages for internal use, such as alerting controllers that incoming planes might begin executing missed approaches again as they had done earlier in the morning."[39] He testified "any pilot flying a plane that day would have been well aware that there was fog all around Logan Airport."[40] Morrissey further testified that he would not consider the internal message, "that fog's coming right back across again, so you can get ready for some, it's real thick again," to be a "significant weather report" within the provisions of the *Terminal Air Traffic Control Manual*.[41] Morrissey believed that any fog coming back in would "be a weather condition that should have been expected by any pilot who had been receiving regular reports while flying that morning."[42]

Jeffrey McDonald worked as the local controller in the tower before the crash. As he cleared Eastern Air Lines Flight 572 to land, he gave the pilot the following information: "The fog is moving back in from the south across the airport and is just approaching Runway 4-R. Your RVR for 4-R is showing more than 6000." When asked about this transmission, McDonald testified that the information was not a "pertinent" airport *condition* within the meaning of the *Terminal Air Traffic Control Manual*, which reads: "Issue airport condition information necessary for an aircraft's safe operations in time for it to be useful to the pilot."[43] Caffrey concluded that "Mr. McDonald gave the explanation, which I accept, that the phrase 'airport condition' in 305 pertains to land mass, construction going on, snow piled along the runway, or a parked aircraft or other vehicle on the runway, but not to weather."[44]

Demetrios J. Merageas worked as the arrival data no. 1 man on July 31, 1973. He testified that he had not heard the message regarding the fog coming back, but "had he done so he would have interpreted it merely as a warning for the controllers to prepare for the possibility that pilots would again execute missed approaches."[45] He did not consider this message as one that should be transmitted to pilots. He testified that he would "advise incoming aircraft of any pertinent major change in the weather but did not consider the return of fog under that day's prevailing weather to be such."[46]

24. "An Unusually Foggy Day" 197

Charles Taylor, the approach controller that day, testified that he issued the most recent weather advisory to Delta Flight 723 moments after it had taken off from Manchester. He transmitted the following: "723 Roger, cleared to Lawrence. No delay. Planned vectors ILS 4 right. The Boston altimeter is 30.11. Weather is partial obscuration, estimate 400 overcast a mile and a half and fog."[47] Taylor testified, and Caffrey credited his testimony, that "this weather advisory was not changed between the time of his transmission to D 723 and the time of the crash."[48] Taylor admitted that he did not hear the internal message regarding the fog coming back nor did anyone tell him about it. Caffrey wrote, "More significantly, he [Taylor] said that if he had heard it, he would not have relayed it to D 723 because, like other controllers who testified, he merely considered it to be an advisory...."[49] Taylor admitted he did not consider it to be a significant change in weather conditions.

Regarding the weather, Caffrey concluded that

> I am not persuaded that any weather information which came to the attention of Mr. Taylor before the crash amounted to a difference [in] weather elements observed from the tower and those reported by the weather station within the meaning of ¶361 of the *Terminal Air Traffic Control Manual* (PX-9) which provides in pertinent part C: "Differences between weather elements observed from the tower and those by the Weather station shall be reported to the official observer for the element concerned."[50]

Caffrey ruled that the air traffic control manual, captioned "*Duty Priority,*" allocates three separate priorities to various duties to be performed by air traffic controllers.

> That section gives *first priority to* separation of aircraft, *second* priority to services which are required but do not involve separation, and *third* [and last] priority to items classified as "additional services." Paragraph 361 of the same manual, *supra* captioned "Disseminating Weather Information," is characterized by the manual as an "additional service." Therefore it is a third priority item.[51]

Caffrey wrote that as it pertains to negligence, he found that "radio transmissions as to fog [that] were or were not made had no causal relationship whatsoever to the crash of D 723."[52] He also found the crew grossly negligent because they "continued their descent (1) without ever mentioning Decision Height [DH] after 11:59 AM, (2) without ever making the required call outs at altitudes above DH and at DH, (3) without ever discussing slant view of the visibility of the runway or its environment prior to or at DH, (4) or without ever reacting in any way to the claimed presence of fog at the approach end of 4-R."[53]

Caffrey also noted the lack of cockpit discipline practiced by Captain Streil. "The four points noted above, and the fact that the CVR shows that the captain undertook to imitate the sound of a bugle at 10:52 AM and again at 11:01, prove that there was a serious lack of discipline in the cockpit of D 723."[54]

Judge Caffrey next dealt with the approach instructions given to Delta Flight 723. The plaintiffs alleged that Delta Flight 723 was provided with nonstandard ATC service and that this failure had a "snowballing" effect on the crew of Delta Flight 723 as the aircraft was on final approach.[55] Caffrey admitted that it could be "inferred" that the flight director was broadcasting erroneous and faulty readings to the crew. Caffrey stated that if this was the case, it might "at least" partially explain why the aircraft did not stabilize on the localizer or glide slope. However, he also said that if the crew was receiving bad information from the flight director, that in no way establishes air traffic control negligence.[56]

Captain Thomas Ball, who retired in 1972 as vice president of flight operations for Delta Air Lines, testified in the trial. Captain Ball admitted that a DC-9 aircraft could land without information from a flight director. This could be done by using the PDI along with radio transmitters on the ground. The flight director, though, provides more information than the PDI. Caffrey used the following example in his opinion: "If the plane were off course to the left, the PDI would merely tell the pilot turn right and you will regain the localizer at some point. The flight director, however, not only tells the pilot to turn right but also computes for him the rate of turn necessary to center his aircraft on the localizer."[57]

Caffrey admitted that evidence existed that the switch of the flight director was found "in or near" the "go-around" mode instead of the "approach" mode. If that was the case, he admitted that the flight director did "indeed provide erroneous course and descent guidance to the crew."[58] However, he also found that a trained crew "should have detected that the flight director was mis-set and would and should have either reset it or ignored its indications" and relied on the PDI.[59]

Judge Caffrey also espoused on the similar locations of the go-around and approach modes on the Collins and Sperry Rand flight directors. He found "more likely than not" that the crew's persistence in following the flight director instead of the PDI can best "be explained rationally by the dual findings (1) that they set the flight director to the wrong mode, and (2) they negligently persisted in following the flight director's indications rather than depending upon the far more reliable information being supplied by the PDI."[60]

Captain Ball stated that none of the nonstandard elements provided by air traffic control, standing alone, would have adversely affected a standard ILS approach. However, he also testified that "he did not know whether, if taken together, these items would preclude a successful landing." He considered that the combination of the nonstandard elements of the approach given by ATC "would be an adverse factor for successful completion."[61]

Captain Herlong Averett, assistant manager of flight training at Delta Air Lines from 1970 to 1974, and then a line captain for Delta on the Lockheed L-1011, agreed with Ball that the PDI is a highly reliable instrument, enough so that if the flight director malfunctioned, pilots could use it to land. Averett also agreed that Delta DC-9 pilots must have enough "proficiency to execute a 45° turn to intercept a localizer."[62] It was also revealed during the trial that "Delta's DC-9 pilots are required to perform as much as 90° intercept angles at other airports."[63]

Captain Everett Nix, manager of flight operations for Delta, testified that the graph of the flight recorder indicated that the approach "deviated significantly from the standards imposed by Delta on its own crews."[64] Caffrey inferred from this that "the deviation was of sufficient magnitude to indicate to a non-negligent crew that a missed approach should be executed forthwith."[65] Captain Nix also testified that the instruments on a DC-9 provide the crew with enough information for them to know their position at any time and that, on approach, Delta pilots are required to know where they are at all times.[66] Caffrey found that the crew was "unaware of their aircraft's location during critical stages of their final approach."[67]

Captain Jack Roseborough worked for the FAA as an airman certification expert and had been flying for thirty-six years. Caffrey found him to be a "qualified and truthful witness and I accept his opinion evidence as factual."[68] He testified that Delta Flight 723 intercepted the localizer properly and that the aircraft began in a good position to continue the approach.[69] However, Roseborough stated, from that point, the aircraft deviated two dots from the localizer. This errant course was followed because the crew continued to follow the instructions of the flight director.[70] Roseborough admitted that there was no evidence that would excuse the crew of Delta Flight 723 from maintaining the localizer center line and acquiring the glide slope. He expressed the opinion that "none of the claimed breaches by ATC ... alone or in a combination were adequate to cause a crash."[71]

The pilots above all corroborated that Delta pilots must have the ability to capture a glide slope from above and must display the ability to do so routinely during an ILS approach.[72] Caffrey ruled that "a pilot is perfectly free to reject any heading assigned to him by ATC if compliance would jeopardize the safety of the aircraft. Should a pilot decide to reject an assigned heading, he should notify the tower of his inability to comply and request an alternate heading."[73]

Caffrey next dealt with the "non-standard, confusing, and distracting radio communications during the final phase of the approach, including the late landing clearance given to D 723."[74] The specific communications are:

> 11:05:39 a.m. D 723: *Ah is seven two three cleared the ILS*
> 11:05:41 a.m. AC: *Yes, seven two three is cleared for the ILS, yes*
> 11:05:43 a.m. D 723: *Alrighty*
>
> * * *
>
> 11:07:14 a.m. AC: *Delta seven two three is cleared to land. Tower one nineteen one*
> 11:07:17 D 723: *Seven two three*
> 11:07:43 D 723: *And Boston tower Delta seven two three final*
> 11:07:45 LC: *Cleared to land four right traffic clearin' at the end, the RVR shows more than six thousand and a fog bank's movin' in, it's pretty heavy across the approach end*[75]

In rendering his decision on these transmissions, Judge Caffrey relied on the testimony of Captains Ball and Roseborough, First Officer Chappell, as well as controllers Tucker and McDonald. He also relied on Edmund Burke, a self-employed consultant in air traffic control matters.

Ball testified that "if this aircraft had stabilized on both the localizer and the glide slope at 15:07:45 he did not think that the communication from the tower which began then would cause it to crash."[76] He also testified that "standing alone the lateness of the instruction from approach controller Taylor to D 723 directing it to switch to tower frequency would not cause the aircraft to crash." He had the same opinion as to the fact that the approach controller did not instruct D 723 to switch to tower frequency prior to its reaching the outer marker. Captain Ball also testified that, while it would be unusual to receive a clearance to land from an approach controller without being told to switch to tower frequency, he would have switched to the tower frequency if it had happened to him when making an approach.[77]

First Officer Keith Chappell of Eastern Air Lines testified that even if his plane were down as low as four hundred feet in the course of an approach, he "would prefer that the controllers relay any change in weather information which has come to their knowledge, rather than that they not relay it. He expressed the opinion that receiving information about a fog bank when as low as 400 feet would not cause a crash."[78]

Roseborough expressed the opinion that "a qualified DC-9 crew would not be distracted by the transmissions which are in evidence in this case as part of the CVR transcript."[79] He testified that "nothing in evidence, in his opinion, including the allegedly late transmissions, either alone or in combination with the other factors complained of, would excuse a pilot from

24. "An Unusually Foggy Day"

maintaining a stabilized position on the center lines of the localizer and the glide slope during the approach."[80]

Daniel Tucker testified that "it is a common occurrence for incoming planes not to be directed to switch over to the tower frequency."[81] Jeffrey McDonald testified that the timing of when he tells pilots to switch over to tower frequency depends on different circumstances. He admitted he does not do it automatically at the outer marker.

Edmund Burke stated that there is nothing unusual about the issuance of a clearance to land to an aircraft which has passed inside the outer marker. He also testified that the "issuance of a clearance by the local controller at 1507:45.5 was reasonable because at that time the local controller was not sure that his earlier request to approach control to issue that clearance had, in fact, been complied with."[82] Burke testified that "this transmission at 1507:45.5, which lasted 3½ seconds, had no adverse effect on the situation, but merely repeated the earlier clearance issued by approach control."[83] He further testified that "none of the transmissions or lack of transmissions from the control tower, or the timing thereof, individually or in combination, in any way caused or contributed to the crash of D 723. I find this testimony to be factual."[84] Caffrey found Burke's testimony credible and believable.

Caffrey then dealt with the Allegheny 666 separation issue. He started out by writing that separation of aircraft is a first priority obligation of ATC. He then continued for several pages in his opinion:

> The United States alleges that the presence of AL 666 at the locations and altitudes established by the record constituted a first priority separation emergency. Mr. Taylor testified that he was very concerned about that particular flight and its potential impact on other traffic from the time it first reported to him at 1502:25 (5 minutes and 40 seconds before the time D 723 crashed) until at least 1509:22 (one minute and 17 seconds after the crash).
>
> Taylor testified, and I find, that the Air Traffic Center had directed AL 666 to go to the Millis holding pattern at an assigned altitude of 9000 feet, but AL 666 first contacted him at 1502:25 and reported its altitude to be 8000 feet at the Millis holding pattern. Taylor immediately realized that he had a potential crisis on his hands because he already knew that EAL 1020 was also assigned to the Millis holding pattern at an altitude of 8000 feet. Taylor in his approximately twenty years as an air traffic controller never had encountered a situation in which two aircraft were in the same holding pattern at the same altitude. He decided to immediately remove EAL 1020 from the holding pattern and to instruct AL 666 to maintain the heading of 220° on which it was then flying. The record is not clear as to exactly where either plane was vis-a-vis the normal holding pattern or vis-a-vis each other. It appears more likely so than not that EAL 1020 was following AL 666 as both planes flew the holding pattern in the same direction.

Taylor instructed EAL 1020 to go to a heading of 070° and make a left turn, which it did. Taking EAL 1020 out of the Millis holding pattern on the heading of 070° caused Taylor to advance the estimated time for its approach clearance by approximately 8 minutes. He had previously given EAL 1020 an estimated landing time of about 1515, but at 1504 he instructed EAL 1020 to intercept the localizer course then, which it did at some point outside the Randolph intersection. At 1507 he cleared EAL 1020 to land and instructed it to continue its descent to an altitude of 2000 feet.

I find that the foregoing did not exhaust Mr. Taylor's legitimate concern with the shenanigans of AL 666. Having dealt with one problem created by AL 666, his continued concern was properly a first priority item for him.

Plaintiffs' Exhibit 32, which includes a transcript of communications between Taylor and AL 666, establishes that after vectoring EAL 1020 out of the holding pattern at 1502:36 he was far from finished with, and was still concerned about and occupied with, potential separation problems posed by AL 666. In fact, he sent an instruction to it at 1502:53 to continue its present heading in the holding pattern. At 1503:28 he instructed AL 666 to reverse course, proceed to the Millis intersection, and hold. This was acknowledged at 1503:32 by AL 666. At 1503:34 Taylor asked AL 666 to identify for him, which AL 666 did at 1503:37.

At 1505:19 (about one and one-half minutes later) Taylor tried to verify that AL 666 had remained at 8000 feet as directed. He got no response to that inquiry. He inquired again at 1505:25, at 1505:29, at 1505:34 and at 1505:46. He received a response from AL 666 at 1505:50, repeated his question as to its altitude at 1505:51, received an unintelligible response from AL 666 at 1505:54, requested a repeat of the answer at 1505:55, got a second unintelligible response at 1505:57, put the question again at 1505:58 and, finally, got an answer from AL 666 verifying the 8000 altitude at 1506:02. He was asked by AL 666 for information as to approach clearance at 1506:04 and he responded at 1506:07, one minute and 58 seconds before the crash. Taylor then cleared D 723 to land and directed it to switch to the tower frequency at 1507:14. I find that concern over AL 666 caused the delay by Taylor in clearing D 723 and in ordering it to switch to tower frequency. D 723 reported to the tower at 1507:43.

Taylor testified, and I find, that while all of the foregoing activity was going on he observed on his radar scope that AL 666 had overshot the Millis intersection by approximately two miles and that it was proceeding in a northerly direction toward a space reserved for departing aircraft. He testified that this necessitated his alerting the departure controller of the course being flown by AL 666 to insure that the departure controller would maintain a separation between AL 666 and any departing aircraft in the airspace under his jurisdiction. After taking this precaution he then contacted AL 666 with instructions to reverse and return to Millis. In all, AL 666 wandered in a northerly direction approximately seven miles away from the holding pattern area.

Taylor further testified that when he first observed AL 666 overshooting the holding pattern he believed that it would not continue off course as far beyond Millis as it in fact did, but that it would discover its own error and reverse its course when two or three miles out from the holding point.

24. "An Unusually Foggy Day"

It has been stipulated that between 1447 and 1514, Taylor was handling the approaches of the following aircraft:

EXEC 1349 TWA 288 TWA 552 DELTA 723 WINNEPESAUKEE 304 EXEC 1343 EASTERN 1020 PILGRIM 152 ALLEGHENY 666 DELTA 986 ALLEGHENY 952 AMERICAN 832 AMERICAN 238 NOVEMBER 731 WHISKEY

On the basis of the foregoing summary of the evidence relating to AL 666, I find that AL 666 was of legitimate concern to Controller Taylor from 1502 to 1509, and that it constituted an emergency situation within the meaning of the *Terminal Air Traffic Control Manual*. In view of AL 666's erratic performance that morning, I further find that maintaining its separation from other aircraft was a first priority item for Mr. Taylor which clearly overrode any obligation he might otherwise have had to perform the third priority additional service of transmitting weather information to D 723.

I find that in light of the potential hazards caused by AL 666, Mr. Taylor's attention was appropriately focused on concentrated communication efforts with that and other aircraft, coordination efforts with other controllers concerning intended routes for other approaching aircraft, the sequence of aircraft being vectored to their approach courses, and the avoidance of potential conflicts with departing aircraft.[85]

In rendering his decision, Judge Caffrey concluded that "I rule that plaintiffs have not proven by a preponderance either that ATC personnel were negligent or that the conduct of ATC, however characterized, was a proximate cause of the crash either in whole or in any part. I find that the sole and exclusive cause of the accident was the negligence of the pilot and copilot of D 723."[86]

25

"Mr. Taylor Simply Forgot About Delta 723"

Caffrey's verdict stunned Delta Air Lines in his overwhelming decision against them. In almost every respect, Caffrey excused the behavior of the controllers and admonished the Delta crew in theirs. This, however, became the foundation of the case to the court of appeals: Delta Air Lines was not on trial. They did not contest their own liability. Delta conceded that crew negligence contributed to the accident. They sought contribution and indemnification from the United States based on the negligence of air traffic controllers who handled the flight.

Delta Air Lines, and several other passengers' estates, appealed to the U.S. Court of Appeals for the First District to overturn Caffrey's opinion. The appellants analyzed Caffrey's rulings and submitted briefs to the appeals court.

The function of approach control is to promote the "safe, orderly and expeditious flow of traffic arriving and departing from a terminal area. Approach controllers operating in these terminal areas, including Boston, do so according to procedures set out in the Federal Aviation Administration's handbook, *Terminal Air Traffic Control* [the *Manual*]."[1] The *Manual* provides that "action verbs in the imperative mean that a procedure is mandatory."[2] The *Manual* also prescribes duty priorities, the first being to separate aircraft, the second to tend to "second priority services" that do not involve air traffic separation, and the third to give "additional services to the extent possible. Included in the last category is the dissemination of weather information."[3] The following information was stipulated as fact by the court of appeals after receiving the appellants' briefs:

> Paragraph 1360 of the *Manual* in use on July 31, 1973, required an approach control to issue certain information and instructions to an aircraft before it reached the so-called approach gate. This would constitute a second priority duty....
> The following information should have been given: (1) D 723's position relative to the outer marker (the final approach fix); (2) a vector to intercept the

final approach course; (3) a clearance for the aircraft to make the instrument approach; and (4) an instruction to go ahead and monitor Boston Local Control (the Tower) then contact it upon reaching the final approach fix or, alternatively, an instruction to switch over to the Tower immediately.... The *Manual* states as a guideline that the maximum localizer interception angle to be given when a plane is 2 miles or more outside the approach gate is 30°. Paragraph 1352 requires, by its use of verbs in the imperative, that the controller "vector aircraft to intercept the localizer course at least 2 miles from the approach gate and at an altitude not above the glide slope." As will be seen, D 723 was never given its position relative to the approach fix and was not turned over to the Tower until well after passing the approach gate. Further, it was given an interception angle larger than 30° and was not instructed to descend to an altitude not above the glide slope.[4]

Plaintiffs argued to the court of appeals that the *Manual* requires a controller to issue certain information and instructions to an aircraft before it reaches the approach gate. Four pieces of information should have been given to Delta Flight 723: "(1) D 723's position relative to the outer marker; (2) a vector to intercept the final approach course; (3) a clearance for the aircraft to make the instrument approach; and (4) an instruction to go ahead and monitor Boston Local Control (the Tower) then contact it upon reaching the final approach fix or, alternatively, an instruction to switch over to the Tower immediately."[5]

Just after 11:04 a.m., approach said to the pilots of Delta Flight 723, "... and Delta seven two three fly heading of zero eight zero [80°] and intercept the localizer course and fly it inbound over."[6]

Captain Streil acknowledged the transmission. This transmission satisfied the second requirement in that it constituted the "vector to intercept the final approach course."[7] However, the angle of intercept given by the controller to the crew was "15° greater than that suggested by the *Manual*."[8] There was also no clearance given to descend the aircraft to two thousand feet, which would be an altitude "not above the glide scope."[9] According to the court of appeals, this was a mandatory procedure.

About thirty seconds before arriving at the approach gate, Captain Streil asked the tower if his flight was "cleared for ILS."[10]

"Yes, seven two three is cleared for ILS, yes," Taylor responded.[11] This conversation satisfied the third mandatory requirement, although it was at the behest of the flight crew, not the tower.[12]

At no time was Delta Flight 723 given the first mandatory instruction (its position relative to the final approach fix) or the fourth required piece of information (to monitor the tower frequency).[13]

The plaintiffs argued that the failure of the controller to have the crew monitor the tower frequency was critical because "a significant weather change had taken place at Logan subsequent to the weather report issued after its take-off from Manchester."[14] Had the crew been told to turn to the tower frequency, they would have heard the following transmission, which was sent to the plane landing ahead of them: "… [T]he fog's movin' back in from the south across the airport now, it's just approaching runway four right."[15] The plaintiffs argued that the excessive speed of the aircraft on approach as well as its inability to align with the localizer was caused by the excessive intercept angle and beginning its approach one thousand feet too high. "Fifty-one seconds before the accident and only at the request of the local control coordinator whose job it was to coordinate approaches, Approach cleared D 723 to land and told it, finally, to go to the Tower frequency."[16] Between that transmission and Streil's acknowledgment of it, the CVR revealed that the pilot warned his copilot that the plane was going too fast and there was a problem with the flight director and to go to "raw data." Just seconds before the plane passed through decision height, the controllers gave the following advisory: "Cleared to land four right, traffic's clearin' at the end, the RVR shows more than six thousand, a fog bank is movin' in, its pretty heavy across the approach end."[17]

Streil responded, "seven two three."[18] Thirteen seconds later he was dead.

The question asked by the plaintiffs was, "Why was Delta 723 not turned over to the tower frequency when Mr. Taylor cleared Delta 723 for the ILS when Delta 723 was more than seven miles from the airport?"[19]

In his testimony, Taylor said that he intended to do so before Delta Flight 723 reached the outer marker but did not. He said he could have turned them over to the tower when he cleared them for ILS, but "he did not consider it important."[20] All Taylor would have had to do was add the words "tower 119.1." Taylor admitted that his standard approach clearance normally would be "Delta 723 turn left heading 080 intercept the localizer course. Cleared for the ILS Tower on 119.1."[21] According to the plaintiffs and Taylor, that would have taken no more than seven seconds. He did concede he did not give Delta 723 a standard approach clearance.[22]

The plaintiffs then discussed the extreme intercept angle and high-altitude approach that Taylor put Delta Flight 723 on. Taylor testified that he "had no reason not to descend Delta 723 to an altitude of 2,000 feet at or before the intercept point."[23] He testified he had never thought of that.[24] The failure of Taylor to order Delta Flight 723 to two thousand feet and capture the glide slope from below placed the additional burden on the pilots to "lose altitude more rapidly than desired in order to cross the outer marker at the prescribed altitude; this factor also resulted in the aircraft having a greater than desired speed due to the rapid descent required while attempting to get down to the required altitude at the outer marker."[25]

25. "Mr. Taylor Simply Forgot About Delta 723"

As for the intercept angle, Taylor testified that he regarded the paragraph that deals with intercept angles as "nothing more than a guide and he did not care whether the angle of intercept was more than 30 degrees or less."[26] Imposing an intercept angle more than the maximum specified by the manual "imposed the burden of additional maneuvering [by the pilots] of the aircraft in order to stabilize on the localizer."[27]

The failure of Taylor to give the crew of Delta Flight 723 its position relative to the outer marker before reaching the approach gate "imposed upon the pilots of Delta 723 the additional burden of having to calculate their distance from the outer marker at a time when they were endeavoring to stabilize the aircraft on the localizer, descend the aircraft to the desired altitude and reduce the speed to the desired value."[28]

The failure of Taylor to issue an approach clearance to Delta 723 until requested by Delta 723 "imposed upon the pilots of Delta 723 the additional burden of inquiring as to the intentions of Mr. Taylor with respect to Delta 723."[29]

Taylor testified that because he had a lot of aircraft to work, some of the items in the *Manual* could be left out because "his first priority of duty is the separation of aircraft."[30] Plaintiffs argued that "there is nothing in paragraph 1360 which gives Mr. Taylor this option as the procedures therein are mandatory."[31]

The plaintiffs offered their own opinion for Taylor's obvious omissions of his duty: "*It seems an incontrovertible conclusion, therefore, that Mr. Taylor simply forgot about Delta 723.*"[32]

Taylor's attorneys at the Caffrey trial argued that Taylor had a higher duty priority at the time he was handling Delta Flight 723, and that was the separation problem with Allegheny 666, and Caffrey agreed. Plaintiffs argued on appeal that "any potential separation problem between Eastern 1020 and Allegheny 666 had been resolved by Mr. Taylor minutes before D 723 had even intercepted the localizer for Runway 4R and prior to the time when Mr. Taylor candidly admits that he could have issued a standard approach clearance to Delta 723."[33]

Controller Taylor admitted that he had "never before failed to render air traffic control services to an aircraft in so many respects as he had done in the case of D 723."[34] Edmund Burke, the self-employed consultant in air traffic control matters whom Judge Caffrey regarded as credible and believable, testified he "had never heard of a situation where an air traffic controller had violated the *Manual* in so many respects in rendering air traffic control service to an aircraft."[35] Plaintiffs argued that Burke's opinion that these omissions by Taylor had "nothing to do with the crash" could not by logically accepted as they had by Judge Caffrey.[36]

The plaintiffs also invoked Captain Ball's testimony. Ball explained that the successful completion of an ILS landing is intended to be distributed over three segments. Taylor's omissions created an "adverse situation during the approach and would tend to push into the final phase of an ILS approach a considerable amount of the workload," which in normal situations should be spread out.[37] Plaintiffs argued that "when non-standard air traffic control services accumulate through each phase of an ILS approach culminating in the crew being confronted with an unexpected loss of visibility less than 13 seconds before intended touchdown, the end result, as in the case of Delta 723, is bound to be disastrous."[38]

Delta Air Lines' procedures require that if a crew loses visual contact with the runway after passing through decision height, the crew must perform a missed approach. Four factors constitute a successful approach:

1. The time at which the awareness of the need for a missed approach is realized,
2. Comprehension by the crew of the situation encountered,
3. The reaction time of the crew to that situation, and
4. The rapidity with which the missed approach procedure is initiated and carried out.[39]

Plaintiffs argued that the "cumulative effect of the non-standard air traffic control services which were rendered to D 723 occurred after the aircraft passed through decision height and entered a dense fog bank halfway across the channel between Castle Island and the airport which totally obscured the approach end to Runway 4R and destroyed the visual contact the crew was satisfied that it previous[ly] had acquired."[40]

Invoking the presumption of due care, which is premised on man's natural instinct for self-preservation and is couched in the theory that an individual will not purposefully expose himself to the possibility of serious bodily harm, plaintiff's wrote that "no pilot in his right mind would descend below decision height if he was not satisfied that he had the runway environment in sight. Since the crew was killed in the accident, it can be presumed that they were exercising due care for their own safety and fulfilling their duties and responsibilities at all times during the approach."[41]

If Taylor had not violated the mandatory procedures in handling Delta Flight 723, plaintiffs surmised that

> the conclusion is inescapable that the aircraft would have been stabilized on the localizer prior to reaching the approach gate, would have been stabilized on the glide slope at the outer marker at the prescribed altitude, would have achieved the desired approach speed at an earlier point in the approach, the crew would have been aware when the aircraft was more than 7 miles from the airport that a new weather factor had been injected, namely a heavy fog bank across the approach end of Runway 4R, the crew would have completed all required radio

frequency changes before reaching the outer marker, the desired objective of the *Manual* and operating pilots.[42]

Plaintiffs alleged that the opinion of the district court placed "considerable preoccupation on the part of the Court with the conduct of the Delta crew rather than with the evidence bearing on the alleged negligence of the United States. The issue of negligence on the part of the United States was the only matter in issue before the District Court."[43]

The plaintiffs implied that "the Court predetermined that the United States should not be held liable and the Opinion was then written to justify this conclusion.... Where the Court was unable to disregard the testimony of competent witnesses, the Court concluded that they simply should not be believed or otherwise discredited their testimony."[44]

Regarding the weather, there was a substantial amount of evidence that indicated a clearly defined fog bank approached and covered Runway 4R several minutes before Delta Flight 723 even began its approach. Air traffic controllers saw it clearly visible to them. Captain Young saw it, but his testimony was discredited because he did not report the condition to the tower.[45]

Plaintiffs noted that "the failure of Mr. Taylor, the Approach Controller, to make a report of an air traffic control 'incident' relating to Allegheny 666 did not cause the Court to discredit Taylor's testimony in that regard."[46]

Captain Ball testified that the initial weather report, "which simply contained the word 'fog,' would not have alerted the crew to the existence of a thick fog bank at the approach end of Runway 4R *was totally discredited by the District Court.*"[47]

Plaintiffs state there was no evidence presented that a fog bank was not there and that the court simply believed it was not there.[48] The court completely discredited the testimony of Harris Cusick, a trained weather observer, because Judge Caffrey believed him to be biased in favor of the plaintiffs because, as Caffrey wrote, "he was friendly with the family of one of the passengers and wanted to see them obtain a recovery."[49] Plaintiffs countered that the Chouinards had already settled their claims with Delta months earlier and this fact was known by the district court. The court chose to believe U.S. Weather Observer Harry Terban, "*who could not even see the approach end of Runway 4R from his observation point on a clear day due to building obstructions.*"[50]

The district court accepted the "skeleton opinion of United States witness Burke that the *Manual* violations of Mr. Taylor did not contribute to the crash of Delta 723,"[51] and those of United States witness Roseborough that if he had heard the word "fog" in the initial weather report, he would expect a fog bank at the end of the runway.[52] Plaintiffs argued that the court appeared to have disregarded or discredited all testimony that emphasized the density of the fog bank and the difference between a general fog condition and a dense fog bank. "It is significant that the District Court elected to believe both United States witnesses Roseborough and Burke on all these matters and rejected the testimony of all other witness which would support a contrary conclusion."[53]

The plaintiffs in Judge Caffrey's trial had called as their expert witness Roys C. Jones, an air safety consultant. Jones possessed extensive qualifications in air traffic control and aviation. He began his career in 1942 as an air traffic controller for the Civil Aeronautics Administration (CAA). He instructed Air Force personnel in the control of air traffic. In 1948, he became a senior controller for the CAA. The CAA chose him as one of four people to develop radar air traffic control for them. He was instrumental in the development of the trombone and "T" pattern of approach control that was still in use in 1973. In the early 1950s, he participated with the Air Defense Command in developing the security control of air traffic throughout the United States. He personally wrote Part 99 of the Federal Air Regulations and participated in drafting some parts of Part 91. In 1957, Jones was transferred to the New York regional office of the CAA as chief of the evaluation branch. During the next three years he was personally responsible for the evaluation and supervision of all ATC facilities in the eastern region. His area of responsibility included performance of ATC personnel and their adherence to standards. During this period, Jones evaluated tower and radar controllers both by flying into various facilities, including Logan, and observing controllers perform. In 1959 he was promoted to chief of the program planning branch in New York, where he worked on the modernization of an ATC plant and the design and construction of new facilities. This work included the design layout of radar equipment and tower positions. He also supervised the layout of the tower cab and TRACON room at Logan Airport. In 1962, he was promoted to the Office of International Affairs, representing the United States' position at international conferences. He was a licensed pilot, who had held a commercial pilot's license, single- and multi-engine ratings, and instrument ratings; he flew forty models of aircraft and had 2,500 hours as a pilot in command as of 1973. He was a member of the Society of Air Safety Investigators, appeared before the NTSB on numerous occasions, and investigated several accidents as a member of a team for the NTSB.[54]

On cross-examination at the original trial, Jones stated that he had never controlled traffic from a tower as an active journeyman controller and never controlled a civilian jet plane. He never qualified as a pilot on a jet plane.[55]

In their appellant brief, plaintiffs pointed out that the court permitted

Jones to testify "conditionally."[56] In his opinion, Judge Caffrey ruled that with respect to his qualifications to express an opinion as to the significance of a vector that directed an aircraft to capture the glide slope from above and at a wide angle of intercept, that Jones "is not qualified to express an opinion of any probative value to the court on this subject."[57] He found Jones's opinion, that the controller's failure to instruct Delta Flight 723 to switch to the tower frequency had a significant effect on the subsequent operations of his aircraft, was "not of a probative value."[58] "The Court totally rejected Mr. Jones' 'speculation as to the effect of AL 666 on Mr. Taylor's responsibilities,'" and gave "no weight" to his opinion that the late weather transmission was distracting to the crew.[59]

The plaintiffs argued that the district court was wrong in finding that the first duty of air traffic controllers was to separate aircraft and that disseminating weather information is of a lower priority where an air traffic controller is rendering air traffic control services to a number of aircraft within his control jurisdiction.

The principle that the duty of air traffic controllers is limited to the separation of aircraft, or that the duty to separate aircraft is the first and foremost duty of air traffic controllers, preempting their responsibilities to furnish information to pilots essential to the safe operation of their aircraft, had not found general judicial acceptance for the past twenty years until the decision of the court below in this case:

> The substantial evidence bearing on the negligence of the United States ... was not properly evaluated by the District Court because of the Court's one-sided view of the evidence in favor of the United States. This appears to have derived from the adherence by the Court to an outdated and no longer judicially acceptable concept of the duties and responsibilities of air traffic controllers.[60]

The outdated concept that plaintiffs believed Judge Caffrey adhered to in his ruling, at the expense of all precedent derived since then, was at the heart of the case he successfully argued twenty years earlier—*Smerdon*.

26

"The Interrelationship Existing Between Pilot and Ground Personnel Can Best Be Characterized as One Requiring Extensive Cooperation"

From the time Andrew Caffrey argued *Smerdon* to 1973 when, as a judge, he made his ruling in the Delta Flight 723 case, much had changed in aviation law, especially that aspect dealing with the responsibilities of air traffic controllers. In their appeal, the plaintiffs cited many cases within those twenty years to bolster their argument that Caffrey had gotten his decision wrong. Plaintiffs wrote, "A wealth of judicial precedent has evolved since *Smerdon* rejecting the traditional position of the United States that the duty of an air traffic controller is limited to 'maintaining control of the airways to prevent collision between aircraft under his control.'"[1]

The first case they cited was *Dickens v. United States* (1974). On April 22, 1970, a twin-engine Beach model D-5 airplane, serial number DH-257, bearing FAA registration number N1661, crashed near Austin Municipal Airport in Texas. Eight people were killed. The air controllers were partly at fault as they did not warn the pilot of the airplane that there was a possibility of wake turbulence from an aircraft that had landed before N1661. In their opinion, the Texas court wrote that "the air traffic controller is legally required to give all the information and warning specified in his manual."[2] Thus, the plaintiffs argued, "The Logan controllers were legally obligated to transmit the change in the weather on Runway 4R."[3]

The next case cited was *Ingham v. Eastern Air Lines, Inc.* (1967). This crash occurred at Idlewild International Airport (now Kennedy International Airport) on the evening of November 30, 1962. Eastern Air Lines Flight 512, a DC-7 aircraft, en route from Charlotte, North Carolina, to New York City, crashed while attempting to land on Runway 4R, which at the time of the accident was engulfed in swirling ground fog. Twenty-one passengers and four crew members perished, while some twenty-eight to thirty other persons were injured. In this case, the pilots of the Eastern airplane were found to be negligent as were the air traffic controllers. The court in this case specifically recognized the duty to warn of weather changes and required controllers to warn incoming pilots of those "subsequent changes which, under all the circumstances, the crew would have considered important both in determining whether to attempt a landing, and in preparing for the weather conditions most likely to be encountered near the runway."[4] There should be no doubt to the reasonable person that the crew of Delta Flight 723 would have considered a visible, moving, dense fog bank at the end of Runway 4R important.

The relationship between a controller and a pilot is a shared one. The case of *Richardson v. United States* (1974) highlights this relationship. A small aircraft crashed into San Francisco Bay after following a Boeing 707. The pilot flew dangerously low and got tangled in the wake vortex of the jet, thus losing control and crashing. Air traffic control did warn the pilot of the wake vortex, but by that time, the plane had crashed. It led to an opinion from the California court regarding the responsibilities between pilot and controller:

> The interrelationship existing between pilot and ground personnel can best be characterized as one requiring extensive cooperation. The pilot is in command of his aircraft and is directly responsible for its operation. However, before he may be held legally responsible for his aircraft, the pilot must be supplied with those pertinent facts that he is not in a position to ascertain for himself. Accordingly, the Air Traffic Controllers are under a duty to provide certain information and warnings to the pilot so that he has the opportunity to make a competent decision as to the operation of his aircraft. Thus the key element in distinguishing the respective duties of pilot and ATC relates to the ability of the former to perceive a potential danger without assistance from the latter. As a result, a balancing process is involved—the vantage point of the pilot will be weighed against the Tower's superior knowledge or awareness of the pilot's danger.[5]

Plaintiffs also cited *Neff v. United States* (1968). In this case, a Martin 404 aircraft took off during a strong thunderstorm and crashed just after liftoff from Rochester (New York) Airport. The court ruled that the pilots were unaware of a storm in the vicinity of the airport but that tower and weather personnel at Rochester Airport were aware of it and did not warn the aircraft about it. Had the pilots known, the court reasoned, they would not have taken off. There is a well-established presumption that airline pilots act with diligence and due care when their lives are at stake. The Washington, D.C., court ruled that,

> The Government had a duty to provide the taxiing plane with all significant relevant weather information. This duty existed whether or not specific regulations

or operating practices required that particular weather information be transmitted. If the Government has new, significant, and immediate relevant information that might have affected the crew's takeoff decision, and there was opportunity to provide it after the plane left the ramp, then the Government will be held liable, even though the regulation did not explicitly require the information to be transmitted.[6]

It is clear that from the time that Caffrey argued *Smerdon* until 1973, the responsibilities and duties of air traffic controllers had expanded and that they were required to provide pilots with information whether the *Manual* instructed them to do so or not. Even if the controllers were not required to provide information, *Ingham v. Eastern Air Lines* affirmed that "when the government undertakes to perform services, which in the absence of specific legislation would not be required, it will, nevertheless, be liable if these activities are performed negligently."[7]

On August 12, 1977, the U.S. court of appeals issued their decision. Questions of fact from a lower court are reviewed under the *clearly erroneous standard* in an appellate court. This standard is based on the proposition that the trial judge had presided over the trial, heard the testimony, and had the best understanding of the evidence. Thus, lower courts receive substantial deference from the appeals court. *Black's Law Dictionary* defines the "clearly erroneous standard." It reads: "Under this standard, a judgment will be upheld unless the appellate court is left with the firm conviction that an error has been committed."[8] In other words, the trial judge receives a wide latitude when making a decision and the Court of Appeals will only overturn if the trial judge has made a huge mistake.

There are two parts that the court of appeals analyzed in determining whether the controllers were concurrently liable (along with Delta Air Lines) in the Delta Flight 723 case. The first issue was whether the approach controller was "under a duty to provide the flight with those services which were omitted."[9] The second issue was whether the failure to give the information and instructions had a "reasonably close causal connection" with the accident.[10] The court of appeals ruled that

> we believe that the approach controller, Mr. Taylor, did have a duty to both the crew and the passengers to comply more fully than he did with the mandatory approach procedures outlined in the *Manual*; and we do not accept the district court's finding that concern about AL 666 was a satisfactory excuse for what was tantamount, on occasion, to forgetting D 723. The district court's finding, however, that the controller's omissions did not proximately cause the accident is not clearly erroneous and we therefore affirm.[11]

Clearly, the court of appeals did not agree with Judge Caffrey that Taylor's preoccupation with AL 666 excused him from performing other duties. They also agreed with the plaintiffs that Taylor "as much has admitted that he had simply forgotten about D 723."[12] However, they did agree with Caffrey that Taylor's omissions did not proximately cause the accident because his ruling was "not clearly erroneous."

When writing about the 45° intercept angle, the court of appeals agreed that because other aircraft had been given the same, or even greater, intercept angles, and because the angles suggested in the *Manual* are guides, and because pilots are free to refuse approaches they may find difficult to handle, the controller had complied with due care.[13]

The three other deviations were of a more serious concern to the court. They started with Taylor's failure to give Delta Flight 723 its position relative to the outer marker, "information which must be given to the crew before it is 3 miles from that point."[14] Delta's expert testified that "the aircraft's distance from the outer marker cannot be determined from aircraft instrumentation, and that that knowledge assists the crew in planning speed reduction in preparation for the approach."[15] Since this mandatory information is "customarily given to all incoming flights, the crew and, more especially, the passengers, were entitled to rely on Approach to give the position report."[16] The court was further troubled by

> the controller's decision to keep D 723 at 3,000 feet which forced [the] pilot to intercept the glide slope from above. While all agreed that occasionally pilots do this in making instrument approaches, there was also expert testimony that pilots are trained to intercept the glide slope from below. Further, the sophisticated instrumentation in airliners is designed with such an intercept in mind. Having to intercept from above greatly increases crew responsibilities and workload. It is, for example, difficult for a jet aircraft to descend rapidly and still keep the speed down to that desired during the approach. It is the purpose of the procedure to achieve the minimum crew workload by making this very exacting phase of flight as uncomplicated and routine as possible. That pilots should be capable of handling the additional problems caused by the intercept does not relieve the controller of his duty to the crew and passengers to adhere to procedures established to make the pilots' tasks simpler and to enhance safety.[17]

The court next dealt with Taylor's actions in not turning Delta Flight 723 over to the tower frequency. The court wrote,

> Mr. Taylor had no reason to keep D 723 on the Approach frequency. Once he discovered the flight was still with him, he turned it over to the Tower instead of undertaking to relay all communications himself. As a result, the crew was required to switch frequencies and to engage in last minute communications with the Tower at a time when concentration should have been focused on the instrument approach and, more particularly, on the mandatory altitude callouts as the aircraft reached decision height. This is the type of distraction that the procedure seeks to prevent.[18]

The court also stated that another consequence of the failure of Taylor to advise the pilot to go to the tower frequency was that the pilot of Delta Flight 723 did not learn of the fog bank on Runway 4R until twenty seconds before the crash.

> This is the kind of information crews can reasonably expect to receive from the local Tower controller who is in a position to observe and relay last minute weather changes that cannot be observed from the cockpit or the radar room. The duty to turn the aircraft over to the Tower at the appropriate time and place arises in part from the desirability of landing aircraft receiving information of a distinctly local character.[19]

The court observed that "the procedures here in question are made mandatory by the Government indicates not only that they are not to be treated casually but that pilots may rely on their being followed. Moreover, it is clear from all the testimony that the three omissions by Mr. Taylor contributed to an increased cockpit workload."[20]

These procedures, the court wrote,

> are important to the safe and efficient termination of flight conducted in instrument flight conditions.... We therefore cannot treat Mr. Taylor's lapses as trivial. Pilots and passengers alike are entitled to expect better service from the air traffic control system and, although pilots are undoubtedly responsible for the safety of their aircraft, controllers are concurrently responsible for adhering to procedures which minimize the difficulties for the crew.[21]

Because of these lapses, the Court ruled that "**the handling of D 723 was negligent**"[22] (emphasis added by author).

The Court then turned to Taylor's handling of AL 666. They came to a startlingly different conclusion than Judge Caffrey.

> After reviewing the record, we are left with a strong conviction that the separation problem created by Allegheny 666 did not justify the controller's failure to give D 723 standard service. Neither the transcripts of radio communications between Approach and the numerous aircraft it was handling, nor the testimony of Mr. Taylor supports the district court's finding that Mr. Taylor was involved in an emergency situation over a seven minute period.
> At approximately two and one half minutes after eleven, AL 666 reported in the Millis holding pattern at 8,000 feet, the same altitude already occupied by EA 1020. [D 723 was at the time on a radar vector flying a heading of 220°.] Approach responded quickly to the potentially serious conflict by directing both aircraft to leave the holding pattern, EA 1020 to the northeast toward Logan Airport and AL 666 to the southwest. It was soon determined that the two aircraft had followed instructions and the immediate problem was resolved. Approach continued to control other aircraft including D 723 to which new vectors were issued. At 11:03 a. m., Approach told AL 666 to reverse its course and to return

to Millis and hold. Mr. Taylor testified that at the time he gave this instruction he was satisfied that, from a separation point of view, it was safe to send AL 666 back to Millis. Almost a full minute later, at 11:04:27 a. m., Approach gave D 723 a final vector to intercept the localizer, but no instruction to descend and to go to Tower frequency, no clearance for the approach and no position report. Not only does it appear from the transcript that there was no reason for Mr. Taylor to withhold a complete standard clearance at that time, but Mr. Taylor himself testified that he had intended to give the full clearance and he didn't know why he had not. Nevertheless, Approach continued to handle the various aircraft in its jurisdiction, vectoring some in readiness for approaches and descending others within the holding pattern. During the early part of minute 11:05 a. m., five attempts to raise AL 666 and to reconfirm its altitude as 8,000 feet were unsuccessful. At 11:05 a. m., D 723 asked if it were cleared for the ILS approach and the response was "Yes, seven two three is cleared for ILS yes." Shortly thereafter, AL 666 reported that it was still at 8,000 feet and Approach took the time to discuss with the flight AL 666's expected approach clearance time. D 723 crossed the outer marker at 11:06:14, after discussion between Approach and AL 666 had, for the moment, ceased, yet Approach still did not turn D 723 over to the Tower and only did so when reminded by the local control coordinator. Mr. Taylor, in his testimony, as much as admitted that he had simply forgotten about D 723.[23]

While Taylor's handling of Delta Flight 723 was negligent, the court of appeals had to decide whether it was a proximate cause of the accident. In order to make this finding, the court must decide if his negligence was actionable. The following is a definition regarding this legal theory: "The actor's negligent conduct is a legal cause of harm to another if (a) his conduct is a substantial factor in bringing about the harm. Thus, it is not enough that the harm would not have occurred had the actor not been negligent. The act must be a 'substantial' cause in bringing about the harm."[24] In defining the term "substantial," courts use the following definition:

> The word "substantial" is used to denote the fact that the defendant's conduct has such an effect in producing the harm as to lead reasonable men to regard it as a cause, using that word in the popular sense, in which there always lurks the idea of responsibility, rather than in the so-called "philosophic sense," which includes every one of the great number of events without which any happening would not have occurred. Each of these events is a cause in the so-called "philosophic sense," yet the effect of many of them is so insignificant that no ordinary mind would think of them as causes.[25]

The court of appeals wrote that "the question of legal cause is for the factfinder; the issue involves essentially no legal judgments. Therefore, we must uphold the district court's finding unless it is clearly erroneous."[26] Delta and the individual plaintiffs "were thus required to convince the district court as factfinder that it was more likely than not that the omissions by Mr. Taylor were a 'substantial' cause of the accident. This they failed to do."[27]

The court of appeals ruled that Judge Caffrey was within his rights to disregard the testimony of Roys C. Jones. The appeals court held that

> The trial court has wide discretion in determining when a purported expert is sufficiently qualified to take the stand and render an opinion in a certain area.
>
> Here the court allowed Jones to testify, but as a factfinder found that his lack of recent experience as a controller and the fact that he had no flying experiences in commercial jets deprived his opinions of probative value. That finding was not clearly erroneous.[28]

The last issue the appeals court dealt with was the weather. The court wrote, "Thus, the really important factual question in this case is whether the crash would not have happened if D 723 had been switched to the Tower frequency at the outer marker and so had learned of the fog bank at the beginning of the final approach instead of a minute and a half later, less than 20 seconds before impact."[29] The court wrote that "there was some testimony that the weather report D 723 received early in its flight estimated 400 feet overcast, 1 ½ miles in fog would not have caused a pilot to be particularly concerned about the possibility of a missed approach, there was other testimony by witnesses for both Delta and the Government that, given the forecast for the area, the weather report received, and the unpredictability of fog, especially near the water, any pilot would be anticipating the possibility of a missed approach that morning."[30]

The pilots did not react to the tower transmission reporting the fog bank. Thus, the court could infer that the pilots did not think it had any bearing on their ability to land. The court continued,

> If, as one might conclude from both the testimony and the evidence of a lack of reaction to the additional weather information, the crew continued for some reason to believe that the weather at the airport was basically as it had been reported to them earlier, the argument that receiving news of the fog a minute and a half sooner would have made the crew act differently is not conclusive. The district court was entitled to find that Delta and the individual plaintiffs did not show by a preponderance of the evidence a causal connection between D 723's having learned of the fog bank only late in the approach and the accident.[31]

The court of appeals concluded that "without an established causal connection, the fact that the controller did not provide proper services in several respects is not a sufficient basis for holding the Government liable.

"*Affirmed.*"[32]

The court of appeals disagreed with Judge Caffrey and determined that there had been negligence on the part of the air traffic controller; however, they ruled that that negligence could not have caused the accident. For the plaintiffs, it was a pyrrhic victory. The plaintiffs made one last appeal to the U.S. Supreme Court, but on Tuesday, February 21, 1978, the Supreme Court refused to review the case and allowed the First District Court of Appeals decision to stand. By appealing to the Supreme Court and losing (again), the plaintiffs had used their last legal option to try and clear the crew of Flight 723 of fault in this accident.

27

"Short Circuits Caused by Particles Produced Mechanical Misalignment"

Or had they? While all legal proceedings had been exhausted in the civil matter against the United States, a product liability case would not fall under the legal concept of double jeopardy, and Sperry Rand could be sued for designing, producing, and marketing a defective flight director.

Boston Attorney Michael Latti had been involved in the Delta case from its beginning, assisting in the main case of *Delta v. United States* as well as its appeal. Latti specialized in maritime law. He got his start in that specialized area right out of law school when, for $25 a week, he followed other maritime lawyers, carrying their briefcases to court and listening to them argue cases at trial. Soon, Latti knew enough to start arguing maritime cases himself.[1]

Latti knew that the proximate cause of the accident in the Delta crash was the faulty flight director. He knew if he could get a judge, or a jury, to focus on the flaws of that flight director rather than on the actions of the crew, he might be able to convince them that the faulty design of the flight director, as well as the mistakes and actions of others, combined enough to distract the crew and cause the accident.

Latti filed the suit on behalf of plaintiff Virginia Streil, wife of Captain Streil; plaintiff Susan Burrill, wife of First Officer Burrill; plaintiff Frances Burrell, wife of trainee Joseph Burrell; plaintiff Ronald Moore, husband of Stewardesses Anna Moore; plaintiff Richard Humphreys, husband of Patricia Humphreys; plaintiffs John and Eloise Wilson, parents of Janice Wilson; and plaintiffs Marla and Robert Meehan, parents of minor passengers Perry Meehan and R. Bradley Meehan.

This product liability case alleged that the flight control system was defectively designed. Latti argued that the defects were "improper electrical loading of the mode selector switch, leading to the pulling off of metal particles within the switch."² Those particles, Latti alleged, caused short circuits, which "caused improper electrical signals to be sent to the command bars, resulting in improper command signals being given to the pilots."³

More specifically, Latti argued that there was a failure of the flight director to identify the operating mode being used, insufficient internal computer checks, and failure to provide a backup system in the event of computer malfunction. Sperry Rand also failed to design an annunciator panel, which would warn a pilot if he or she had selected the wrong mode, and they also failed to design a "reasonable interlock design in the mode selection."⁴ Sperry Rand also did not design the wiring to handle the "gains on the system which produced a coupling of the pitch and bank command signal either due to the mode selector switch or other malfunction."⁵

Latti also complained of the "inability of the system to warn of malfunctions in the mode selector switch." He stated that this particular flight director system "required an annunciator panel because of the bad switchology and potential malfunction of the switches."⁶

To successfully argue a product liability case, an attorney must establish that

1. The defendant owed the plaintiff a duty of care.
2. That the defendant was negligent in the discharge of that duty.
3. That defendant's negligence was the cause of plaintiff's damage
4. Plaintiff's actual and special damage.⁷

The law, in defining a duty of care, states that a

manufacturer or person who owns or controls an instrumentality which it knows, or with reasonable care should know, is dangerous in its nature or is in a dangerous condition and who disposes of it in a manner that it foresees, or in the exercise of reasonable care ought to foresee, will probably carry that thing into contact with some person, known or unknown, who will be ignorant of the danger, owes a legal duty to every such person to use reasonable care to prevent injury to him.⁸

The amount of care required of a manufacturer increases as the risk of injury increases. A product causing lesser harm will not require the same duty of care as that which may cause greater harm. It would be less.

Once the duty of care has been proven to be breached, "the plaintiff must show that his injury resulted from the dangerous design of the product."⁹ There is a difference, though, between a design defect and a manufacturer defect. In the case of a manufacturer defect, it is possible that the defect happened after the product left the manufacturer's hands. "If there is negligence of design it is apparent that the danger was not created by any subsequent handling of the product or by the wearing out with the lapse of time."¹⁰ The *American Law of Product Liability* states that

[t]he burden of proof of defective product design in a products liability case is on the plaintiff, and sufficient proof of the plaintiff's case is made when it is proved that the injury occurred while the product was being used in the way it was intended to be used, as a result of the defect in design and manufacture, of which the injured person was not aware, that made the product unsafe for its intended use.[11]

An interrogatory is a formal device used by attorneys to gather information. It is a written question that must be answered by the opposing party. Latti used his interrogatories of Sperry Rand representatives to devastating effect in proving design defects of their flight director. In question 18 of his interrogatory, he asked Sperry Rand officials to "[p]lease state whether the subject type flight director can be operating in a mode other than that indicated by the mode selector switch at a given time."[12]

Sperry Rand representatives answered that "[t]he Z5-534 Flight Director Computer can be operating in a mode other than that indicated by the position of the mode selector switch."[13] They went on to explain in the BL (blue left) position, there would be a heading error until the localizer deviation is less than 165 millivolts when the computer will switch to the localizer back course mode. They explained that in the VOR/LOC position, the "roll guidance will be heading error until the VOR deviation is less than 75 millivolts or the localizer deviation is less than 165 millivolts when the computer will switch to the VOR or localizer mode depending upon whether a VOR or localizer frequency has been selected."[14] In the "VOR/LOC position there will be no pitch guidance [bar biased from view] until the computer is in the localizer mode and the glide slope deviation is less than 22.5 millivolts, when the pitch guidance will be in the glide path mode. If the G/A [go-around] mode is selected the computer will remain in the go-around mode until the mode switch is moved to the FI [flight instruments] position or BL position, or SB [standby] position."[15]

Sperry Rand representatives also explained that to regain the APP mode from the G/A mode, a pilot must "rotate the switch counterclockwise to the FI, BL or SB position and then clockwise back to the APP position."[16]

Interrogatory question 22 underscored why the Sperry Rand flight director was so dangerous to passengers and crew: "[I]n which guidance mode [will] the command bars ... display command information when the mode selector switch has been turned from APP to G/A and then directly back to APP?"[17]

Sperry Rand officials replied that "[w]hen the mode switch has been turned from APP to G/A and then directly back to APP, the Z5-534 Flight Director Computer will generate signals in the G/A mode."[18] The APP mode and the G/A mode will give different commands for the pilot to follow. If he thinks he is in the APP mode but is really in the G/A mode, he will follow faulty commands that could lead to disaster.

Latti revealed how such a sophisticated device as a flight director could have so many defects in its design.

> The design defects and/or malfunctions associated with Sperry's Mode Selector Switch are the inappropriate electrical loading and mechanical misalignment of the Janco Component inducing unusual wear resulting in particles in the switch. Short circuits caused by particles produced by mechanical misalignment and/or improperly compensated inductive loads could have been precluded by proper electrical design and by separating the pitch and roll commands to separate wafers—a procedure introduced by Delta maintenance and now recommended but still not adhered to by Sperry. The failure to do this resulted in the coupling of the pitch and bank command signal.
>
> Further, any small inadvertent displacement of the switch out of the approach detent will inadvertently select the go-around mode even when the switch is returned to approach. Recycling of the switch is necessary in order to get a proper approach signal. This is further complicated by the fact that the detent is not pronounced on the mode selector switch.[19]

These design flaws led to the flight director exhibiting incorrect displays to the pilot. Without an annunciator panel warning them of the incorrect display or signifying what mode the selector switch was supposed to display, pilots would receive erroneous information from the director, which, if followed, could cause a plane to crash. In the case of Flight 723, Latti argued that "the incorrect display confused the crew, caused 'pilot overload' and directed an unstabilized approach which was causally related to the impact of the Delta Craft 222 with the sea wall before reaching the displaced threshold of Runway 4R at Logan Airport…."[20] Latti further stated that "[t]he conclusion that the Flight Director System, and Sperry Mode Selector Switch were not functioning properly at the start of the approach [at] 11:05:23 AM is based upon the unsuitability of the flight path set forth in the Flight Profile of the aircraft, Appendix G of the NTSB report."[21]

Clearly, Michael Latti's arguments that the flight director's design was defective reached the duty of care and negligence thresholds. Proving them in front of a jury was the least of Latti's worries. His biggest hurdle in winning this case rested with the trial judge because the trial judge in this case was the same as the one in the previous case of *Delta v. United States*, Judge Andrew Caffrey, and Caffrey had already ruled that the cause of the crash was the actions of the Delta Air Lines pilots. Latti's main legal strategy would be keeping opinions, conclusions, and findings of fact from that prior case from seeping over into this one as it would taint the jurors' impartiality. Neither Delta Air Lines nor the pilots of the aircraft had anything to do with this product liability case. With Caffrey as the judge again, if Latti could not keep Caffrey's opinions from that case out, he would have a difficult time winning this one.

The case, *Frances A. Burrell v. Delta Air Lines Inc., McDonnell Douglas Corp., Sperry Rand Corp., and Kollsman Instrument Corp.*, began on September 20, 1977, more than four years after the crash. Judge Caffrey empaneled six jurors and two alternates to render a verdict on the case. The first day of the trial encompassed opening arguments from both sides. From the call to order by the bailiff, the inclusion of the testimony from Captain Ball and other Delta pilots was uppermost in Caffrey's mind. Captain Ball had admitted in the previous trial that "a DC-9 aircraft could land without information from a flight director and that none of the non-standard elements provided by Air Traffic Control, standing alone, would have adversely affected a standard ILS approach."[22] This could be done by using a PDI along with radio transmitters on the ground.

As Latti revealed proposed testimony from one of his expert witnesses on conducting an ILS approach, the opposing attorney Maurice Noyer objected. Caffrey motioned for both men to approach the bench. Agreeing with Noyer, Caffrey warned Latti: "You have had enough background to know there's been a lot of—that the NTS [National Transportation Safety] Board has made a finding on this matter, and I made another; and what Delta did is extremely material to this case as is very clear."[23] It seemed that Judge Caffrey welcomed bringing the actions of the Delta crew into this product liability case.

When Latti tried to explain about customs and practices of using a flight director, Caffrey interrupted that Latti's proposed testimony was "directly contrary to the testimony of Captain Ball."[24] Michael Latti now had no doubt that Judge Caffrey would not exclude opinions, conclusions, and findings of fact from the first case from this trial. Latti had two strategies to contemplate: The first was to persuade Judge Caffrey to change his mind, and that was highly unlikely. The second was to move to have Caffrey recused from this case because he was biased and prejudicial to the plaintiffs. While the second alternative would be more desirable to Latti, it would take time and involve many others... unless he could persuade Caffrey to recuse himself.

The first day of the trial ended on a discordant note, and it concerned the transcripts of the cockpit voice recorder (CVR). Both attorneys had met prior to the trial and stipulated to, and filed with the court, a list of exhibits for both sides, which would allow two sets of CVR transcripts into evidence without objection. One of those exhibits was a transcript prepared by Latti's expert witness, Captain Donald McClure, a long-time captain for Eastern Air Lines and prominent member of ALPA. The NTSB prepared the other

27. "Short Circuits ... Produced Mechanical Misalignment"   225

set of transcripts for the defendants, which had been used in the previous trial. This agreement was mentioned in the defense's opening statement, and copies were given to the jury and Judge Caffrey without question.

Caffrey called both attorneys to the bench.

"I may be getting old and gray, but I have a distinct memory that the transcript which was put in evidence at the previous [trial] had cockpit area microphone number one as the source of the bugle call not once but twice. I noticed with interest that this has a question mark as to where it is coming from and I am curious <u>how we lost the identity of the microphone</u> between the previous trial and now," he said (emphasis in original transcript).[25]

"We haven't," Noyer responded. "This is Mr. McClure's. We also have in evidence the same transcript of the last trial," he explained.

"This doesn't jog my memory," Caffrey replied, holding up McClure's transcripts in his hand. "<u>A lot seems to be omitted</u>" (emphasis in original transcript).

"It is a difference of different interpretations," Noyer added eloquently.

"If this man prepared the transcript, <u>I hope he prepared a complete one</u> and <u>it looks like a lot of omissions to me</u>," Caffrey responded with displeasure (emphasis in original transcript).

Latti chimed in. "This is his interpretation as an expert."

"Who ruled him as an expert on cockpit voice recorders, sir?" Caffrey retorted.

"It is marked as an exhibit," Latti said smoothly.

"It hasn't been offered as an exhibit and," Caffrey explained, "<u>there are so many discrepancies between the one used by the National Transportation Safety Board and between Delta and the U.S.</u> that I have serious reservations about whether the jury should get <u>a tape that is so hacked up</u>," Caffrey retorted, frustrated with Latti (emphasis in original transcript).[26]

"As far as my understanding goes," Latti replied, "I thought all these documents that we have labeled are exhibits."

"I don't know what made them exhibits," Caffrey replied. "They are not exhibits until they are offered and ruled admissible," he added sharply.

Latti knew the procedures used to offer exhibits and evidence in trial. "It was by agreement of counsel that the exhibits were marked," he said.

"Counsel can agree to one and one being 902," Caffrey responded. "But unless some judge says okay that goes into evidence as 902, then they are not exhibits."

"All right," Latti conceded. "That changes our understanding, your Honor."

"I didn't have any understanding," Caffrey retorted. "The fact that they have been premarked doesn't ordinarily make them admissible."

"My understanding was that it was without objection."

Caffrey became indignant. "I am going to try to get the truth before this jury, if possible" (emphasis in original transcript).

"That is what I am doing," Latti replied.

"*I have some doubts this transcript here will help you to get a lot of truth,*" Caffrey replied, obviously piqued at Latti (emphasis in original transcript).

Latti tried explaining. "I think you can hear many of the transcriptions Mr. McClure has found and—"

Judge Caffrey cut him off. "We may have to have a voir dire," he said.[27] That meant Judge Caffrey would bring in Captain McClure and question him regarding his qualifications as a transcriber of CVRs. "I have heard it at least twice previously and had the transcripts under my nose for a long period of time and this transcript is quite surprising, very frankly, and that is what I am calling counsel here for, and I suggest you talk to your brother overnight," Caffrey explained, pointing to Noyer, "and see what you can do to resolve this."[28]

Latti responded dryly. "This would be the transcript we would offer, your Honor, as to what he would testify, and I will offer it through the Rules of Evidence."[29]

Caffrey had had enough of this issue. "I want to know what the other transcripts are which were available and who prepared them, because there is a substantial discrepancy and the question of whether the Captain is indicating bugle calls goes a long way as to whether he had a negative flippant attitude and that was a fact in an earlier decision" (emphasis in original transcript).[30]

Judge Caffrey was not going to exclude the opinions, conclusions, and findings of fact from the first case from this trial. If Caffrey persisted in this quest, Latti knew it might be grounds for an appeal if he lost. It could also lead to Caffrey's recusal from the case. Latti would be patient and wait a few days to see what course he would need to pursue.

28

"You Are Not Going to Get Rid of Me, Mike"

Michael Latti did not have to wait very long. Judge Caffrey entered the courtroom at 10:25 a.m. on September 21, 1977, a disappointed man. There was no doubt that he had been thinking about the first trial and his ruling against Delta. He obviously felt himself to be impartial enough in this case to render a verdict independent of the first one, although the plaintiffs would probably argue he could not. What he could not do, however, was pass the same standard he placed on himself to members of the jury if they knew about his prior verdict. Whether someone had mentioned it to him the night before or earlier that morning, or if he had merely figured it out himself, Caffrey realized he might have a problem with his continuance on the case.

Caffrey addressed the jury as the bailiff brought the court to order. "Before we resume the trial I have a question to ask the members of the jury: Since the beginning of this trial yesterday morning there has been some publicity about this case in the media, and by 'media' I include television, radio and the newspapers. I would like to know whether or not any member now sitting in the jury box has had any of the publicity come to his or her attention, the publicity which was in the media."[1]

"I saw the morning *Herald*," one of the jurors responded.

"I saw something in the Cambridge edition of the *Herald*," said another.

"Is there anybody else who saw anything?"

"The *Boston Globe*, this morning's *Globe*," said another.

Caffrey asked attorneys Latti and Noyer to approach the bench. He then called over the jurors who admitted they had read something in the morning papers. "Tell me what you saw," he asked one of the jurors.

"It said that the jury was selected and identified Sperry as the defendant and it gave the number of plaintiffs and said they claim that a piece of the Sperry equipment was defective, causing the accident," he told the judge.[2]

The next juror, incredibly, had brought the article he read into the courtroom and handed it to the judge. "This is what I read, your honor."

Another juror told Caffrey, "I read the article in which your name was mentioned."

Caffrey then asked the question that had bothered him the most. "Were you aware of the previous decision that was made in this case?"

"Yes," the juror replied.[3]

Both attorneys asked for that juror's dismissal.

Caffrey handed the decision of whether to continue to the attorneys. "Do you want to run for luck with this jury, or what do you want to do? You can walk over and tell him he is excused, in any event. The question is whether or not you can rely on his saying that he hasn't—"[4]

Noyer quickly chimed in. "I think we can, very frankly. I think that he was being very straight forward and candid." Noyer knew he had a sympathetic judge for his case. He did not want to lose Judge Caffrey.

"The question is whether the rest of them will go out and buy a *Globe* when they see the guy that has read the *Globe* has taken off," Caffrey explained.

Michael Latti saw his opening. Unlike Noyer, Latti had an unsympathetic judge for his case. He did not want to keep Judge Caffrey. "I would just as soon, your Honor, and I don't know how to say this, but I don't think you can avoid the problem except by transferring the case."[5]

Caffrey ignored Latti's statement as the clerk of the court walked over to Caffrey and told him three other jurors glanced at the articles also.[6] Half of the jurors had read the articles regarding the prior case. They all admitted they had read the *Herald*.

Caffrey thought for a minute. "The only thing I think is, if you want to kick it over a couple of weeks, we could talk to the *Globe* guy and say, 'Would you mind not putting this early a case in your coverage?' Maybe he doesn't realize that. He ought to know what he is doing. The reporters seem to be fairly decent around here. I was really taken by surprise when I read the thing.'"[7]

"May I suggest, your Honor," Latti began, "that, possibly, a transfer of the case to another jurisdiction might make more sense because of the publicity that has followed this case continually, and, also, there has been numerous articles in the newspaper during the time that your case was tried concerning the United States and the decision that you made and also the fact that it was mentioned in the newspaper that it was pilot error, and then we have the Circuit Court decision when it came down. We have copies of that."[8]

Caffrey thought how he could move the case yet not lose it himself. He wanted to remain on it. "I could transfer it to New Hampshire. I am on

28. "You Are Not Going to Get Rid of Me, Mike"   229

standby designation in New Hampshire. I won't have to find another judge. That is the problem: Sticking another judge with the case," he explained. Looking at the two attorneys he said, "I think you have enough of a question that we ought to have a mistrial, but I don't want to lose it. I don't want to put it off indefinitely, any more than you do, or presumably, do," he said looking at Latti.[9]

Noyer was getting nervous. A different judge would not help his case. "We have stipulations that have been made based upon prior testimony, which is going to require, in my estimation, someone who has a knowledge of the background of the case to try it. It would be impossible to go to a strange judge with this case and try it," he confessed.[10]

"I think if we went to New Hampshire the odds of getting that kind of publicity would be substantially lessened," Caffrey replied.[11]

Neither New Hampshire nor Judge Caffrey would do for Michael Latti. He kept on point regarding Judge Caffrey's lack of impartiality in the case. "I don't think Maine has had any contact with it at all, you Honor. Judge Genoux is up in Portland and he has a little familiarity with the case."[12]

Caffrey knew where Latti was going with his line of reasoning and admonished him. "You are not going to get rid of me, Mike, by transferring the case. If it goes to Maine, I will go to Maine with it. I would just as soon go to New Hampshire as go to Maine, although they are both up the road."[13]

Stung by Caffrey's response, Latti said, "I don't know why you apply [imply] that."[14]

"I think you know why I apply [imply] it. You haven't had too good a batting average on the earlier go-arounds."[15]

Latti held his ground. "I think if you hear this evidence that you will change your mind, the evidence that will come in, you will change your mind somewhat with respect to another cause of the accident."

"I didn't hear that thing about the little particles," Caffrey admitted. "That is a new claim. I am not going to find the facts, in any event, and I don't like—"[16]

"Excuse me, your Honor," Latti interrupted. "The only problem, your Honor, is if it is transferred to New Hampshire it would be awful. It might create a hardship on these plaintiffs to put their case together. There are ten or eleven experts from MIT that are going to testify."[17]

Caffrey considered that a lame excuse. "Well, from Boston to Concord is 75 miles. That is not a big deal. It is less of a deal than going to Portland, Maine, for your experts."

Noyer chimed in with his vote for Caffrey and Boston. "Since your Honor has indicated that we are going to be together still, I'd just as soon stay in Boston."

Caffrey agreed. "I would just as soon stay here and talk to the press and call them in before we start another trial and say, 'Look. Would you guys mind not putting this in.' I think they are fairly decent people."

"Right," Noyer responded.

"I can't believe they wouldn't do it, if we ask them," Caffrey insisted.[18]

This was not the issue for Michael Latti and the plaintiffs. They wanted a judge who would be impartial in this case and not rely on prior opinions or conclusions from a case not related to this product liability case. "About the prior ruling of the Court—"[19]

Caffrey shut him down. "I think it might be more effective than an instruction not to listen to the media or press. I think it might be more effective for me to ask the press people to just not put the prior decision in, so the jury will know about it. I think that would take care of it."[20] He then asked his clerk when they could reschedule the case.

"November 7," the clerk responded.

"All right," Caffrey said, satisfied he would still be on the case. "Does anyone want to move for a mistrial or do you want me to do it on my motion?"[21]

"It isn't my motion, your Honor," Noyer confessed. He wanted to stay with this jury and try the case now. "I don't think we have any choice."

"I think that unless, there be any doubt about it, on my own motion," Caffrey began, "where counsel seem to be uncertain of which way to move, that, in view of this publicity, I will declare a mistrial and reassign the case to start November 7th. I will undertake to contact the reporters that are in the building and ask them not to publicize this."[22] Caffrey admitted to the jury that he did not know that the probable cause of the accident recorded by the NTSB was publicized but stated he knew it from the non-jury trial he conducted and admitted to them he concluded the cause of the crash was pilot error. "I am going to declare a mistrial because of the publicity about the fact that in an earlier trial I made a ruling that pilot error was the cause of this crash. We will excuse you ladies and gentlemen from any further participation on this case. You are free to leave."[23]

Latti and Caffrey continued to go back and forth on the issue of impartiality and moving the case to another state. "Could your Honor also consider a very substantial voir dire by the Court concerning this, regardless of where the case is tried—whether it is here or in New Hampshire—to try to get some impartiality on this."[24]

"I will check this out with the reporters and I would tell them that we would like to try this case here. We can transfer it elsewhere if we have to. I will ask them if it will cause any great inhibition for them not to say what the previous decisions were, because the jury read it."[25]

Latti continued to ask about moving the trial to New Hampshire. Caffrey responded that they would just have to be more careful when interviewing the jurors for the next trial and ask them if they knew anything about the prior decisions in the previous case. Judge Caffrey could still not admit that he caused the mistrial by remaining as the presiding judge on the case.

* * *

Michael Latti had six weeks to maneuver Judge Caffrey off the case. Transcripts of the first day of the trial had been filed immediately, and Latti obtained a copy to start his motion against Judge Caffrey. He had Frances Burrell sign an affidavit on everything Judge Caffrey said regarding the prior case on the first day of the trial. One month later, on October 18, 1977, the transcripts of the second day of the trial were published, and Latti took them and incorporated all the prejudicial pretrial publicity the jurors shared at court on that day. On October 20, Latti filed his motion to have Judge Caffrey recused.

Caffrey did not want to transfer this case. He had been with it from the beginning and, from his spoken words, felt it needed a judge who had familiarity with the case so as not to start over. Surely, he also might have felt that if Latti won the case, then perhaps others would think that his original decision in *Delta v. United States* was wrong. He had some of his reputation riding on seeing this case through to the end; but Caffrey was a jurist first and foremost. His main obligation had always been to uphold the law no matter the outcome. Caffrey must have read the transcripts, as well as Latti's motion of recusal, and realized that, no matter what or how he ruled, another mistrial was likely due to his involvement in the first case. In the pursuit of justice, Andrew Caffrey put the law above his own desires. On October 21, one day after Latti filed his motion, Judge Caffrey, without comment, disqualified himself from the case.[26]

Judge Garrity next drew the case but was not able to take it. The Massachusetts District Court was slim on judges, and it was not until 1979 that, on the recommendation of Senator Ted Kennedy, President Jimmy Carter nominated David Nelson to the bench. He drew the case.

Judge Nelson was the first African American to serve as a federal judge in Massachusetts. He received his bachelor's degree in 1957 from Boston College and studied for the Roman Catholic priesthood before he entered Boston College Law School. After graduation, he joined the law firm of Crane, Inker, & Oteri. In 1971, Judge Nelson became chief of the Consumer Protection Division in the Office of the Attorney General in Massachusetts. In 1973, Governor Francis Sargent appointed him to the Massachusetts Superior Court where he remained until he became a district judge.[27]

Judge Nelson was an ideal appointment for Michael Latti. Through his work with the Consumer Protection Division, Nelson was familiar with product liability cases; but, even better, he did not know much, if anything, about the crash of Delta Flight 723. As the pretrial hearings got underway, Latti explained the history of the case.

"There was never any trial?" Judge Nelson asked as he looked through his notes on the case.[28]

"Myself and Mr. Tompkins brought a case against the United States, against the controllers," Michael Latti explained. Judge Caffrey wrote an opinion and found that they were not negligent. The case was appealed to the Circuit Court—[29]

Judge Nelson interrupted Latti. "He directed a verdict?"

"No," Latti answered. "It was jury waived, your Honor, as against the U.S. And what happened in that case, it went up to the Circuit Court of Appeals, and the Circuit Court of Appeals found negligence but found that it was not the proximate cause … so the case was tried to completion, and a great deal was written about it."[30]

Nelson asked what the plaintiffs alleged in this current case. Latti responded that "it is basically twofold: They were negligent in the manner in which they wired this switch, meaning the wire leading up to this mode selector switch; and, also, they were further careless and negligent in failing to give the crew a warning for the malfunction which was not easily recognizable," he said, summing up his argument.[31]

Latti then explained exactly what Sperry Rand had done with their wiring. "It is a basic engineering principle, known to all engineers, that when you have two contact points coming together—metal contact points—you are going to get wear and, over a period of years, you will get grinding off of metal particles."[32]

Giving a hint of the exhibits he would show at trial, Latti described his argument further. "Now, Sperry Rand knew this. Any good, competent engineer knows this. What the plaintiffs are saying is that Sperry Rand, and the wiring and the schematic drawings will show this, in the wiring of this switch they put in excessive inductive load, or, simply stated, at times there was too much current flowing through this switch."[33]

Latti explained how the switch worked. He spoke of the little points on the rotor switch being like the distributor on a car. He showed how you "rotate this switch and it touches little buttons and there is a rotor and that has little points on it also, and as you turn this, the rotor comes in contact with stationary points which is what they call a stator."[34] When someone turned it, you would break contact between the contact points and get a sudden discharge of energy or current, and the current that was discharged would arc and spark between the contact points. This would cause pitting, and now the points would become rough. "The rougher the points," he cautioned, "the more metal particles are ground off."[35] The particles would fuse together to the contact points, and every time the switch was rotated, the particles would move and create a kaleidoscope effect.

"At times you got a true reading and other times when you switched, you have different spots on the dial, you would have a short circuiting. And that's what happened here.... It was too much for them to handle and that's what happened here. And that's what we will find."[36]

"Guilty," Judge Nelson joked.

"Send them away," Latti retorted with a respectful grin.[37]

The courtroom laughed.

"The defense is that there is no evidence of any defect in the flight director?" Nelson asked Noyer.

"Yes, your Honor. The defense is that the flight director was working properly at the time of the accident; that the flight crew had mispositioned a switch which they are to use to get whatever signal, particular signal they want; that the switch was in the wrong position and it was determined by posit accident examination of the switch and also the defense, that the cause of the accident was solely and clearly pilot error."[38] Noyer still relied on the prior rulings of Judge Caffrey and the NTSB for his defense.

The legal maneuvering to get to trial on this case lasted several years with each side preparing depositions, interrogatories, interviewing witnesses, and readying exhibits. Latti lined up a *Who's Who* of witnesses to bolster his case—MIT professors, a former Apollo astronaut, NASA engineers.[39] They would testify that the pilots of Flight 723 became oversaturated with cockpit issues not of their own making, and they lost orientation and control of their aircraft.

Throughout 1980, there was not a lot of movement on the case as the attorneys prepared and practiced their legal maneuvers and Judge Nelson sat on other cases. By the spring of 1981, Latti filed a motion for a speedy trial. Nelson set a conference date of October 21 with the trial scheduled for November 16, 1981. The defendants filed a motion to extend the trial date to January 4, 1982, and Nelson granted it.[40] Each party put pressure on the other to reach a settlement before trial. The longer the defendants delayed the trial, the more impatient the plaintiffs may get for a quick settlement. Latti wanted to go to trial soon because he felt he had a strong case. The huge question for Latti, though, was whether Judge Nelson would allow any opinions, conclusions, or findings of fact from the first trial into this trial. If he did allow it, then Latti's case could be in tatters.

In the fall of 1981, the defendant, Sperry Rand, asked Judge Nelson for a summary judgment. A summary judgment is defined as "[a] judgment granted on a claim or defense about which there is no genuine issue of material fact and upon which the movant is entitled to prevail as a matter of law."[41] A summary judgment means that there are no disputed facts in the case that can be reasonably disputed, and in light of those facts, the party asking for the summary judgment feels they are entitled to judgment under the law. The attorneys for Sperry Rand asked for the summary judgment because they felt the case had already been decided by two courts and the evidence could not be reasonably disputed. They wanted Judge Nelson to forgo a trial and deliver a verdict in their favor.

On January 25, 1982, Judge Nelson ruled on the defendant's summary judgment motion. He denied it and ruled on the issue regarding the previous trials: "The facts found by the District Court and the decision of the Court of Appeals in the prior case cannot be construed to be determinative of the facts and issues in this case," Judge Nelson wrote.[42]

Judge Nelson had delivered the death blow to the defendants. They now knew that Latti had the upper hand. He had the expert witnesses, the record of malfunctions and the copy of the transcripts prepared by his expert witness that caused Judge Caffrey such consternation.

Judge Nelson advised the two parties to seek a settlement. Latti did not have to wait long for the offer. On February 5, 1982, the parties reported a settlement to Judge Nelson.

Sitting in his chambers, Judge Nelson asked Latti, "Are you prepared then to tell me the terms of the agreement, or what is it that you want to place on the record?"[43]

"Yes, Your Honor," Latti replied. "The total fund that has been created for settlement is 1.1 million dollars."[44]

"So, 1.1 million dollars," Nelson replied.

"Further," Latti responded, "I would like to report that that sum of money has been approved by all clients and referring counsel as well as the personal representatives of each one of the estates."[45]

On February 9, 1982, Judge Nelson approved the settlement and finally, after almost nine years of litigation, closed the case.[46] Michael Latti had achieved what the NTSB, the Massachusetts Aeronautical Commission, and Delta Air Lines and their attorneys could not. He showed that a defective design in the wiring of the flight director on Delta Ship 222 fed the pilots improper information and directions, which led to them flying their aircraft into the seawall short of Runway 4R, killing eighty-nine people.

Chapter Notes

Chapter 1

1. *The Fisheries of Gloucester from the First Catch by the English in 1623, to the Centennial Year, 1876* (Gloucester, MA: Procter Brothers, 1876), 58.
2. Marvin Bomber, Intra-Company Memo, Flight 723/31 Jul, August 2, 1973, 1.
3. "Wives Give Thanks for Impatience," *Brattleboro Reformer* (Vermont), August 1, 1973.
4. Marvin Bomber, Intra-Company Memo, Flight 723/31 Jul, August 2, 1973, 2.
5. "The Boeing 707," *The Aeroplane*, September 12, 1958, 457.
6. Terry Waddington, *McDonnell Douglas DC-9* (Miami, FL: World Transport Press, 1998), 11.
7. *Ibid.*, 10.
8. *Ibid.*, 11.
9. *Ibid.*, 15.
10. *Ibid.*, 19.
11. *Ibid.*
12. *Ibid.*
13. *Ibid.*
14. Rene J. Francillon, "The Early DC-9s: Success that Kills," *Airliners*, no. 77 (Sept./Oct. 2002): 66.
15. Terry Waddington, *McDonnell Douglas DC-9* (Miami, FL: World Transport Press, 1998), 123.
16. Rene J. Francillon, "The Early DC-9s: Success that Kills," *Airliners*, no. 77 (Sept./Oct. 2002): 66.
17. *Aircraft Accident Report: Delta Air Lines Inc. Douglas DC-9-31, N975NE, Boston, Massachusetts, July 31, 1973*, NTSB-AAR-74-3 (Washington, D.C.: National Transportation Safety Board, 1974), 35.

Chapter 2

1. *Report of Minor Accident, Accident No. 45-11-27-208, Army Air Forces* (Bryan, TX: AAFIS [IP], 1974).
2. *Ibid.*
3. *Aircraft Accident Report: Delta Air Lines Inc. Douglas DC-9-31, N975NE, Boston, Massachusetts, July 31, 1973*, NTSB-AAR-74-3 (Washington, D.C.: National Transportation Safety Board, 1974), 32.
4. Benjamin Taylor, "Crashed Jet's Co-Pilot Teethed on Airplanes," *Boston Globe*, August 2, 1973.
5. *Ibid.*
6. *Aircraft Accident Report: Delta Air Lines Inc. Douglas DC-9-31, N975NE, Boston, Massachusetts, July 31, 1973*, NTSB-AAR-74-3 (Washington, D.C.: National Transportation Safety Board, 1974), 32–33.
7. *Ibid.*, 33.
8. *Ibid.*, 33–34.
9. In Re Air Crash Disaster at Boston, Mass, Etc., 415 F. Supp. 206 (D. Mass. 1976).
10. *Ibid.*
11. *Ibid.*
12. *Ibid.*
13. *Ibid.*
14. *Ibid.*
15. *Ibid.*
16. *Ibid.*
17. "ICC, State Officials Die in Jet Crash," *Nashua Telegraph* (New Hampshire), August 1, 1973.
18. Gerard Weidmann, "Passengers on Ill-Fated Flight 723 Had Diverse Backgrounds," *Boston Globe*, August 2, 1973.
19. "ICC, State Officials Die in Jet Crash," *Nashua Telegraph* (New Hampshire), August 1, 1973.

20. Albert Nettel, "Cheats Death Earlier, Dies in Plane Crash," *Union Leader* (New Hampshire), August 1, 1973.
21. "Obituaries: Mass for Crash Victim John J. Ruane Is Today," *Boston Globe*, August 4, 1973.
22. "3 Burlington Architects Victims of Plane Crash," *Burlington Free Press*, August 1, 1973.
23. Gerard Weidmann, "Passengers on Ill-Fated Flight 723 Had Diverse Backgrounds," *Boston Globe*, August 2, 1973.
24. "Would-Be Travelers on Plane Feel Lucky," *Burlington Free Press*, August 2, 1973.
25. "3 Vermont Doll Collectors Die," *Burlington Free Press*, August 1, 1973.
26. "Winooskian Loses 3 in Crash," *Burlington Free Press*, August 1, 1973.
27. Brenda Newton McSweeney, Interviewed by Author, September 28, 2019, Boone, NC.
28. "Would-Be Travelers on Plane Feel Lucky," *Burlington Free Press*, August 2, 1973.
29. "Young Bride Is Victim in Tragedy," *Burlington Free Press*, August 1, 1973.
30. "Rites Planned for 4 Victims of Plane Crash," *Burlington Free Press*, August 7, 1973.
31. John Robinson and David Rogers, "Crash Victims Were Traveling on Business, Vacations, Errands," *Boston Globe*, August 2, 1973.
32. Al Larkin, "N.H. Aide and ICC Official among Crash Victims," *Boston Globe*, August 1, 1973.
33. "Sheridan Couple on Ill-Fated Plane," *Montana Standard*, August 1, 1973.
34. John Robinson and David Rogers, "Crash Victims Were Traveling on Business, Vacations, Errands," *Boston Globe*, August 2, 1973.
35. *Ibid.*
36. "$2 Million Suit in Boston Crash," *Rutland Daily Herald* (Vermont), August 24, 1973.
37. List of Victims, *Union Leader* (New Hampshire), August 1, 1973.
38. *Ibid.*
39. *Ibid.*
40. "Bennington Native Killed, among 88 Disaster Victims," *Bennington Banner* (Vermont), August 1, 1973.
41. Bill Cahill, "3d Tragedy Hits Gloucester Native," *Boston Globe*, August 3, 1973.
42. "Deaths and Funerals," *Burlington Free Press*, August 3, 1973.
43. List of Victims, *Union Leader* (New Hampshire), August 1, 1973.
44. "Ex-Middlebury Couple Die in Boston Plane Crash," *Hartford Courant* (Connecticut), August 3, 1973.
45. "Epping Woman, Miriam Jackson, Dies in Airliner," *Portsmouth Herald* (New Hampshire), August 1, 1973.
46. List of Victims, *Union Leader* (New Hampshire), August 1, 1973.
47. *Ibid.*
48. "Executive, Salesman among DC9 Victims," *Hartford Courant* (Connecticut), August 2, 1973.
49. John Robinson and David Rogers, "Crash Victims Were Traveling on Business, Vacations, Errands," *Boston Globe*, August 2, 1973.
50. List of Victims, *Union Leader* (New Hampshire), August 1, 1973.
51. *Ibid.*
52. Merrill Lockhard, "9 Area Residents Crash Victims," *Nashua Telegraph* (New Hampshire), August 1, 1973.
53. Marvin Bomber, Intra-Company Memo, Flight 723/31 Jul, August 2, 1973, 2.

Chapter 3

1. *Hearing before the Subcommittee on Investigations and Review of the Committee on Public Works and Transportation, House of Representatives, Ninety-Fourth Congress, on Adequacy of Air Service to New England*, Robert E. Jones, Chairman (Washington, D.C.: U.S. Government Printing Office, 1976), 4.
2. Air Commerce Act of 1926.
3. Civil Aeronautics Act of 1938.
4. John M. Lindsey, "The Legislative Development of Civil Aviation, 1938–1958," *Journal of Air Law and Commerce*, no. 28 (1962): 1.
5. Claude E. Puffer, *Air Transportation* (Philadelphia: Blakiston Books, 1941), 94.
6. *Ibid.*
7. Dorothy Campbell Culver, *Civil and Commercial Aviation, A Guide to Federal Legislation and Administrative Agencies* (Berkeley: Bureau of Public Administration, University of California, 1940), 59.
8. Federal Aviation Act of 1958.
9. *Ibid.*
10. *Ibid.*
11. Charles Schultze, *Hearings before the Committee on Government Operations,*

United States Senate, Eighty-Ninth Congress, on a Bill to Establish a Department of Transportation, and for Other Purposes, John L. McClellan, Chairman (Washington, D.C.: U.S. Government Printing Office, 1966), 79.

12. Ibid., 268.

13. Hearings before the Committee on Commerce, United States Senate, Ninety-Third Congress, on Activities of the National Transportation Safety Board, Warren Magnuson, Chairman (Washington, D.C.: U.S. Government Printing Office, 1973), 58.

14. Ibid., 594.

15. Ibid.

16. Ibid., 269.

17. Department of Transportation Act: Report to Accompany 15963, United States Congress, House Committee on Government Operations.

18. Hearing before the Subcommittee on Investigations and Review of the Committee on Public Works and Transportation, House of Representatives, Ninety-Fourth Congress, on Adequacy of Air Service to New England, Robert E. Jones, Chairman (Washington, D.C.: U.S. Government Printing Office, 1976), 4.

19. Ibid., 43.

20. Hearing before the Subcommittee on Aviation of the Committee on Commerce, United States Senate, Ninety-Third Congress, on Adequacy of Northern New England Air Service, Warren Magnuson, Chairman (Washington, D.C.: U.S. Government Printing Office, 1972), 337.

21. Ibid.

22. Civil Aeronautics Board Reports, Economic Cases of the CAB Mar–Jul, 1972 (Washington, D.C.: U.S. Government Printing Office, 1972), 651.

23. Ibid., 653.

24. Ibid., 624.

25. Hearing before the Subcommittee on Investigations and Review of the Committee on Public Works and Transportation, House of Representatives, Ninety-Fourth Congress, on Adequacy of Air Service to New England, Robert E. Jones, Chairman (Washington, D.C.: U.S. Government Printing Office, 1976), 105.

CHAPTER 4

1. In Re Air Crash Disaster at Boston, Mass., July 31, 1973, 412 F. Supp. 959 (D. Mass. 1976).

2. "Would-Be Travelers on Plane Feel Lucky," Burlington Free Press, August 2, 1973.

3. Marvin Bomber, Intra-Company Memo, Flight 723/31 Jul, August 2, 1973, 2.

4. Dorothy Nelkin, JETPORT: The Boston Airport Controversy (New Brunswick, NJ: Transaction Books, 1974), 47.

5. Ibid., 49.

6. Ibid.

7. Ibid., 50.

8. Ibid.

9. Ibid., 52.

10. Ibid., 53.

11. Ibid., 52.

12. Ibid., 55.

13. Ibid.

14. Ibid., 56.

15. Ibid.

16. Ibid., 63.

17. Ibid., 64.

18. Ibid., 80.

19. Ibid., 69.

20. Ibid., 70–71.

21. Ibid., 71.

22. Ibid.

23. Ibid., 74.

24. Ibid., 83.

25. Ibid.

26. Ibid.

27. Ibid., 84.

28. Ibid., 107.

29. Ibid., 111.

30. Ibid.

31. Ibid., 110.

32. Ibid., 114.

33. Ibid., 115.

34. Ibid.

CHAPTER 5

1. Charles Taylor, Excerpts from Fourth Day of Trial, January 2, 1976, In Re Air Crash Disaster at Boston, Mass., July 31, 1973, 412 F. Supp. 959 (D. Mass. 1976).

2. Brief for Plaintiffs, Appellants, Karen Haelsig McMaster, Etc. v. United States of America, Appeal from the United States District Court for the District of Massachusetts, No. 76–1270, 561 F.2d 381 (1st Cir. 1977).

3. Charles Taylor, Excerpts from Fourth Day of Trial, January 2, 1976, In Re Air Crash Disaster at Boston, Mass., July 31, 1973, 412 F. Supp. 959 (D. Mass. 1976).

4. Jeffrey McDonald, Excerpts from Fourth Day of Trial, January 2, 1976, In Re

Air Crash Disaster at Boston, Mass., July 31, 1973, 412 F. Supp. 959 (D. Mass. 1976).
  5. *Ibid.*
  6. Harry Terban, Excerpts from Fourth Day of Trial, January 2, 1976, In Re Air Crash Disaster at Boston, Mass., July 31, 1973, 412 F. Supp. 959 (D. Mass. 1976).
  7. *Ibid.*
  8. *Ibid.*
  9. Stephanie M. Peters, "Charles Arena, 76; Fire Chief at Logan Was Safety Expert," *Boston Globe*, October 23, 2009.
  10. Geoffrey Keating, Excerpts from Fourth Day of Trial, January 2, 1976, In Re Air Crash Disaster at Boston, Mass., July 31, 1973, 412 F. Supp. 959 (D. Mass. 1976).
  11. Harris Cusick, Excerpts from Fourth Day of Trial, January 2, 1976, In Re Air Crash Disaster at Boston, Mass., July 31, 1973, 412 F. Supp. 959 (D. Mass. 1976).
  12. *Ibid.*
  13. *Ibid.*
  14. *Ibid.*
  15. *Ibid.*
  16. *Ibid.*
  17. National Transportation Safety Board, "Transcription of Cockpit Voice Recorder Data, Fairchild A-100, S/N 2634, Delta Airlines Douglas Model DC-9–31, N975NE, Flight 723, Logan International Airport, Boston, Massachusetts, July 31, 1973," 1.
  18. *Ibid.*, 3.
  19. Jean Theodore Lee and Carl Max Reber, *Pilots' Weather Handbook* (Washington, D.C.: U.S. Government Printing Office, 1955), 74.
  20. National Weather Service, Definition of Advection Fog.
  21. National Transportation Safety Board, "Transcription of Cockpit Voice Recorder Data, Fairchild A-100, S/N 2634, Delta Airlines Douglas Model DC-9–31, N975NE, Flight 723, Logan International Airport, Boston, Massachusetts, July 31, 1973," 3.
  22. In Re Air Crash Disaster at Boston, Mass, Etc., 415 F. Supp. 206 (D. Mass. 1976).
  23. National Transportation Safety Board, "Transcription of Cockpit Voice Recorder Data, Fairchild A-100, S/N 2634, Delta Airlines Douglas Model DC-9–31, N975NE, Flight 723, Logan International Airport, Boston, Massachusetts, July 31, 1973," 3.
  24. *Ibid.*, 6.

Chapter 6

  1. National Transportation Safety Board, "Transcription of Cockpit Voice Recorder Data, Fairchild A-100, S/N 2634, Delta Airlines Douglas Model DC-9–31, N975NE, Flight 723, Logan International Airport, Boston, Massachusetts, July 31, 1973," 6.
  2. *Ibid.*
  3. *Ibid.*, 7.
  4. *Ibid.*
  5. *Ibid.*
  6. *Ibid.*
  7. *Ibid.*
  8. *Ibid.*
  9. *Ibid.*, 9.
  10. *Ibid.*, 10.
  11. *Ibid.*
  12. *Ibid.*
  13. *Ibid.*, 11.
  14. *Ibid.*
  15. *Ibid.*, 12.
  16. *Ibid.*, 13.
  17. *Ibid.*
  18. *Ibid.*, 14.
  19. *Ibid.*
  20. *Ibid.*
  21. *Ibid.*, 15.
  22. *Ibid.*
  23. *Ibid.*
  24. *Ibid.*
  25. Charles Taylor, Excerpts from Fourth Day of Trial, January 2, 1976, In Re Air Crash Disaster at Boston, Mass., July 31, 1973, 412 F. Supp. 959 (D. Mass. 1976).
  26. *Ibid.*
  27. *Ibid.*
  28. *Ibid.*, 491–492.
  29. Charles Taylor, Approach Control Transmission, Channel 1, Logan Airport, July 31, 1973.

Chapter 7

  1. Jeffrey McDonald, Local Control Transmission, Logan Airport, July 31, 1973.
  2. *Ibid.*
  3. Charles Taylor, Approach Control Transmission, Logan Airport, July 31, 1973.
  4. National Transportation Safety Board, "Transcription of Cockpit Voice Recorder Data, Fairchild A-100, S/N 2634, Delta Airlines Douglas Model DC-9–31, N975NE, Flight 723, Logan International Airport, Boston, Massachusetts, July 31, 1973," 13.
  5. *Ibid.*

6. *Ibid.*
7. Charles Taylor, Approach Control Transmission, Logan Airport, July 31, 1973.
8. *Ibid.*
9. *Ibid.*, 14.
10. *Ibid.*
11. *Ibid.*
12. *Ibid.*
13. *Ibid.*, 15.
14. *Ibid.*
15. Daniel Tucker, Excerpts from Fourth Day of Trial, January 2, 1976, In Re Air Crash Disaster at Boston, Mass., July 31, 1973, 412 F. Supp. 959 (D. Mass. 1976), 422a.
16. *Ibid.*
17. National Transportation Safety Board, "Transcription of Cockpit Voice Recorder Data, Fairchild A-100, S/N 2634, Delta Airlines Douglas Model DC-9-31, N975NE, Flight 723, Logan International Airport, Boston, Massachusetts, July 31, 1973," 15.
18. *Ibid.*
19. Jeffrey McDonald, Excerpts from Fourth Day of Trial, January 2, 1976, In Re Air Crash Disaster at Boston, Mass., July 31, 1973, 412 F. Supp. 959 (D. Mass. 1976), 392a.
20. Daniel Tucker, Excerpts from Fourth Day of Trial, January 2, 1976, In Re Air Crash Disaster at Boston, Mass., July 31, 1973, 412 F. Supp. 959 (D. Mass. 1976), 428a.
21. National Transportation Safety Board, "Transcription of Cockpit Voice Recorder Data, Fairchild A-100, S/N 2634, Delta Airlines Douglas Model DC-9-31, N975NE, Flight 723, Logan International Airport, Boston, Massachusetts, July 31, 1973," 15.
22. *Ibid.*
23. *Ibid.*
24. *Ibid.*
25. "Wheels Fail, Plane Lands Safely Here: Foam on Runway Aids Viscount Carrying 23 from Boston," *Baltimore Sun*, September 5, 1961.
26. *Ibid.*
27. *Ibid.*
28. *Ibid.*
29. *Ibid.*
30. National Transportation Safety Board, "Transcription of Cockpit Voice Recorder Data, Fairchild A-100, S/N 2634, Delta Airlines Douglas Model DC-9-31, N975NE, Flight 723, Logan International Airport, Boston, Massachusetts, July 31, 1973," 18.
31. *Ibid.*
32. *Ibid.*
33. *Ibid.*
34. *Ibid.*
35. Warren Hutchins, Excerpts from First Day of Trial, December 29, 1975, In Re Air Crash Disaster at Boston, Mass., July 31, 1973, 412 F. Supp. 959 (D. Mass. 1976), 166a.
36. Richard Giroux, Excerpts from First Day of Trial, December 29, 1975, In Re Air Crash Disaster at Boston, Mass., July 31, 1973, 412 F. Supp. 959 (D. Mass. 1976), 176a.
37. *Ibid.*
38. Thomas Karakoudas, Excerpts from First Day of Trial, December 29, 1975, In Re Air Crash Disaster at Boston, Mass., July 31, 1973, 412 F. Supp. 959 (D. Mass. 1976), 186a.
39. William Rae, Excerpts from First Day of Trial, December 29, 1975, In Re Air Crash Disaster at Boston, Mass., July 31, 1973, 412 F. Supp. 959 (D. Mass. 1976), 188a.
40. *Ibid.*, 190a.
41. National Transportation Safety Board, "Transcription of Cockpit Voice Recorder Data, Fairchild A-100, S/N 2634, Delta Airlines Douglas Model DC-9-31, N975NE, Flight 723, Logan International Airport, Boston, Massachusetts, July 31, 1973," 18.
42. *Ibid.*, 19.
43. *Aircraft Accident Report: Delta Airlines Inc. Douglas DC-9-31, N975NE, Boston, Massachusetts, July 31, 1973*, NTSB-AAR-74-3 (Washington, D.C.: National Transportation Safety Board, 1974), 11.

CHAPTER 8

1. Mark Dunton, "October 1973—The End of the Sixties?," *The National Archives* (blog), October 14, 2013, https://blog.nationalarchives.gov.uk/october-1973-the-end-of-the-sixties/.
2. J. Anthony Lukas, *Common Ground* (New York: Random House, 1985), 27.
3. *Ibid.*
4. *Ibid.*
5. *Ibid.*
6. *Ibid.*
7. Geoffrey Keating, Excerpts from Fourth Day of Trial, January 2, 1976, In Re

Air Crash Disaster at Boston, Mass., July 31, 1973, 412 F. Supp. 959 (D. Mass. 1976).
8. *Ibid.*
9. *Ibid.*
10. *Aircraft Accident Report: Delta Airlines Inc. Douglas DC-9-31, N975NE, Boston, Massachusetts, July 31, 1973*, NTSB-AAR-74-3 (Washington, D.C.: National Transportation Safety Board, 1974), 73.
11. Federal Aviation Administration, "Transcription of Local and Ground Controller Channels," Logan Airport Tower, July 31, 1973.
12. *Ibid.*
13. *Ibid.*
14. *Ibid.*
15. *Ibid.*
16. Geoffrey Keating, Excerpts from Fourth Day of Trial, January 2, 1976, In Re Air Crash Disaster at Boston, Mass., July 31, 1973, 412 F. Supp. 959 (D. Mass. 1976).

Chapter 9

1. Harry Terban, Excerpts from Fourth Day of Trial, January 2, 1976, In Re Air Crash Disaster at Boston, Mass., July 31, 1973, 412 F. Supp. 959 (D. Mass. 1976), 608a.
2. *Ibid.*
3. *Ibid.*, 610a.
4. *Ibid.*, 613a.
5. *Aircraft Accident Report: Delta Airlines Inc. Douglas DC-9-31, N975NE, Boston, Massachusetts, July 31, 1973*, NTSB-AAR-74-3 (Washington, D.C.: National Transportation Safety Board, 1974), 25.
6. *Ibid.*
7. Harry Terban, Excerpts from Fourth Day of Trial, January 2, 1976, In Re Air Crash Disaster at Boston, Mass., July 31, 1973, 412 F. Supp. 959 (D. Mass. 1976), 632a.
8. Federal Aviation Administration, "Transcription of Local and Ground Controller Channels," Logan Airport Tower, July 31, 1973.
9. *Ibid.*
10. *Ibid.*
11. *Ibid.*
12. *Ibid.*
13. *Ibid.*
14. *Ibid.*
15. *Ibid.*
16. *Ibid.*
17. *Ibid.*
18. Charles T. Arena, Excerpts from First Day of Trial, December 29, 1975, In Re Air Crash Disaster at Boston, Mass., July 31, 1973, 412 F. Supp. 959 (D. Mass. 1976), 608a.
19. Federal Aviation Administration, "Transcription of Local and Ground Controller Channels," Logan Airport Tower, July 31, 1973.
20. *Ibid.*
21. *Ibid.*
22. *Ibid.*
23. *Ibid.*
24. *Ibid.*
25. *Ibid.*
26. *Ibid.*
27. *Ibid.*
28. *Ibid.*
29. *Ibid.*
30. *Ibid.*
31. *Ibid.*

Chapter 10

1. Ed Susman and Marshall Molloy, "Vermont Survivor Found Fully Conscious," *Burlington Free Press*, August 1, 1973.
2. *Ibid.*
3. Harris Cusick, Excerpts from First Day of Trial, December 29, 1975, In Re Air Crash Disaster at Boston, Mass., July 31, 1973, 412 F. Supp. 959 (D. Mass. 1976), 221a.
4. Brenda Newton McSweeney, Interviewed by Author, September 28, 2019, Boone, NC.
5. *Ibid.*
6. Harris Cusick, Excerpts from First Day of Trial, December 29, 1975, In Re Air Crash Disaster at Boston, Mass., July 31, 1973, 412 F. Supp. 959 (D. Mass. 1976), 221a.
7. Herber Black, "Plane Crash Survivor Fights for Life," *Boston Globe*, August 3, 1973.
8. Boston Fire Department, Data Processing and Records Memo, Subject: Delta Airline Disaster, September 10, 1973.
9. Mike Barnicle, "'I Never Felt so Helpless…,'" *Boston Globe*, August 1, 1973.
10. *Ibid.*
11. *Ibid.*
12. *Ibid.*
13. "Obituaries: Frank Mahoney, *Globe* Reporter Known for Fire Expertise; Dead at 63," *Boston Globe*, December 10, 1991.
14. *Ibid.*
15. "NATO Defense Plans Found in

Wreckage of Delta Jet," *Boston Globe*, August 1, 1973.
16. Joe Pilati, "Papers from Delta Crash to Go to Washington," *Boston Globe*, August 2, 1973.
17. *Ibid.*
18. *Ibid.*
19. "NATO Defense Plans Found in Wreckage of Delta Jet," *Burlington Free Press*, August 1, 1973.
20. Jean Cole, "A Grim and Lengthy Ritual Is Conducted as Casualties Are Brought to Mortuary," *Boston Herald American*, August 1, 1973.
21. *Ibid.*
22. Michael Luongo, Medical Examiner for Suffolk County, Memo to Edward T. Sullivan, November 13, 1973.
23. *Ibid.*
24. *Ibid.*
25. *Ibid.*
26. *Ibid.*
27. *Ibid.*

Chapter 11

1. *Hearings before the Committee on Commerce, United States Senate, Ninetieth Congress, First Session, on Nominations of Joseph P. O'Connell, Francis H. McAdams, Rear Adm. Louis N. Thayer, John H. Reed, Oscar Laurel, Warren G. Magnuson, Chairman* (Washington, D.C.: U.S. Government Printing Office, 1967), 1.
2. *Ibid.*
3. *Ibid.*, 10.
4. *Ibid.*
5. *Ibid.*, 3.
6. *Ibid.*, 4.
7. *Ibid.*, 5.
8. *Ibid.*, 12.
9. "Safety Board Free From 'Pressures,'" *Austin American* (Texas), June 16, 1969.
10. *Ibid.*
11. Jack Anderson, "Brother Act," *Bell-McClure Syndicate*, August 1, 1967. Accessed from American University Archives & Special Collections.
12. *Ibid.*
13. *Ibid.*
14. *Ibid.*
15. *Ibid.*
16. *Ibid.*
17. "Safety Board Free From 'Pressures,'" *Austin American* (Texas), June 16, 1969.
18. *Ibid.*

19. *Hearings before the Committee on Commerce, United States Senate, Ninety-First Congress, First Session, on Nomination of Isabel Burgess to Be a Member of the National Transportation Safety Board, Warren G. Magnuson, Chairman* (Washington, D.C.: U.S. Government Printing Office, 1969), 39.
20. Jean Tro Williams, "The Senator Is Going to Washington," *Arizona Republic*, September 7, 1969.
21. *Hearings before the Committee on Commerce, United States Senate, Ninety-First Congress, First Session, on Nomination of Isabel Burgess to Be a Member of the National Transportation Safety Board, Warren G. Magnuson, Chairman* (Washington, D.C.: U.S. Government Printing Office, 1969), 41.
22. *Ibid.*
23. *Ibid.*
24. *Ibid.*
25. *Hearings before the Committee on Commerce, United States Senate, Ninety-Third Congress, First Session, on Activities of the National Transportation Safety Board, Warren G. Magnuson, Chairman* (Washington, D.C.: U.S. Government Printing Office, 1973), 77.
26. *Aircraft Accident Report: Allegheny Airlines Inc. Douglas DC-9, N988VJ, and a Forth Corporation Piper PA-28, N7374J, Near Fairland, Indiana, September 9, 1969*, NTSB-AAR-70-15 (Washington, D.C.: National Transportation Safety Board, 1970), 2.
27. "Shelby Crash Report Delay Request Told," *Indianapolis Star*, October 7, 1970.
28. "FAA Asks Safety Board to Alter Critical Report," *Miami Herald*, October 14, 1970.
29. *Hearings before the Committee on Commerce, United States Senate, Ninety-Third Congress, First Session, on Activities of the National Transportation Safety Board, Warren G. Magnuson, Chairman* (Washington, D.C.: U.S. Government Printing Office, 1973), 78.
30. *Ibid.*
31. *Ibid.*
32. *Ibid.*
33. *Ibid.*

Chapter 12

1. Richard P. Nathan, *The Plot that Failed: Nixon and the Administrative*

Presidency (New York: John Wiley & Sons, 1975), 8.
2. *Ibid.*, 50.
3. *Hearings before the Committee on Commerce, United States Senate, Ninety-Third Congress, First Session, on Activities of the National Transportation Safety Board, Warren G. Magnuson, Chairman* (Washington, D.C.: U.S. Government Printing Office, 1973), 81.
4. *Ibid.*, 77.
5. Richard P. Nathan, *The Plot that Failed: Nixon and the Administrative Presidency* (New York: John Wiley & Sons, 1975), 69.
6. *Ibid.*
7. *Hearings before the Committee on Commerce, United States Senate, Ninety-Third Congress, First Session, on Activities of the National Transportation Safety Board, Warren G. Magnuson, Chairman* (Washington, D.C.: U.S. Government Printing Office, 1973), 57.
8. *Ibid.*, 112.
9. *Ibid.*, 60.
10. *Ibid.*, 110.
11. *Ibid.*, 111.
12. *Ibid.*, 10.
13. *Ibid.*, 49.
14. *Ibid.*, 84.
15. *Ibid.*, 70.
16. *Ibid.*, 8.
17. *Ibid.*, 9.
18. *Ibid.*, 12.
19. *Ibid.*
20. *Ibid.*, 14.
21. *Ibid.*
22. James McCord, Letter to the Honorable Judge John Sirica, March 19, 1973.
23. *Hearings before the Committee on Commerce, United States Senate, Ninety-Third Congress, First Session, on Activities of the National Transportation Safety Board, Warren G. Magnuson, Chairman* (Washington, D.C.: U.S. Government Printing Office, 1973), 82.
24. *Ibid.*, 105–106.
25. John Harris, "Boston Democrat May Second Nixon," *Boston Globe*, August 22, 1956.
26. *Hearings before the Committee on Commerce, United States Senate, Ninety-Third Congress, First Session, on Activities of the National Transportation Safety Board, Warren G. Magnuson, Chairman* (Washington, D.C.: U.S. Government Printing Office, 1973), 24.
27. *Ibid.*, 22.
28. *Ibid.*, 139.
29. David J. Wimer, Letter to General Alexander Haig, Subject: National Transportation Safety Board (Non-Republican Vacancy), Undated.
30. *Ibid.*
31. *Ibid.*
32. *Ibid.*
33. *Ibid.*

CHAPTER 13

1. Robert Anglin, "88 Killed in Crash at Fogbound Logan; Delay in Alarm Is Target of Probers," *Boston Globe*, August 1, 1973.
2. Dr. Joshua Tofield, Interviewed by Author, November 16, 2019, Telephone.
3. Jeffrey R. Saffle, MD, "The 1942 Fire at Boston's Cocoanut Grove Nightclub," *The American Journal of Surgery* 166 (December 1993).
4. Dr. Charles Lund and Dr. Newton Browder, "Estimation of the Area of Burns," Lund and Browder Chart.
5. Dr. Joshua Tofield, Interviewed by Author, November 16, 2019, telephone.
6. *Ibid.*
7. *Ibid.*
8. *Ibid.*
9. Eric Perez, MD, Maryann Foley, and Ronald Karlin, MD, "Classification of Burns," *Health Encyclopedia*, University of Rochester Medical Center. Accessed November 20, 2019. https://www.urmc.rochester.edu/encyclopedia/content.aspx?ContentTypeID=90&ContentID=P09575.
10. Dr. Joshua Tofield, Interviewed by Author, November 16, 2019, telephone.
11. *Ibid.*
12. *Ibid.*
13. "Person Next to Him Saved His Life," *Brattleboro Reformer* (Vermont), August 3, 1973.
14. Jude Aldo and John W. King, "The Management of Burns with Silver Nitrate Solution," *Journal of the National Medical Association* 58, no. 3 (1966): 165.
15. *Ibid.*
16. Ray and Leona Chouinard, Interviewed by Author, July 17, 2019.
17. Brenda Newton McSweeney, Interviewed by Author, September 28, 2019, Boone, NC.
18. Dr. Joshua Tofield, Interviewed by Author, November 16, 2019, Telephone.

19. Brenda Newton McSweeney, Interviewed by Author, September 28, 2019, Boone, NC.
20. *Ibid.*
21. Bryan Marquard, "Obituary: John Constable; Brought Surgery Talents to Remote Villages," *Boston Globe*, August 5, 2016.
22. Bob Hohler, "'73 Delta Crash, the Reality Lingers," *Boston Globe*, July 31, 1993.
23. Prudy Cullen, Interviewed by Author, November 11, 2020, Telephone.

Chapter 14

1. Michael Luongo, Medical Examiner for Suffolk County, Memo to Edward T. Sullivan, November 13, 1973.
2. *Ibid.*
3. Boston Fire Department, Data Processing and Records Memo, Subject: Delta Airline Disaster, September 10, 1973.
4. *Ibid.*
5. *Ibid.*
6. Michael Luongo, Medical Examiner for Suffolk County, Memo to Edward T. Sullivan, November 13, 1973.
7. Robert J. DiGrazia, Police Commissioner, Letter to Director Edward T. Sullivan, Administrative Services, September 26, 1973.
8. Francis Guiney, Executive Director, Health and Hospitals, Departmental Communication, Subject: Air Disaster, August 28, 1973.
9. James Donohue, "Flight from Burlington Ends in Catastrophe at Boston; 88 Die as Plane Crashes in Fog," *Rutland Daily Herald* (Vermont), August 1, 1973.
10. *Hearing before the Committee on Commerce, United States Senate, Ninety-Fourth Congress, First Session, on Nomination of Isabel Burgess, to Be a member of the National Transportation Safety Board, Warren G. Magnuson, Chairman* (Washington, D.C.: U.S. Government Printing Office, 1975), 5.
11. *Ibid.*, 31.
12. *Ibid.*, 41.
13. Michael McGovern, "'Thousands of Pieces' in Boston Jet Crash," *Daily News*, August 2, 1973.
14. *Ibid.*
15. *Ibid.*
16. "Board Says Crash Study to Take about 6 Months," *Burlington Free Press*, August 2, 1973.
17. *Ibid.*
18. Nancy Green, "Kennedy Told Logan Traffic Control Chaotic," *Boston Globe*, March 13, 1970.
19. *Ibid.*
20. *Ibid.*
21. *Ibid.*
22. *Ibid.*
23. *Ibid.*
24. *Ibid.*
25. *Ibid.*
26. "Sharp Takeoff Rule," *Spokesman-Review* (Washington state), October 31, 1970.
27. *Ibid.*
28. *Ibid.*
29. Jerry Moskel, "FAA Orders New Flying Procedures," *Battle Creek Enquirer* (Michigan), October 31, 1970.
30. *Ibid.*
31. *The Long Range Needs of Aviation: Report of the Aviation Advisory Commission*, Crocker Snow, Chairman, January 1973.
32. Crocker Snow, Letter to Isabel Burgess, August 3, 1973.
33. "Editorials: Logan Crash Raises Questions," *North Adams Transcript* (Massachusetts), August 3, 1973.
34. *Ibid.*
35. *Ibid.*
36. *Ibid.*
37. *Ibid.*
38. U.S. Environmental Protection Agency, *Public Hearings on Noise Abatement and Control, Vol. VII, Physiological and Psychological Effects, Boston Massachusetts, October 28 and 29, 1971* (Washington, D.C.: U.S. Government Printing Office, 1971).
39. Isabel Burgess, Letter to Crocker Snow, August 13, 1973.

Chapter 15

1. *Hearings before the Committee on Interstate and Foreign Commerce, House of Representatives, and the Sub-Committee on Transportation and Aeronautics on Aviation Safety, Ninetieth Congress, First and Second Sessions* (Washington, D.C.: U.S. Government Printing Office, 1968), 30.
2. *Ibid.*
3. *Ibid.*
4. *Ibid.*
5. *Ibid.*

6. *Ibid.*
7. *Ibid.*
8. *Ibid.*
9. *Ibid.*
10. *Ibid.*
11. *Ibid.*, 39.
12. *Hearings before the Committee on Interstate and Foreign Commerce, House of Representatives, on Aviation Facilities Maintenance and Development, Ninety-First Congress, First Session* (Washington, D.C.: U.S. Government Printing Office, 1969), 84.
13. *Ibid.*
14. *Ibid.*
15. William Kling, "Tells Steps to Cut Landing Air Crashes," *Chicago Tribune*, January 22, 1969.
16. "Crashes in Landing Spur Demand for Greater Vigilance," *Miami Herald*, January 23, 1969.
17. *Aircraft Accident Report: Piedmont Airlines Fairchild-Hiller 2276, N712U, Charleston, West Virginia, August 10, 1968*, NTSB-AAR-69-6 (Washington, D.C.: National Transportation Safety Board, 1969), 11.
18. Bill Eaton, "850 Feet Too Low at Coyote Pt.," *Oakland Tribune*, November 27, 1968.
19. *Aircraft Accident Report: North Central Airlines, Inc., Convair 580, N2045, O'Hare International Airport, Chicago, Illinois, December 27, 1968*, NTSB-AAR-70-27 (Washington, D.C.: National Transportation Safety Board, 1970), 1.
20. "NWMC Forms Plan, Zoning Committee," *Daily Herald* (Illinois), February 23, 1968.
21. "Claim Radar Could Have Avoided NC Plane Crash," *Oshkosh Northwestern* (Wisconsin), January 9, 1969.
22. *Ibid.*
23. "Crash Investigation Starts," *Billings Gazette* (Montana), December 29, 1968.
24. Marvin Miles, "Airport May Be Death Trap by 1975, Controllers Claim," *Los Angeles Times,* February 4, 1969.
25. *Ibid.*
26. *Ibid.*
27. Andrew Wilson, "MP Joins Pilots' Radar Protest," *Observer* (United Kingdom), January 19, 1969.
28. George Rhodes, "Approach Radar Reactivated by FAA," *San Francisco Examiner*, February 5, 1969.
29. *Ibid.*

Chapter 16

1. "Statement," *Manchester Union Leader* (New Hampshire), August 1, 1973.
2. "Mayor Sets Civic Tribute for Plane Crash Victims," *Manchester Union Leader* (New Hampshire), August 2, 1973.
3. "Vermont Churches Mourn Victims of Plane Crash," *Brattleboro Reformer* (Vermont), August 4, 1973.
4. Richard Weintraub, "Services in 3 States for Crash Victims," *Boston Globe*, August 5, 1973.
5. *Ibid.*
6. *Ibid.*
7. "Delta in Court Action; Marshfield Man 'Stable,'" *Rutland Daily Herald* (Vermont), August 8, 1973.
8. John Reed, Chairman, NTSB, Letter to FBI Director William Ruckelshaus, June 5, 1973.
9. Margo Miller, "Delta to Get Crash Tapes after FAA," *Boston Globe*, August 7, 1973.
10. *Ibid.*
11. Vern Haughland, "Changes Recommended for TriStar Airliners," *York Dispatch* (Pennsylvania), May 3, 1973.
12. "'Simple Device' Missing from Ill-Fated Jumbo Jet," *Akron Beacon Journal* (Ohio), March 9, 1973.
13. Verne O. Williams, "EAL Failed to Get New Warning Unit," *Miami News*, March 8, 1973.
14. "'Simple Device' Missing from Ill-Fated Jumbo Jet," *Akron Beacon Journal* (Ohio), March 9, 1973.
15. *Ibid.*
16. *Ibid.*
17. "New Field for Ralph Nader," *Herald News*, March 17, 1973.
18. Robert Anglin, "Runway Reopens as Secrecy Shrouds Probe of Logan Crash," *Boston Globe*, August 3, 1973.
19. William Hines, "Commercial Flying's Big Problem: Safety in Last Few Minutes," *Morning News*, August 8, 1973.
20. *Ibid.*
21. Robert Anglin, "Runway Reopens as Secrecy Shrouds Probe of Logan Crash," *Boston Globe*, August 3, 1973.
22. *Ibid.*

Chapter 17

1. James H. Hammond, "Logan's Prob-

lem: One Safety System and Two Runways," *Boston Globe*, May 13, 1974.
2. *Ibid.*
3. *Ibid.*
4. *Ibid.*
5. *Ibid.*
6. Kenneth Campbell, "Safety, Costs on 2 Runways," *Boston Globe*, May 9, 1974.
7. James H. Hammond, "Logan's Problem: One Safety System and Two Runways," *Boston Globe*, May 13, 1974.
8. "Tragic Hub Airport Crash Boiling into Political Battle," *Fitchburg Sentinel* (Massachusetts), August 4, 1973.
9. *Ibid.*
10. *Ibid.*
11. *Ibid.*
12. "Safety Improvements Get Priority at Logan," *Burlington Free Press*, August 4, 1973.
13. *Aircraft Accident Report: Delta Airlines Inc. Douglas DC-9-31, N975NE, Boston, Massachusetts, July 31, 1973*, NTSB-AAR-74-3 (Washington, D.C.: National Transportation Safety Board, 1974), 18.
14. *Ibid.*, 63.
15. *Ibid.*
16. *Ibid.*
17. *Ibid.*, 64.
18. *Ibid.*
19. *Ibid.*
20. Thomas Oliphant, "Bad Weather Limits Urged on Delta DC9s," *Boston Globe*, August 30, 1973.
21. *Aircraft Accident Report: Delta Airlines Inc. Douglas DC-9-31, N975NE, Boston, Massachusetts, July 31, 1973*, NTSB-AAR-74-3 (Washington, D.C.: National Transportation Safety Board, 1974), 65.
22. *Ibid.*

CHAPTER 18

1. Dr. Joshua Tofield, Interviewed by Author, November 16, 2019, Telephone.
2. "Passenger Who Perished May Have Saved Chouinard's Life," *Bennington Banner* (Vermont), August 4, 1973.
3. *Ibid.*
4. *Ibid.*
5. *Ibid.*
6. "Marshfield Is Hopeful Chouinard Will Survive," *Burlington Free Press*, August 6, 1973.
7. *Ibid.*

8. Brenda Newton McSweeney, Interviewed by Author, September 28, 2019, Boone, NC.
9. *Ibid.*
10. *Ibid.*
11. Ray and Leona Chouinard, Interviewed by Author, July 17, 2019.
12. "Boston Crash Survivor Said in 'Good Spirits,'" *Bennington Banner* (Vermont), August 21, 1973.
13. *Ibid.*
14. *Ibid.*
15. *Ibid.*
16. *Ibid.*
17. Gloria Negri, "While City Sleeps, Drama at MGH," *Boston Globe*, September 17, 1973.
18. "Debridement of a Wound, Infection, or Burn," Reasons of Procedure, *Health Library*, Beth Israel Lahey Health, Winchester Hospital. Accessed April 19, 2019. www.winchesterhospital.org/health-library/article?id=2010813273.
19. Dr. Joshua Tofield, Interviewed by Author, November 16, 2019, Telephone.
20. *Ibid.*
21. *Ibid.*
22. *Ibid.*
23. "Sgt. Chouinard Keeps Up Lengthy Fight for Life," *Burlington Free Press*, September 17, 1973.
24. *Ibid.*
25. *Ibid.*
26. *Ibid.*
27. *Ibid.*
28. *Ibid.*
29. *Ibid.*
30. *Ibid.*

CHAPTER 19

1. *Hearings before the Committee on Commerce, United States Senate, Ninety-Third Congress, First Session, on Activities of the National Transportation Safety Board*, Warren G. Magnuson, Chairman (Washington, D.C.: U.S. Government Printing Office, 1973), 133.
2. Department of Transportation Act: Report to Accompany 15963, United States Congress, House Committee on Government Operations.
3. Francis McAdams, *Notation 120-A-A Aircraft Accident Report—Piedmont Airlines Inc., Boeing 727/Lanseair Inc. Cessna 310*

N3121S Mid-Air Collision, Hendersonville, North Carolina, July 19, 1967 (Washington, D.C.: Department of Transportation, National Transportation Safety Board, November 15, 1968), 1–2.

4. C.O. Miller, "The Bureau of Aviation Safety and the Accident Prevention System," Remarks at the Flight Safety Foundation Luncheon, Anaheim, California, October 9, 1968.

5. Ibid.

6. J.J. O'Connell, "The Bureau of Aviation Safety and the Accident Prevention System," Remarks at the Flight Safety Foundation Luncheon, Anaheim, California, October 9, 1968.

7. C.O. Miller, "The Bureau of Aviation Safety and the Accident Prevention System," Remarks at the Flight Safety Foundation Luncheon, Anaheim, California, October 9, 1968.

8. *Hearings before the Committee on Commerce, United States Senate, Ninety-Third Congress, First Session, on Activities of the National Transportation Safety Board, Warren G. Magnuson, Chairman* (Washington, D.C.: U.S. Government Printing Office, 1973), 116.

9. Ibid.
10. Ibid.
11. Ibid.
12. Ibid.
13. Ibid.

14. *Hearings, Committee on Commerce, United States Senate, Ninety-Third Congress, Second Session, "To Amend the DOT Act in Order to Establish the National Transportation Safety Board as an Independent Agency in the Executive Branch of the Government"* (Washington, D.C.: U.S. Government Printing Office, 1974), 1.

15. Ibid.
16. Ibid.

17. *An Aircraft Accident Involving Piedmont Airlines Inc., Boeing 727, N68650, and Lanseair, Cessna 310, N3121S, at Hendersonville, North Carolina, July 19, 1967*, Public Hearing, Docket No. SA-400 (Washington, D.C.: Department of Transportation, 1967), 600.

18. Ibid.

19. William Ringle, "Hearing Starts Tuesday on Fatal Burlington-to-Boston Flight," *Burlington Free Press*, September 14, 1973.

20. Robert E. Walsh, "Delta Pilot Knew Plane Off Course, Prober Testifies," *Boston Globe*, September 18, 1973.

21. Ibid.
22. Ibid.

23. David Rogers, "Delta Log Reveals Pilots Knew They Were Off Course," *Boston Globe*, September 19, 1973.

24. Robert E. Walsh, "Delta Pilot Knew Plane Off Course, Prober Testifies," *Boston Globe*, September 18, 1973.

25. *Aircraft Accident Report: Delta Airlines Inc. Douglas DC-9-31, N975NE, Boston, Massachusetts, July 31, 1973*, NTSB-AAR-74-3 (Washington, D.C.: National Transportation Safety Board, 1974), 7.

26. Robert E. Walsh, "Delta Pilot Knew Plane Off Course, Prober Testifies," *Boston Globe*, September 18, 1973.

27. Ibid.
28. Ibid.
29. Ibid.

30. Betsy Buechner, "Delta Jet Told of Fog 20 Seconds before Crash," *Burlington Free Press*, September 20, 1973.

31. Ibid.

32. Betsy Buechner, "Final Minute Apparently Crucial for Delta Pilots," *Burlington Free Press*, September 19, 1973.

33. Betsy Buechner, "Delta Jet Told of Fog 20 Seconds before Crash," *Burlington Free Press*, September 20, 1973.

34. Ibid.
35. Ibid.
36. Ibid.

37. *Aircraft Accident Report: Delta Airlines Inc. Douglas DC-9-31, N975NE, Boston, Massachusetts, July 31, 1973*, NTSB-AAR-74-3 (Washington, D.C.: National Transportation Safety Board, 1974).

38. Betsy Buechner, "Delta Jet Told of Fog 20 Seconds before Crash," *Burlington Free Press*, September 20, 1973.

39. David Rogers, "Shifting Fog Bank May Have Cut Down Delta Jet's Visibility," *Boston Globe*, September 20, 1973.

40. "Malfunctions, Misunderstandings Plague Logan Tower at Time of Delta Crash," *Berkshire Eagle* (Massachusetts), September 20, 1973.

41. Ibid.

42. Robert Walsh, "Pilot Says Visibility Good Just Prior to Delta Crash," *Boston Globe*, September 20, 1973.

43. Ibid.
44. Ibid.
45. Ibid.

Chapter 20

1. Robert E. Walsh, "Despite Crash Testimony of Others: Five Delta Pilots Say Equipment in Order," *Boston Globe*, September 21, 1973.
2. *Ibid.*
3. *Ibid.*
4. "Pilot Error Blamed for DC-9 Crash," *Brattleboro Reformer* (Vermont), September 25, 1973.
5. *Ibid.*
6. *Ibid.*
7. "State Report on Delta Crash Termed Surprising," *Boston Globe*, September 25, 1973.
8. *Ibid.*
9. *Ibid.*
10. *Aircraft Accident Report: Delta Airlines Inc. Douglas DC-9-31, N975NE, Boston, Massachusetts, July 31, 1973*, NTSB-AAR-74-3 (Washington, D.C.: National Transportation Safety Board, 1974), 7.
11. William Ringle, "Runway Visibility Reports Can Suffer from Time Lag," *Burlington Free Press*, September 26, 1973.
12. *Aircraft Accident Report: Delta Airlines Inc. Douglas DC-9-31, N975NE, Boston, Massachusetts, July 31, 1973*, NTSB-AAR-74-3 (Washington, D.C.: National Transportation Safety Board, 1974), 7.
13. *Ibid.*, 17–18.
14. *Ibid.*, 16.
15. *Ibid.*, 69.
16. *Ibid.*, 14.
17. *Ibid.*, 69.
18. *Ibid.*, 15–16.
19. *Ibid.*
20. *Ibid.*, 16.
21. *Ibid.*
22. *Ibid.*, 17.
23. David Rogers, "Delta Crew Skipped 3 Altitude Reports, Panel Told," *Boston Globe*, September 26, 1973.
24. *Ibid.*
25. *Ibid.*
26. William Ringle, "Pilot Told Seconds before Crash that Visibility Was 6,000 Feet," *El Paso Times*, September 27, 1973.
27. *Ibid.*
28. *Ibid.*
29. *Ibid.*
30. David Rogers, "Delta Crew Skipped 3 Altitude Reports, Panel Told," *Boston Globe*, September 26, 1973.
31. William Ringle, "Delta Introduces Some Surprise Evidence," *Burlington Free Press*, September 27, 1973.
32. *Ibid.*
33. *Ibid.*
34. *Ibid.*
35. *Ibid.*
36. *Ibid.*
37. David Rogers, "Federal Hearings on Delta Crash Recessed 'Indefinitely,'" *Boston Globe*, September 28, 1973.
38. *Ibid.*
39. *Ibid.*
40. *Ibid.*
41. David Rogers, Interviewed by Author, April 7, 2020, Telephone.

Chapter 21

1. David Rogers, "13 Were Impatient, Decided Not to Sit, Wait for Flight 723," *Boston Globe*, August 1, 1973.
2. *Ibid.*
3. Betty Sproston, "Marion Smith Estate Described as Collectors' Treasure Trove," *Burlington Free Press*, October 3, 1973.
4. *Ibid.*
5. *Ibid.*
6. Dr. Thomas Dodson, Interviewed by Author, November 14, 2019, Telephone.
7. *Ibid.*
8. *Ibid.*
9. Dr. Joshua Tofield, Interviewed by Author, November 16, 2019, Telephone.
10. *Ibid.*
11. Brenda Newton McSweeney, Interviewed by Author, September 28, 2019, Boone, NC.
12. *Ibid.*
13. Harris Cusick, Excerpts from First Day of Trial, December 29, 1975, In Re Air Crash Disaster at Boston, Mass., July 31, 1973, 412 F. Supp. 959 (D. Mass. 1976).
14. *Ibid.*
15. Nancy Pomerene, "Chouinard's Death Moves Man Who Found Him," *Boston Globe*, December 13, 1973.
16. Brenda Newton McSweeney, Interviewed by Author, September 28, 2019, Boone, NC.
17. *Ibid.*
18. Tim Maclay, Interviewed by Author, May 11, 1973, Telephone.
19. *Ibid.*
20. David Rogers, "No Metal Particles Found in Switch Taken from Wrecked Delta Jetliner," *Boston Globe*, October 4, 1973.
21. *Ibid.*

Chapter 22

1. "Chouinard Improving, Is Taking Solid Food," *Burlington Free Press*, November 29, 1973.
2. *Ibid.*
3. Ray and Leona Chouinard, Interviewed by Author, July 17, 2019.
4. Dr. Joshua Tofield, Interviewed by Author, November 16, 2019, Telephone.
5. Brenda Newton McSweeney, Interviewed by Author, September 28, 2019, Boone, NC.
6. Ray and Leona Chouinard, Interviewed by Author, July 17, 2019.
7. "The Condition of Crash Survivor at Lowest Point," *Rutland Daily Herald* (Vermont), December 5, 1973.
8. *Ibid.*
9. "Chouinard Loses Battle for Life," *Burlington Free Press,* December 12, 1973.
10. Nancy Pomerene, "Chouinard's Death Moves Man Who Found Him," *Boston Globe*, December 13, 1973.
11. Brenda Newton McSweeney, Interviewed by Author, September 28, 2019, Boone, NC.
12. "Chouinard Buried with Honors," *Burlington Free Press*, December 17, 1973.
13. Dr. Joshua Tofield, Interviewed by Author, November 16, 2019, Telephone.
14. Ken Botwright, "Return of Special Logan Radar Urged," *Boston Globe*, December 24, 1973.
15. *Ibid.*
16. *Ibid.*
17. *Ibid.*
18. *Ibid.*
19. *Ibid.*
20. *Ibid.*
21. *Ibid.*
22. "Delta Claims FAA Fault in Logan Crash Suit," *Rutland Daily Herald* (Vermont), January 15, 1974.
23. *Ibid.*
24. *Ibid.*

Chapter 23

1. *Aircraft Accident Report: Delta Airlines Inc. Douglas DC-9-31, N975NE, Boston, Massachusetts, July 31, 1973*, NTSB-AAR-74-3 (Washington, D.C.: National Transportation Safety Board, 1974), 1.
2. *Ibid.*, 13.
3. *Ibid.*
4. *Ibid.*
5. *Ibid.*
6. *Ibid.*, 14.
7. *Ibid.*
8. *Ibid.*
9. *Ibid.*, 19.
10. *Ibid.*
11. *Ibid.*
12. *Ibid.*
13. *Ibid.*, 20.
14. *Ibid.*, 21.
15. *Ibid.*
16. *Ibid.*
17. *Ibid.*, 22.
18. *Ibid.*
19. *Ibid.*
20. *Ibid.*, 23.
21. *Ibid.*
22. *Ibid.*
23. *Ibid.*, 24.
24. *Ibid.*, 25.
25. *Ibid.*
26. *Ibid.*
27. *Ibid.*
28. *Ibid.*, 20.
29. *Ibid.*, 21.
30. *Ibid.*, 27.
31. *Ibid.*, 67.
32. *Ibid.*
33. *Ibid.*, 73.
34. *Ibid.*
35. *Ibid.*, 74.
36. *Ibid.*
37. *Ibid.*, 74–75.
38. *Ibid.*, 76.
39. *Ibid.*
40. *Ibid.*
41. *Ibid.*
42. *Ibid.*, 69.
43. *Ibid.*
44. *Ibid.*
45. Letter from Alexander Butterfield, Administrator Federal Aviation Administration, to John Reed, Chairman, National Transportation Safety Board, June 26, 1974.

Chapter 24

1. "Delta Settles 11 Lawsuits," *Times Argus* (Vermont), June 30, 1975.
2. *Ibid.*
3. "Caffrey, Andrew Augustine," Federal Judicial Center. Accessed on May 15, 2019. fjc.gov/node/1378706.
4. Smerdon v. United States, 135 F. Supp. 929 (D. Mass. 1955). https://law.justia.com/

cases/federal/district-courts/FSupp/135/929/1617569/.
5. *Ibid.*
6. *Ibid.*
7. *Ibid.*
8. *Ibid.*
9. *Ibid.*
10. *Ibid.*
11. *Ibid.*
12. *Ibid.*
13. *Ibid.*
14. *Ibid.*
15. *Ibid.*
16. *Ibid.*
17. *Ibid.*
18. *Ibid.*
19. *Ibid.*
20. *Ibid.*
21. In re Aircrash Dis. at Boston, Mass., July 31, 1973, 412 F. Supp. 959, 998 (D. Mass. 1976). https://law.justia.com/cases/federal/district-courts/FSupp/412/959/2368195/.
22. *Ibid.*
23. *Ibid.*
24. *Ibid.*
25. *Ibid.*
26. *Ibid.*
27. *Ibid.*
28. *Ibid.*
29. *Ibid.*
30. *Ibid.*
31. *Ibid.*
32. *Ibid.*
33. *Ibid.*
34. *Ibid.*
35. *Ibid.*
36. *Ibid.*
37. *Ibid.*
38. *Ibid.*
39. *Ibid.*
40. *Ibid.*
41. *Ibid.*
42. *Ibid.*
43. *Ibid.*
44. *Ibid.*
45. *Ibid.*
46. *Ibid.*
47. *Ibid.*
48. *Ibid.*
49. *Ibid.*
50. *Ibid.*
51. *Ibid.*
52. *Ibid.*
53. *Ibid.*
54. *Ibid.*
55. *Ibid.*
56. *Ibid.*
57. *Ibid.*
58. *Ibid.*
59. *Ibid.*
60. *Ibid.*
61. *Ibid.*
62. *Ibid.*
63. *Ibid.*
64. *Ibid.*
65. *Ibid.*
66. *Ibid.*
67. *Ibid.*
68. *Ibid.*
69. *Ibid.*
70. *Ibid.*
71. *Ibid.*
72. *Ibid.*
73. *Ibid.*
74. *Ibid.*
75. *Ibid.*
76. *Ibid.*
77. *Ibid.*
78. *Ibid.*
79. *Ibid.*
80. *Ibid.*
81. *Ibid.*
82. *Ibid.*
83. *Ibid.*
84. *Ibid.*
85. *Ibid.*
86. *Ibid.*

Chapter 25

1. Delta Airlines Inc. v. United States of America; Karen Haelsig McMaster v. United States of America; No. 76-1269, No. 76-1270; United States Court of Appeals for the First Circuit, 561 F.2d 381 (1st Cir. 1977), 5.
2. *Ibid.*
3. *Ibid.*
4. *Ibid.*
5. *Ibid.*
6. *Ibid.*, 5-6.
7. *Ibid.*, 6-7.
8. *Ibid.*, 7.
9. *Ibid.*
10. *Ibid.*
11. *Ibid.*
12. *Ibid.*
13. *Ibid.*
14. *Ibid.*
15. *Ibid.*, 8.
16. *Ibid.*, 9.
17. *Ibid.*, 10.

18. *Ibid.*
19. Brief for Appellant Delta Airlines, Inc., Delta Airlines, Inc., Plaintiff, Appellant v. United States of America, Defendant, Appellee; Helen M. Hall, et al., Plaintiff v. Delta Airlines, Inc., Defendant; Third-Party Plaintiff-Appellant v. United States of America Third-Party Defendant-Appellee, United States Court of Appeals for the First Circuit, No. 76-1269.
20. *Ibid.*
21. *Ibid.*, 29.
22. *Ibid.*, 30.
23. *Ibid.*, 31.
24. *Ibid.*, 32.
25. *Ibid.*, 39.
26. *Ibid.*, 31.
27. *Ibid.*, 39.
28. *Ibid.*
29. *Ibid.*, 40.
30. *Ibid.*, 31.
31. *Ibid.*
32. *Ibid.*, 33.
33. *Ibid.*, 34.
34. *Ibid.*, 40.
35. *Ibid.*
36. *Ibid.*
37. *Ibid.*, 41.
38. *Ibid.*
39. *Ibid.*, 41-42.
40. *Ibid.*, 42.
41. *Ibid.*
42. *Ibid.*, 42-43.
43. *Ibid.*, 43.
44. *Ibid.*, 44.
45. Karen Haelsig McMaster, Etc., et al., Plaintiffs, Appellants v. United States of America, Defendant, Appellee; Appeal from the United States District Court for the District of Massachusetts. Brief for Plaintiffs, Appellants (1976), 15.
46. Brief for Appellant Delta Airlines, Inc., Delta Airlines, Inc., Plaintiff, Appellant v. United States of America, Defendant, Appellee; Helen M. Hall, et al., Plaintiff v. Delta Airlines, Inc., Defendant; Third-Party Plaintiff-Appellant v. United States of America Third-Party Defendant-Appellee; United States Court of Appeals for the First Circuit, No. 76-1269, 45.
47. *Ibid.*
48. *Ibid.*
49. *Ibid.*, 46.
50. *Ibid.*, 45.
51. *Ibid.*, 46.
52. *Ibid.*, 46-47.
53. *Ibid.*, 47.
54. Karen Haelsig McMaster, Etc., et al., Plaintiffs, Appellants v. United States of America, Defendant, Appellee; Appeal from the United States District Court for the District of Massachusetts. Brief for Plaintiffs, Appellants (1976), 47-51.
55. *Ibid.*
56. *Ibid.*, 52.
57. *Ibid.*, 53.
58. *Ibid.*
59. *Ibid.*
60. Brief for Appellant Delta Airlines, Inc., Delta Airlines, Inc., Plaintiff, Appellant v. United States of America, Defendant, Appellee; Helen M. Hall, et al., Plaintiff v. Delta Airlines, Inc., Defendant; Third-Party Plaintiff-Appellant v. United States of America Third-Party Defendant-Appellee; United States Court of Appeals for the First Circuit, No. 76-1269, 47.

Chapter 26

1. Brief for Appellant Delta Airlines, Inc., Delta Airlines, Inc., Plaintiff, Appellant v. United States of America, Defendant, Appellee; Helen M. Hall, et al., Plaintiff v. Delta Airlines, Inc., Defendant; Third-Party Plaintiff-Appellant v. United States of America Third-Party Defendant-Appellee; United States Court of Appeals for the First Circuit, No. 76-1269, 20.
2. Brief for Plaintiffs, Appellants, Karen Haelsig McMaster, Etc., Et Al., Plaintiffs, Appellants v. United States of America, Defendant, Appellee; Appeal from the United States District Court for the District of Massachusetts (1976), 22.
3. *Ibid.*, 22-23.
4. *Ibid.*, 23.
5. *Ibid.*, 24.
6. *Ibid.*, 25.
7. *Ibid.*, 18-23.
8. Bryan A. Garner, ed., *Black's Law Dictionary*, 3rd pocket ed. (St. Paul, MN: West Publishing Co., 1996), 107.
9. Delta Airlines Inc. v. United States of America; Karen Haelsig McMaster v. United States of America; No. 76-1269, No. 76-1270; United States Court of Appeals for the First Circuit, 561 F.2d 381 (1st Cir. 1977), 14.
10. *Ibid.*
11. *Ibid.*
12. *Ibid.*, 22.

13. *Ibid.*, 17.
14. *Ibid.*
15. *Ibid.*, 18.
16. *Ibid.*
17. *Ibid.*, 19.
18. *Ibid.*
19. *Ibid.*, 20.
20. *Ibid.*, 20–22.
21. *Ibid.*
22. *Ibid.*
23. *Ibid.*, 20–22.
24. *Ibid.*, 24.
25. *Ibid.*
26. *Ibid.*, 25.
27. *Ibid.*
28. *Ibid.*, 25.
29. *Ibid.*, 29.
30. *Ibid.*
31. *Ibid.*, 30.
32. *Ibid.*

Chapter 27

1. Attorney Michael Latti, Latti & Anderson LLP. Accessed September 1, 2021. https://www.lattianderson.com/about-our-firm/attorney-michael-latti/.
2. Plaintiff's Complaint, Virginia A. Streil v. Sperry Rand Corp., McDonnell Douglas Corp., and Kollsman Instrument Corp., No. 75-1420C, United States District Court, District of Massachusetts (1975), 3.
3. *Ibid.*
4. Interrogatory of Frances A. Burrell by Sperry Rand, Frances A. Burrell v. Sperry Rand Corp., Civil Action No. 74-4399-C, United States District Court, District of Massachusetts (1977), 2.
5. Plaintiff's Complaint, Virginia A. Streil v. Sperry Rand Corp., McDonnell Douglas Corp., and Kollsman Instrument Corp., No. 75-1420C, United States District Court, District of Massachusetts (1975), 3.
6. Interrogatory of Frances A. Burrell by Sperry Rand, Frances A. Burrell v. Sperry Rand Corp., Civil Action No. 74-4399-C, United States District Court, District of Massachusetts (1977), 2.
7. Plaintiff's Complaint, Virginia A. Streil v. Sperry Rand Corp., McDonnell Douglas Corp., and Kollsman Instrument Corp., No. 75-1420C, United States District Court, District of Massachusetts (1975), 6.
8. *Ibid.*
9. *Ibid.*, 9.
10. *Ibid.*
11. *Ibid.*
12. Interrogatory of Sperry Rand by Frances Burrell, Frances A. Burrell v. Sperry Rand Corp., Civil Action No. 74-4399-C, United States District Court, District of Massachusetts (1977).
13. *Ibid.*
14. *Ibid.*
15. *Ibid.*
16. *Ibid.*
17. *Ibid.*
18. *Ibid.*
19. Interrogatory of Frances A. Burrell by Sperry Rand, Frances A. Burrell v. Sperry Rand Corp., Civil Action No. 74-4399-C, United States District Court, District of Massachusetts (1977), 3.
20. *Ibid.*
21. *Ibid.*
22. In re Aircrash Disaster at Boston, Mass., July 31, 1973, 412 F. Supp. 959, 998 (D. Mass. 1976). https://law.justia.com/cases/federal/district-courts/FSupp/412/959/2368195/.
23. Frances A. Burrell, Affidavit, October 18, 1977, 2.
24. *Ibid.*, 3.
25. *Ibid.*, 6.
26. *Ibid.*, 7.
27. *Ibid.*, 8.
28. *Ibid.*
29. *Ibid.*
30. *Ibid.*

Chapter 28

1. Frances A. Burrell v. Delta Airlines, Inc., McDonnell Douglas Corporation, Sperry Rand Corporation, and Kollsman Instrument Corporation, Second Day of Jury Trial, MDL No. 160-49, United States District Court, District of Massachusetts (September 21, 1977), 2-2.
2. *Ibid.*, 2-2-2-3.
3. *Ibid.*, 2-3-2-4.
4. *Ibid.*, 2-5.
5. *Ibid.*
6. *Ibid.*
7. *Ibid.*, 2-5-2-6.
8. *Ibid.*, 2-6.
9. *Ibid.* 2-6-2-7.
10. *Ibid.*, 2-7.
11. *Ibid.*
12. *Ibid.*, 2-8.
13. *Ibid.*, 2-8-2-9.
14. *Ibid.*, 2-9.

15. *Ibid.*
16. *Ibid.*, 2–9.
17. *Ibid.*
18. *Ibid.*, 2–9–2–10.
19. *Ibid.*, 2–10.
20. *Ibid.*, 2–11.
21. *Ibid.*
22. *Ibid.*
23. *Ibid.*, 2–12–2–13.
24. *Ibid.*
25. *Ibid.*
26. Court Docket, Frances A. Burrell v. Sperry Rand Corp., Civil Action No. 74–4399-C, United States District Court, District of Massachusetts.
27. "The Honorable David S. Nelson," *Long Road to Justice: The African American Experience in the Massachusetts Court.* Accessed September 1, 2021. http://www.longroadtojustice.org/topics/leadership/david-nelson.php.
28. Pretrial Conference, Frances A. Burrell v. Sperry Rand, Inc., United States District Court, District of Massachusetts, July 10, 1979.
29. *Ibid.*, 11.
30. *Ibid.*
31. *Ibid.*, 10.
32. *Ibid.*
33. *Ibid.*
34. *Ibid.*, 11.
35. *Ibid.*, 11–12.
36. *Ibid.*, 17.
37. *Ibid.*
38. *Ibid.*, 12.
39. Plaintiff's Exhibits, Frances A. Burrell v. Sperry Rand Corp., Civil Action No. 74–4399-C, United States District Court, District of Massachusetts (1977).
40. Court Docket, Frances A. Burrell v. Sperry Rand Corp., Civil Action No. 74–4399-C, United States District Court, District of Massachusetts (1982).
41. Bryan A. Garner, ed., *Black's Law Dictionary*, 3rd pocket ed. (St. Paul, MN: West Publishing Co., 1996), 690.
42. Plaintiff's Supplemental Memorandum in Support of Its Motion in Limine—RE: Previous Litigation, Frances A. Burrell v. Sperry Rand Corp., Civil Action No. 74–4399-C, United States District Court, District of Massachusetts (1982).
43. Settlement, Frances A. Burrell v. Sperry Rand Corp., MDL No. 160, United States District Court, District of Massachusetts (1982).
44. *Ibid.*
45. *Ibid.*
46. Court Docket, Frances A. Burrell v. Sperry Rand Corp., Civil Action No. 74–4399-C, United States District Court, District of Massachusetts.

Bibliography

Air Commerce Act of 1926.
An Aircraft Accident Involving Piedmont Airlines Inc., Boeing 727, N68650, and Lanseair, Cessna 310, N3121S, at Hendersonville, North Carolina, July 19, 1967. Public Hearing. Docket No. SA-400. Washington, D.C.: Department of Transportation, 1967.
Aircraft Accident Report: Allegheny Airlines Inc. Douglas DC-9, N988VJ, and a Forth Corporation Piper PA-28, N7374J, Near Fairland, Indiana, September 9, 1969. NTSB-AAR-70-15. Washington, D.C.: National Transportation Safety Board, 1970.
Aircraft Accident Report: Delta Airlines Inc. Douglas DC-9-31, N975NE, Boston, Massachusetts, July 31, 1973. NTSB-AAR-74-3. Washington, D.C.: National Transportation Safety Board, 1974.
Aircraft Accident Report: North Central Airlines, Inc., Convair 580, N2045, O'Hare International Airport, Chicago, Illinois, December 27, 1968. NTSB-AAR-70-27. Washington, D.C.: National Transportation Safety Board, 1970.
Aircraft Accident Report: Piedmont Airlines Fairchild-Hiller 2276, N712U, Charleston, West Virginia, August 10, 1968. NTSB-AAR-69-6. Washington, D.C.: National Transportation Safety Board, 1969.
Aldo, Jude, and John W. King. "The Management of Burns with Silver Nitrate Solution." *Journal of the National Medical Association* 58, no. 3 (1966): 165.
Anderson, Jack. "Brother Act." *Bell-McClure Syndicate*, August 1, 1967. Accessed from American University Archives & Special Collections.
Anglin, Robert. "88 Killed in Crash at Fogbound Logan." *Boston Globe*, August 1, 1973.

Anglin, Robert. "Runway Reopens as Secrecy Shrouds Probe of Logan Crash." *Boston Globe*, August 3, 1973.
Arena, Charles T. Excerpts from First Day of Trial, December 29, 1975. In Re Air Crash Disaster at Boston, Mass., July 31, 1973, 412 F. Supp. 959 (D. Mass. 1976).
Barnicle, Mike. "'I Never Felt so Helpless....'" *Boston Globe*, August 1, 1973.
"Bennington Native Killed, among 88 Disaster Victims." *Bennington Banner* (Vermont), August 1, 1973.
Black, Herber. "Plane Crash Survivor Fights for Life." *Boston Globe*, August 3, 1973.
"Board Says Crash Study to Take about 6 Months." *Burlington Free Press*, August 2, 1973.
"The Boeing 707." *The Aeroplane*, September 12, 1958.
Bomber, Marvin. Intra-Company Memo. Flight 723/31 Jul. August 2, 1973.
"Boston Crash Survivor Said in 'Good Spirits.'" *Bennington Banner* (Vermont), August 21, 1973.
Boston Fire Department. Data Processing and Records Memo. Subject: Delta Airline Disaster, September 10, 1973.
Botwright, Ken. "Return of Special Logan Radar Urged." *Boston Globe*, December 24, 1973.
Brief for Appellant Delta Airlines, Inc. Delta Airlines, Inc., Plaintiff, Appellant v. United States of America, Defendant, Appellee; Helen M. Hall, et al., Plaintiff v. Delta Airlines, Inc., Defendant; Third-Party Plaintiff-Appellant v. United States of America Third-Party Defendant-Appellee. United States Court of Appeals for the First Circuit. No. 76-1269.
Brief for Plaintiffs, Appellants. *Karen Haelsig*

McMaster, Etc. v. United States of America. Appeal from the United States District Court for the District of Massachusetts, No. 76–1270, 561 F.2d 381 (1st Cir. 1977).

Buechner, Betsy. "Delta Jet Told of Fog 20 Seconds before Crash." *Burlington Free Press*, September 20, 1973.

Buechner, Betsy. "Final Minute Apparently Crucial for Delta Pilots." *Burlington Free Press*, September 19, 1973.

Burgess, Isabel. Letter to Crocker Snow. August 13, 1973.

Burrell, Frances A. Affidavit. October 18, 1977.

Butterfield, Alexander, Administrator, Federal Aviation Administration. Letter to John Reed, Chairman, National Transportation Safety Board. June 26, 1974.

"Caffrey, Andrew Augustine." Federal Judicial Center. Accessed on May 15, 2019. fjc.gov/node/1378706.

Cahill, Bill. "3d Tragedy Hits Gloucester Native." *Boston Globe*, August 3, 1973.

Campbell, Kenneth. "Safety, Costs on 2 Runways." *Boston Globe*, May 9, 1974.

"Chouinard Buried with Honors." *Burlington Free Press*, December 17, 1973.

"Chouinard Improving, Is Taking Solid Food." *Burlington Free Press*, November 29, 1973.

"Chouinard Loses Battle for Life." *Burlington Free Press*, December 12, 1973.

Chouinard, Ray and Leona. Interviewed by Author. July 17, 2019.

Civil Aeronautics Act of 1938.

Civil Aeronautics Board Reports. *Economic Cases of the CAB Mar-Jul, 1972*. Washington, D.C.: U.S. Government Printing Office, 1972.

"Claim Radar Could Have Avoided NC Plane Crash." *Oshkosh Northwestern* (Wisconsin), January 9, 1969.

"Cocoanut Grove Fire." *Wikipedia*. Accessed November 20, 2019. https://en.wikipedia.org/wiki/Cocoanut_Grove_fire.

Cole, Jean. "A Grim and Lengthy Ritual Is Conducted as Casualties Are Brought to Mortuary." *Boston Herald American*, August 1, 1973.

"The Condition of Crash Survivor at Lowest Point." *Rutland Daily Herald* (Vermont), December 5, 1973.

Court Docket. *Frances A. Burrell v. Sperry Rand Corp.* Civil Action No. 74–4399-C. United States District Court, District of Massachusetts (1977).

"Crash Investigation Starts." *Billings Gazette* (Montana), December 29, 1968.

"Crashes in Landing Spur Demand for Greater Vigilance." *Miami Herald*, January 23, 1969.

Cullen, Prudy. Interviewed by Author. November 11, 2020. Telephone.

Culver, Dorothy Campbell. *Civil and Commercial Aviation, A Guide to Federal Legislation and Administrative Agencies*. Berkeley: Bureau of Public Administration, University of California, 1940.

Cusick, Harris. Excerpts from First Day of Trial, December 29, 1975. In Re Air Crash Disaster at Boston, Mass., July 31, 1973, 412 F. Supp. 959 (D. Mass. 1976).

Cusick, Harris. Excerpts from Fourth Day of Trial, January 2, 1976. In Re Air Crash Disaster at Boston, Mass., July 31, 1973, 412 F. Supp. 959 (D. Mass. 1976).

"Deaths and Funerals." *Burlington Free Press*, August 3, 1973.

"Debridement of a Wound, Infection, or Burn," Reasons of Procedure. *Health Library*. Beth Israel Lahey Health, Winchester Hospital. Accessed April 19, 2019. www.winchesterhospital.org/health-library/article?id=2010813273.

Delta Airlines Inc. v. United States of America; Karen Haelsig McMaster v. United States of America. No. 76–1269, No. 76–1270. United States Court of Appeals for the First Circuit, 561 F.2d 381 (1st Cir. 1977).

"Delta Claims FAA Fault in Logan Crash Suit." *Rutland Daily Herald* (Vermont), January 15, 1974.

"Delta in Court Action; Marshfield Man 'Stable.'" *Rutland Daily Herald* (Vermont), August 8, 1973.

"Delta Settles 11 Lawsuits." *Times Argus* (Vermont), June 30, 1975.

Department of Transportation Act: Report to Accompany 15963. United States Congress. House Committee on Government Operations.

DiGrazia, Robert J., Police Commissioner. Letter to Director Edward T. Sullivan, Administrative Services. September 26, 1973.

Dodson, Dr. Thomas. Interviewed by Author. November 14, 2019. Telephone.

Donohue, James. "Flight from Burlington Ends in Catastrophe at Boston; 88 Die as Plane Crashes in Fog." *Rutland Daily Herald* (Vermont), August 1, 1973.

Dunton, Mark. "October 1973—The End of the Sixties?" *The National Archives* (blog), October 14, 2013. https://blog.nationalarchives.gov.uk/october-1973-the-end-of-the-sixties/.

Eaton, Bill. "850 Feet Too Low at Coyote Pt." *Oakland Tribune*, November 27, 1968.

"Editorials: Logan Crash Raises Questions." *North Adams Transcript* (Massachusetts), August 3, 1973.

"Epping Woman, Miriam Jackson, Dies in Airliner." *Portsmouth Herald* (New Hampshire), August 1, 1973.

"Executive, Salesman among DC9 Victims." *Hartford Courant*, August 2, 1973.

"Ex-Middlebury Couple Die in Boston Plane Crash." *Hartford Courant*, August 3, 1973.

"FAA Asks Safety Board to Alter Critical Report." *Miami Herald*, October 14, 1970.

Federal Aviation Act of 1958.

Federal Aviation Administration. "Transcription of Local and Ground Controller Channels." Logan Airport Tower. July 31, 1973.

The Fisheries of Gloucester from the First Catch by the English in 1623, to the Centennial Year, 1876. Gloucester, MA: Procter Brothers, 1876.

Frances A. Burrell v. Delta Airlines, Inc., McDonnell Douglas Corporation, Sperry Rand Corporation, and Kollsman Instrument Corporation. Second Day of Jury Trial. MDL No. 160-49. United States District Court, District of Massachusetts (1977).

Francillon, Rene J. "The Early DC-9s: Success that Kills." *Airliners*, no. 77 (Sept./Oct. 2002).

Garner, Bryan A., ed. *Black's Law Dictionary*, 3rd pocket ed. St. Paul, MN: West Publishing Co., 1996.

Giroux, Richard. Excerpts from First Day of Trial, December 29, 1975. In Re Air Crash Disaster at Boston, Mass., July 31, 1973, 412 F. Supp. 959 (D. Mass. 1976).

Green, Nancy. "Kennedy Told Logan Traffic Control Chaotic." *Boston Globe*, March 13, 1970.

Guiney, Francis, Executive Director, Health and Hospitals. Departmental Communication. Subject: Air Disaster. August 28, 1973.

Hammond, James H. "Logan's Problem: One Safety System and Two Runways." *Boston Globe*, May 13, 1974.

Harris, John. "Boston Democrat May Second Nixon." *Boston Globe*, August 22, 1956.

Haughland, Vern. "Changes Recommended for TriStar Airliners." *York Dispatch* (Pennsylvania), May 3, 1973.

Hearing before the Subcommittee on Aviation of the Committee on Commerce, United States Senate, Ninety-Third Congress, on Adequacy of Northern New England Air Service, Warren Magnuson, Chairman. Washington, D.C.: U.S. Government Printing Office, 1972.

Hearing before the Subcommittee on Investigations and Review of the Committee on Public Works and Transportation, House of Representatives, Ninety-Fourth Congress, on Adequacy of Air Service to New England, Robert E. Jones, Chairman. Washington, D.C.: U.S. Government Printing Office, 1976.

Hearings before the Committee on Commerce, United States Senate, Ninetieth Congress, First Session, on Nominations of Joseph P. O'Connell, Francis H. McAdams, Rear Adm. Louis N. Thayer, John H. Reed, Oscar Laurel, Warren G. Magnuson, Chairman. Washington, D.C.: U.S. Government Printing Office, 1967.

Hearings before the Committee on Commerce, United States Senate, Ninety-First Congress, First Session, on Nomination of Isabel Burgess to Be a Member of the National Transportation Safety Board, Warren G. Magnuson, Chairman. Washington, D.C.: U.S. Government Printing Office, 1969.

Hearings before the Committee on Commerce, United States Senate, Ninety-Third Congress, on Activities of the National Transportation Safety Board, Warren Magnuson, Chairman. Washington, D.C.: U.S. Government Printing Office, 1973.

Hearings before the Committee on Government Operations, United States Senate, Eighty-Ninth Congress, on a Bill to Establish a Department of Transportation, and for Other Purposes, John L. McClellan, Chairman. Washington, D.C.: U.S. Government Printing Office, 1966.

Hearings before the Committee on Interstate and Foreign Commerce, House of Representatives, and the Sub-Committee on Transportation and Aeronautics on Aviation Safety, Ninetieth Congress, First and Second Sessions. Washington, D.C.: U.S. Government Printing Office, 1968.

Hearings before the Committee on Interstate and Foreign Commerce, House of Representatives, on Aviation Facilities Maintenance and Development, Ninety-First Congress, First Session. Washington, D.C.: U.S. Government Printing Office, 1969.

Hearings, Committee on Commerce, United States Senate, Ninety-Third Congress, Second Session, "To Amend the DOT Act in Order to Establish the National Transportation Safety Board as an Independent Agency in the Executive Branch of the Government." Washington, D.C.: U.S. Government Printing Office, 1974.

Hines, William. "Commercial Flying's Big Problem: Safety in Last Few Minutes." *Morning News*, August 8, 1973.

Hohler, Bob. "'73 Delta Crash, the Reality Lingers." *Boston Globe*, July 31, 1993.

Hutchins, Warren. Excerpts from First Day of Trial, December 29, 1975. In Re Air Crash Disaster at Boston, Mass., July 31, 1973, 412 F. Supp. 959 (D. Mass. 1976).

"ICC, State Officials Die in Jet Crash." *Nashua Telegraph* (New Hampshire), August 1, 1973.

In Re Air Crash Disaster at Boston, Mass., July 31, 1973, 412 F. Supp. 959 (D. Mass. 1976).

In Re Air Crash Disaster at Boston, Mass, Etc., 415 F. Supp. 206 (D. Mass. 1976).

In Re Aircrash Disaster, 412 F. Supp. 959, 998 (D. Mass. 1976). https://law.justia.com/cases/federal/district-courts/FSupp/412/959/2368195/.

Interrogatory of Frances A. Burrell by Sperry Rand. Frances A. Burrell v. Sperry Rand Corp. Civil Action No. 74–4399-C. United States District Court, District of Massachusetts (1977).

Interrogatory of Sperry Rand by Frances Burrell. Frances A. Burrell v. Sperry Rand Corp. Civil Action No. 74–4399-C. United States District Court, District of Massachusetts (1977).

Karakoudas, Thomas. Excerpts from First Day of Trial, December 29, 1975. In Re Air Crash Disaster at Boston, Mass., July 31, 1973, 412 F. Supp. 959 (D. Mass. 1976).

Keating, Geoffrey. Excerpts from Fourth Day of Trial, January 2, 1976. In Re Air Crash Disaster at Boston, Mass., July 31, 1973, 412 F. Supp. 959 (D. Mass. 1976).

Kling, William. "Tells Steps to Cut Landing Air Crashes." *Chicago Tribune*, January 22, 1969.

Larkin, Al. "N.H. Aide and ICC Official among Crash Victims." *Boston Globe*, August 1, 1973.

Lee, Jean Theodore, and Carl Max Reber. *Pilots' Weather Handbook*. Washington, D.C.: U.S. Government Printing Office, 1955.

Lindsey, John M. "The Legislative Development of Civil Aviation, 1938–1958." *Journal of Air Law and Commerce*, no. 28 (1962).

List of Victims. *Union Leader* (New Hampshire), August 1, 1973.

Lockhard, Merrill. "9 Area Residents Crash Victims." *Nashua Telegraph* (New Hampshire), August 1, 1973.

The Long Range Needs of Aviation: Report of the Aviation Advisory Commission. Crocker Snow, Chairman. January, 1973.

Lukas, J. Anthony. *Common Ground*. New York: Random House, 1985.

Lund, Dr. Charles, and Dr. Newton Browder. "Estimation of the Area of Burns." Lund and Browder Chart.

Luongo, Michael, Medical Examiner for Suffolk County. Memo to Edward T. Sullivan. November 13, 1973.

Maclay, Tim. Interviewed by Author. May 11, 2019. Telephone.

"Malfunctions, Misunderstandings, Plague Logan Tower at Time of Delta Crash." *Berkshire Eagle* (Massachusetts), September 20, 1973.

Marquard, Bryan. "Obituary: John Constable; Brought Surgery Talents to Remote Villages." *Boston Globe*, August 05, 2016.

"Marshfield Is Hopeful Chouinard Will Survive." *Burlington Free Press*, August 6, 1973.

"Mayor Sets Civic Tribute for Plane Crash Victims." *Manchester Union Leader* (New Hampshire), August 2, 1973.

McAdams, Francis. *Notation 120-A-A Aircraft Accident Report—Piedmont Airlines Inc., Boeing 727/Lanseair Inc. Cessna 310 N3121S Mid-Air Collision, Hendersonville, North Carolina, July 19, 1967.* Washington, D.C.: Department of Transportation, National Transportation Safety Board, November 15, 1968.

McCord, James. Letter to the Honorable Judge John Sirica. March 19, 1973.

McDonald, Jeffrey. Excerpts from Fourth Day of Trial, January 2, 1976. In Re Air Crash Disaster at Boston, Mass., July 31, 1973, 412 F. Supp. 959 (D. Mass. 1976).

McDonald, Jeffrey. Local Control Transmission. Logan Airport. July 31, 1973.

McGovern, Michael. "'Thousands of Pieces' in Boston Jet Crash." *Daily News*, August 2, 1973.

McSweeney, Brenda Newton. Interviewed by Author. September 28, 2019. Boone, NC.

Miles, Marvin. "Airport May Be Death Trap by 1975, Controllers Claim." February 4, 1969.

Miller, C.O. "The Bureau of Aviation Safety and the Accident Prevention System." Remarks at the Flight Safety Foundation Luncheon, Anaheim, California, October 9, 1968.

Miller, Margo. "Delta to Get Crash Tapes after FAA." *Boston Globe*, August 7, 1973.

Moskel, Jerry. "FAA Orders New Flying Procedures." *Battle Creek Enquirer* (Michigan), October 31, 1970.

Nathan, Richard P. *The Plot That Failed: Nixon and the Administrative Presidency*. New York: John Wiley & Sons, 1975.

National Transportation Safety Board. "Transcription of Cockpit Voice Recorder Data, Fairchild A-100, S/N 2634, Delta Airlines Douglas Model DC-9-31, N975NE, Flight 723, Logan International Airport, Boston, Massachusetts, July 31, 1973."

National Weather Service. Definition of Advection Fog.

"NATO Defense Plans Found in Wreckage of Delta Jet." *Boston Globe*, August 1, 1973.

Negri, Gloria. "While City Sleeps, Drama at MGH." *Boston Globe*, September 17, 1973.

Nelkin, Dorothy. *JETPORT: The Boston Airport Controversy*. New Brunswick, NJ: Transaction Books, 1974.

Nettel, Albert. "Cheats Death Earlier, Dies in Plane Crash." *Union Leader* (New Hampshire), August 1, 1973.

"New Field for Ralph Nader." *Herald News*. March 17. 1973.

"NWMC Forms Plan, Zoning Committee." *Daily Herald* (Illinois), February 23, 1968.

"Obituaries: Frank Mahoney, *Globe* Reporter Known for Fire Expertise; at 63." *Boston Globe*, December 10, 1991.

"Obituaries: Mass for Crash Victim John J. Ruane Is Today." *Boston Globe*, August 4, 1973.

O'Connell, J.J. "The Bureau of Aviation Safety and the Accident Prevention System." Remarks at the Flight Safety Foundation Luncheon, Anaheim, California, October 9, 1968.

Oliphant, Thomas. "Bad Weather Limits Urged on Delta DC9s." *Boston Globe*, August 30, 1973.

"Passenger Who Perished May Have Saved Chouinard's Life." *Bennington Banner* (Vermont), August 4, 1973.

Perez, Eric MD, Maryann Foley, and Ronald Karlin, MD. "Classification of Burns." *Health Encyclopedia*. University of Rochester Medical Center. Accessed November 20, 2019. https://www.urmc.rochester.edu/encyclopedia/content.aspx?ContentTypeID=90&ContentID=P09575.

"Person Next to Him Saved His Life." *Brattleboro Reformer* (Vermont), August 3, 1973.

Peters, Stephanie. "Charles Arena, 76; Fire Chief at Logan Was Safety Expert." *Boston Globe*, October 23, 2009.

Pilati, Joe. "Papers from Delta Crash to Go to Washington." *Boston Globe*, August 2, 1973.

"Pilot Error Blamed for DC-9 Crash." *Brattleboro Reformer* (Vermont), September 25, 1973.

Plaintiff's Complaint. *Virginia A. Streil v. Sperry Rand Corp., McDonnell Douglas Corp., and Kollsman Instrument Corp.* No. 75–1420C. United States District Court, District of Massachusetts (1975).

Plaintiff's Exhibits. *Frances A. Burrell v. Sperry Rand Corp.* Civil Action No. 74–4399-C. United States District Court, District of Massachusetts (1977).

Plaintiff's Supplemental Memorandum in Support of Its Motion in Limine—RE: Previous Litigation. *Frances A. Burrell v. Sperry Rand Corp.* Civil Action No. 74–4399-C. United States District Court, District of Massachusetts (1982).

Pomerene, Nancy. "Chouinard's Death Moves Man Who Found Him." *Boston Globe*, December 13, 1973.

Pretrial Conference. *Frances A. Burrell v. Sperry Rand, Inc.* United States District Court, District of Massachusetts (1979).

Puffer, Claude E. *Air Transportation*. Philadelphia: Blakiston Books, 1941.

Rae, William. Excerpts from First Day of Trial, December 29, 1975. In Re Air Crash Disaster at Boston, Mass., July 31, 1973, 412 F. Supp. 959 (D. Mass. 1976).

Reed, John, Chairman, NTSB. Letter to FBI Director William Ruckelshaus. June 5, 1973.
Report of Minor Accident, Accident No. 45-11-27-208, Army Air Forces (Bryan, TX: AAFIS [IP]).
Rhodes, George. "Approach Radar Reactivated by FAA." *San Francisco Examiner*, February 5, 1969.
Ringle, William. "Delta Introduces Some Surprise Evidence." *Burlington Free Press*, September 27, 1973.
Ringle, William. "Hearing Starts Tuesday on Fatal Burlington-to-Boston Flight." *Burlington Free Press*, September 14, 1973.
Ringle, William. "Pilot Told Seconds before Crash that Visibility Was 6,000 Feet." *El Paso Times*, September 27, 1973.
Ringle, William. "Runway Visibility Reports Can Suffer from Time Lag." *Burlington Free Press*, September 26, 1973.
"Rites Planned for 4 Victims of Plane Crash." *Burlington Free Press*, August 7, 1973.
Robinson, John, and David Rogers. "Crash Victims Were Traveling on Business, Vacations, Errands." *Boston Globe*, August 2, 1973.
Rogers, David. "Delta Crew Skipped 3 Altitude Reports, Panel Told." *Boston Globe*, September 26, 1973.
Rogers, David. "Delta Log Reveals Pilots Knew They Were Off Course." *Boston Globe*, September 19, 1973.
Rogers, David. "Federal Hearings on Delta Crash Recessed 'Indefinitely.'" *Boston Globe*, September 28, 1973.
Rogers, David. Interviewed by Author. November 16, 2019. Telephone.
Rogers, David. "No Metal Particles Found in Switch Taken from Wrecked Delta Jetliner." *Boston Globe*, October 4, 1973.
Rogers, David. "Shifting Fog Bank May Have Cut Down Delta Jet's Visibility." *Boston Globe*, September 20, 1973.
Rogers, David. "13 Were Impatient, Decided Not to Sit, Wait for Flight 723." *Boston Globe*, August 1, 1973.
"Safety Board Free from 'Pressures.'" *Austin American* (Texas), June 16, 1969.
"Safety Improvements Get Priority at Logan." *Burlington Free Press*, August 4, 1973.
Saffle, Jeffrey R., MD. "The 1942 Fire at Boston's Cocoanut Grove Nightclub." *The American Journal of Surgery* 166 (December 1993).

Settlement. Frances A. Burrell v. Sperry Rand Corp. MDL No. 160. United States District Court, District of Massachusetts (1982).
"Sgt. Chouinard Keeps Up Lengthy Fight for Life." *Burlington Free Press*, September 17, 1973.
"Sharp Takeoff Rule." *Spokesman-Review* (Washington state), October 31, 1970.
"Shelby Crash Report Delay Request Told." *Indianapolis Star*, October 7, 1970.
"Sheridan Couple on Ill-Fated Plane." *Montana Standard*, August 1, 1973.
"'Simple Device' Missing from Ill-Fated Jumbo Jet." *Akron Beacon Journal* (Ohio), March 9, 1973.
Smerdon v. United States, 135 F. Supp. 929 (D. Mass. 1955). https://law.justia.com/cases/federal/district-courts/FSupp/135/929/1617569/.
Snow, Crocker. Letter to Isabel Burgess. August 3, 1973.
Sproston, Betty. "Marion Smith Estate Described as Collectors' Treasure Trove." *Burlington Free Press*, October 3, 1973.
"State Report on Delta Crash Termed Surprising." *Boston Globe*, September 25, 1973.
"Statement." *Manchester Union Leader* (New Hampshire), August 1, 1973.
Susman, Ed, and Marshall Molloy. "Vermont Survivor Found Fully Conscious." *Burlington Free Press*, August 1, 1973.
Taylor, Benjamin. "Crashed Jet's Co-Pilot Teethed on Airplanes." *Boston Globe*, August 2, 1973.
Taylor, Charles. Approach Control Transmission, Channel 1. Logan Airport. July 31, 1973.
Taylor, Charles. Excerpts from Fourth Day of Trial, January 2, 1976. In Re Air Crash Disaster at Boston, Mass., July 31, 1973, 412 F. Supp. 959 (D. Mass. 1976).
Terban Harry. Excerpts from Fourth Day of Trial, January 2, 1976. In Re Air Crash Disaster at Boston, Mass., July 31, 1973, 412 F. Supp. 959 (D. Mass. 1976).
"3 Burlington Architects Victims of Plane Crash." *Burlington Free Press*, August 1, 1973.
"3 Vermont Doll Collectors Die." *Burlington Free Press*, August 1, 1973.
Tofield, Dr. Joshua. Interviewed by Author. November 16, 2019. Telephone.
"Tragic Hub Airport Crash Boiling into Political Battle." *Fitchburg Sentinel* (Massachusetts), August 4, 1973.

Tucker, Daniel. Excerpts from Fourth Day of Trial, January 2, 1976. In Re Air Crash Disaster at Boston, Mass., July 31, 1973, 412 F. Supp. 959 (D. Mass. 1976).

"$2 Million Suit in Boston Crash." *Rutland Daily Herald* (Vermont), August 24, 1973.

U.S. Environmental Protection Agency. *Public Hearings on Noise Abatement and Control, Vol. VII, Physiological and Psychological Effects, Boston Massachusetts, October 28 and 29, 1971.* Washington, D.C.: U.S. Government Printing Office, 1971.

"Vermont Churches Mourn Victims of Plane Crash." *Brattleboro Reformer* (Vermont), August 4, 1973.

Waddington, Terry. *McDonnell Douglas DC-9.* Miami, FL: World Transport Press, 1998.

Walsh, Robert. "Delta Pilot Knew Plane Off Course, Prober Testifies." *Boston Globe*, September 18, 1973.

Walsh, Robert E. "Despite Crash Testimony of Others: Five Delta Pilots Say Equipment in Order." *Boston Globe*, September 21, 1973.

Walsh, Robert E. "Pilot Says Visibility Good Just Prior to Delta Crash." *Boston Globe*, September 20, 1973.

Weidmann, Gerard. "Passengers on Ill-Fated Flight 723 Had Diverse Backgrounds." *Boston Globe*, August 2, 1973.

Weintraub, Richard. "Services in 3 States for Crash Victims." *Boston Globe*, August 5, 1973.

"Wheels Fail, Plane Lands Safely Here: Foam on Runway Aids Viscount Carrying 23 from Boston." *Baltimore Sun*, September 5, 1961.

Williams, Jean Tro. "The Senator Is Going to Washington." *Arizona Republic*, September 7, 1969.

Williams, Verne O. "EAL Failed to Get New Warning Unit." *Miami News*, March 8, 1973.

Wilson, Andrew. "MP Joins Pilots' Radar Protest." *The Observer* (United Kingdom), January 19, 1969.

Wimer, David J. Letter to General Alexander Haig. Subject: National Transportation Safety Board (Non-Republican Vacancy). Undated.

"Winooskian Loses 3 in Crash." *Burlington Free Press*, August 1, 1973.

"Wives Give Thanks for Impatience." *Brattleboro Reformer* (Vermont), August 1, 1973.

"Would-Be Travelers on Plane Feel Lucky." *Burlington Free Press*, August 2, 1973.

"Young Bride Is Victim in Tragedy." *Burlington Free Press*, August 1, 1973.

Index

Air Canada Flight 675 71–72
Air Commerce Act of 1926 24
Air Line Pilot's Association (ALPA) 19, 89, 119, 129, 136–137, 161, 224
Air Safety Board 24, 25, 26, 87
Alaska Airlines 117
Aldo, Dr. Jude 107
Allegheny Flight 415 67
Allegheny Flight 666 51–53, 155–156, 201, 203, 207, 216
Allegheny Airlines Flight 853 92
Allen, Bobbie 90, 150
ALPA 17, 89, 119, 129, 136, 137, 161, 224
Altshuler, Alan 39, 136, 138
American Airlines Flight 400 66
American Transport Association (ATA) 135
Approach Light System (ALS) 65, 186–187
Arena, Chief Charles 42, 67, 70–72, 74, 76, 79–81, 85, 154
Averett, Capt. Herlong 17, 164–165, 199
Aviation Consumer Action Program (ACAP) 132

BAC-111 12–13
Bachman, Richard 132
Baker, Bertha 20
Ball, Capt. Thomas 198–200, 207, 209, 224
Bander, Martin 175
Bean, Mrs. Frances 23
Bergeron, Mr. & Mrs. William 22
Boeing 12, 15, 31, 51, 89, 117, 129, 213
Bomber, Marvin 10, 11, 15, 23, 35
Bonita, Walter 85
Boriello, Paul 54, 65–67, 71–76, 157
Borman, Frank 134
Boston, MA 10–11, 14, 16, 18–22, 29–33, 35–39, 42, 44, 46, 48–49, 51, 55, 57, 59–60, 63–64, 67, 72–74, 76–77, 83, 86, 104, 110–111, 113–116, 119, 122, 131–132, 135–138, 167–168, 175, 182, 187, 190, 193–194, 197, 200, 204, 229, 231; *see also* Logan Airport
Boston City Hospital 85, 104

Boston City Hospital (BCH) 85, 104–105
Boston Fire Department 81, 85, 114–115
Boston Globe 16, 83, 113, 145, 164, 166, 227; *see also* Rogers, David
Boston Harbor 35–37, 41, 44, 58–60, 64–65, 78, 136–138, 160, 190
Boston Police Department 86, 115
Boston Red Sox 20, 34
Boston School Committee 64
Boston Strangler 85
Boyle, Susan 21
Braniff 12
Brau, Charles 22
Brinegar, Claude 97, 99
British Aircraft Company 12
Brother Act 89–90
Brothman, Mr. & Mrs Maurice 22
Browder, Newton 105–106
Brown dermatome 146
Brown v. Board of Education 63
Burgess, Isabel 91, 92, 99, 100, 102; leads on-site investigation 116–118, 120–122, 134–135, 139, 149
Burke, Edmund 200–201, 207, 209
Burochoff, S. Arthur 83
Burrell, Frances 220, 231
Burrell, Joseph 16, 44–45, 47, 49, 50, 54, 55, 58, 60, 165, 220, 224, 231; training 17–18
Burrill, FO Sidney 11, 16, 44–50, 54–55, 57–58, 60, 154, 157, 164, 220
Burrill, Susan 16, 220
busing 63–64, 132
Butterfield, Alexander 33, 97, 139, 140, 173

Caffrey, Andrew 189–190, 192–204, 207, 209–212, 214–216, 218, 223–234
Caldwell, John 56
Cameron, David 19
Cannon, Sen. Howard 93, 102–103, 151–152
Caravelle 12
Carpentiere, Winston 23
Cary, Adeline 19

261

Index

Castle Island 48, 58–59, 154, 195, 208
Category (CAT) II 136–138, 188
Chappell, Capt. Keith 157–158, 195–196, 200
Chouinard, Laurette 108–109, 169
Chouinard, Leo 20–21, 79; admitted to MGH 104–108, 111, 112, 113, 118, 141, 142, 145, 147, 148, 168, 169; death 175; found on runway 80–81; funeral 176
Chouinard, Leona 20, 111–112, 176
Chouinard, Ray 20, 174
Chouinard, Roger 144, 175–176
Chouinard family 111, 142, 144, 174–175
Civil Aeronautics Authority (CAA) 25, 26, 192, 210
Civil Aeronautics Board (CAB) 24, 26–32, 87, 118–120, 152–153, 191
Cockpit Voice Recorder (CVR) 116, 118, 138, 153, 160, 162, 197, 200, 206, 224–226
Cocoanut Grove Fire 85, 104–105
Collins Flight Director (FD) 162, 164, 166, 184, 198
Colonial Airlines 29
Commerce Act of 1887 18
Constable, Dr. John 111–113, 141, 169
Coolidge, Calvin 24, 61, 143
Cotton, Howard 91
Cotton, Norris 18, 30
Court of Appeals 204–205, 214, 217–218, 232, 234
Cousins Properties 19
Cox, Archibald 33, 173
CREEP 101
Crowley, Jeannette 22
Cullen, Prudy 113
Cummings, Robert 19
Cusick, Harris 42, 43, 70 131, 159; finds Leo Chouinard 78–81; meets with Chouinard family 169–171, 176, 195, 209

D'Arcy, G. Minot 22
Davis, Richard 143–144
DC-9 11–14, 16–17, 31–32, 45, 49, 51, 60, 64–65, 76, 92, 117–118, 120, 128, 138–140, 153–154, 161–162, 164–165, 185–186, 188, 195, 198–200, 224
Dean, John 95, 101, 173
Debridement 145–147
Delta Airlines 140, 186
Delta Flight 623 65–66, 76, 157, 187
Delta Flight 723 15, 18, 22, 44, 50, 54–55, 59–60, 66, 122, 134, 149, 150–152, 157–158, 160, 166, 178–179, 193, 195, 197–199, 205–209, 211–217, 232; see also Ship 222
Department of Commerce 26
Department of Health and Hospitals 115
Department of Transportation (DOT) 27–29, 37, 86–89, 91–93, 97–103, 116, 135, 152, 199

Dickens v. United States 212
Dodson, Dr. Thomas 168–169
Douglas Aircraft Company 11–15, 89, 149, 190, 224; *see also* DC-9
Drew, George 119, 137
Dupuis, Sylvio 130

Eastern Air Lines 31, 133, 134, 224
Eastern Airlines Flight 401 133
Eastern Airlines Flight 572 52–53, 55, 67, 76, 195–196
Eastern Airlines Flight 945 195
Eastern Airlines Flight 1020 51–52, 66, 203, 207
Eastern Airlines Flight 1043 67
Ehrlichman, John 95–97, 101
Eisenhower, Dwight 26, 62, 96, 102, 189
Ellsberg, Daniel 96
Ennis, Marion 142
Ervin, Senator Sam 101
Executive Air Flight 1350 76

Federal Aviation Act 26
Federal Aviation Administration (FAA) 16, 26–28, 33, 38, 40, 84, 87, 89, 92–93, 95, 97–98, 100, 116, 118–120, 122–129, 131–140, 154, 157, 159, 161, 165, 172–173, 178, 181, 185–188, 192, 196, 199, 204, 212
Federal Highway Administration 27
Federal Maritime Administration 27
Federal Railroad Administration 27
Flemming, Harry 96
Fleury, Patricia 21
flight director 54–55, 57–58, 60, 139–140, 153–155, 158–160, 162–163, 172–173, 180–181, 183–185, 187–188, 193, 198–199, 206, 220–224, 233–234
Flight Safety Foundation (FAF) 149
Fog Warning 9
Fort Independence 58
Fuller, Mr. & Mrs. Joseph 21

Gainer, Hubert 131
Garrity, Judge W. Arthur 64, 132, 231
"Get 'Em High, Keep 'Em High" 119–121
Gilliland, Whitney 87
Giroux, Richard 59
glide slope 54, 57, 127–129, 162, 164, 180–183, 193, 198–201, 205–206, 208, 211, 215, 222
Gosselin, Mary 21
Gosselin, Thomas 21
Grenier Field 10, 11, 14, 19; *see also* Manchester Airport
Grey, L Patrick 101
Ground Proximity Warning System (GPWS) 133–135
Gummere, Phyllis 22

Index

Hadik, Laszlo 18, 84
Haldeman, H.R. 95-97, 101
Haley, William 99, 100, 102, 139
Hall, Clarence 22
Hartigan, Laurence 19
Hayes, James 119
Heffelfinger, William S. 97, 100
Henrickson, Capt. Richard 160
Hetterman, D.P. 165
Hoag, Margaret 19, 82
Holstine, Arnold 116-118, 138-139, 154
Holzscheiter, Albert 22
Howland, Ferris 178
Hubbell, Charles 22
Humberto, Medeiros Cardinal 131
Humphreys, Patricia 16, 220
Humphreys, Richard 220
Hunt, E. Howard 96, 132
Hunting Aircraft Company 12
Hutchins, Warren 58

Iberia Airlines Flight 933 177-178
Ingham v. Eastern Air Lines, Inc. 212, 214
Instrument Landing System (ILS) 6, 44, 48, 51-53, 70, 119, 126-129, 136, 156, 163-164, 184, 187, 197-199, 205-206, 208, 217, 220, 224
Interstate Commerce Commission (ICC) 18, 25

Jackson, Miriam 22
Japan Airlines 87, 127
Johnson, Lyndon 27, 29, 87, 88, 91, 96, 125, 128, 177
Jones, Danny 128
Jones, Roys C. 210-211, 218

Kapopoulos, Ora 23
Karakoudas, Thomas 59, 154
Keating, Geoffrey 42, 64-67, 70, 74, 78, 131, 154, 170, 195
Kennedy, Sen. Edward 119, 231
Kennedy, Pres. John F. 62
Kennedy, Maureen 82
Kennedy, Sen. Robert F. 63
Kennedy International Airport (JFK) 127, 133, 212
Kennett, Linnell 22
Kester, John G. 22
King, Edward 37, 39, 131, 138
King, Dr. John 107
King, Dr. Martin Luther 63
Kmiecek, Leonard 128
Knapp, Dennis 22
Koteff, Jay 23
Koteff, Tracy 23

Krogh, Egil "Bud" 96-97, 100-101, 132; *see also* Plumbers

Lafontaine, George 22
Laguardia Airport 119
Lake Central Airlines 87
Latti, Michael 220-234
Laurel, Oscar 87-88, 102
Leffingwell, S. L. 17
localizer 38, 50-51, 57, 154, 162-164, 166, 180-183, 185, 192-193, 198-202, 205-208, 217, 222
Logan Airport 10, 34; founding 35-36, 50-51, 58-59, 81-82, 85, 114, 116, 117, 119, 121, 130-131, 136, 138, 155, 167, 176-178, 186-187, 190, 192-194, 196, 210, 216, 223; weather conditions 39-45, 54, 70-71
Longchamp, Michael 19
Lubbock, Eric 129
Lund, Charles 105-106
Luongo, Dr. Michael 85-86, 114-115, 155
Lyman, Stanley 119, 128, 177-178
Lyons, Kenneth 177-178

MacArthur, Roger 23
Maclay, Timothy 172
Mahoney, Frank 83; finds nuclear defense NATO plans 84-85
Malek, Frederick 96
Manchester Airport 10-11, 19, 20-23, 33, 44, 46, 49, 55, 58, 76-77, 110, 131, 167-168, 193, 194, 197, 206
Massachusetts Aeronautics Commission (MAC) 30, 120, 160, 161
Massachusetts General Hospital (MGH) 81, 107-108, 111, 113, 145, 168, 176
Massachusetts Institute of Technology (MIT) 39, 149
MASSPORT 36, 37, 38, 39, 42, 66, 67, 72, 73, 81, 131, 136, 137, 138
Mayflower Airlines 29
McAdams, Francis 87-88, 92-93, 98-100, 102-103, 139, 149-150, 153, 156-157, 159-161, 166
McBride, Neil 132-135
McClure, Capt. Donald 224-226
McCord, James 101
McDonald, Jeffrey 41, 54-55, 156, 196
McKee, William 123-125, 128
Mealy, Charles 19, 34-35
Meehan, Marla 220
Meehan, Perry 21, 220
Meehan, R. Bradley 21, 220
Meehan, Robert 220
Merageas, Jim 54, 196
Metz, Lisa 19
Metz, Robert 19

Index

Miller, Charles 97, 103, 139, 149–150, 165
Millis Intersection 51–53, 201, 202, 216–217
Mohawk 12
Molin, Mr. & Mrs. Wilbur 22
Mooney, Richard 119
Moore, Anna 16, 220
Moore, Ronald 220
Moran, Patricia 19
Moran, Robert 19
Morrissey, Jimmy 71–73, 76–77, 196
Murphy, Sen. George 102
Murphy, Timothy 98, 102–103
Murtaugh, George Rev. 176
Muscato, Thomasina 22

N975NE 14, 134, 139, 163
Nader, Ralph 132–133
National Airways 29
National Association of Government Employees (NAGE) 128, 177
National Transportation Safety Board (NTSB) 16, 27–29, 70, 87–93, 97–101, 103, 116–119, 126, 132–135, 138–140, 149–155, 159, 161, 163–164, 170, 172–173, 180–182, 184–187, 189, 192, 195, 210, 223–225, 230, 233–234
Neff v. United States 213
Nelson, Hon. David 231–234
Neptune Road 36, 38
New York City 10–11, 19–21, 22, 29–30, 55, 116, 167, 210, 212
New York Times 96
New York Yankees 20, 34
Newton, Brenda 20, 108, 110–112, 143, 169, 175–176
Newton, Bud 108, 142, 170
Newton, Lorraine 108
Nix, Capt. Everett 199
Nixon, Pres. Richard 18, 29, 33, 62, 90–91, 93–103, 117, 120, 125, 135, 149, 152, 173, 178, 180, 185
noise pollution 118, 122
North Adams Transcript 121
North Central Airlines 127–128
Northeast Airlines 14–16, 24, 29–32, 45, 55, 139, 153–154, 161–162, 164–165, 184–185
Noyer, Maurice 224–230, 233

O'Connell, Joseph 87–92, 102, 126, 150
Office of Accident Investigation (OAI) 28–29
Our Lady of the Airways 131
Outer Marker (OM) 40–41, 48, 50–51, 53, 58, 157, 165, 180–182, 200–201, 204–208, 215, 217–218

party system 89, 93, 132, 134–135, 178
Patunoff, Yvette 19, 82

Paull, Mr. & Mrs Willis 22
Penney, Albert 22
Pentagon Papers 96
pictorial deviation indicator (PDI) 57, 60, 163, 181, 198–199, 224
Piedmont Airlines 89–90, 123, 126
Pilot's Weather Handbook 45
plumbers 96–97, 100–101
Poseidon Adventure 34
precision approach radar (PAR) 6, 122, 126–129, 177–178
probable cause 27–28, 89, 92–93, 98, 150, 153, 180, 230, 260
Provost, Michael 21
proximate cause 150, 191, 203, 217, 220, 232
public hearing 90, 93, 133, 135, 149, 151–153, 170, 172, 182, 185
Pucinski, Roman 127

Queener, Capt. Ralph 157–158

Race, Scott 20, 34
Race, Shirley 20
Rae, William 59
Reed, John H. 87–88, 91, 93, 99–103, 132–135, 137, 139, 153
Richards, Norman 23
Richardson, Elliot 173
Richardson v. United States 213
Ritchie, the Rev. Donald 176
Rock, Francis 172
Rogers, David 164, 166, 172
Rogers, Paul 123–124
Rooney, Fred 124–125
Roosevelt, Franklin D. 24–26, 61
Roseborough, Capt. Jack 199–200, 209–210
Rox, Frank 131–134, 136, 147, 150, 154–157, 159–161, 165, 172
Ruane, John J., 19
Runway 4R 36, 40–42, 44, 48–49, 51, 53–55, 58, 60, 64–75, 81–82, 136–137, 153–154, 156–159, 161, 169–170, 178, 184, 192, 195–196, 207–210, 212–213, 216, 223, 234
Runway 15R 36, 38, 136–137
Runway 33L 36, 38, 177
RVR 43, 53, 58, 69–70, 154, 156–157, 161, 184–185, 196, 200, 206

St. Pierre, the Rev. Roland 176
Samuels, Sidney 11, 167–168
Sargent, Gov. Frank 39, 136–137, 231
Saturday Night Massacre 173, 178
Sauters, Elizabeth 22
Schaffer, Richard 166
Schultze, Charles 27
Schwartz, Dr. Stanley 86
segregation 63, 64

Senate Commerce Committee 30, 101, 123, 151
Shaffer, John 93, 119–120, 125
Ship 222 11, 14, 21, 33, 44, 138–139, 162–165, 172, 234
silver nitrate solution 107–108, 111, 145, 147, 177
Slattery, Edward 153
Smerdon v. United States 190–192
Smith, Capt. C.A. 17, 45
Smith, Judy 19
Smith, Kenneth 93
Smith, Marion 19, 82, 168
Snow, Crocker 30, 120, 122, 137, 160
Spears, Richard 97, 99, 101–103, 116, 151
Sperry Rand 162–166, 172, 184, 187–188, 198, 220–224, 227, 232, 234
State Airport Management Board 36
Streil, Capt. John 11, 33, 35, 44–46, 48–55, 57–58, 60, 138, 154–157, 161–162, 164, 166, 183, 189, 197, 205–206, 220; Flight 177 55–56; funeral 131; military background 15–16
Streil, Virginia 220

Tallant, Harold 56
tannic acid 104–105
Taylor, Charles 40, 51, 53, 76, 155, 197
Terban, Harry 41–43, 69–70, 159, 170, 194, 209
Terminal Air Traffic Control Manual 192, 196–197, 203–205, 207, 209, 214–215
Terrain Avoidance System 133–134
Thayer, Louis 87–88, 98–100, 102, 139
Theriault, Richard 19
Thomas, David 123–124

Thompson, Robert 22
Tierney, Nancy 56
Tofield, Dr. Joshua 104–108, 111–112, 141, 145–148, 169, 172, 174, 177
TRACON 40–41, 53–54, 196, 210
Trans World Airlines (TWA) 31, 51, 128, 133–134, 203
transmissometer 43, 69, 70, 156, 159, 184, 195; *see also* runway visual range (RVR)
Tucker, Daniel 54–55, 71–72, 76–77, 200–201

Vallancourt, Robert 19
VHF Omni Range (VOR) 46, 72, 74, 79, 162–164, 166, 168, 180, 183, 187, 195, 222
Vickers Viscount 15, 55, 164
Vietnam War 62, 88, 96, 122, 125
Volpe, John 38, 97–99, 102

Walsh, Mary Allen 56
Warren, Lourde 22
Watergate 5, 33, 63, 95–96, 101, 117, 132, 173
Watts, Sandy 21
Weiss, Eric 101–102
White, Mayor Kevin 38, 39
White 12 106, 111, 143
Wiggin, Chester 18, 30
Wilson, Eloise 220
Wilson, Janice 16, 220
Wilson, John 220
Wood Island Park 38
Worcester, MA 10

Yom Kippur War 62
Young, Capt. Vernon 195, 209

www.ingramcontent.com/pod-product-compliance
Ingram Content Group UK Ltd.
Pitfield, Milton Keynes, MK11 3LW, UK
UKHW041932140426
5217IPUK00014B/435